NANA

Vol. 21

Shojo Beat

Contents

Chapter 78 3
Chapter 79 81
Junko's Place 173

The Story of Nana

Hachi's psyched that Ren came up with a name for her baby. She promises to celebrate Nana's birthday with her and gets ready to join Nana in Osaka.

Ren can't kick his drug habit and threatens to quit Trapnest. Takumi and Reira try to talk Ren into staying, but Ren won't listen. Reira goes AWOL to buy Ren some time to rest and get clean, and Takumi has a minor breakdown when she ditches the band. Hachi can't leave Takumi alone at a time like this, so she decides to stay in Tokyo. Nana gets really depressed that Hachi isn't coming to see her in Osaka.

The day before Nana's birthday, Ren finally makes up his mind to go see Nana. But first he drives to see Reira. The paparazzi chase him through the snow, so Ren drives crazy, and...?!

♥For the complete story, please check out *Nana*, volumes 1 - 20. Available in bookstores everywhere!!

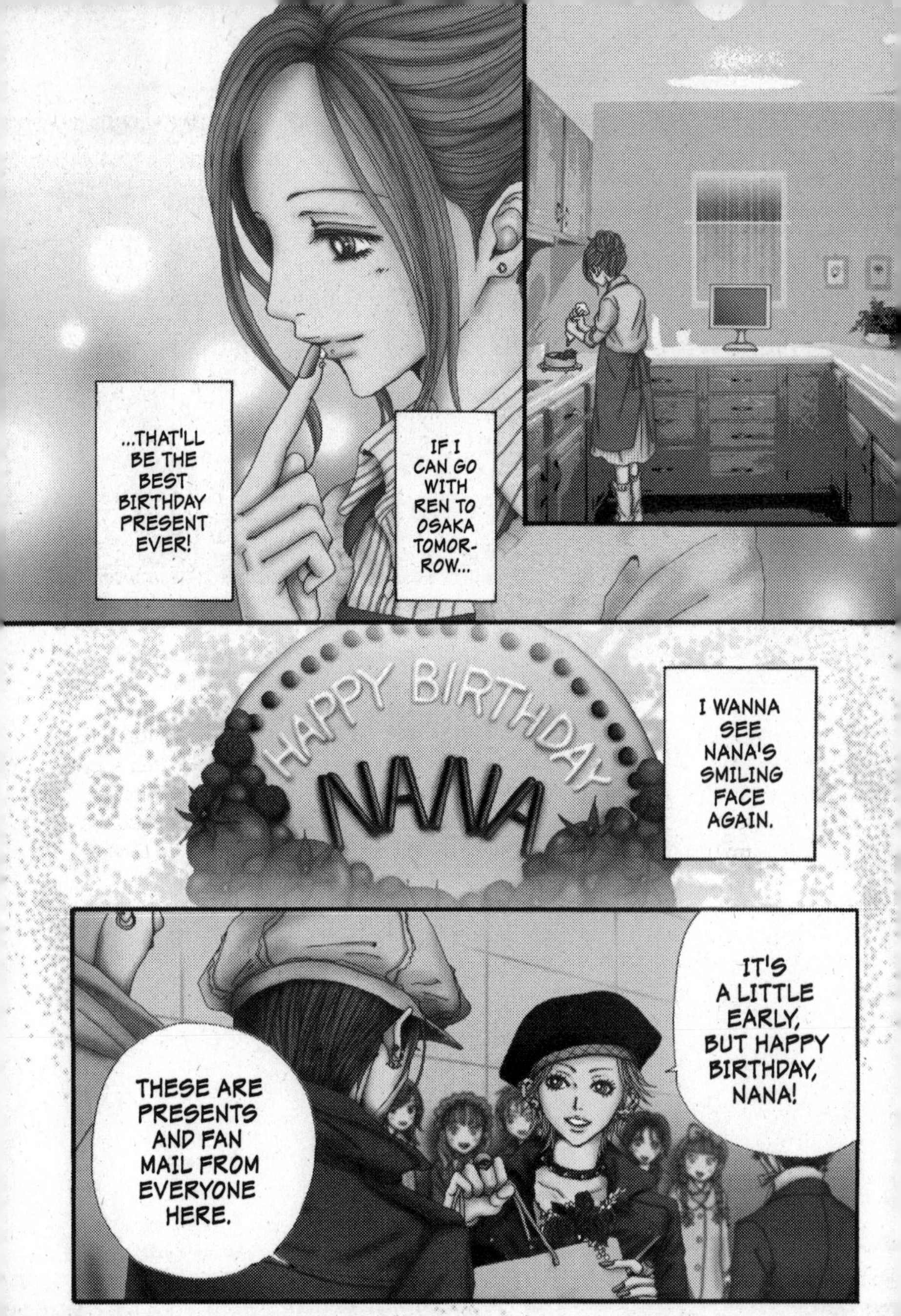
IF I CAN GO WITH REN TO OSAKA TOMORROW...
...THAT'LL BE THE BEST BIRTHDAY PRESENT EVER!
I WANNA SEE NANA'S SMILING FACE AGAIN.
HAPPY BIRTHDAY
NANA
IT'S A LITTLE EARLY, BUT HAPPY BIRTHDAY, NANA!
THESE ARE PRESENTS AND FAN MAIL FROM EVERYONE HERE.

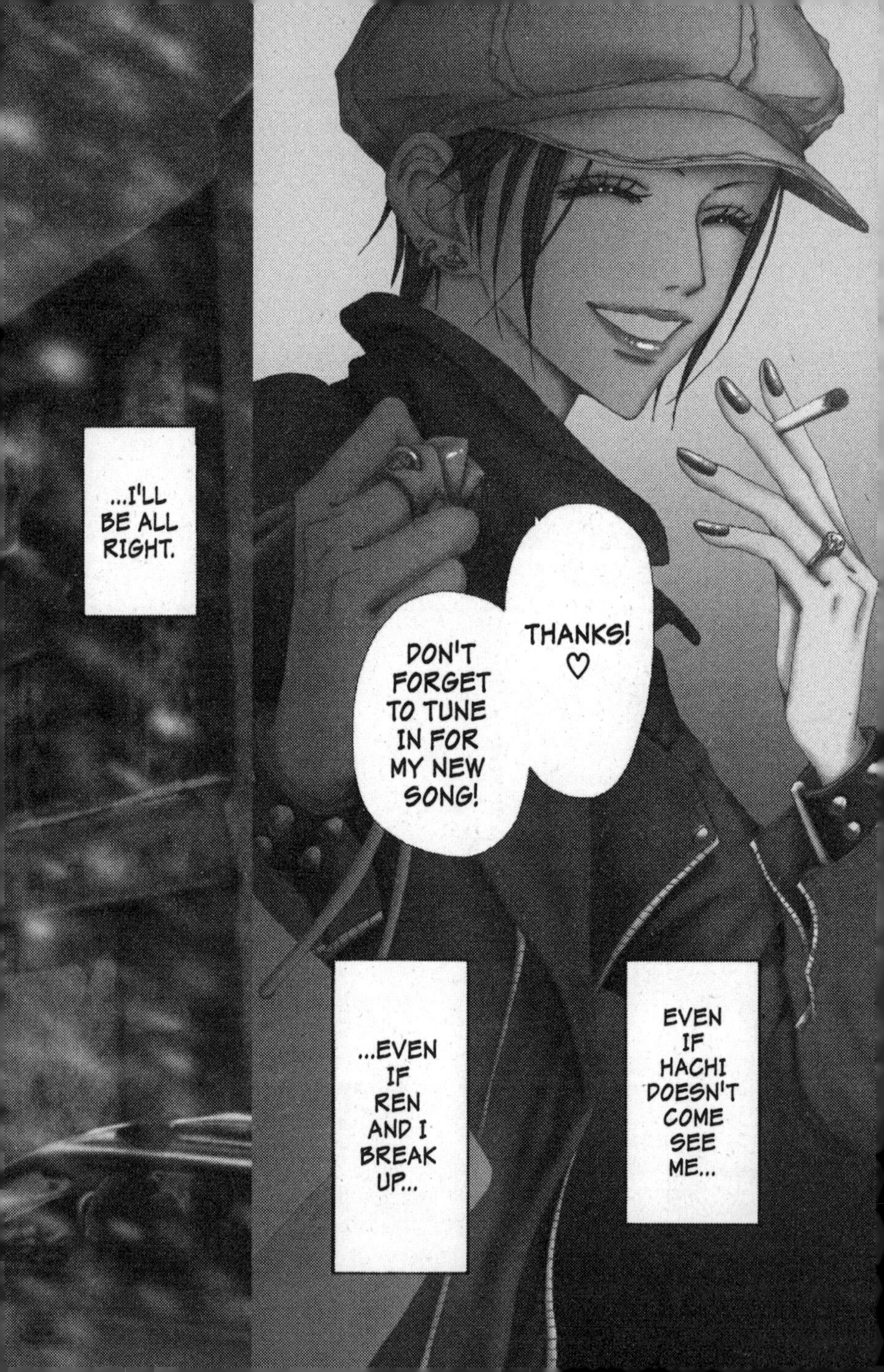
THANKS! ♡
DON'T FORGET TO TUNE IN FOR MY NEW SONG!
EVEN IF HACHI DOESN'T COME SEE ME...
...EVEN IF REN AND I BREAK UP...
...I'LL BE ALL RIGHT.

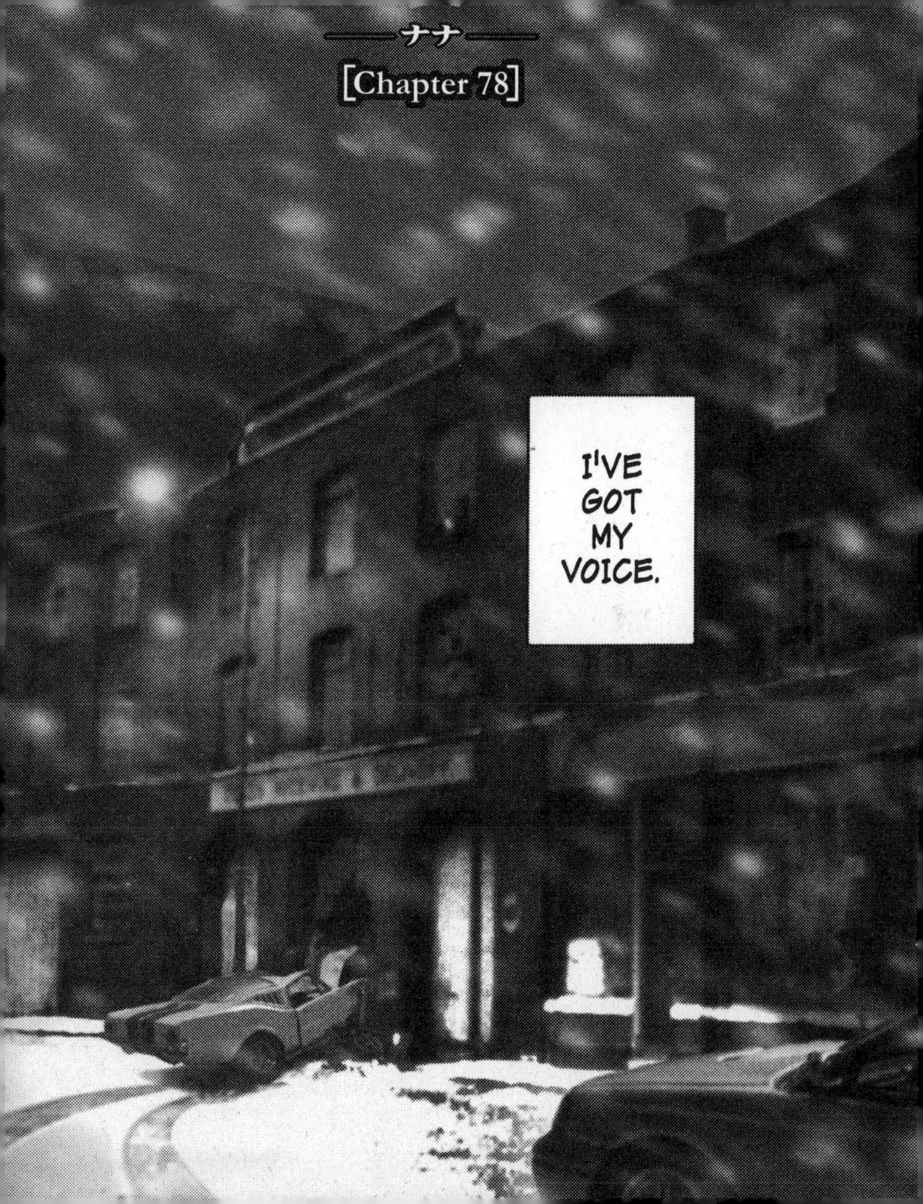
ナナ
[Chapter 78]
I'VE GOT MY VOICE.

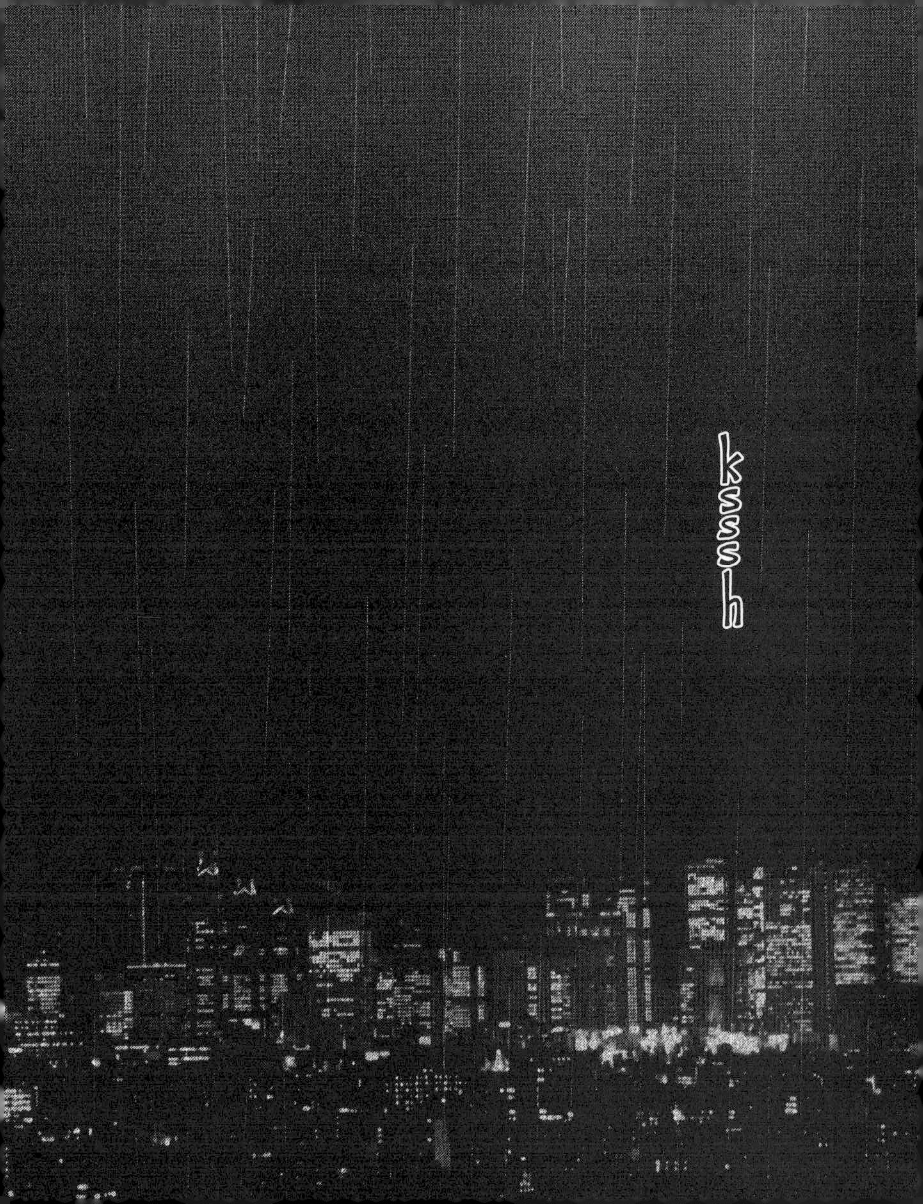
ksssh

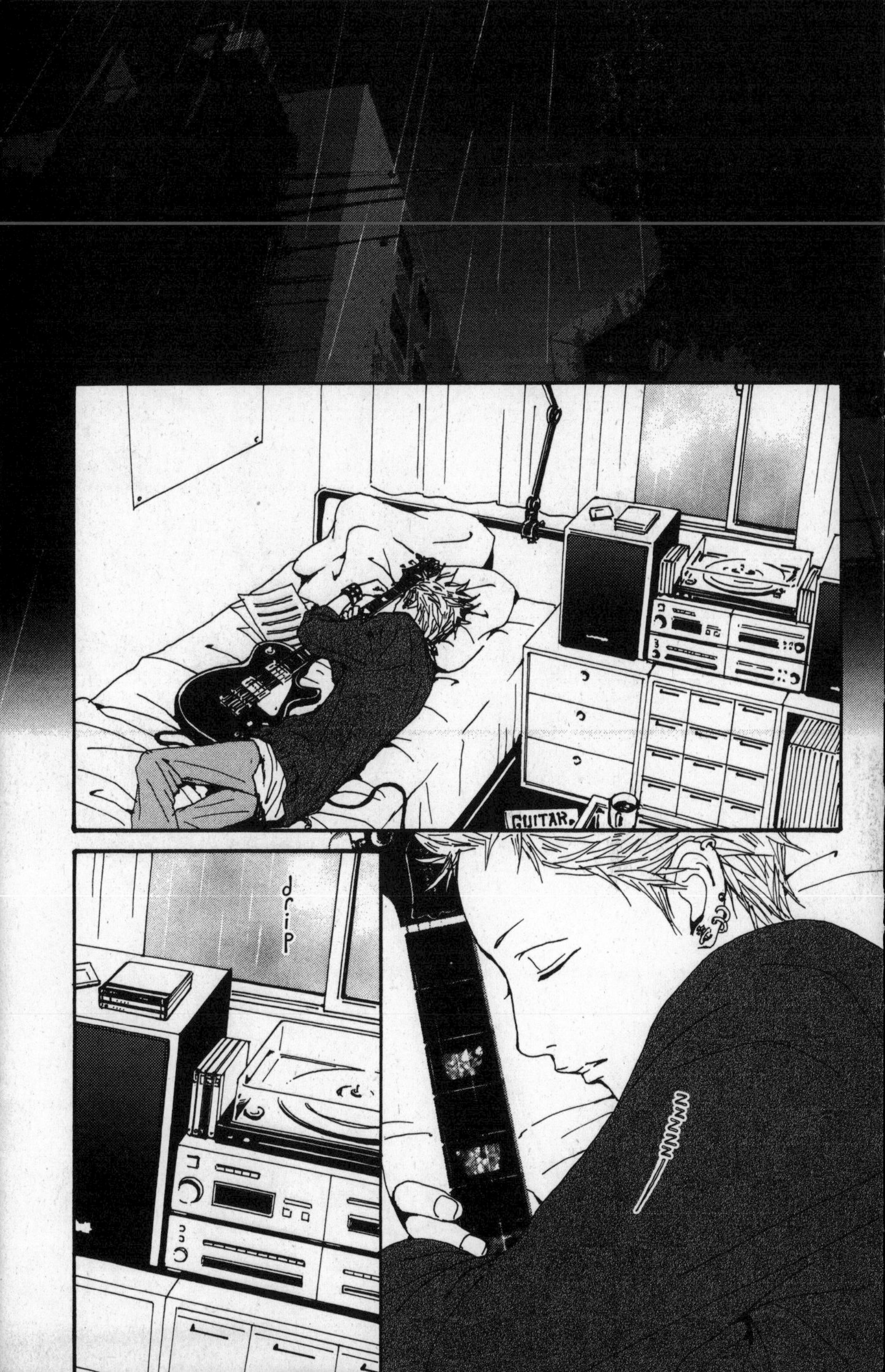
GUITAR.
NNNNN
drip

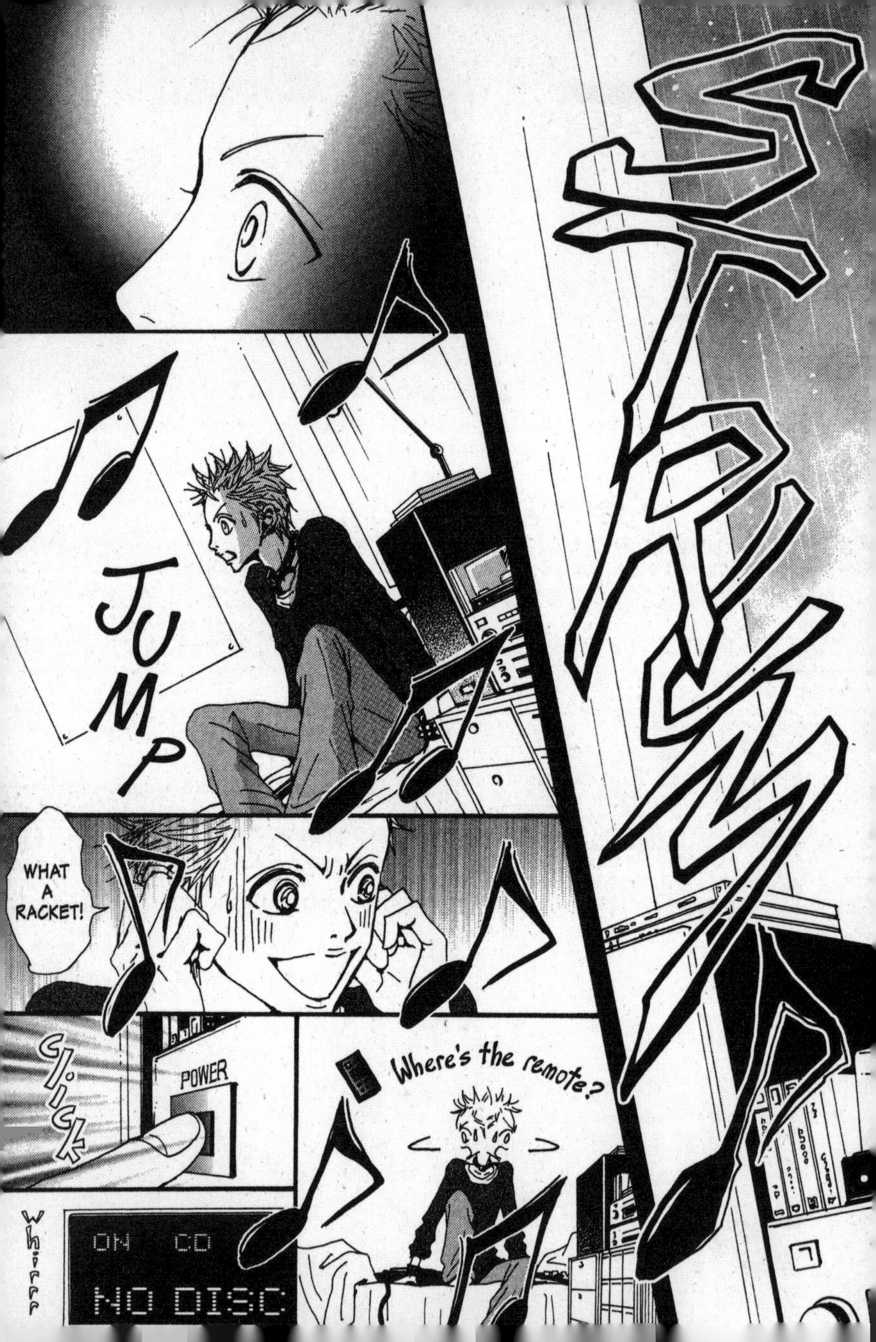
JUMP
WHAT A RACKET!
Where's the remote?
Click
POWER
Whirrr
ON CD
NO DISC

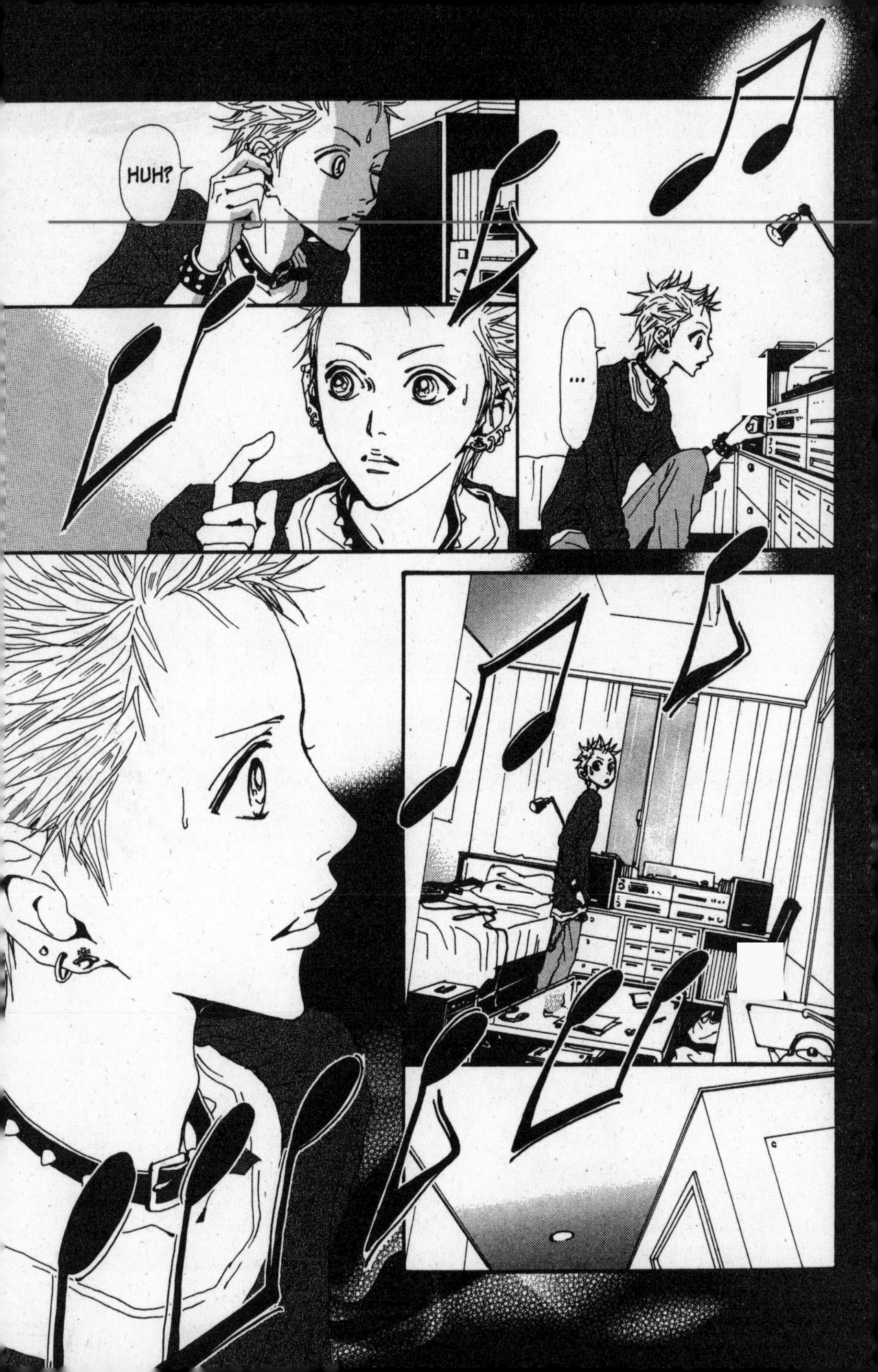
...
HUH?

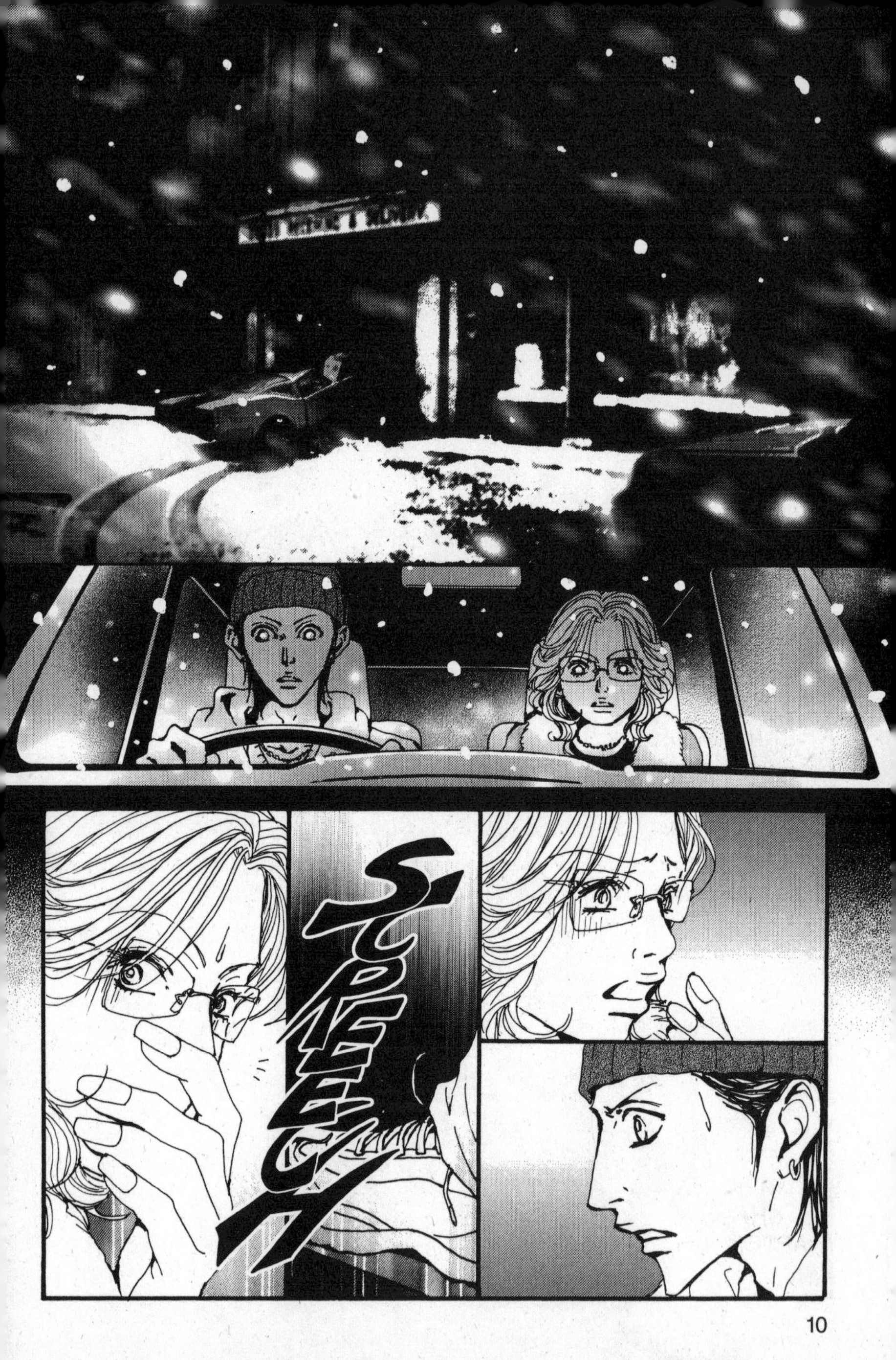
SCREEECH

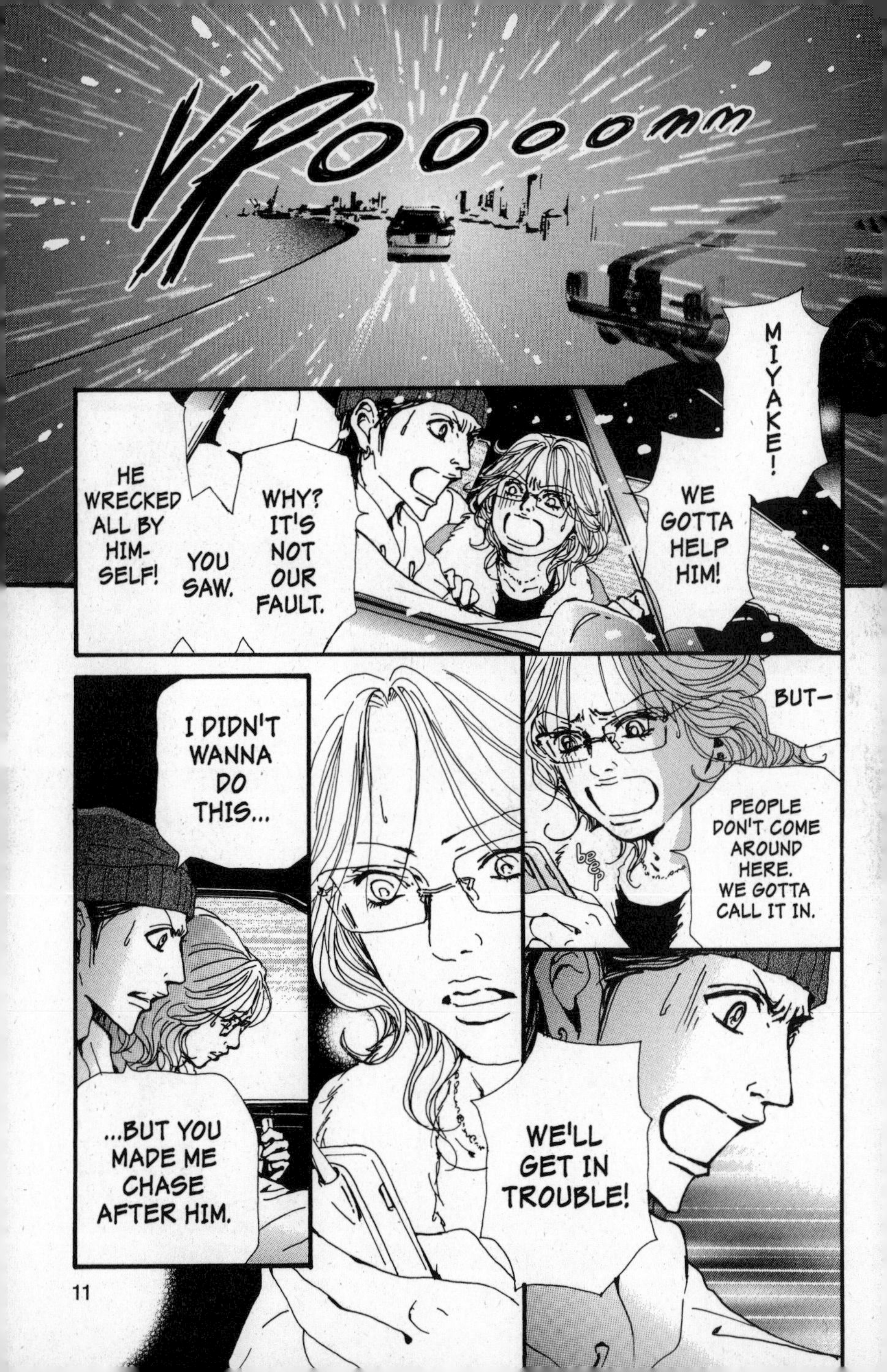
VROOOOMM
MIYAKE!
WE GOTTA HELP HIM!
WHY? IT'S NOT OUR FAULT.
YOU SAW.
HE WRECKED ALL BY HIM-SELF!
BUT—
beep
PEOPLE DON'T COME AROUND HERE. WE GOTTA CALL IT IN.
WE'LL GET IN TROUBLE!
I DIDN'T WANNA DO THIS...
...BUT YOU MADE ME CHASE AFTER HIM.

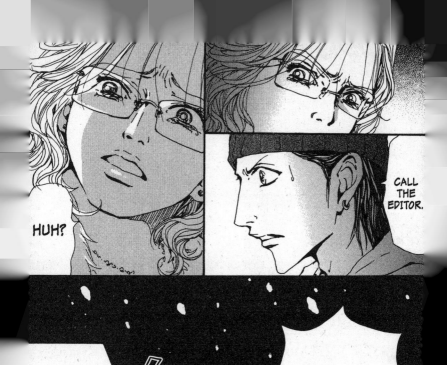

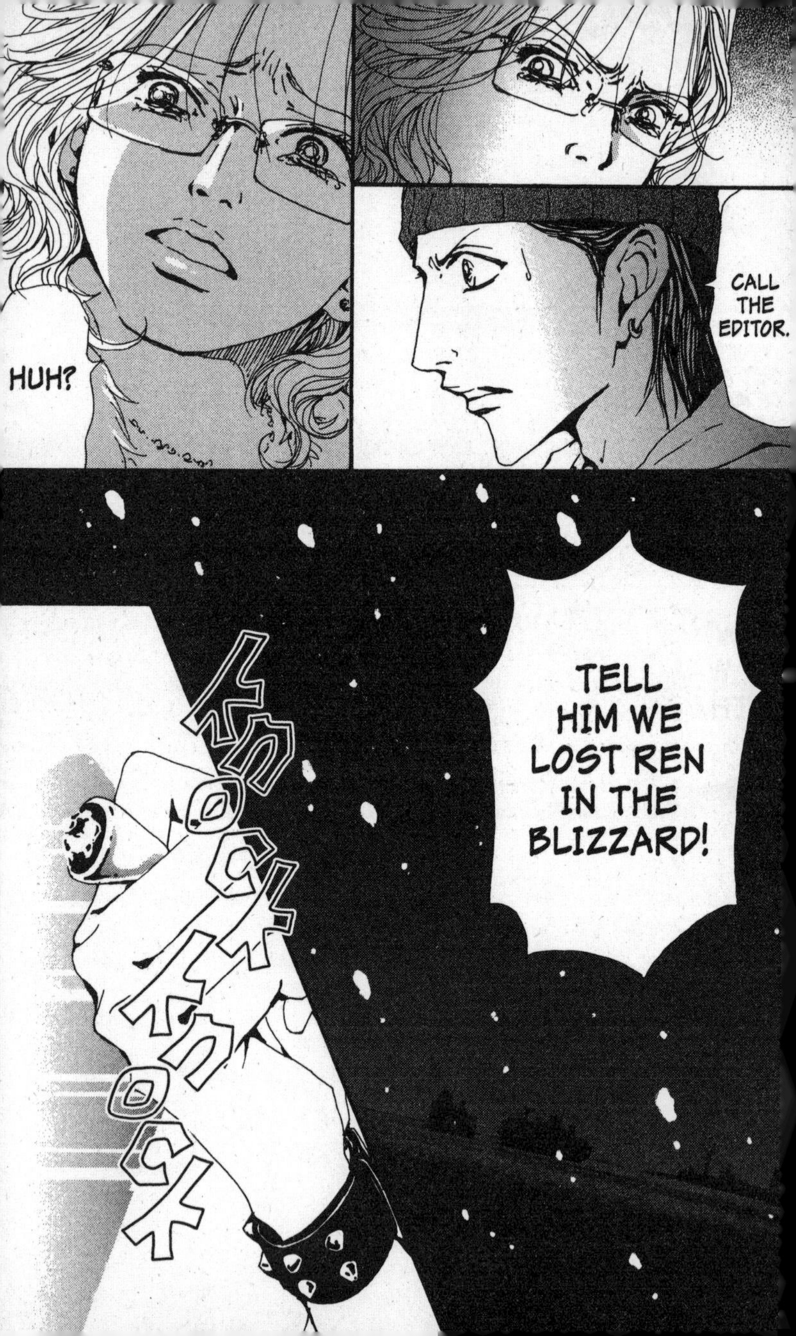
CALL THE EDITOR.
HUH?
TELL HIM WE LOST REN IN THE BLIZZARD!
KNOCK KNOCK

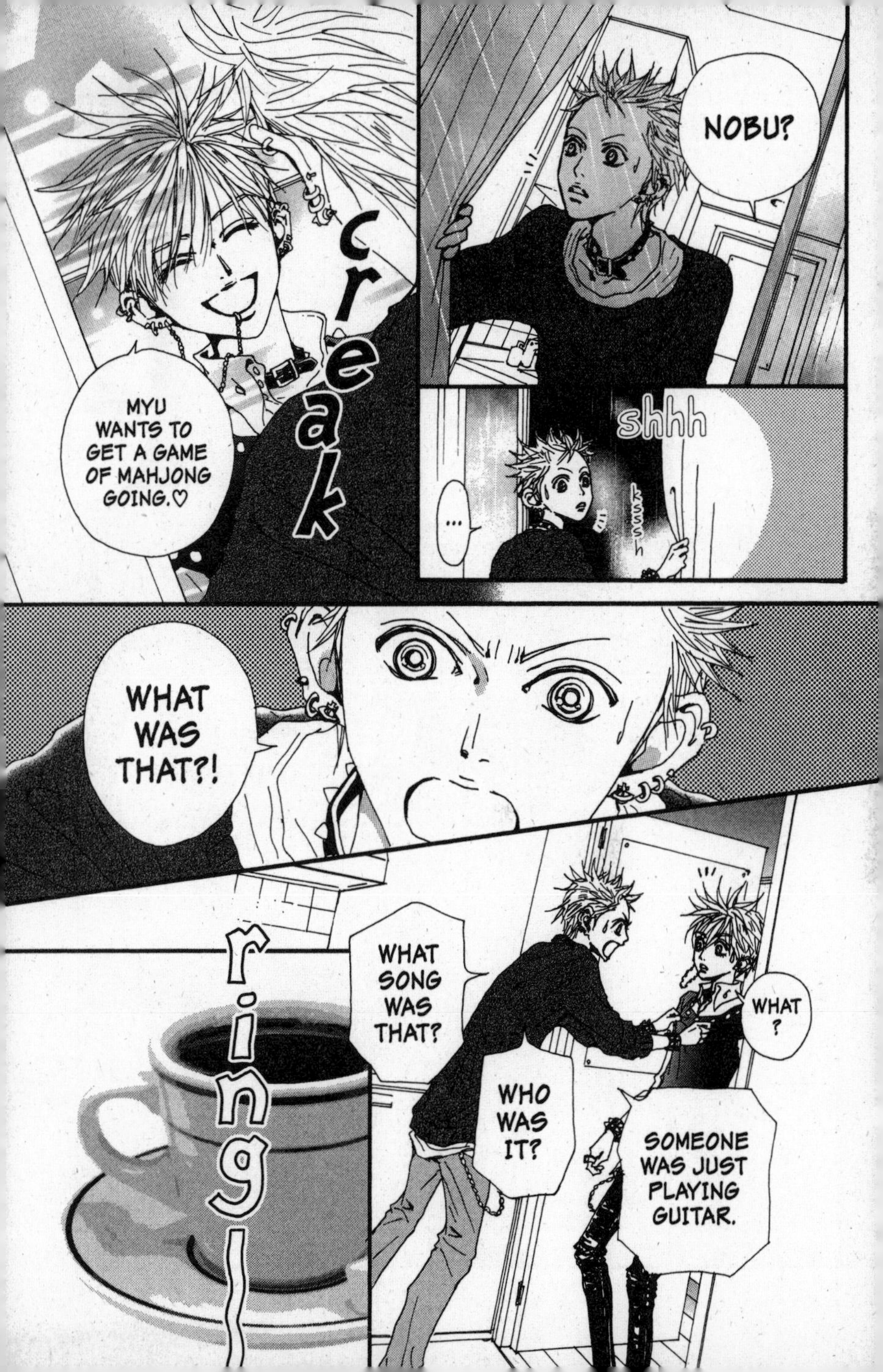
NOBU?
shhh
...
ksssh
creak
MYU WANTS TO GET A GAME OF MAHJONG GOING.♡
WHAT WAS THAT?!
WHAT?
WHAT SONG WAS THAT?
WHO WAS IT?
SOMEONE WAS JUST PLAYING GUITAR.
ring

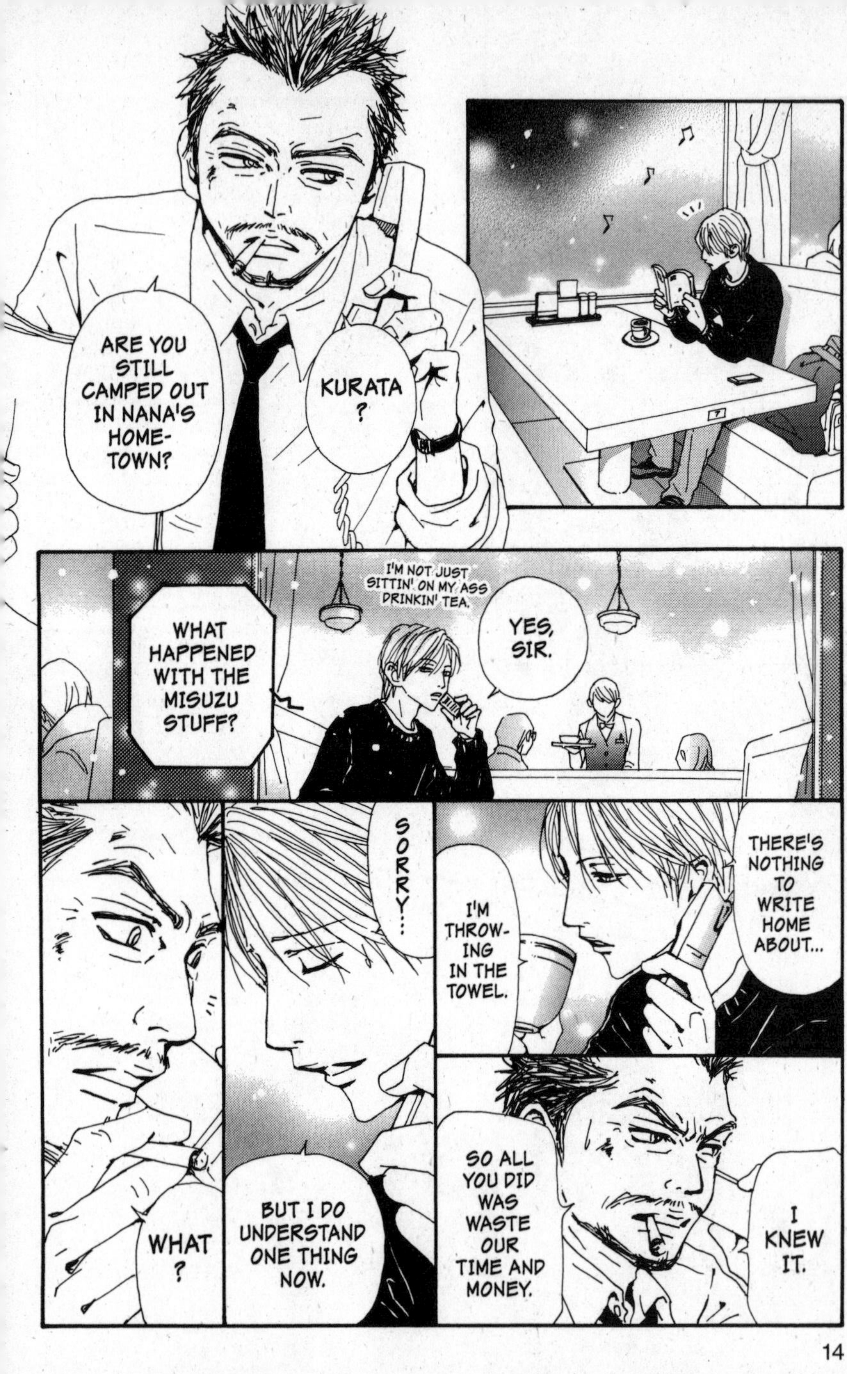
KURATA?
ARE YOU STILL CAMPED OUT IN NANA'S HOME-TOWN?
YES, SIR.
I'M NOT JUST SITTIN' ON MY ASS DRINKIN' TEA.
WHAT HAPPENED WITH THE MISUZU STUFF?
THERE'S NOTHING TO WRITE HOME ABOUT...
I'M THROW-ING IN THE TOWEL.
I KNEW IT.
SO ALL YOU DID WAS WASTE OUR TIME AND MONEY.
SORRY...
BUT I DO UNDERSTAND ONE THING NOW.
WHAT?

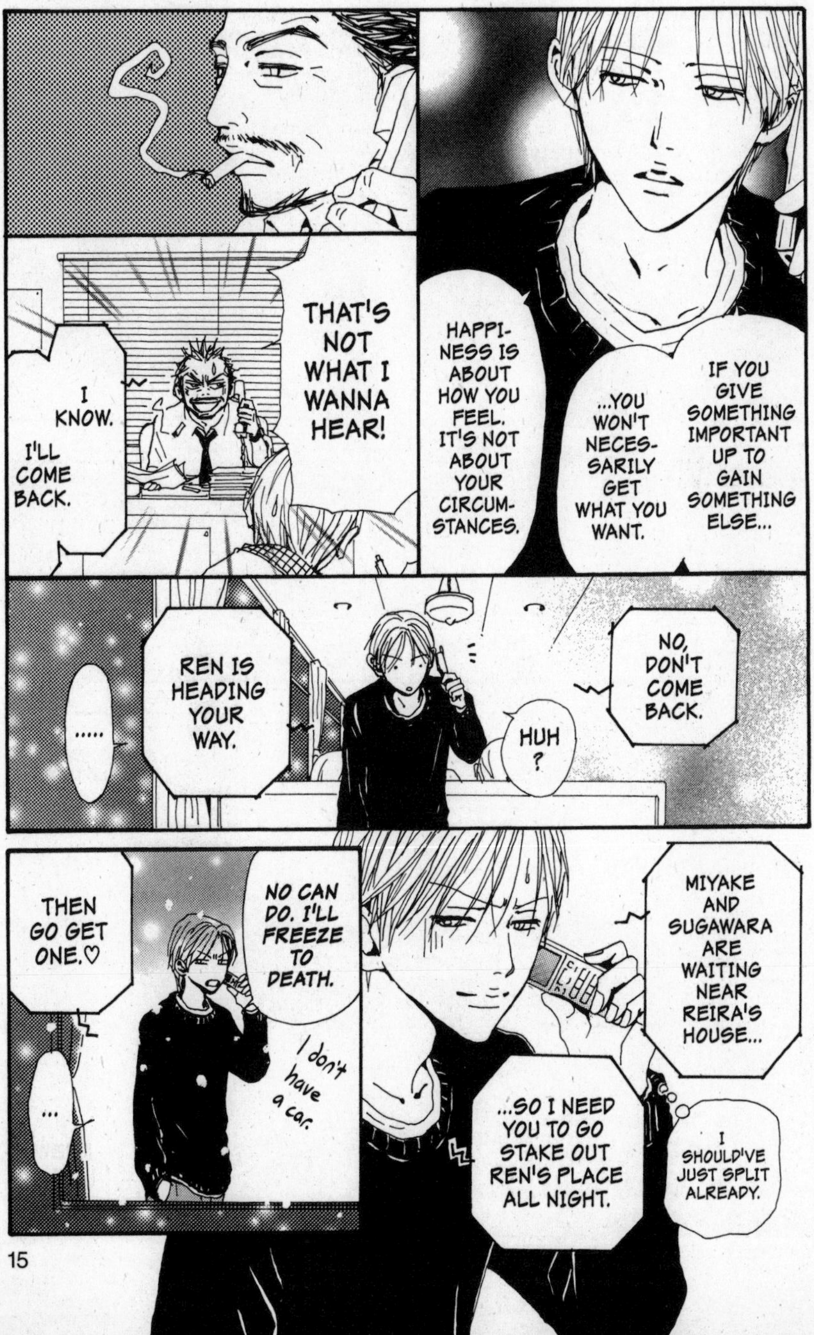

IF YOU GIVE SOMETHING IMPORTANT UP TO GAIN SOMETHING ELSE...
...YOU WON'T NECES-SARILY GET WHAT YOU WANT.
HAPPI-NESS IS ABOUT HOW YOU FEEL. IT'S NOT ABOUT YOUR CIRCUM-STANCES.
THAT'S NOT WHAT I WANNA HEAR!
I KNOW.
I'LL COME BACK.
NO, DON'T COME BACK.
HUH?
REN IS HEADING YOUR WAY.
.....
MIYAKE AND SUGAWARA ARE WAITING NEAR REIRA'S HOUSE...
...SO I NEED YOU TO GO STAKE OUT REN'S PLACE ALL NIGHT.
I SHOULD'VE JUST SPLIT ALREADY.
NO CAN DO. I'LL FREEZE TO DEATH.
I don't have a car.
THEN GO GET ONE.♡
...

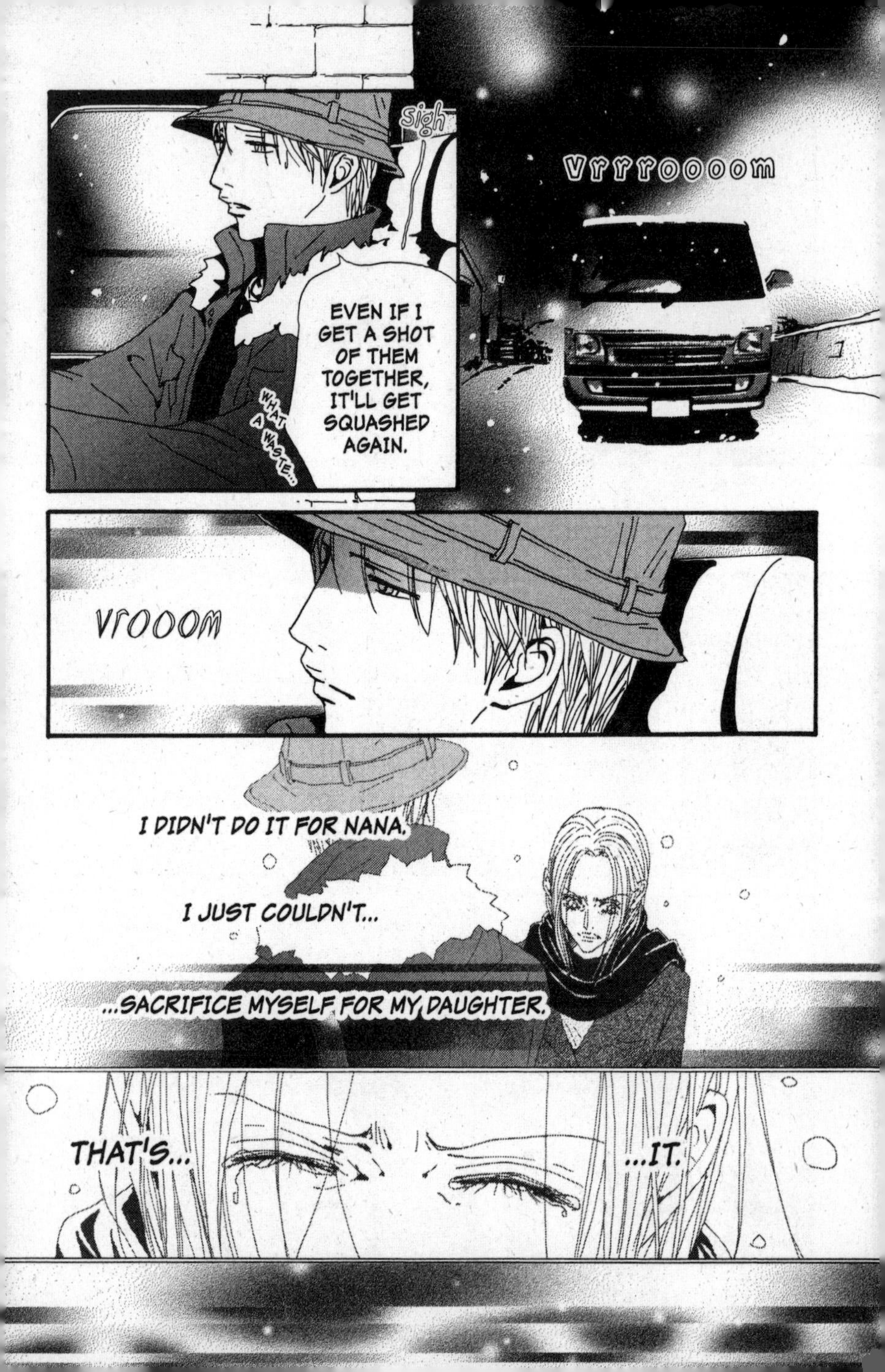
Vrrroooom
Sigh
EVEN IF I GET A SHOT OF THEM TOGETHER, IT'LL GET SQUASHED AGAIN.
WHAT A WASTE...
VROOOM
I DIDN'T DO IT FOR NANA.
I JUST COULDN'T...
...SACRIFICE MYSELF FOR MY DAUGHTER.
THAT'S...
...IT.

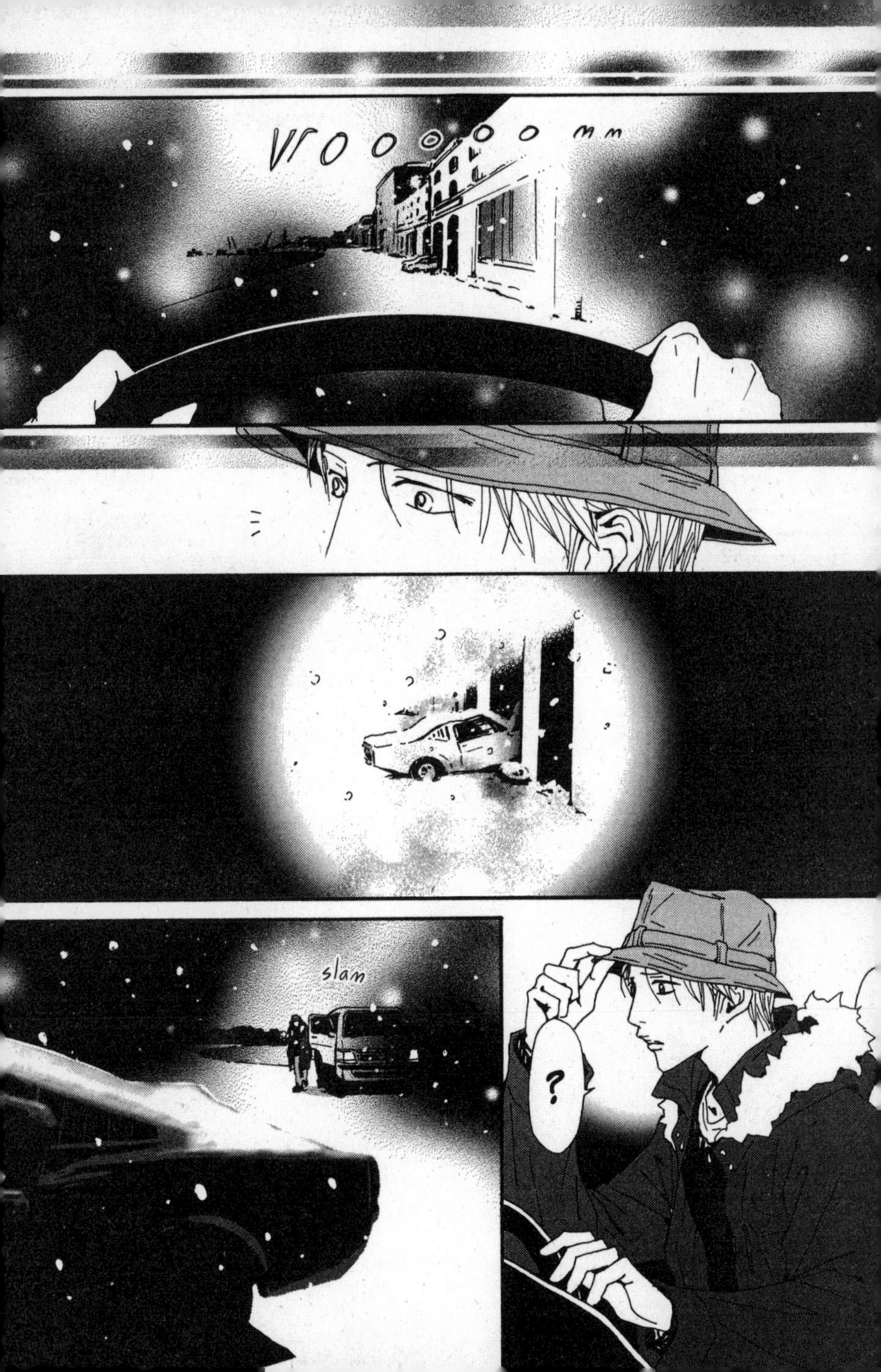
Vrooooomm
slam
?

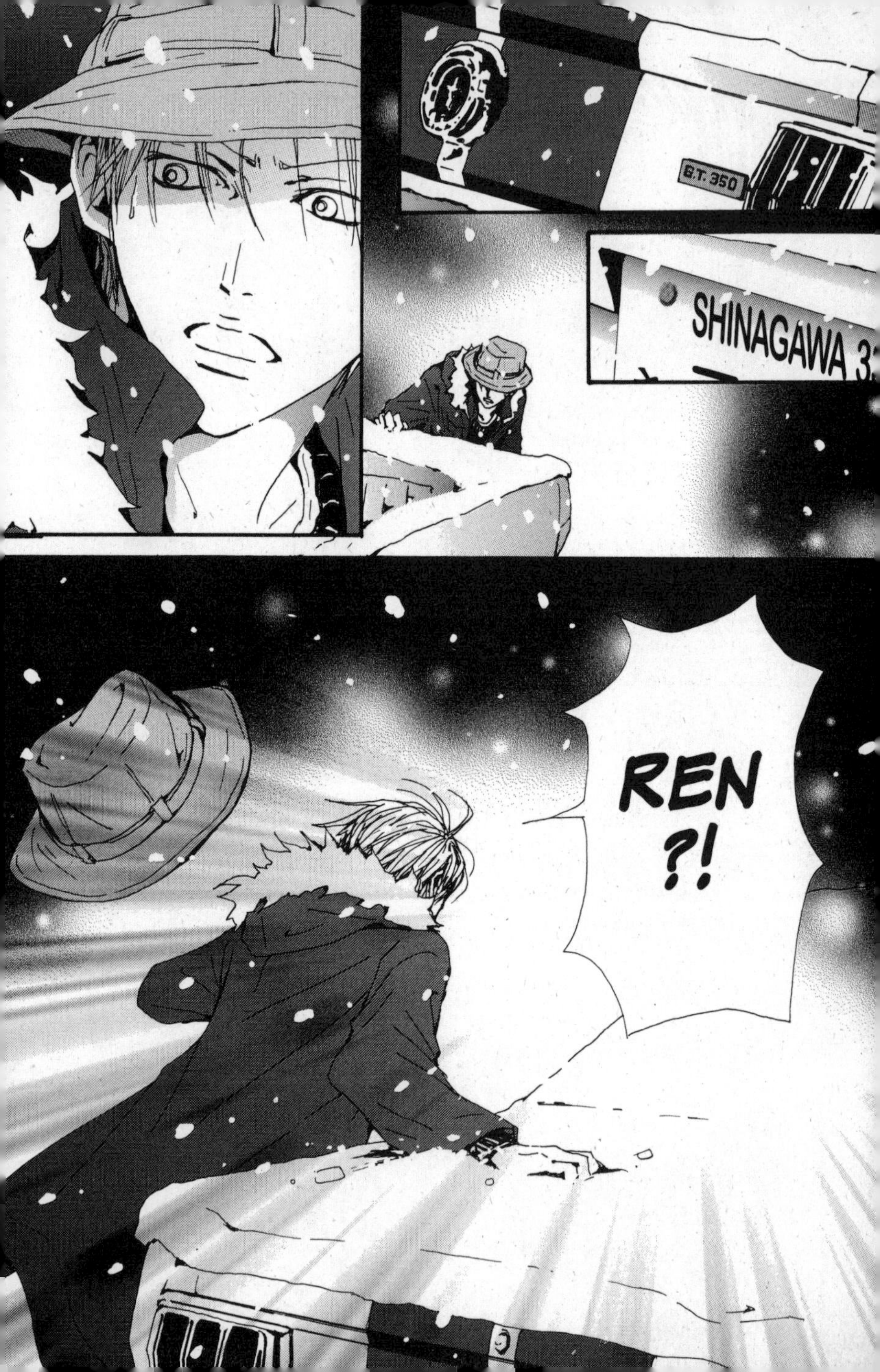
B.T. 350
SHINAGAWA 3
REN ?!

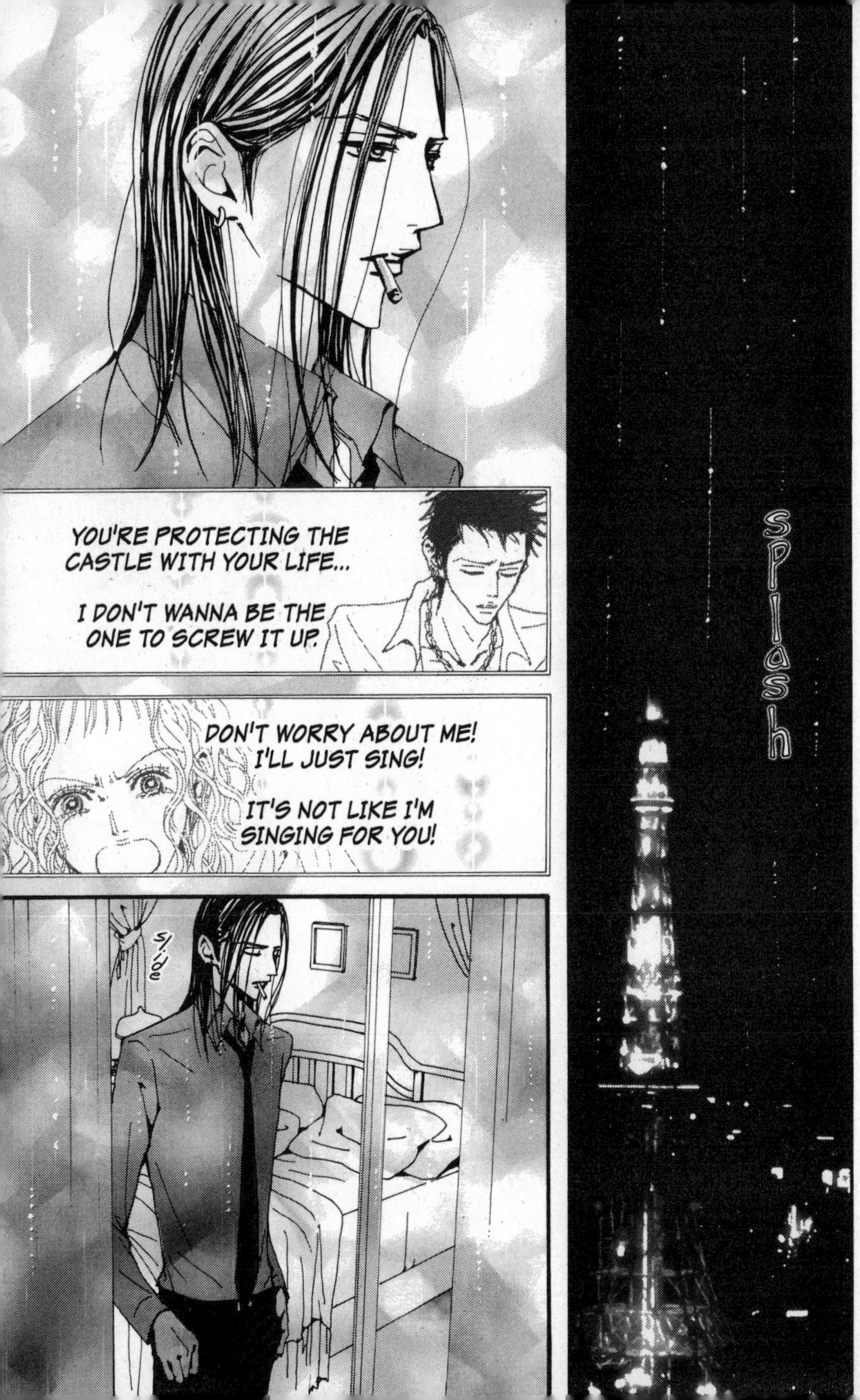
splash
YOU'RE PROTECTING THE CASTLE WITH YOUR LIFE...
I DON'T WANNA BE THE ONE TO SCREW IT UP.
DON'T WORRY ABOUT ME! I'LL JUST SING!
IT'S NOT LIKE I'M SINGING FOR YOU!
slide

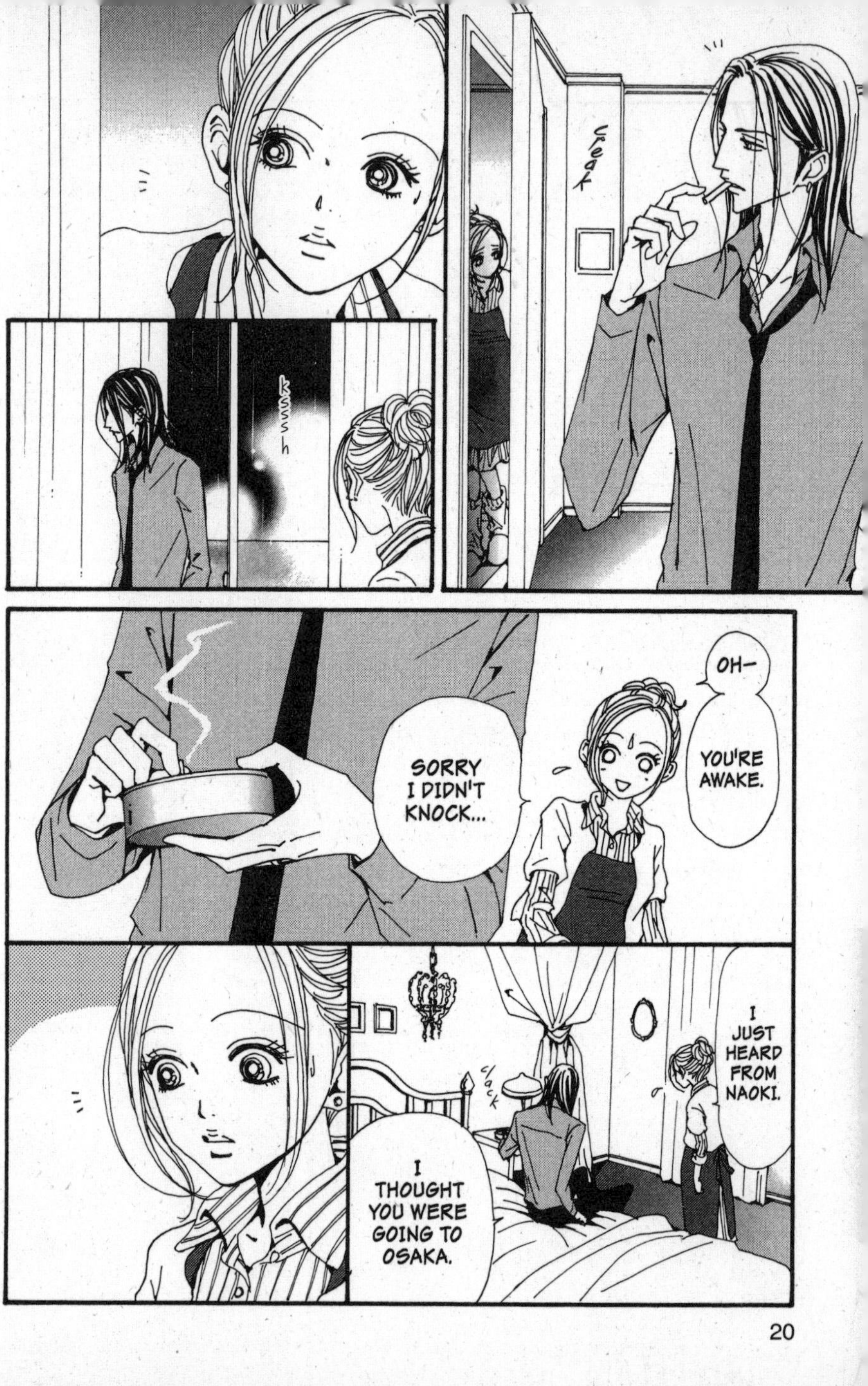
creak
ksssh
OH—
YOU'RE AWAKE.
SORRY I DIDN'T KNOCK...
I JUST HEARD FROM NAOKI.
clack
I THOUGHT YOU WERE GOING TO OSAKA.

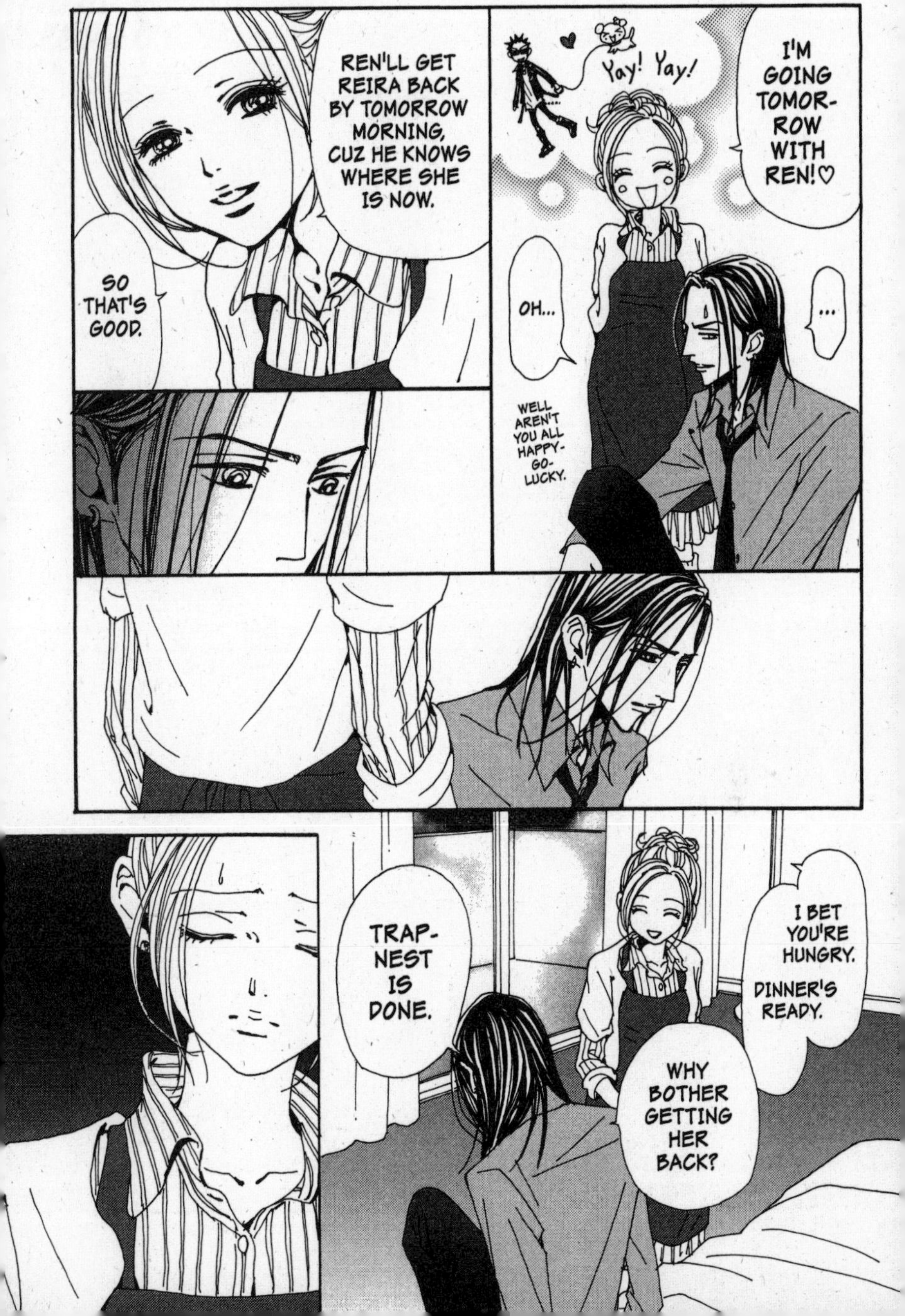
I'M GOING TOMORROW WITH REN!♡
Yay! Yay!
...
OH...
WELL AREN'T YOU ALL HAPPY-GO-LUCKY.
REN'LL GET REIRA BACK BY TOMORROW MORNING, CUZ HE KNOWS WHERE SHE IS NOW.
SO THAT'S GOOD.
I BET YOU'RE HUNGRY.
DINNER'S READY.
TRAP-NEST IS DONE.
WHY BOTHER GETTING HER BACK?

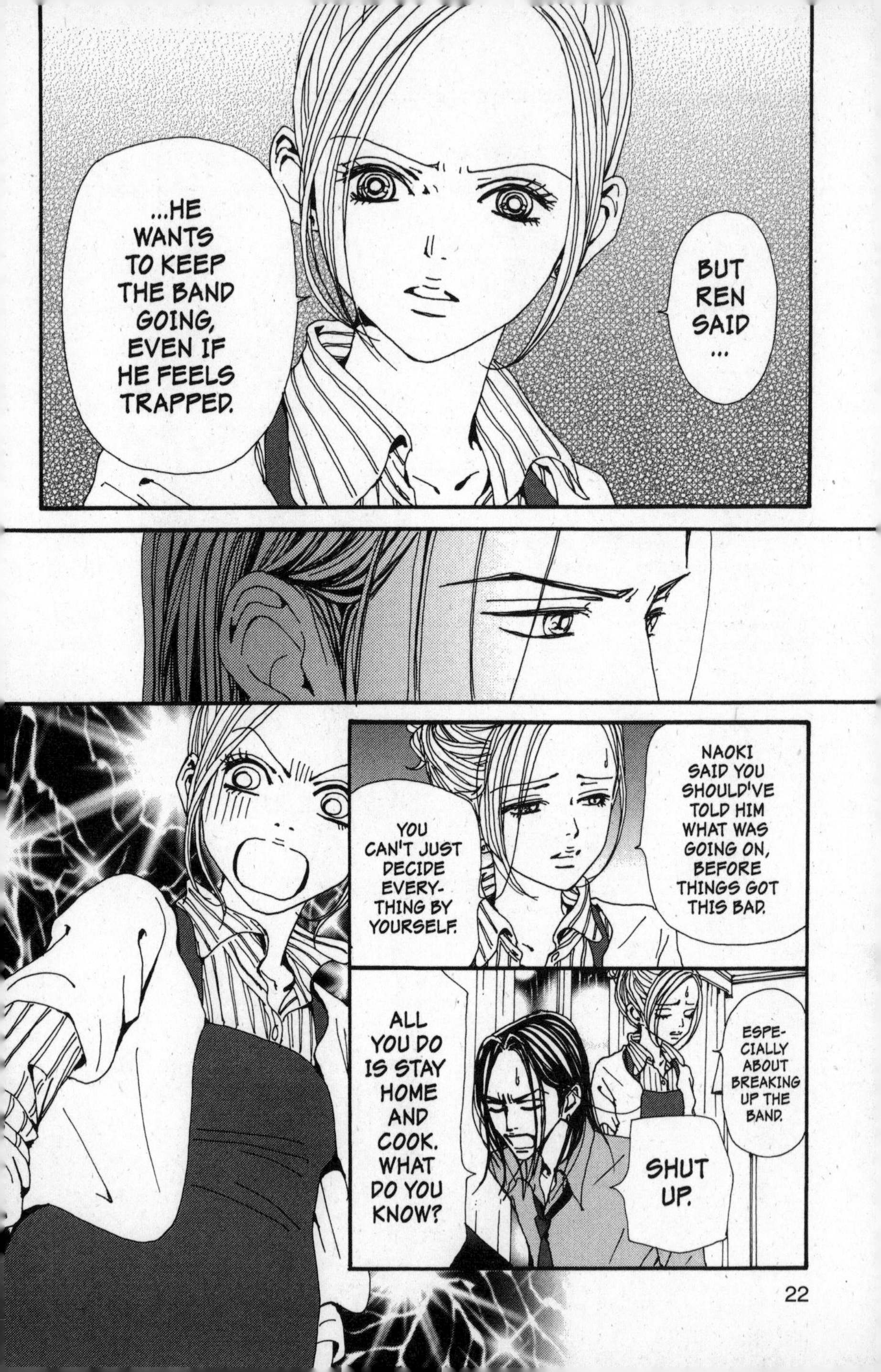
BUT REN SAID ...
...HE WANTS TO KEEP THE BAND GOING, EVEN IF HE FEELS TRAPPED.
NAOKI SAID YOU SHOULD'VE TOLD HIM WHAT WAS GOING ON, BEFORE THINGS GOT THIS BAD.
YOU CAN'T JUST DECIDE EVERY-THING BY YOURSELF.
ESPE-CIALLY ABOUT BREAKING UP THE BAND.
SHUT UP.
ALL YOU DO IS STAY HOME AND COOK. WHAT DO YOU KNOW?

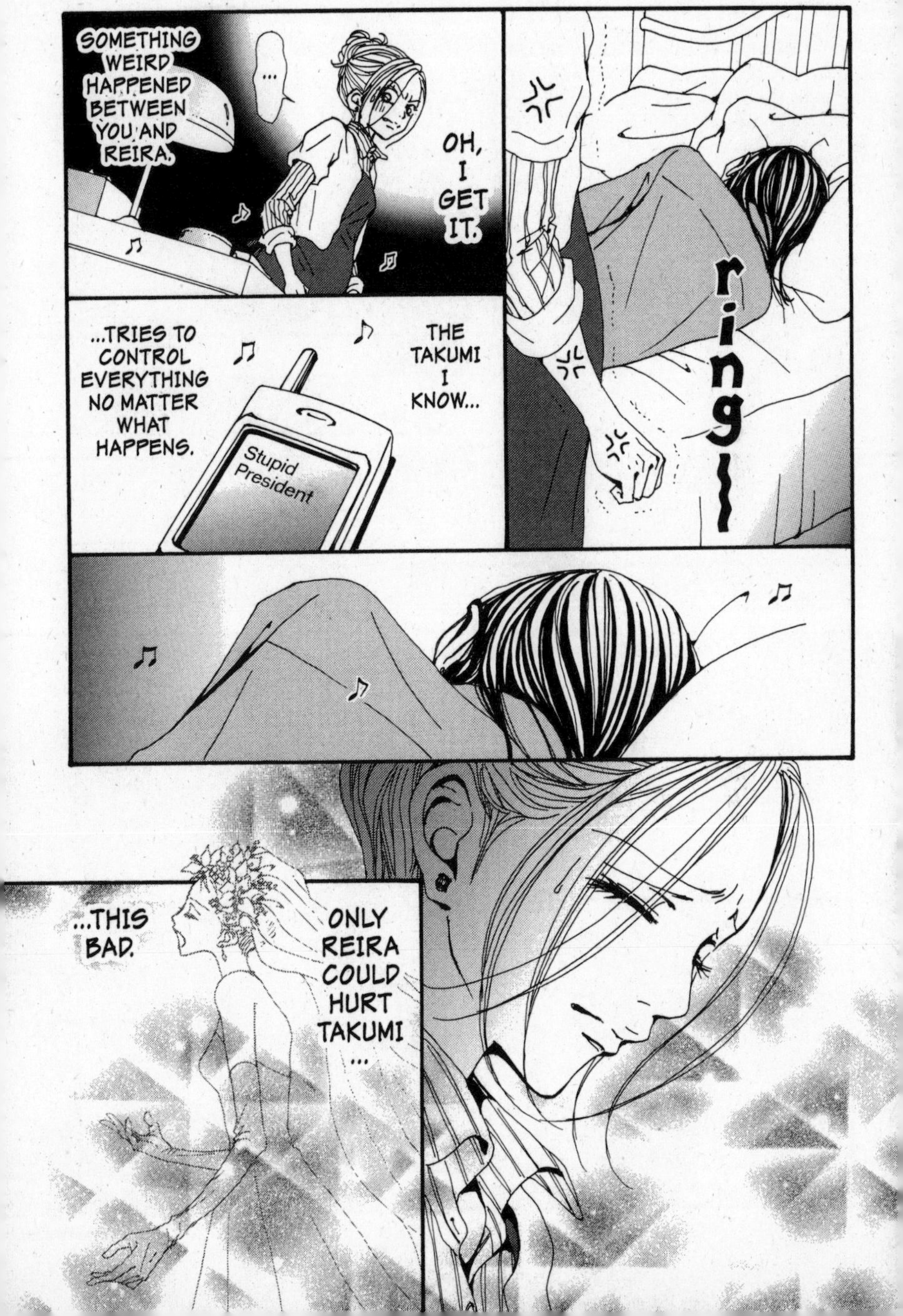
ring~
OH, I GET IT.
...
SOMETHING WEIRD HAPPENED BETWEEN YOU AND REIRA.
THE TAKUMI I KNOW...
...TRIES TO CONTROL EVERYTHING NO MATTER WHAT HAPPENS.
Stupid President
ONLY REIRA COULD HURT TAKUMI...
...THIS BAD.

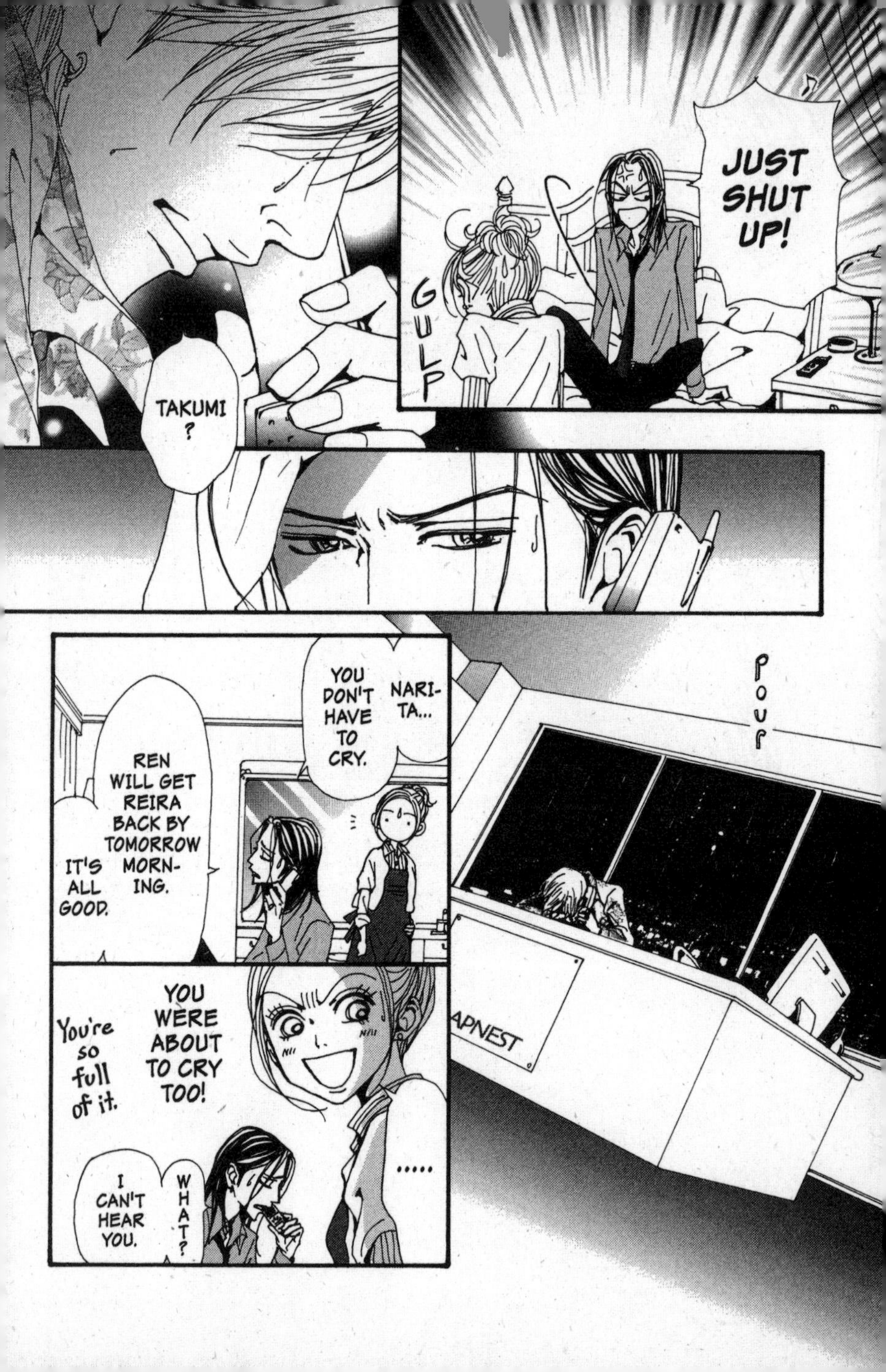
JUST SHUT UP!
GULP
TAKUMI?
POUR
APNEST
NARI-TA...
YOU DON'T HAVE TO CRY.
REN WILL GET REIRA BACK BY TOMORROW MORN-ING.
IT'S ALL GOOD.
YOU WERE ABOUT TO CRY TOO!
You're so full of it.
.....
WHAT?
I CAN'T HEAR YOU.

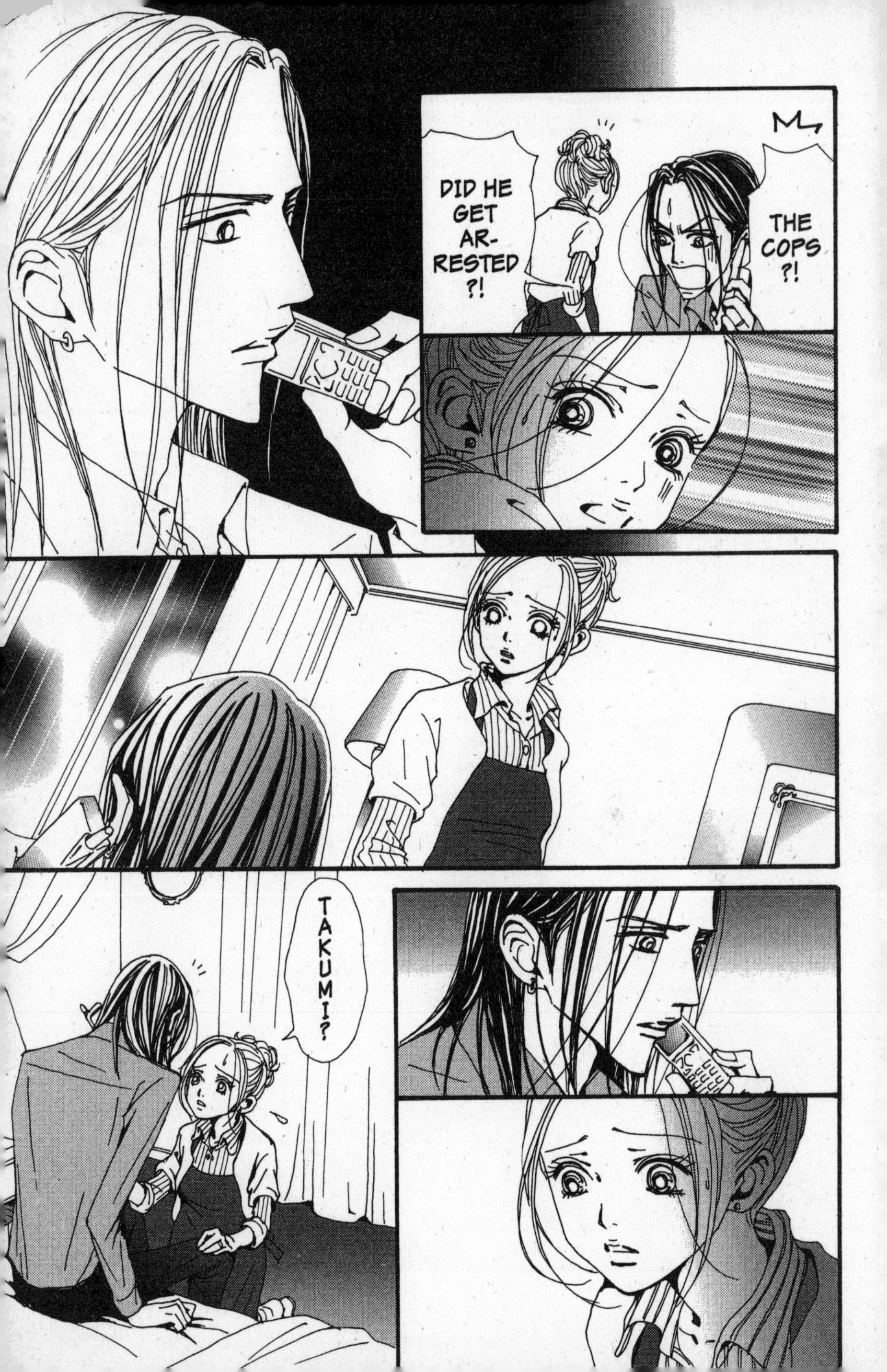
THE COPS ?!
DID HE GET AR-RESTED ?!
TAKUMI?

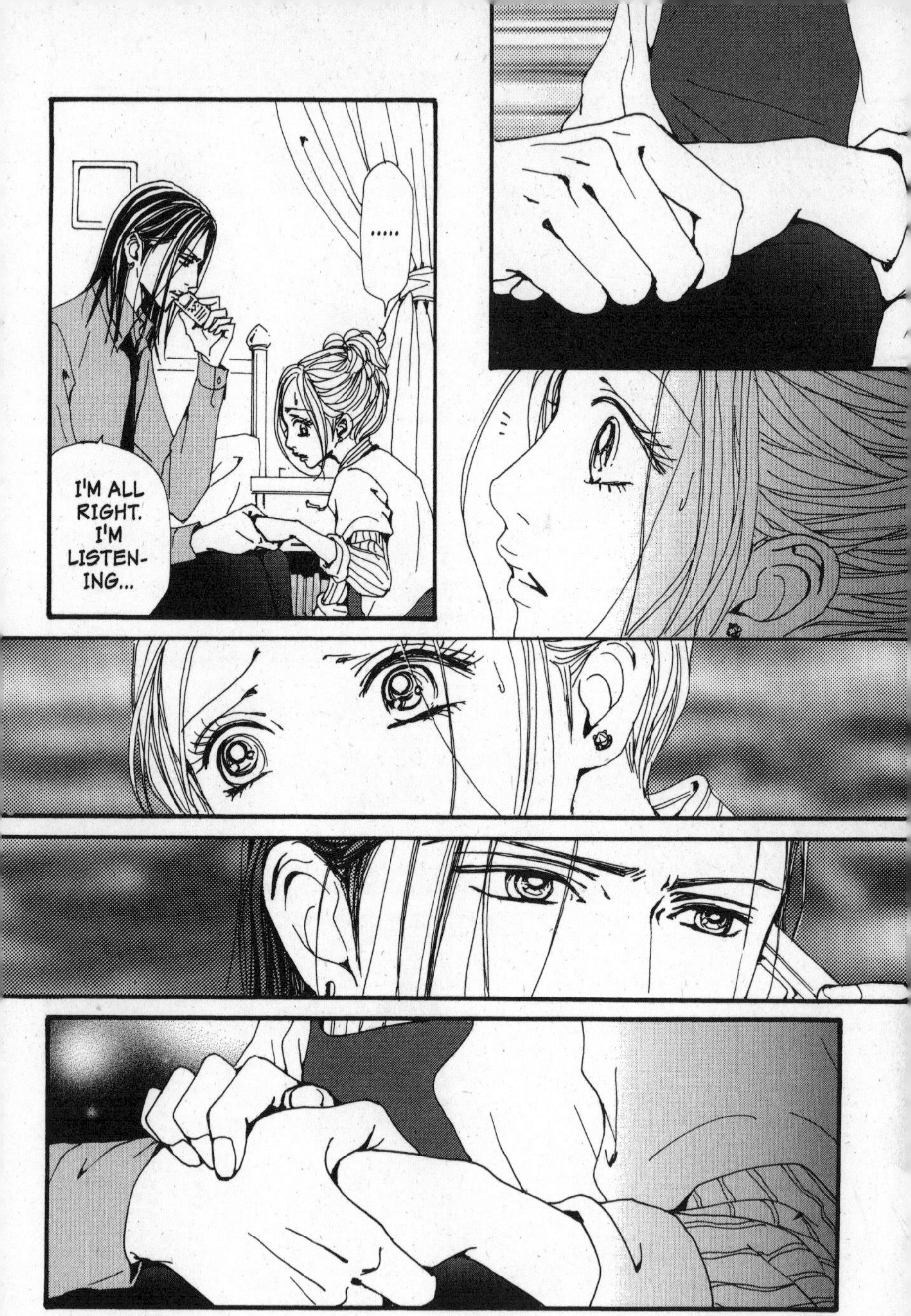
.....
I'M ALL RIGHT. I'M LISTEN-ING...

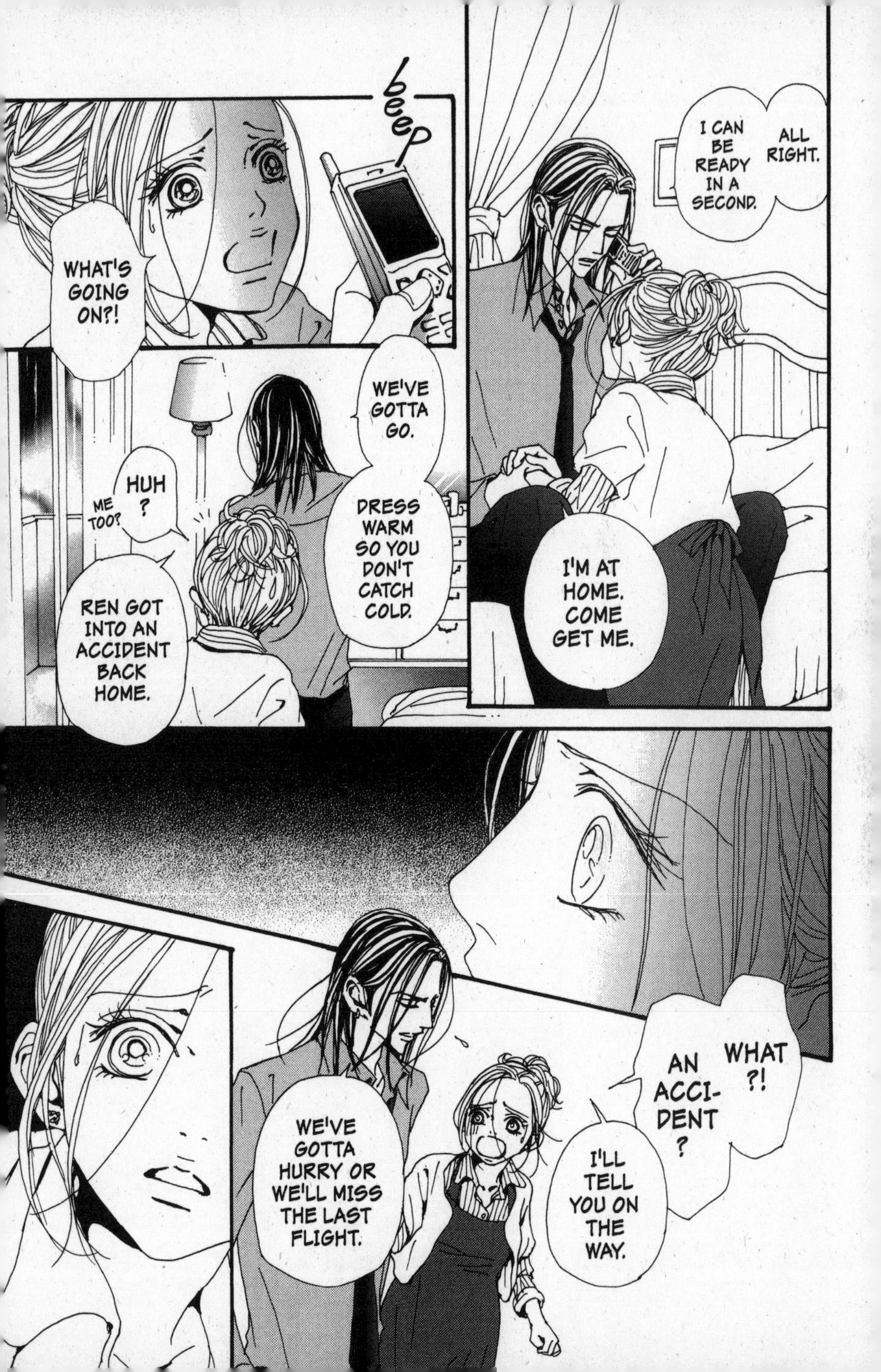
ALL RIGHT.
I CAN BE READY IN A SECOND.
I'M AT HOME. COME GET ME.
beep
WHAT'S GOING ON?!
WE'VE GOTTA GO.
DRESS WARM SO YOU DON'T CATCH COLD.
HUH?
ME TOO?
REN GOT INTO AN ACCIDENT BACK HOME.
WHAT?!
AN ACCI-DENT?
I'LL TELL YOU ON THE WAY.
WE'VE GOTTA HURRY OR WE'LL MISS THE LAST FLIGHT.

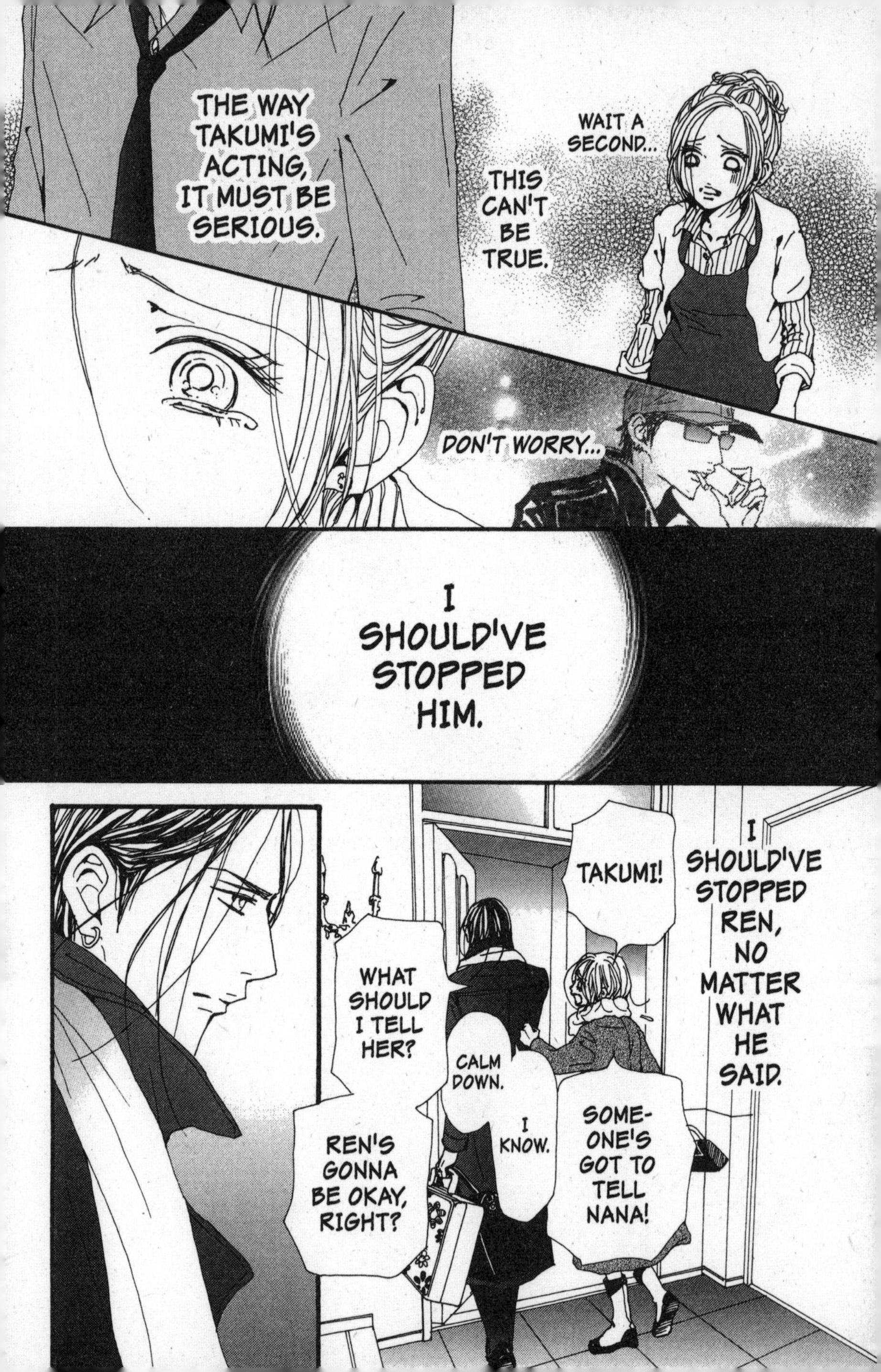
WAIT A SECOND...
THIS CAN'T BE TRUE.
THE WAY TAKUMI'S ACTING, IT MUST BE SERIOUS.
DON'T WORRY...
I SHOULD'VE STOPPED HIM.
I SHOULD'VE STOPPED REN, NO MATTER WHAT HE SAID.
TAKUMI!
SOME-ONE'S GOT TO TELL NANA!
I KNOW.
CALM DOWN.
WHAT SHOULD I TELL HER?
REN'S GONNA BE OKAY, RIGHT?

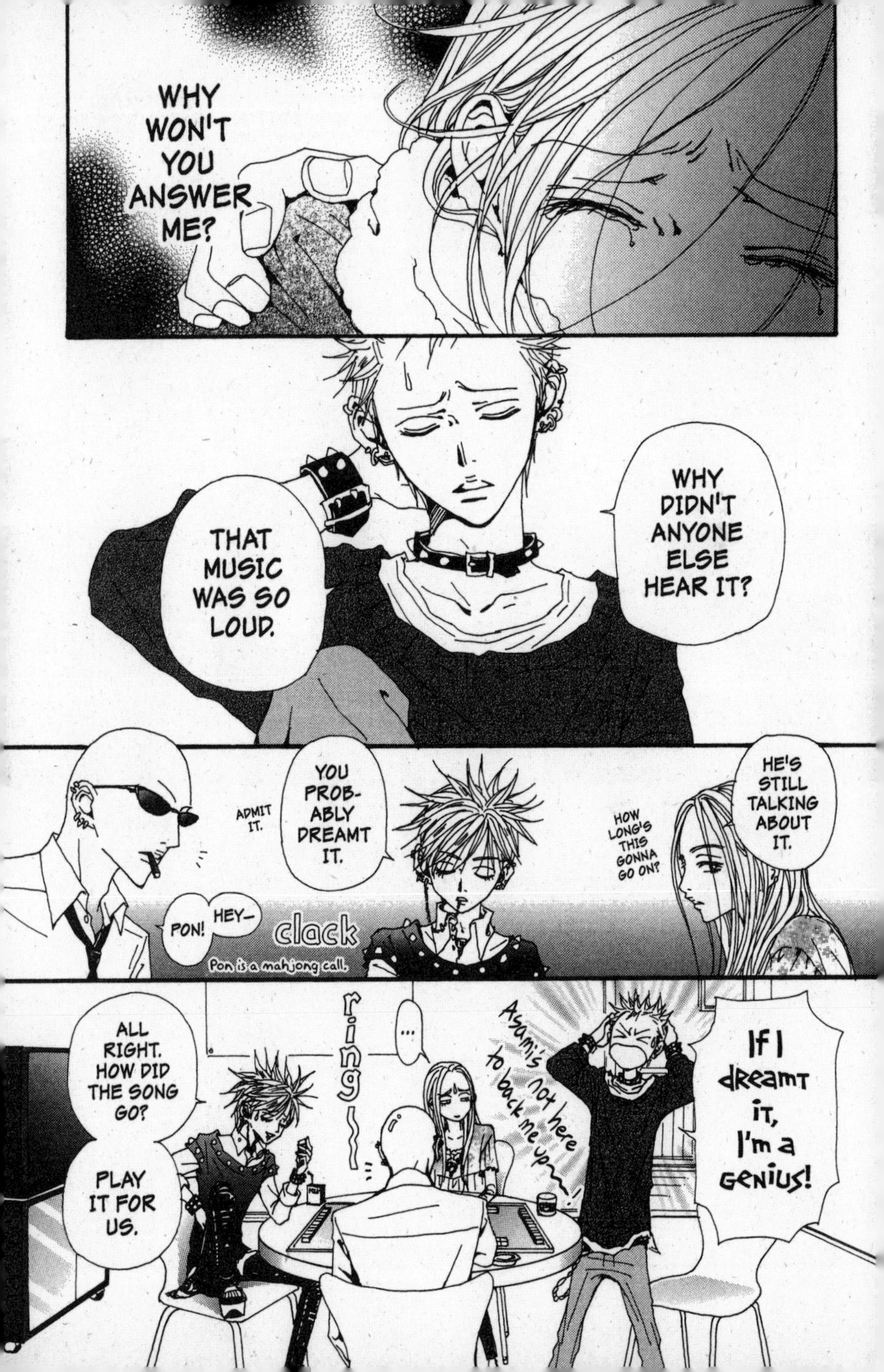
WHY WON'T YOU ANSWER ME?
WHY DIDN'T ANYONE ELSE HEAR IT?
THAT MUSIC WAS SO LOUD.
HE'S STILL TALKING ABOUT IT.
HOW LONG'S THIS GONNA GO ON?
YOU PROBABLY DREAMT IT.
ADMIT IT.
HEY—
PON!
clack
Pon is a mahjong call.
If I dreamt it, I'm a genius!
Asami's not here to back me up~!
...
ring~
ALL RIGHT. HOW DID THE SONG GO?
PLAY IT FOR US.

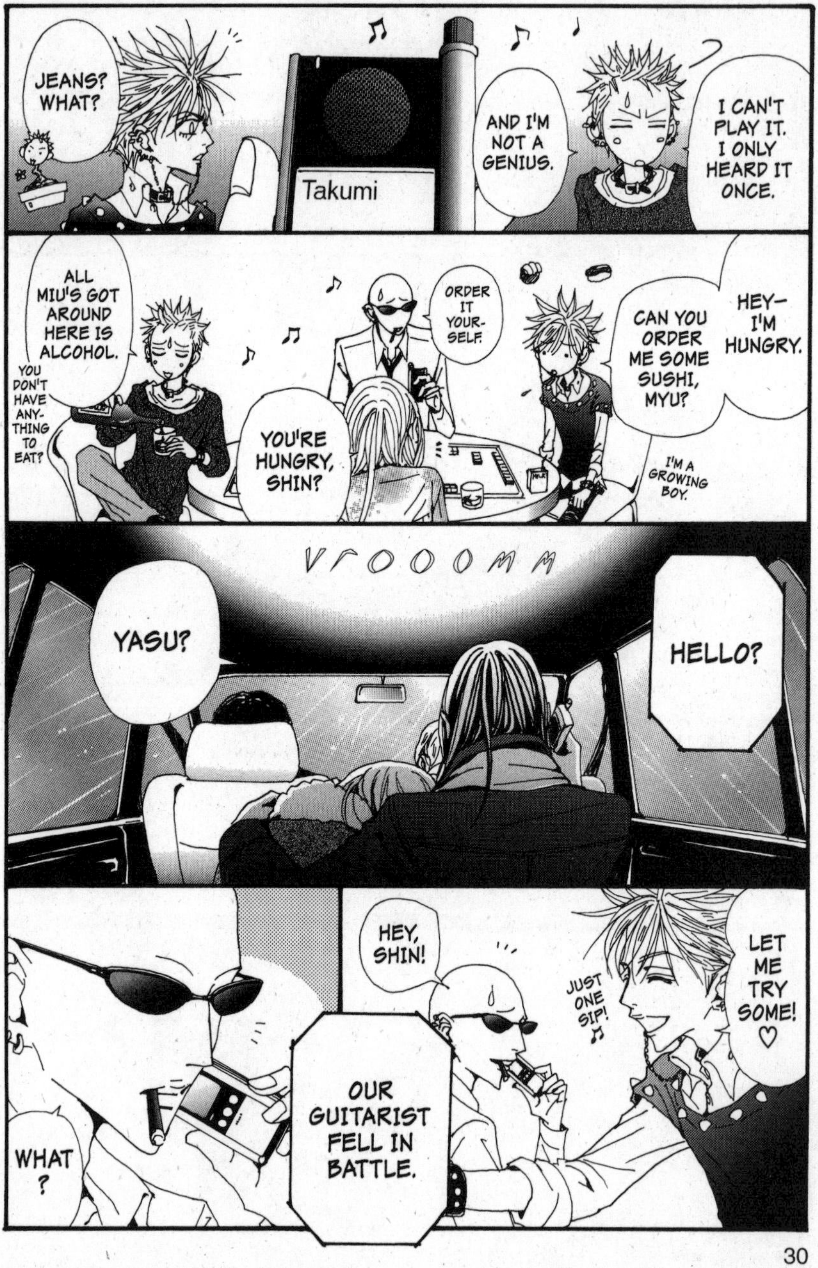
I CAN'T PLAY IT. I ONLY HEARD IT ONCE.
AND I'M NOT A GENIUS.
Takumi
JEANS? WHAT?
HEY— I'M HUNGRY.
CAN YOU ORDER ME SOME SUSHI, MYU?
I'M A GROWING BOY.
ORDER IT YOURSELF.
YOU'RE HUNGRY, SHIN?
ALL MIU'S GOT AROUND HERE IS ALCOHOL.
YOU DON'T HAVE ANYTHING TO EAT?
VROOOMM
HELLO?
YASU?
LET ME TRY SOME! ♡
JUST ONE SIP! ♪
HEY, SHIN!
OUR GUITARIST FELL IN BATTLE.
WHAT?

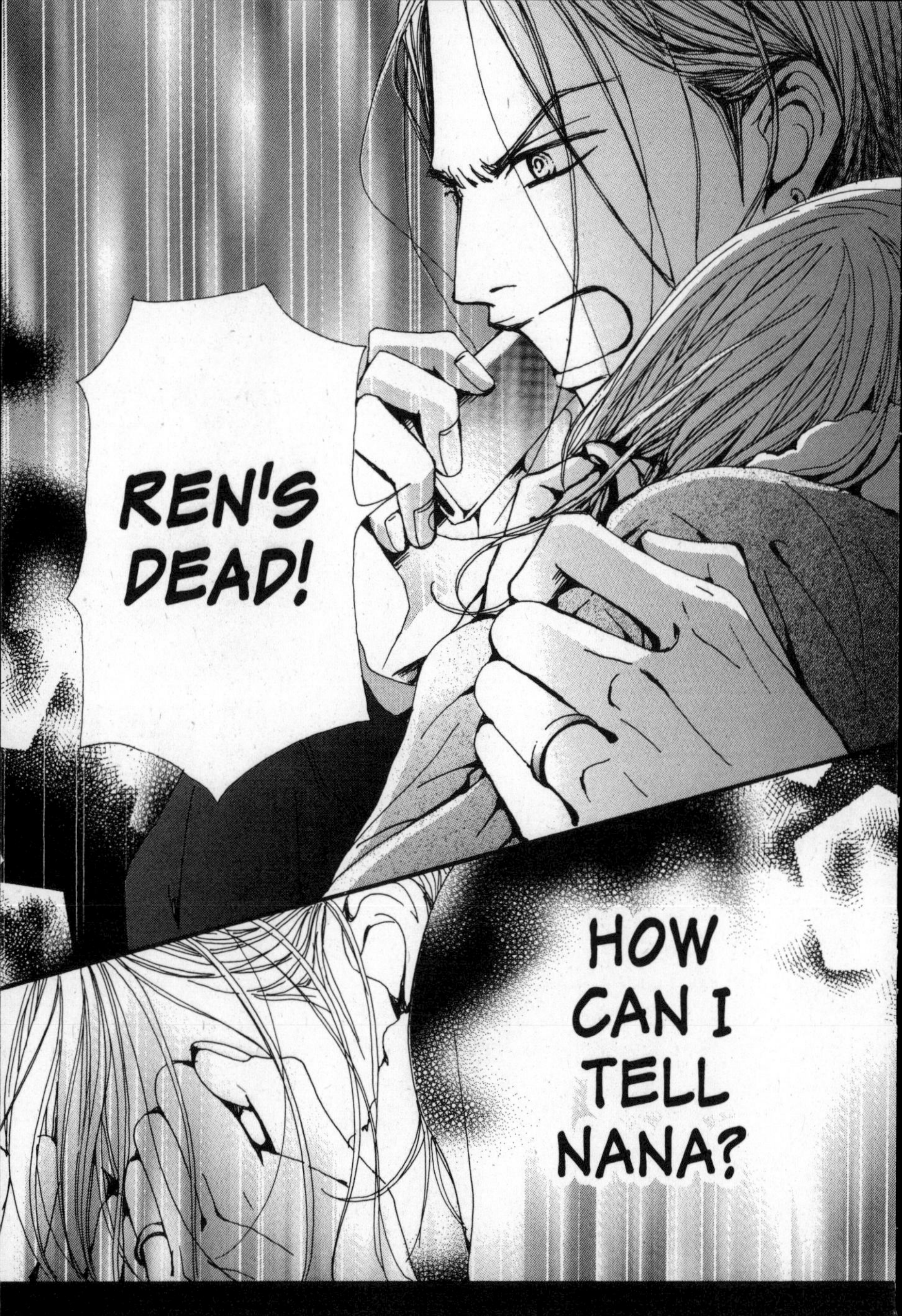
REN'S DEAD!
HOW CAN I TELL NANA?

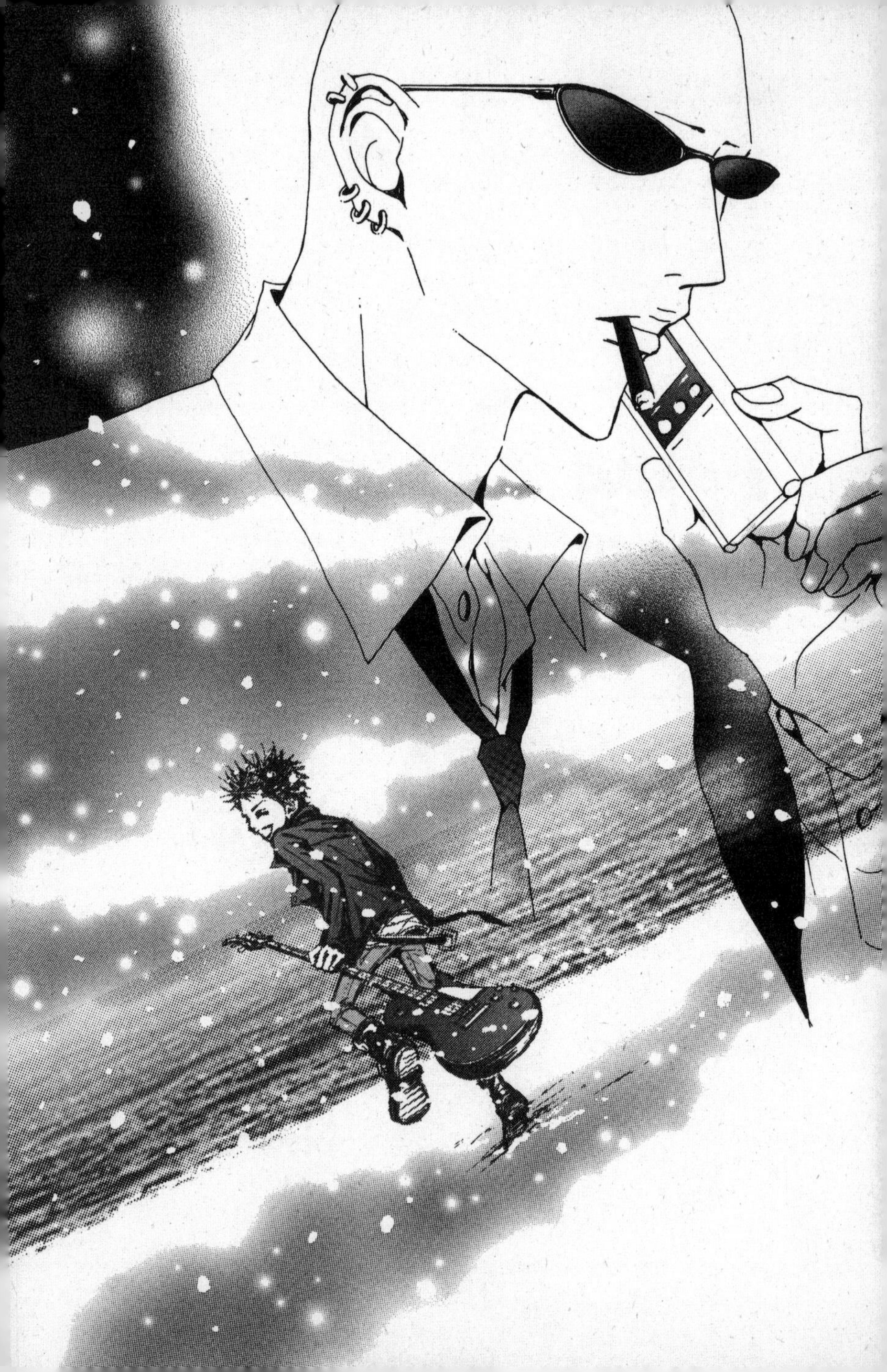

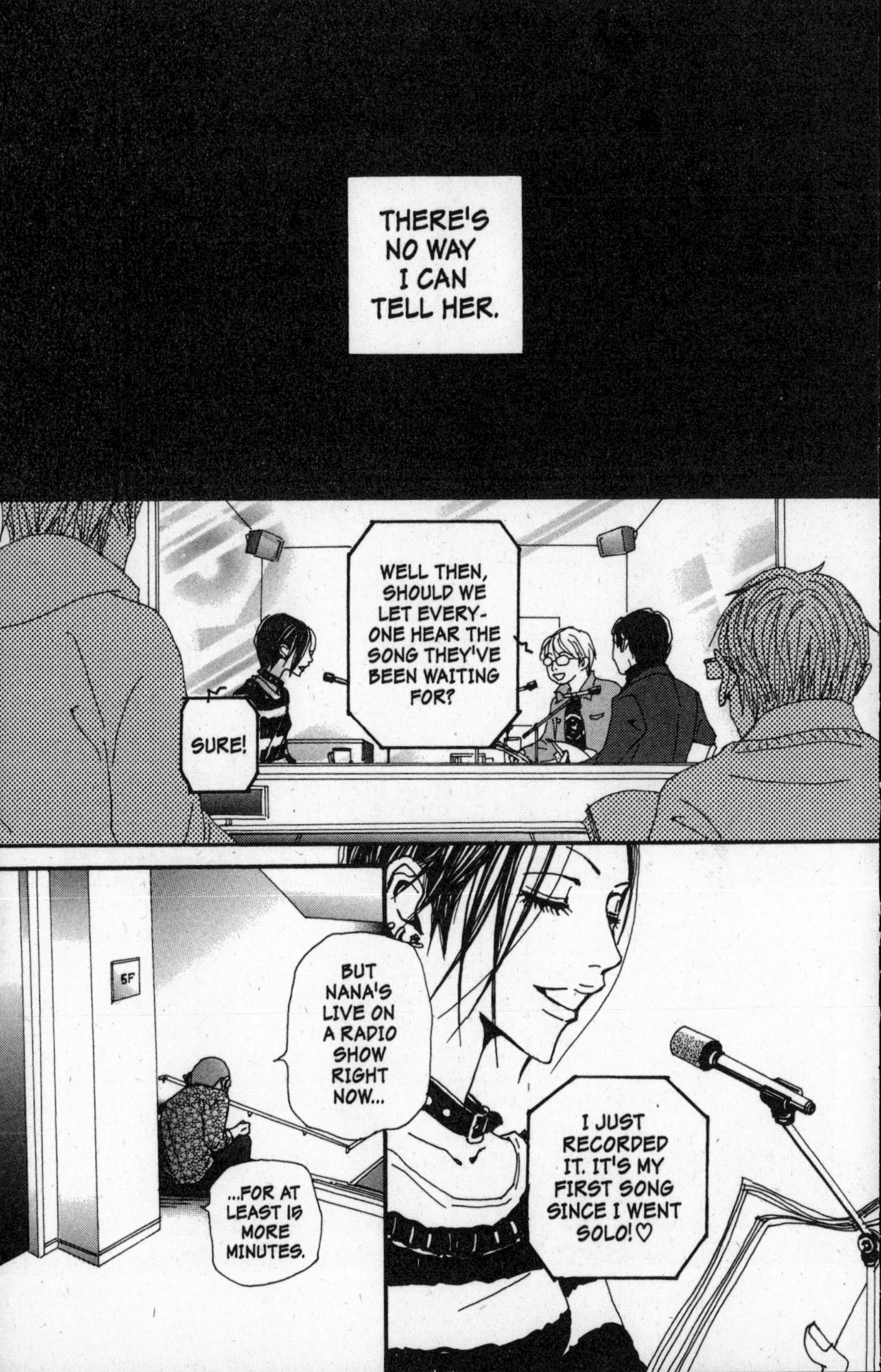

THERE'S NO WAY I CAN TELL HER.
WELL THEN, SHOULD WE LET EVERY-ONE HEAR THE SONG THEY'VE BEEN WAITING FOR?
SURE!
I JUST RECORDED IT. IT'S MY FIRST SONG SINCE I WENT SOLO! ♡
BUT NANA'S LIVE ON A RADIO SHOW RIGHT NOW...
...FOR AT LEAST 15 MORE MINUTES.
5F

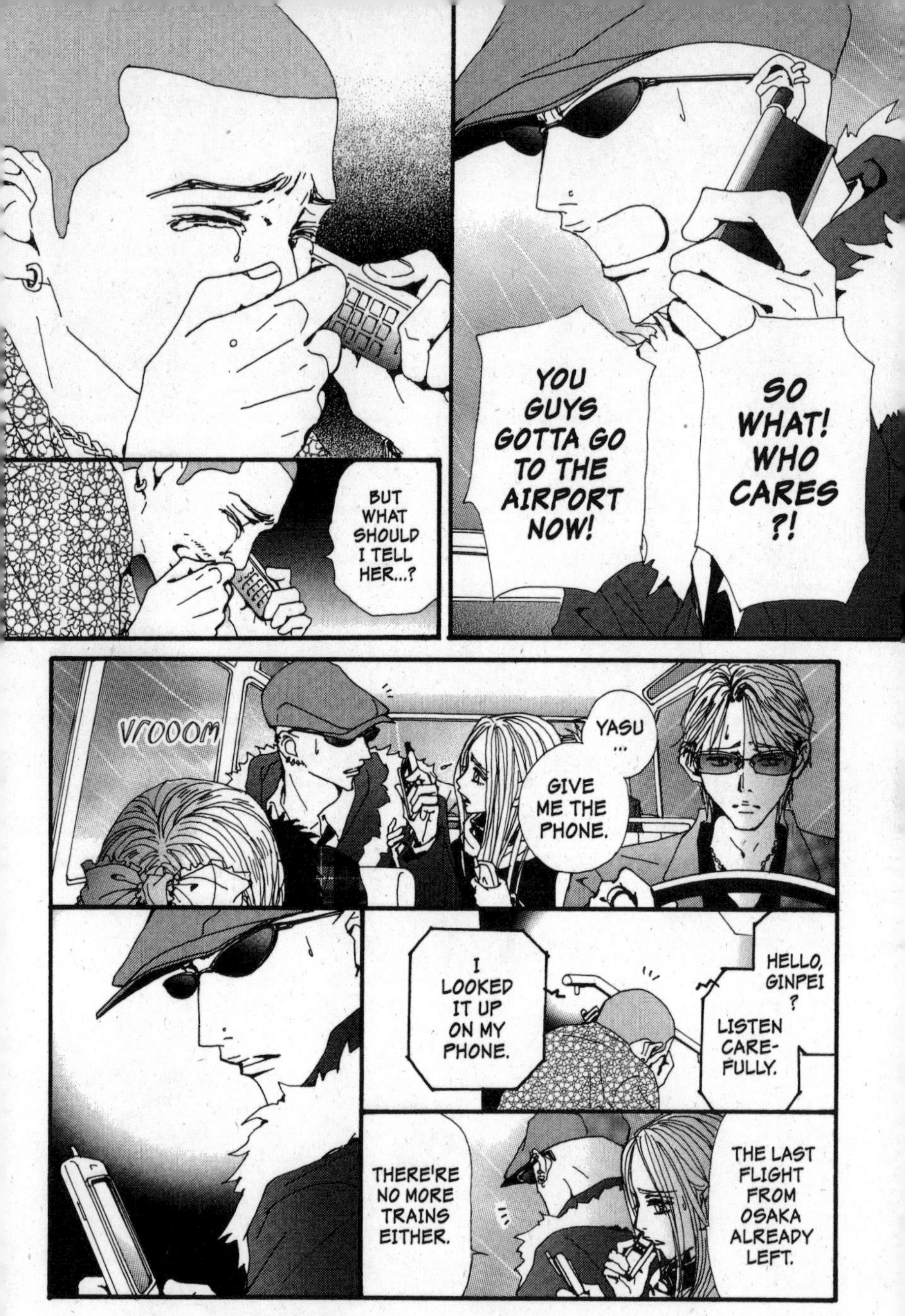
SO WHAT! WHO CARES?!
YOU GUYS GOTTA GO TO THE AIRPORT NOW!
BUT WHAT SHOULD I TELL HER...?
YASU ...
GIVE ME THE PHONE.
VROOOM
HELLO, GINPEI?
LISTEN CAREFULLY.
I LOOKED IT UP ON MY PHONE.
THE LAST FLIGHT FROM OSAKA ALREADY LEFT.
THERE'RE NO MORE TRAINS EITHER.

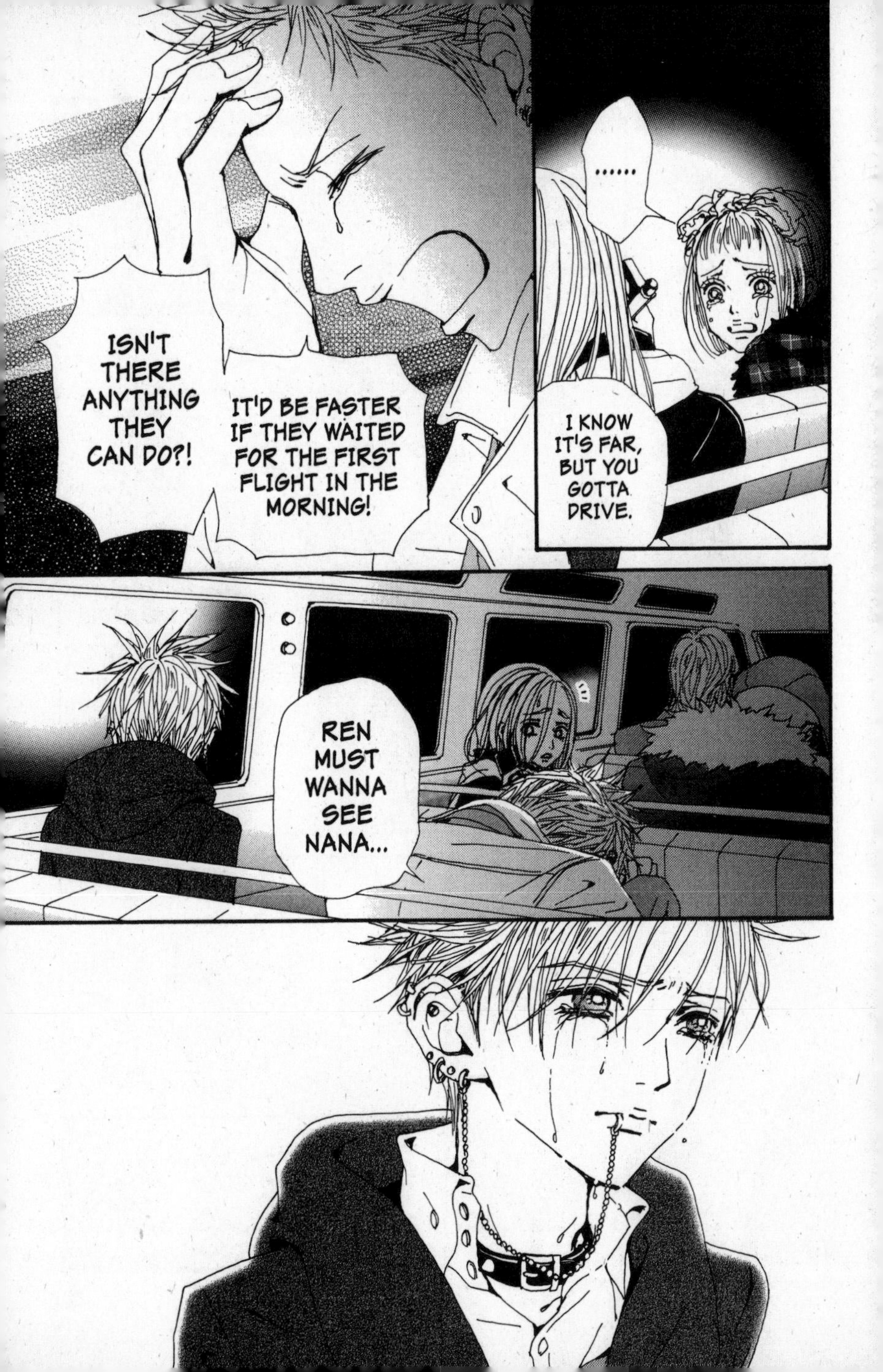
......
I KNOW IT'S FAR, BUT YOU GOTTA DRIVE.
IT'D BE FASTER IF THEY WAITED FOR THE FIRST FLIGHT IN THE MORNING!
ISN'T THERE ANYTHING THEY CAN DO?!
REN MUST WANNA SEE NANA...

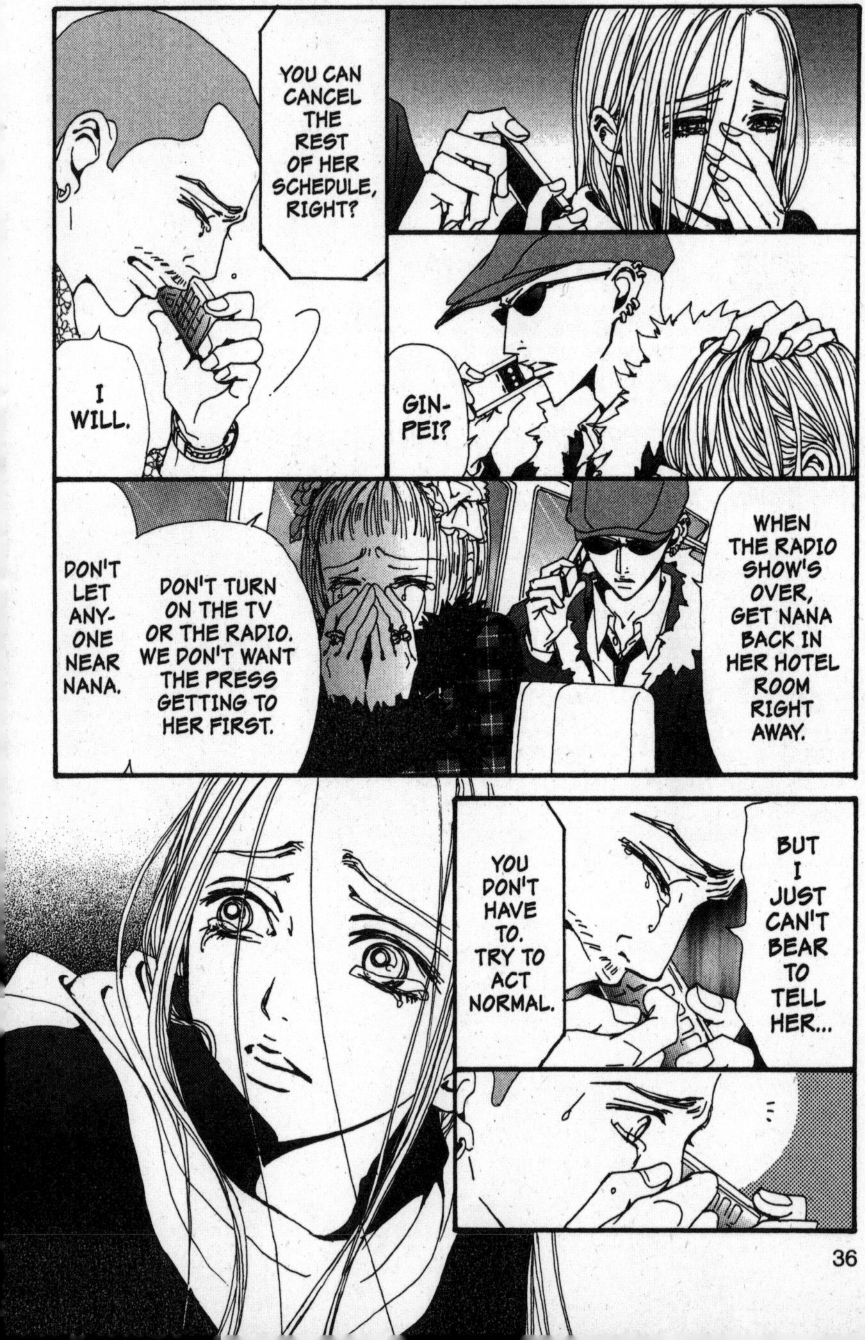
GIN-PEI?
YOU CAN CANCEL THE REST OF HER SCHEDULE, RIGHT?
I WILL.
WHEN THE RADIO SHOW'S OVER, GET NANA BACK IN HER HOTEL ROOM RIGHT AWAY.
DON'T TURN ON THE TV OR THE RADIO. WE DON'T WANT THE PRESS GETTING TO HER FIRST.
DON'T LET ANY-ONE NEAR NANA.
BUT I JUST CAN'T BEAR TO TELL HER...
YOU DON'T HAVE TO. TRY TO ACT NORMAL.
...

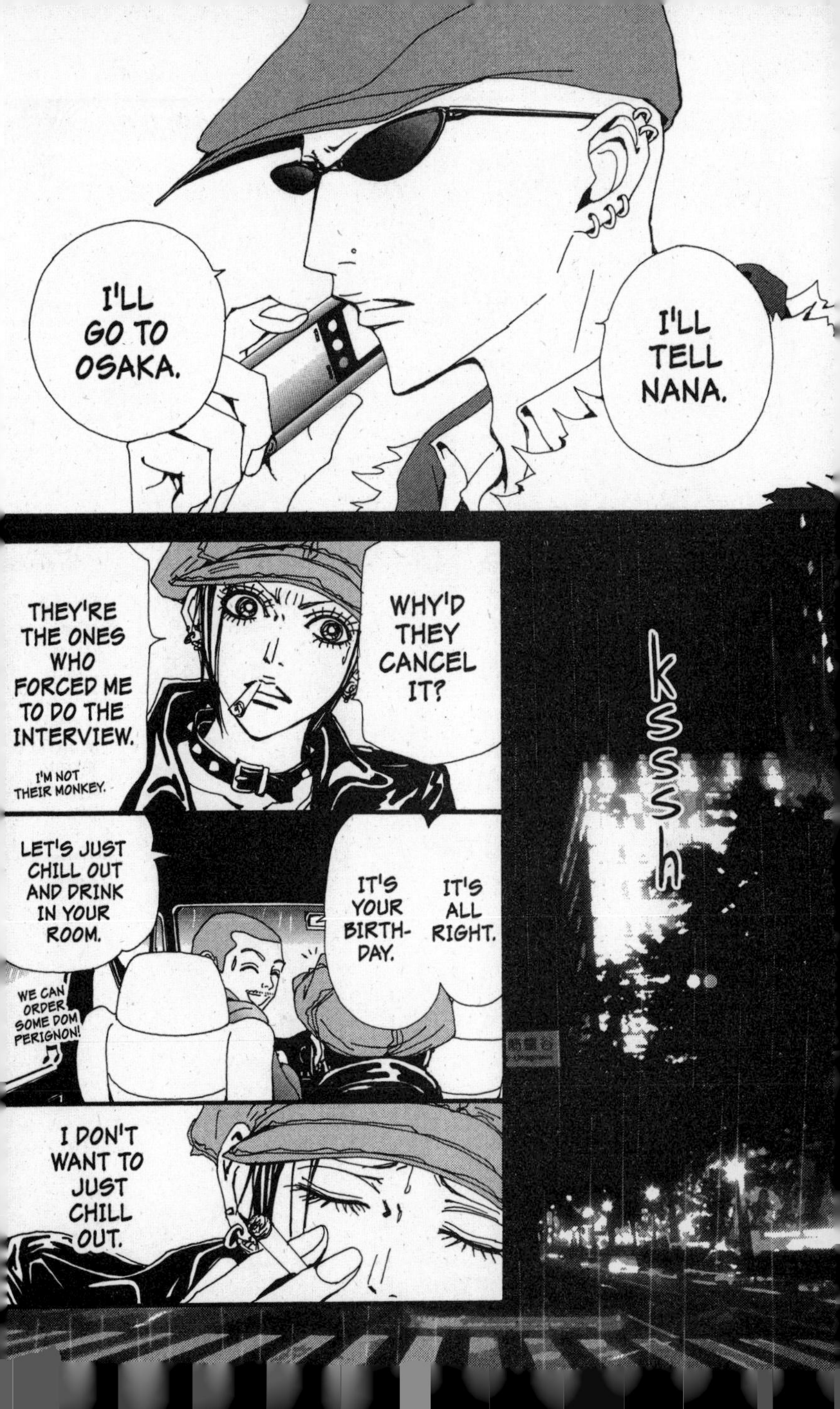
I'LL TELL NANA.
I'LL GO TO OSAKA.
KSSSH
WHY'D THEY CANCEL IT?
THEY'RE THE ONES WHO FORCED ME TO DO THE INTERVIEW.
I'M NOT THEIR MONKEY.
IT'S ALL RIGHT.
IT'S YOUR BIRTHDAY.
LET'S JUST CHILL OUT AND DRINK IN YOUR ROOM.
WE CAN ORDER SOME DOM PERIGNON!
I DON'T WANT TO JUST CHILL OUT.

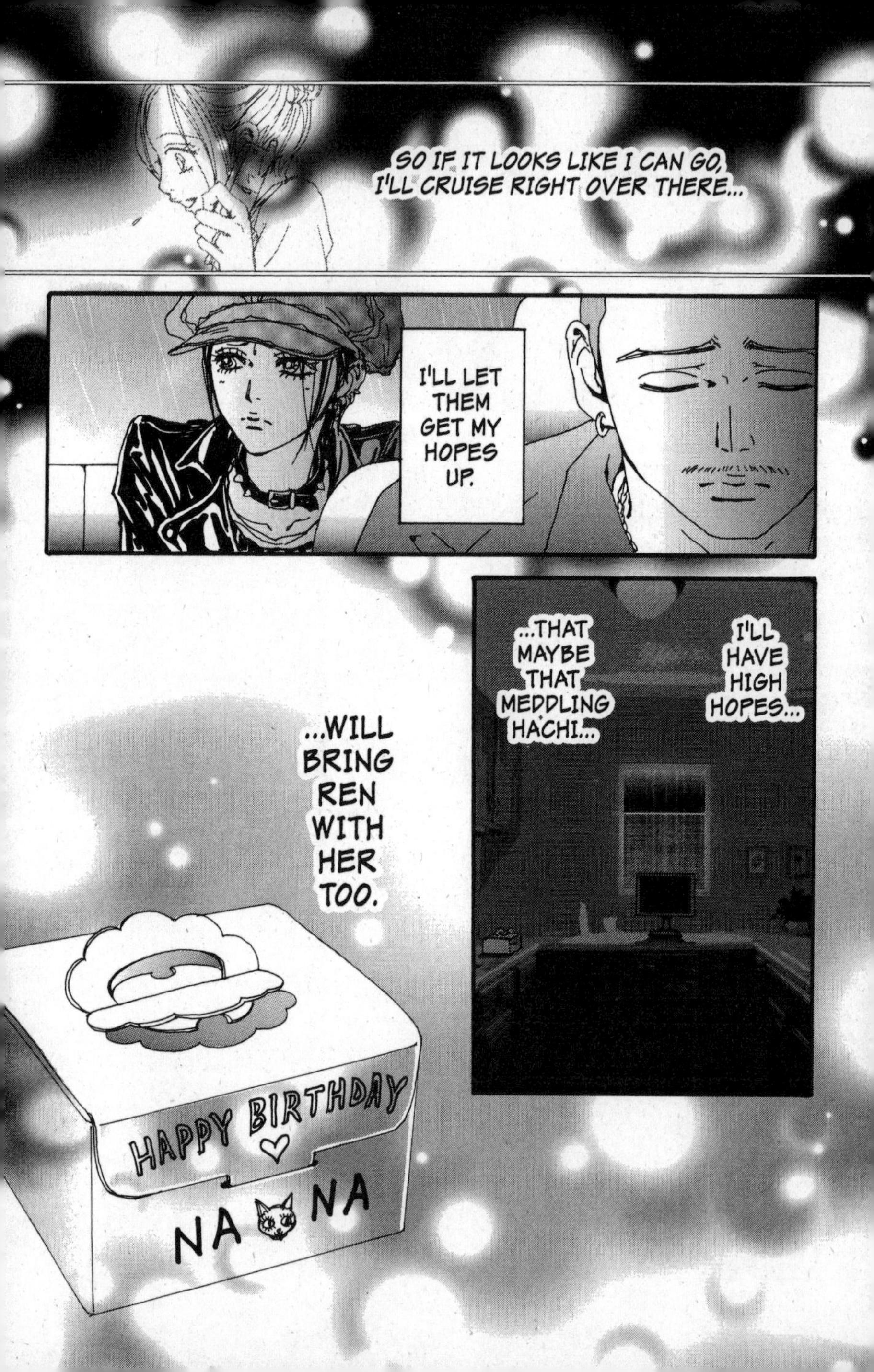
SO IF IT LOOKS LIKE I CAN GO, I'LL CRUISE RIGHT OVER THERE...
I'LL LET THEM GET MY HOPES UP.
I'LL HAVE HIGH HOPES...
...THAT MAYBE THAT MEDDLING HACHI...
...WILL BRING REN WITH HER TOO.
HAPPY BIRTHDAY ♥
NA NA

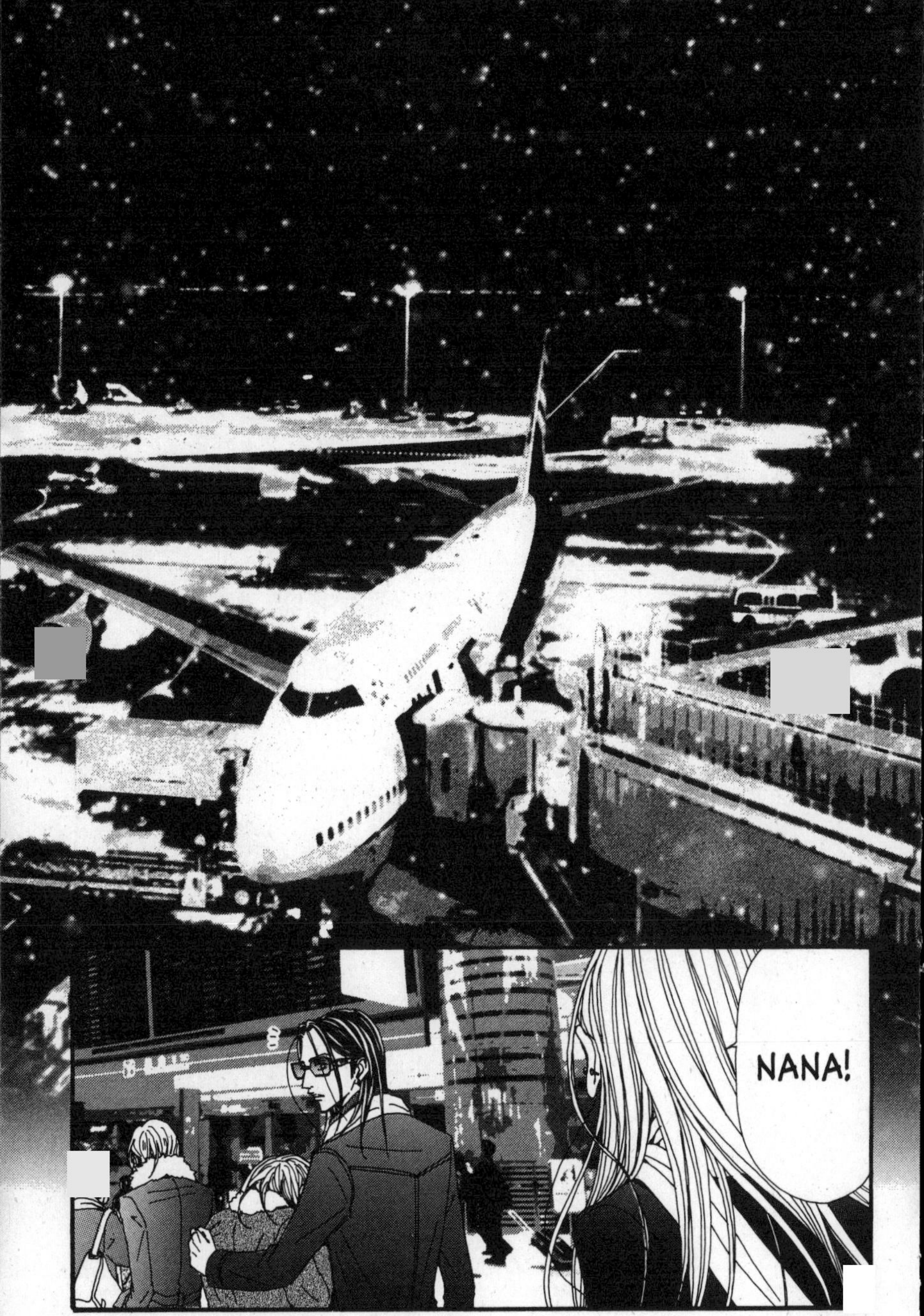
NANA!

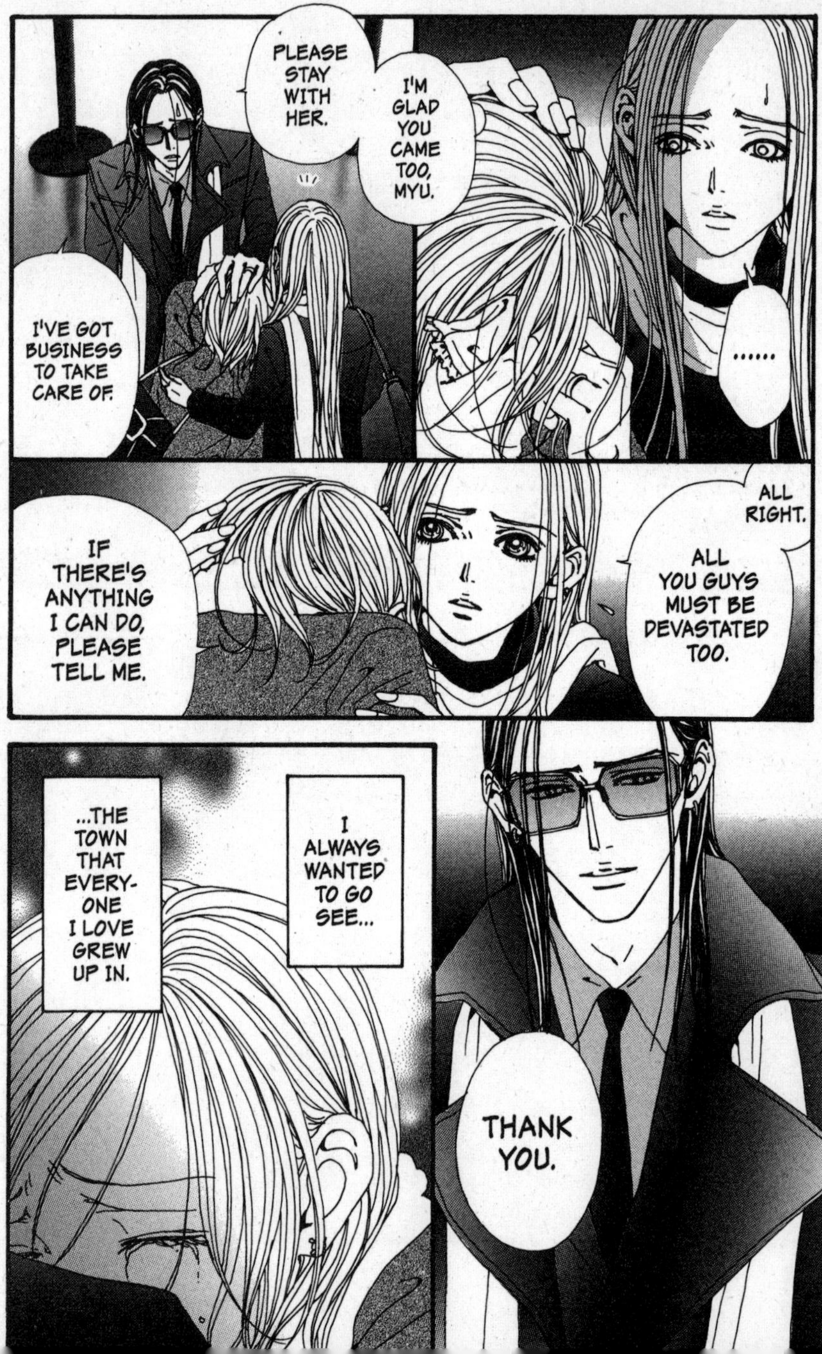
......
I'M GLAD YOU CAME TOO, MYU.
PLEASE STAY WITH HER.
I'VE GOT BUSINESS TO TAKE CARE OF.
ALL RIGHT.
ALL YOU GUYS MUST BE DEVASTATED TOO.
IF THERE'S ANYTHING I CAN DO, PLEASE TELL ME.
THANK YOU.
I ALWAYS WANTED TO GO SEE...
...THE TOWN THAT EVERY-ONE I LOVE GREW UP IN.

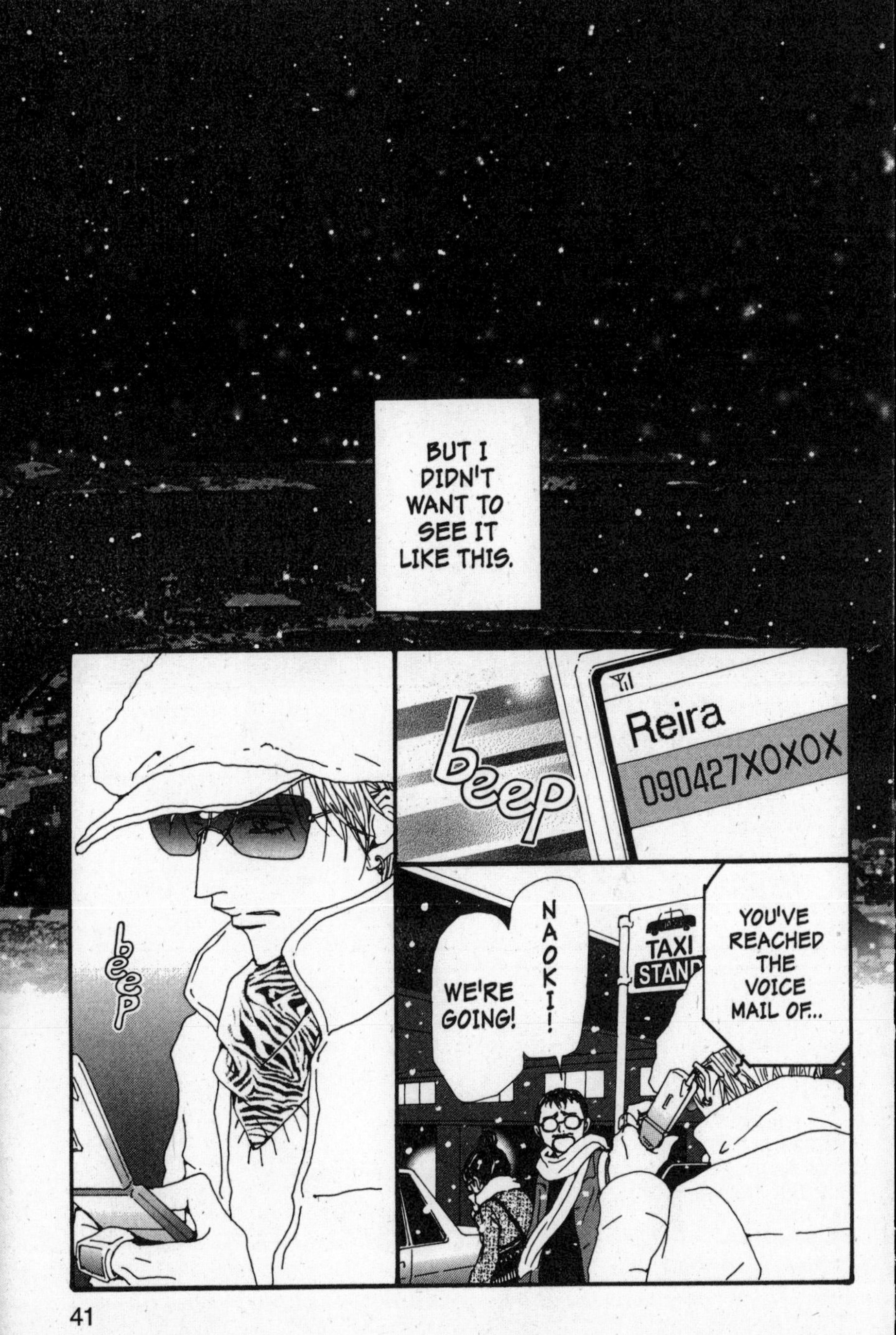
BUT I DIDN'T WANT TO SEE IT LIKE THIS.
Reira
090427XOXOX
beep
YOU'VE REACHED THE VOICE MAIL OF...
TAXI
STAND
NAOKI!
WE'RE GOING!
beep

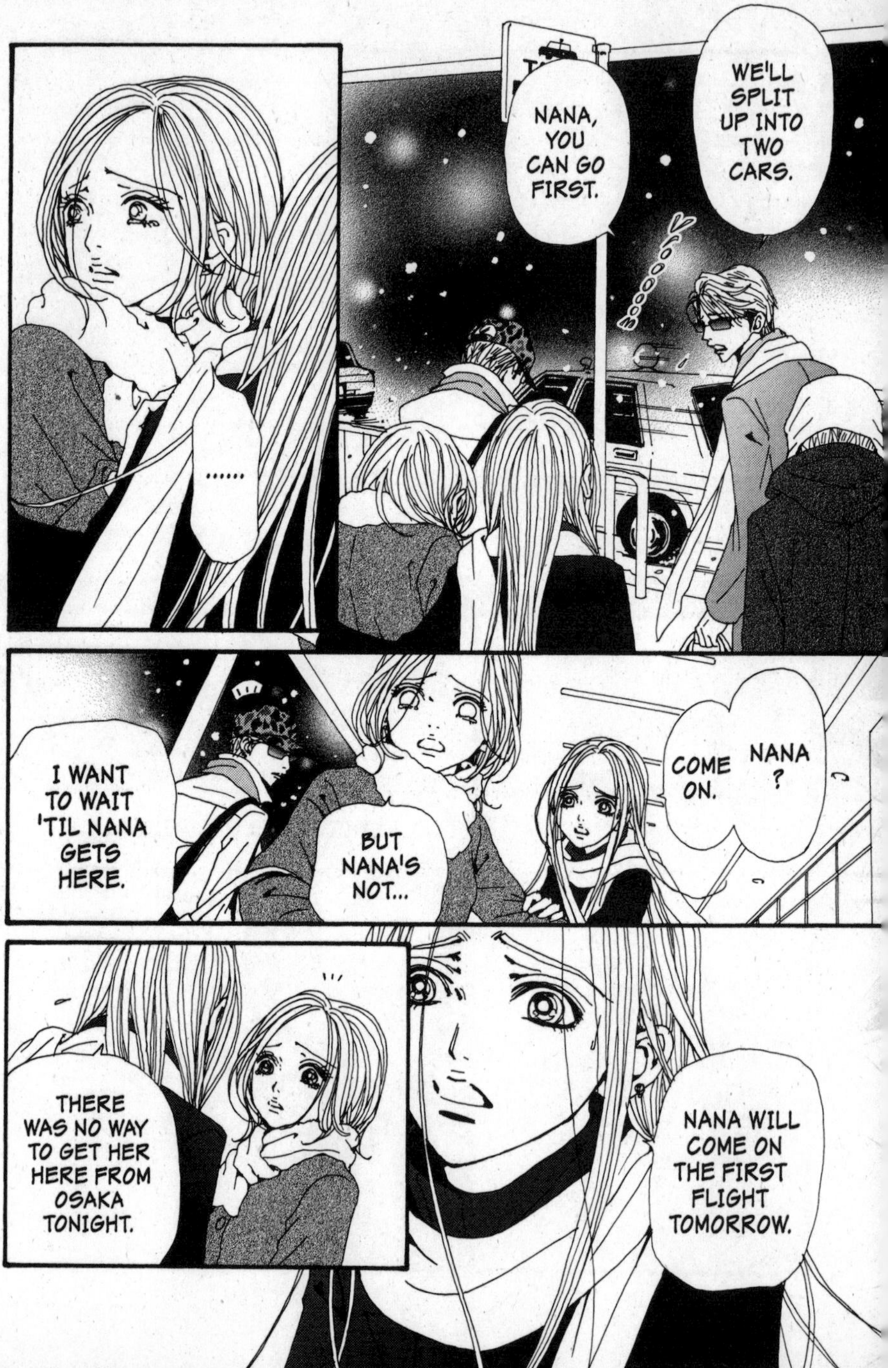
WE'LL SPLIT UP INTO TWO CARS.
NANA, YOU CAN GO FIRST.
Vroooooom
......
NANA ?
COME ON.
BUT NANA'S NOT...
I WANT TO WAIT 'TIL NANA GETS HERE.
NANA WILL COME ON THE FIRST FLIGHT TOMORROW.
THERE WAS NO WAY TO GET HER HERE FROM OSAKA TONIGHT.

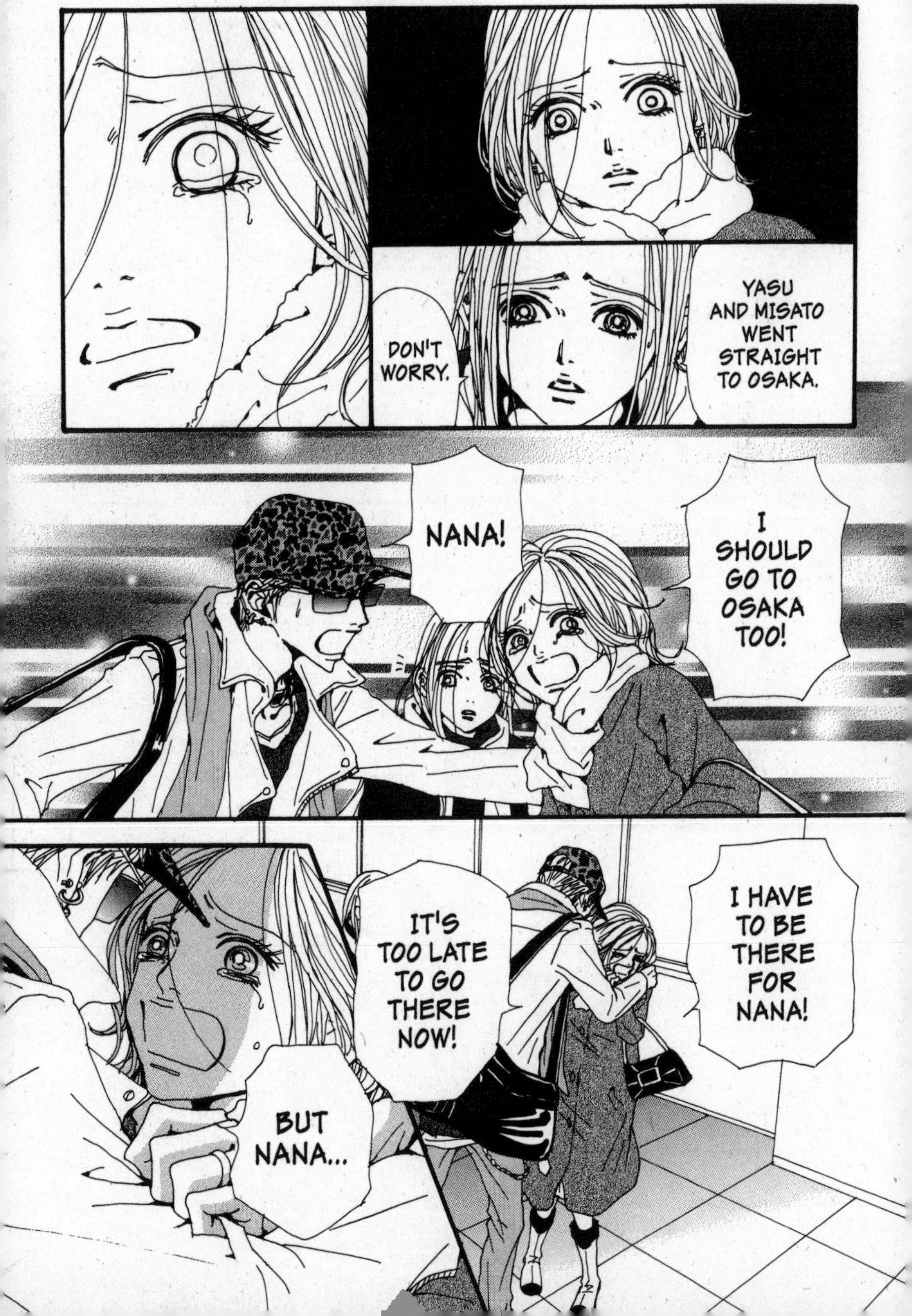
YASU AND MISATO WENT STRAIGHT TO OSAKA.
DON'T WORRY.
I SHOULD GO TO OSAKA TOO!
NANA!
I HAVE TO BE THERE FOR NANA!
IT'S TOO LATE TO GO THERE NOW!
BUT NANA...

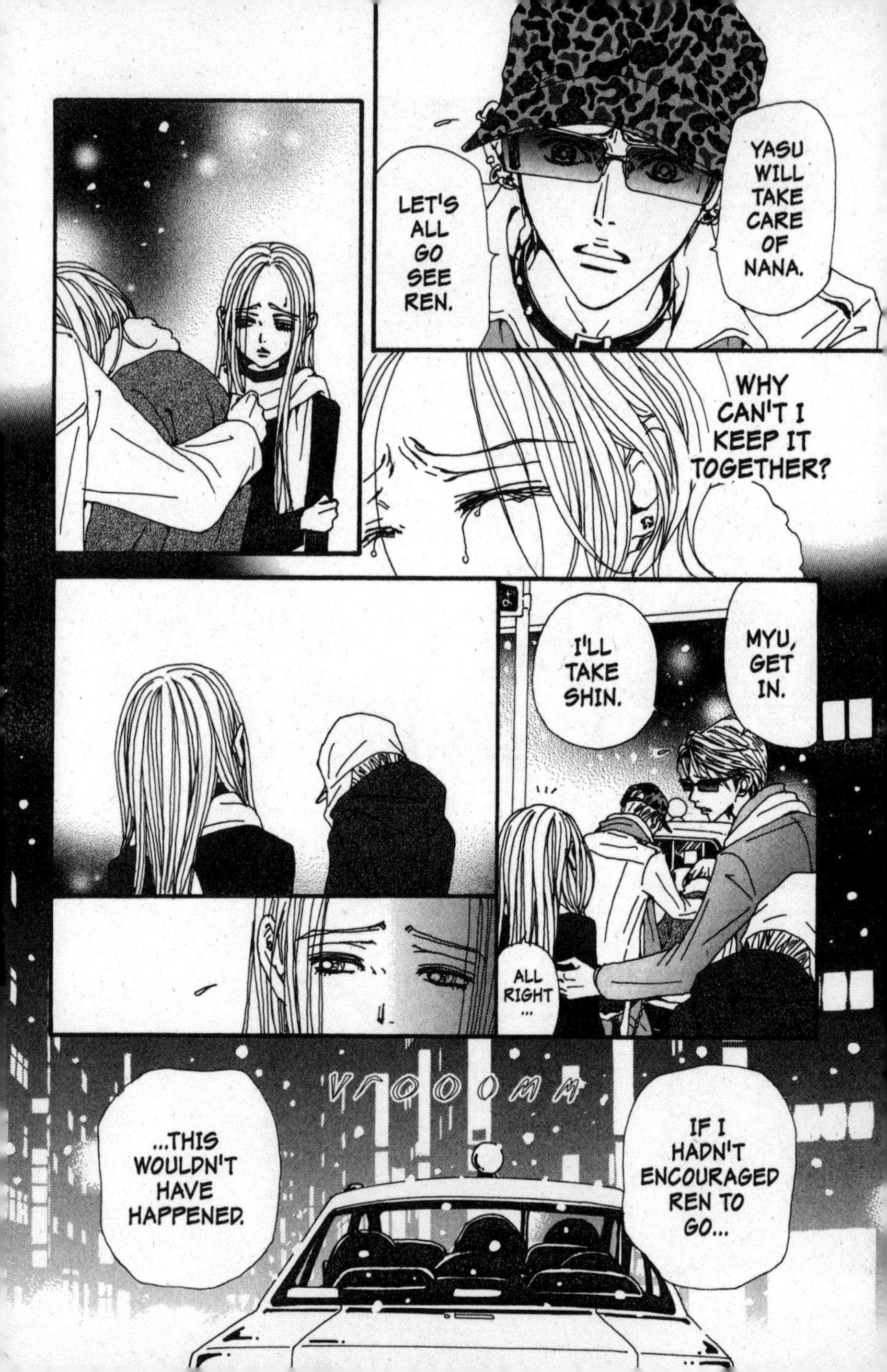
YASU WILL TAKE CARE OF NANA.
LET'S ALL GO SEE REN.
WHY CAN'T I KEEP IT TOGETHER?
MYU, GET IN.
I'LL TAKE SHIN.
ALL RIGHT ...
VROOOMM
IF I HADN'T ENCOURAGED REN TO GO...
...THIS WOULDN'T HAVE HAPPENED.

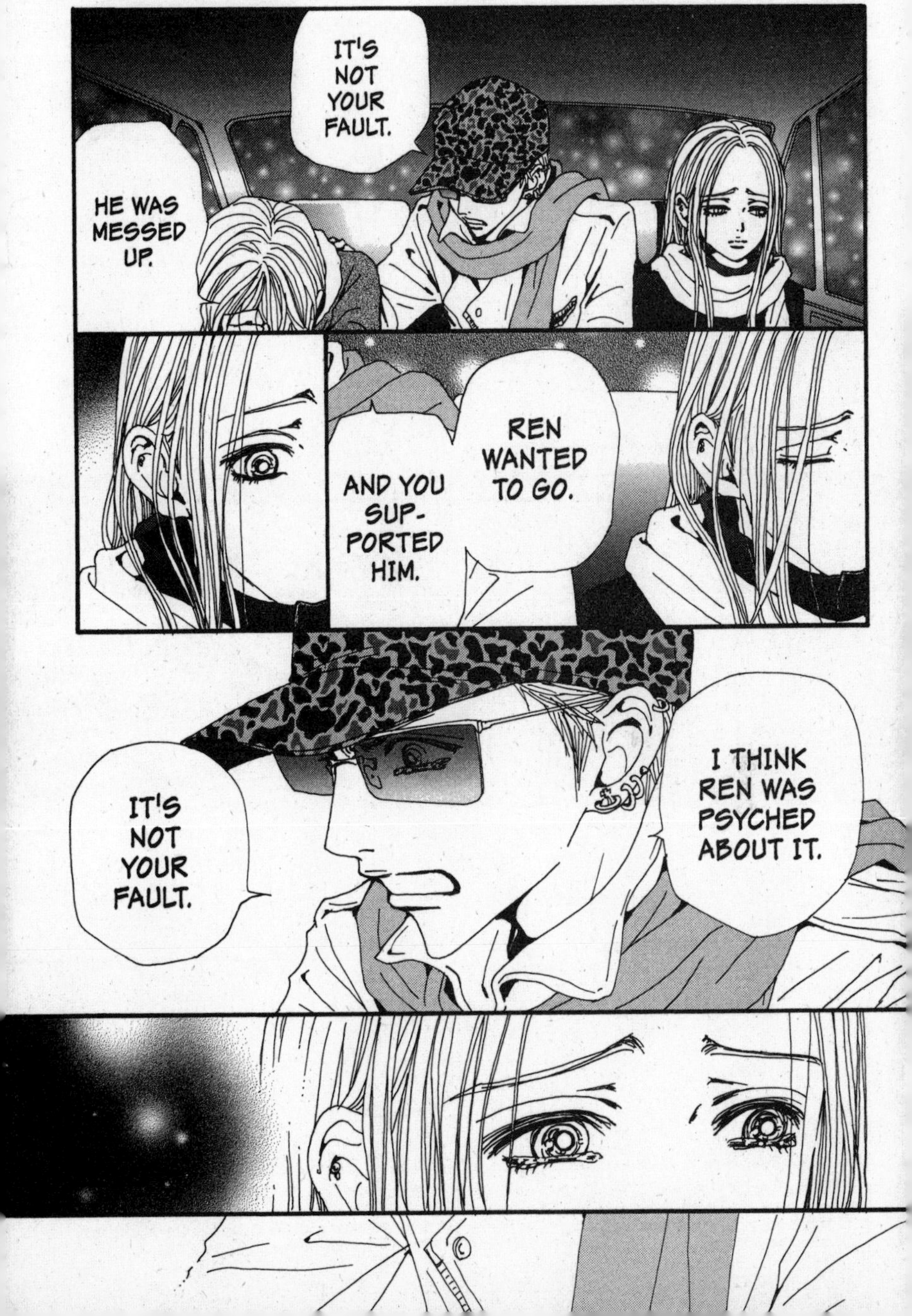
IT'S NOT YOUR FAULT.
HE WAS MESSED UP.
REN WANTED TO GO.
AND YOU SUP-PORTED HIM.
I THINK REN WAS PSYCHED ABOUT IT.
IT'S NOT YOUR FAULT.

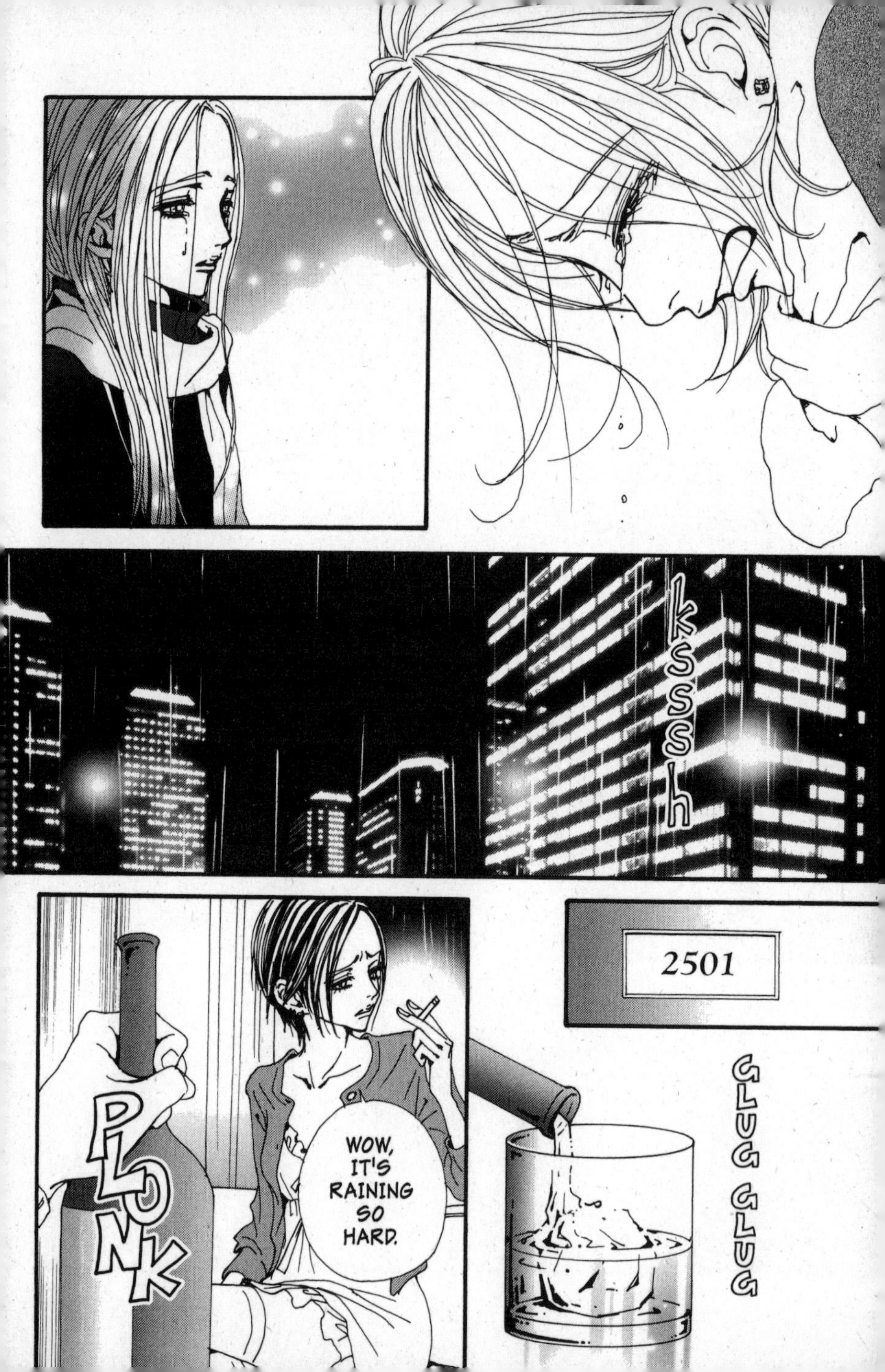
ksssh
2501
GLUG GLUG
WOW, IT'S RAINING SO HARD.
PLONK

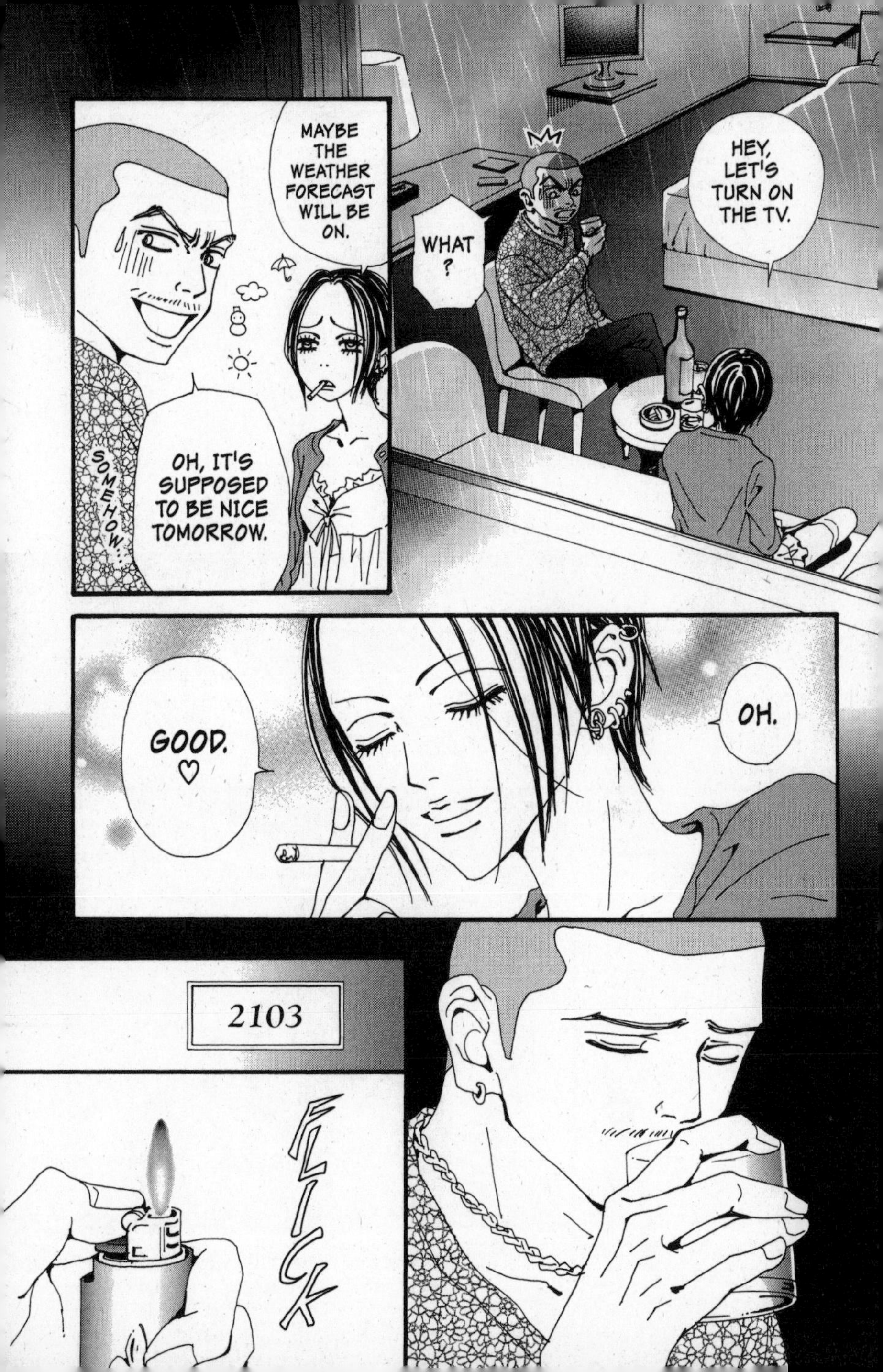
HEY, LET'S TURN ON THE TV.
WHAT?
MAYBE THE WEATHER FORECAST WILL BE ON.
OH, IT'S SUPPOSED TO BE NICE TOMORROW.
SOMEHOW...
OH.
GOOD. ♡
2103
FLICK

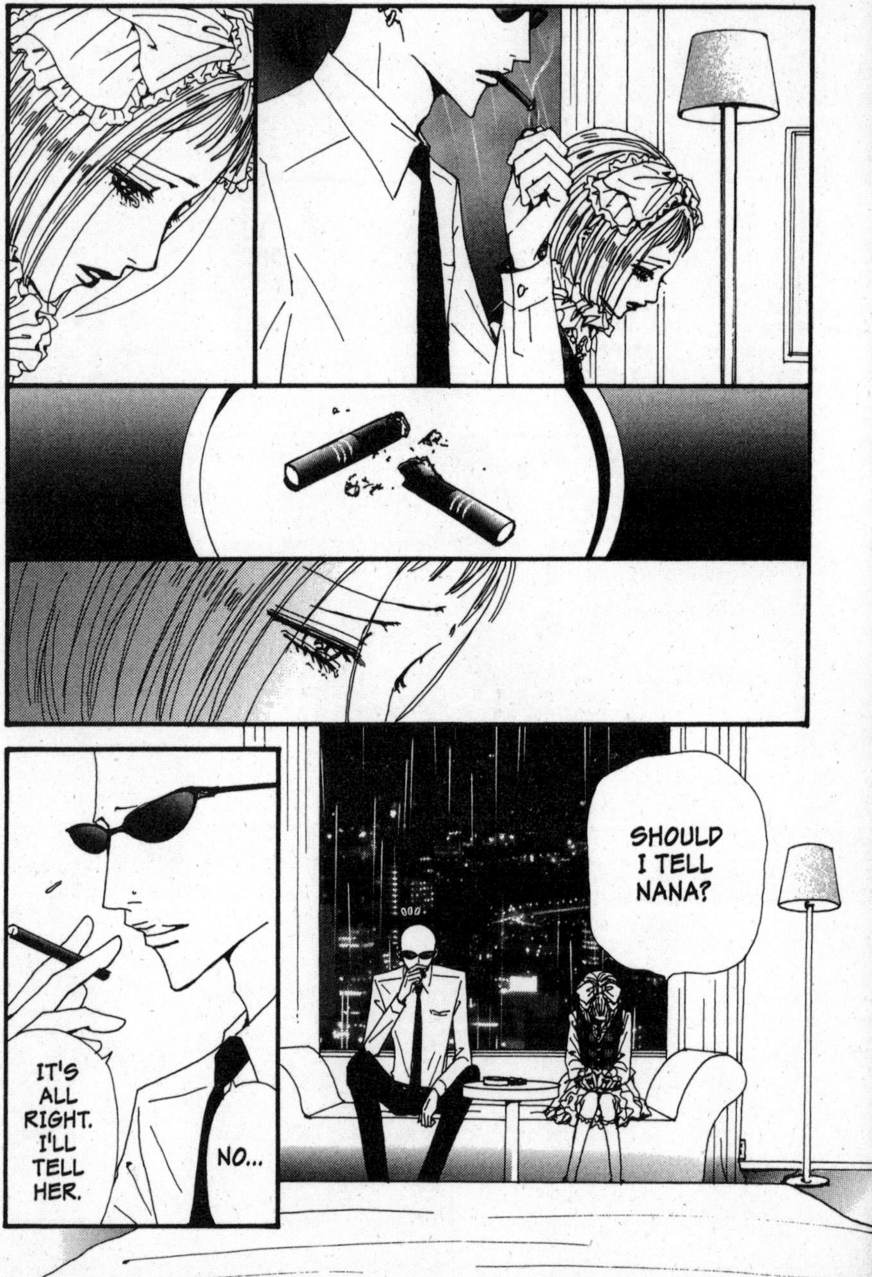
SHOULD I TELL NANA?
NO...
IT'S ALL RIGHT. I'LL TELL HER.

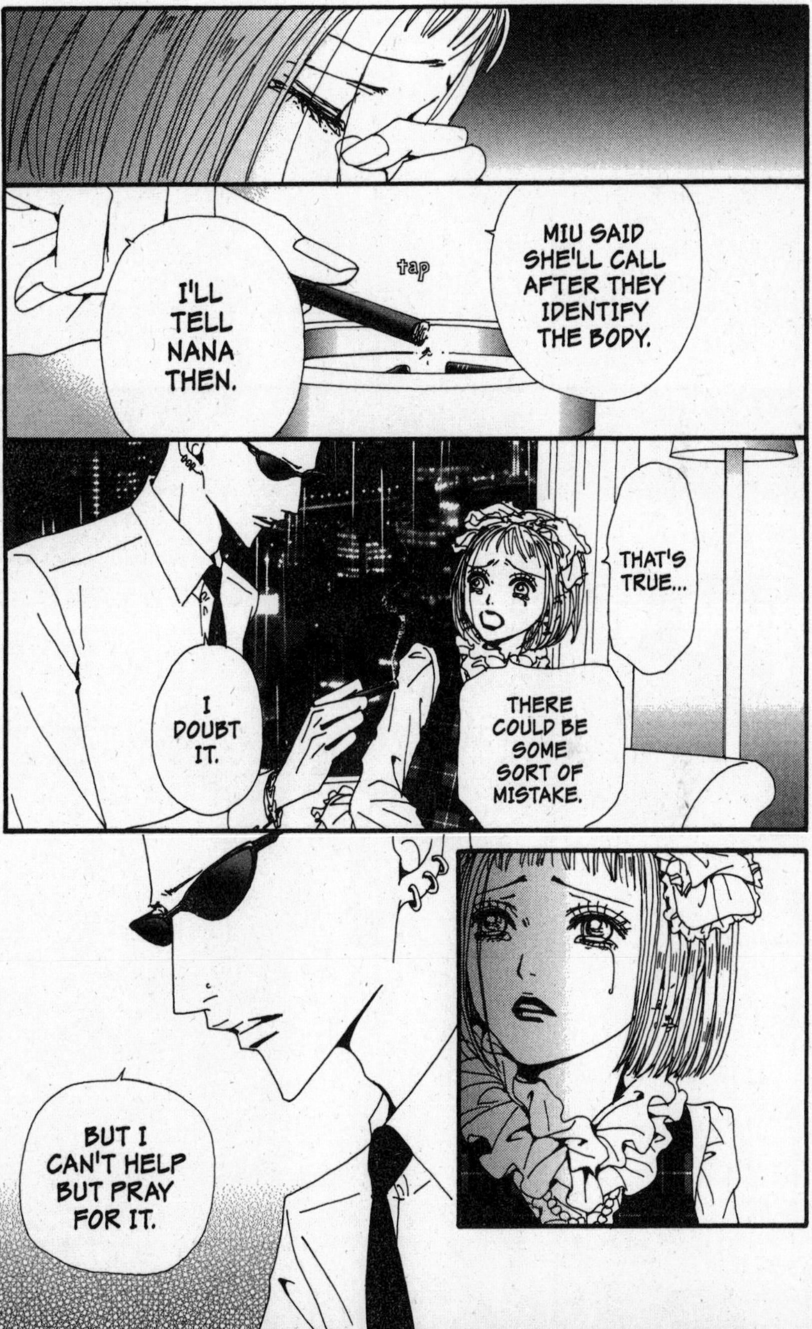
MIU SAID SHE'LL CALL AFTER THEY IDENTIFY THE BODY.
tap
I'LL TELL NANA THEN.
THAT'S TRUE...
THERE COULD BE SOME SORT OF MISTAKE.
I DOUBT IT.
BUT I CAN'T HELP BUT PRAY FOR IT.

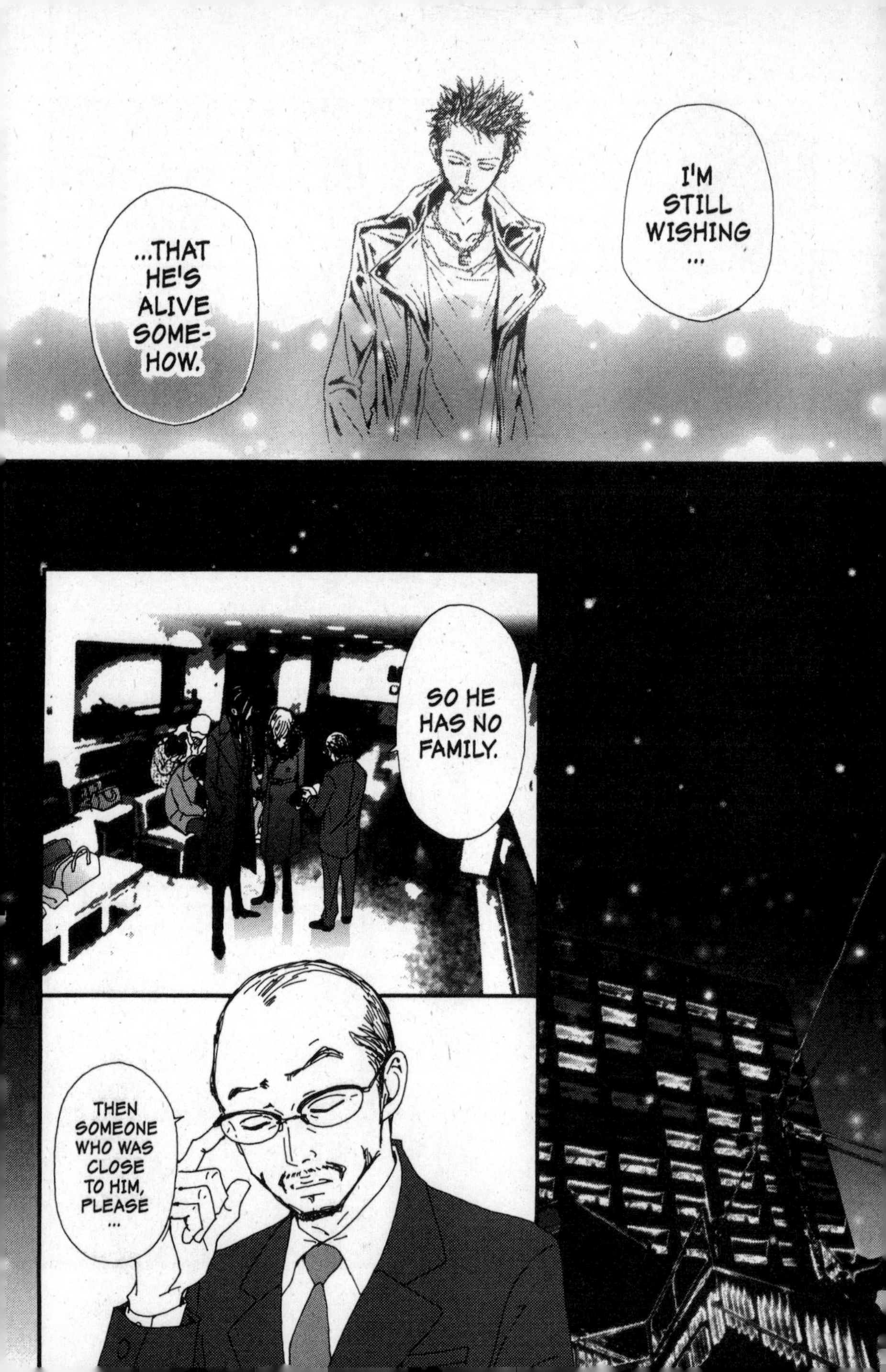
I'M STILL WISHING...
...THAT HE'S ALIVE SOME-HOW.
SO HE HAS NO FAMILY.
THEN SOMEONE WHO WAS CLOSE TO HIM, PLEASE...

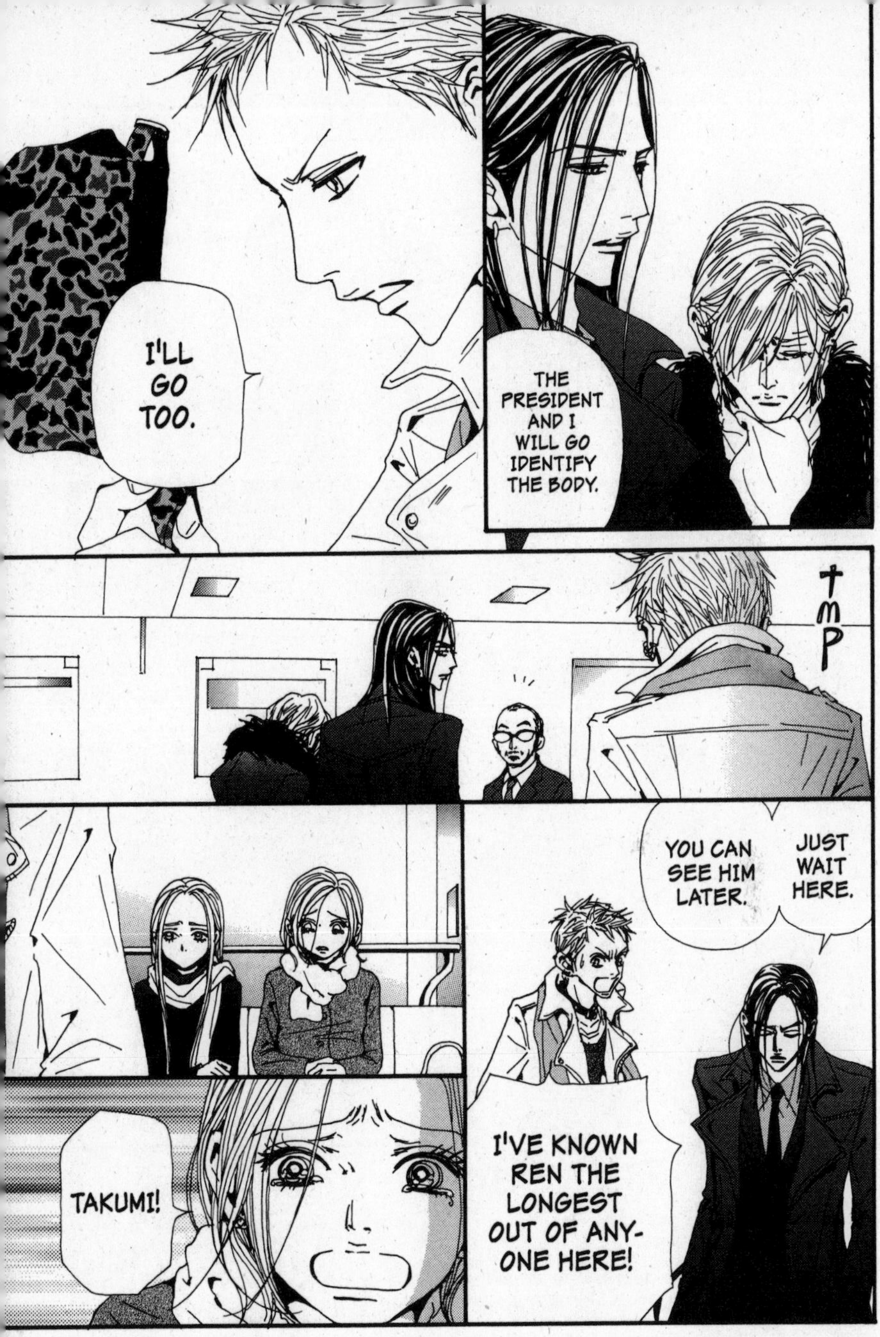
THE PRESIDENT AND I WILL GO IDENTIFY THE BODY.
I'LL GO TOO.
TMP
JUST WAIT HERE.
YOU CAN SEE HIM LATER.
I'VE KNOWN REN THE LONGEST OUT OF ANY-ONE HERE!
TAKUMI!

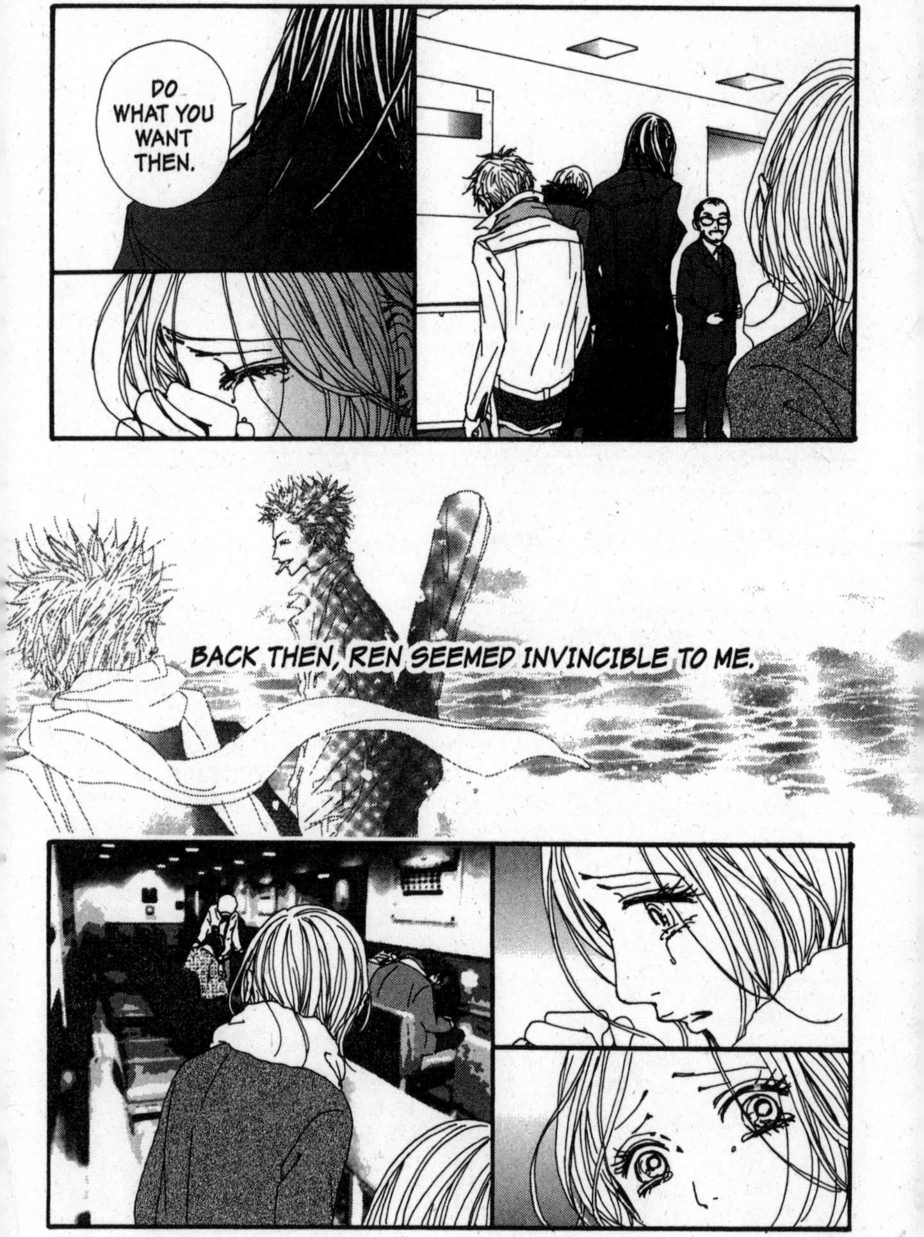
DO WHAT YOU WANT THEN.
BACK THEN, REN SEEMED INVINCIBLE TO ME.

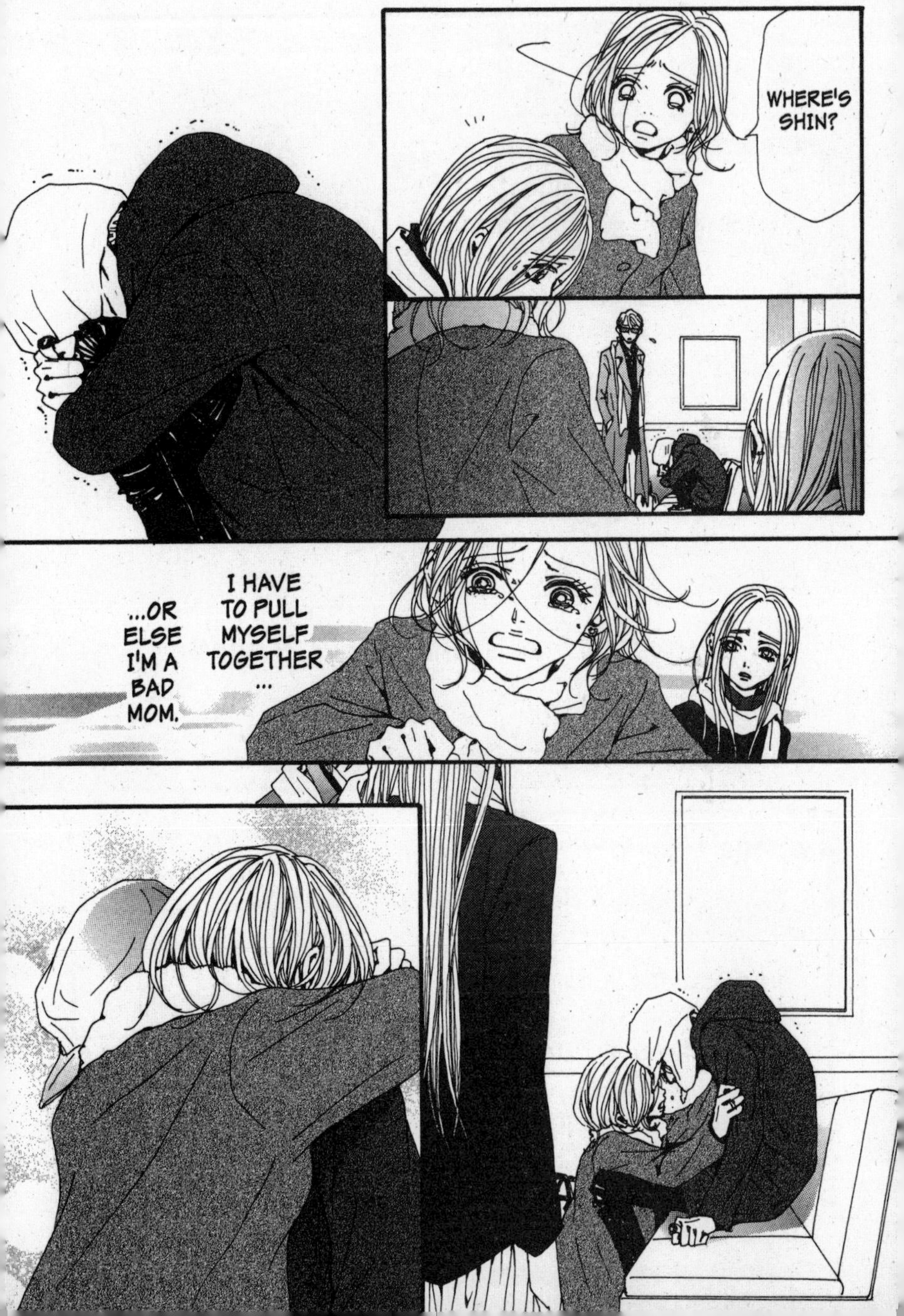
WHERE'S SHIN?
I HAVE TO PULL MYSELF TOGETHER ...
...OR ELSE I'M A BAD MOM.

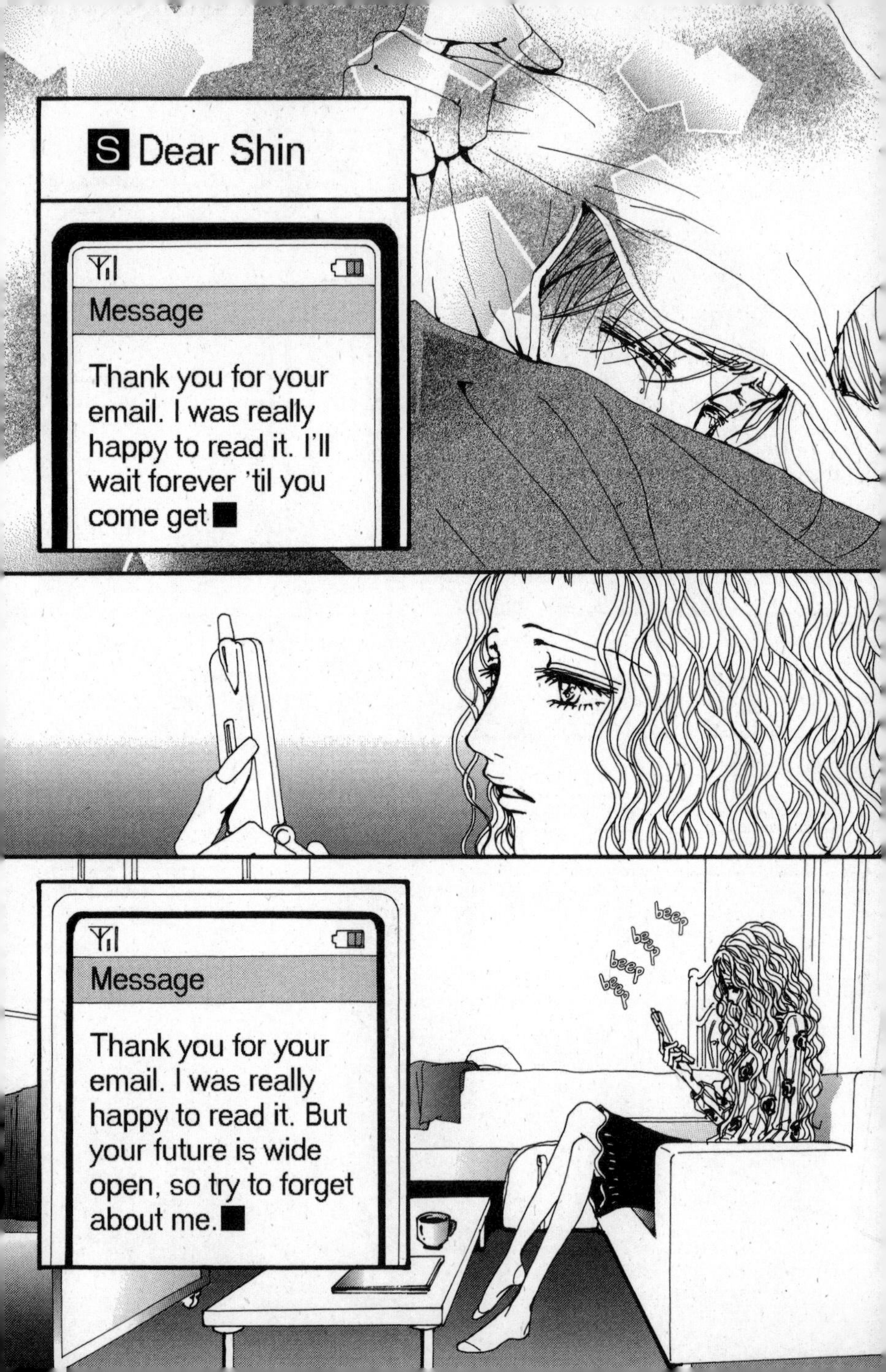
S Dear Shin
Message
Thank you for your email. I was really happy to read it. I'll wait forever 'til you come get
beep
beep
beep
beep
Message
Thank you for your email. I was really happy to read it. But your future is wide open, so try to forget about me.

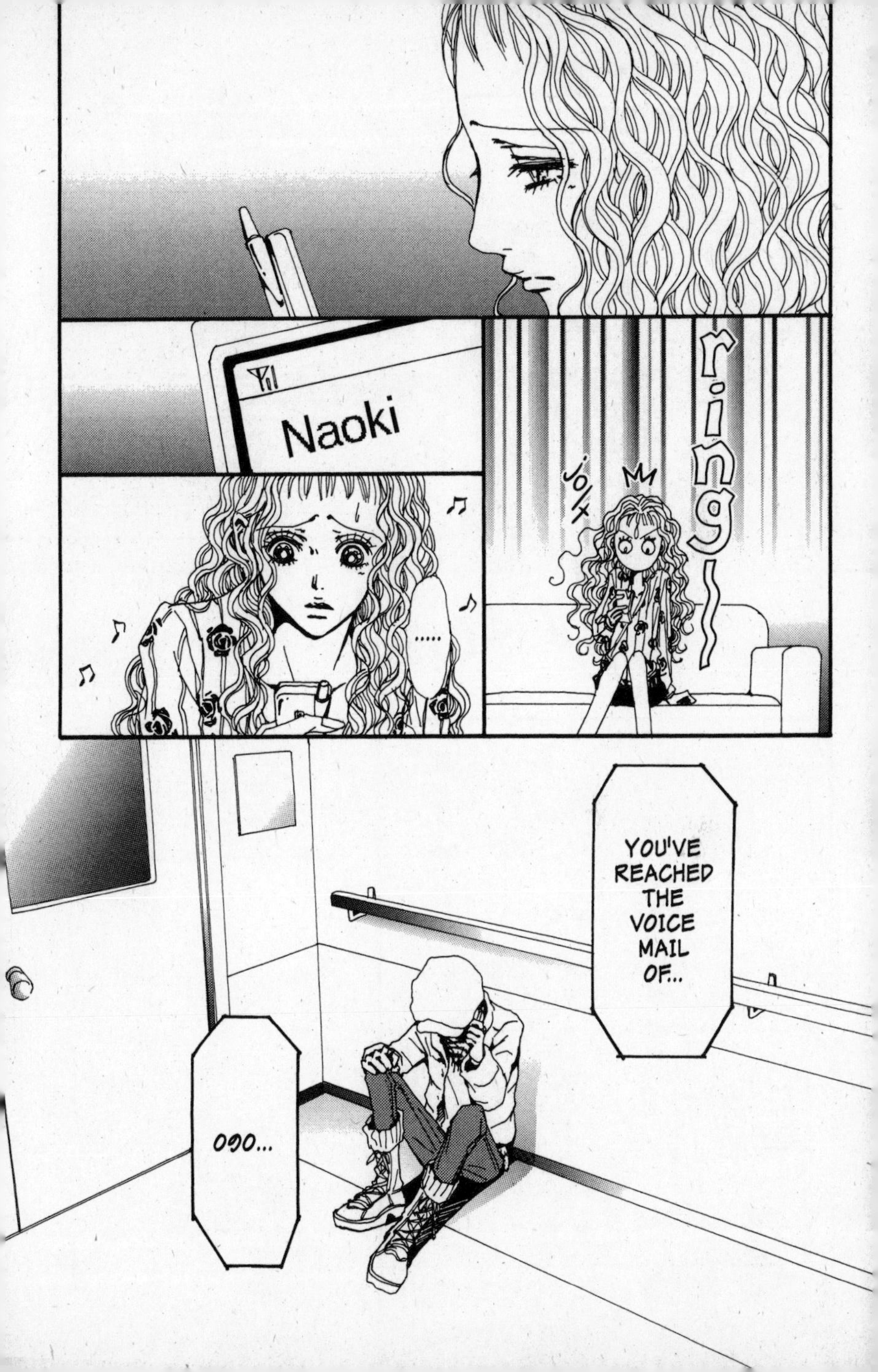
ring~
jolt
Naoki
......
YOU'VE REACHED THE VOICE MAIL OF...
ODO...

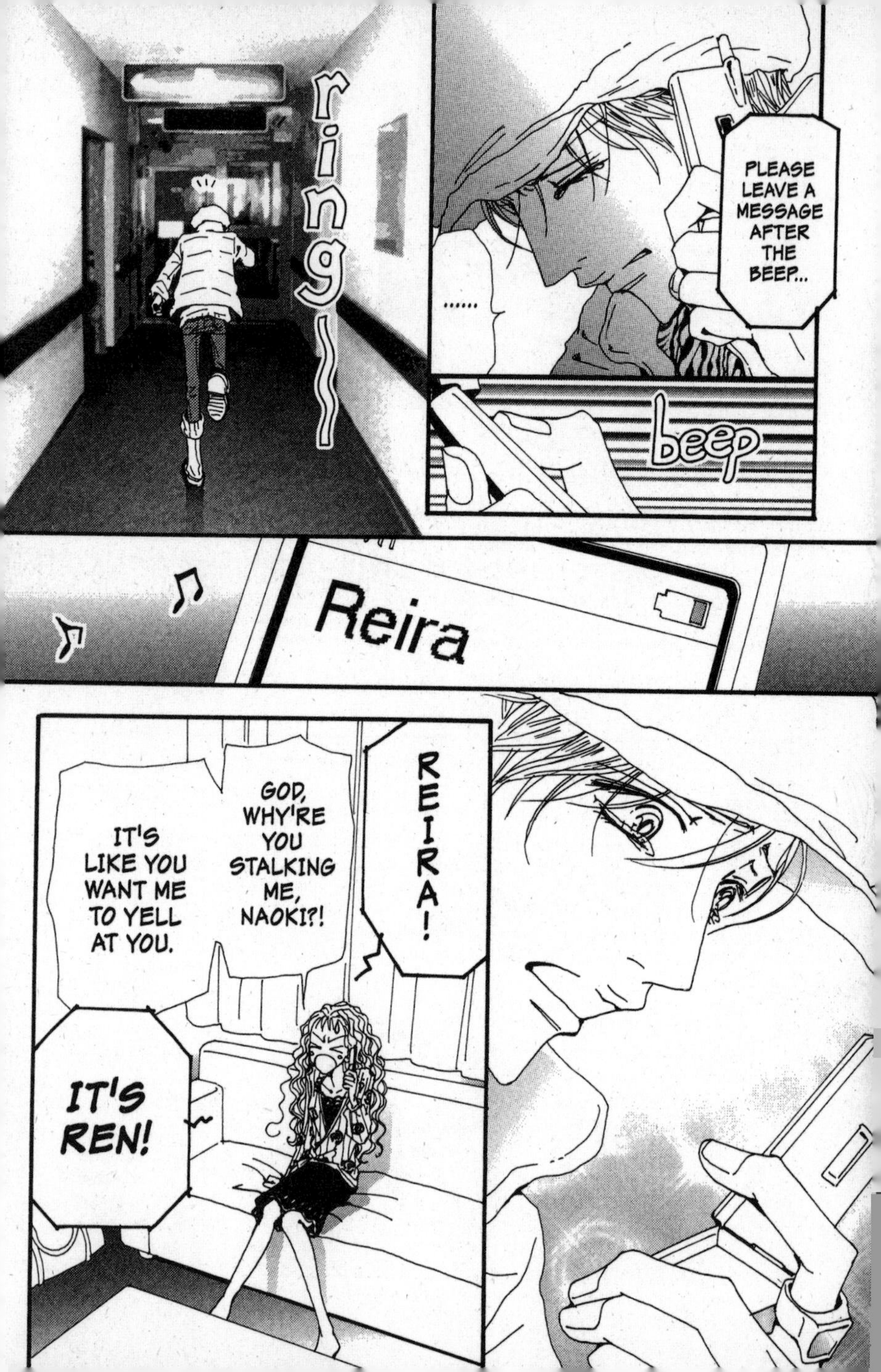
PLEASE LEAVE A MESSAGE AFTER THE BEEP...
......
beep
ring~
Reira
REIRA!
GOD, WHY'RE YOU STALKING ME, NAOKI?!
IT'S LIKE YOU WANT ME TO YELL AT YOU.
IT'S REN!

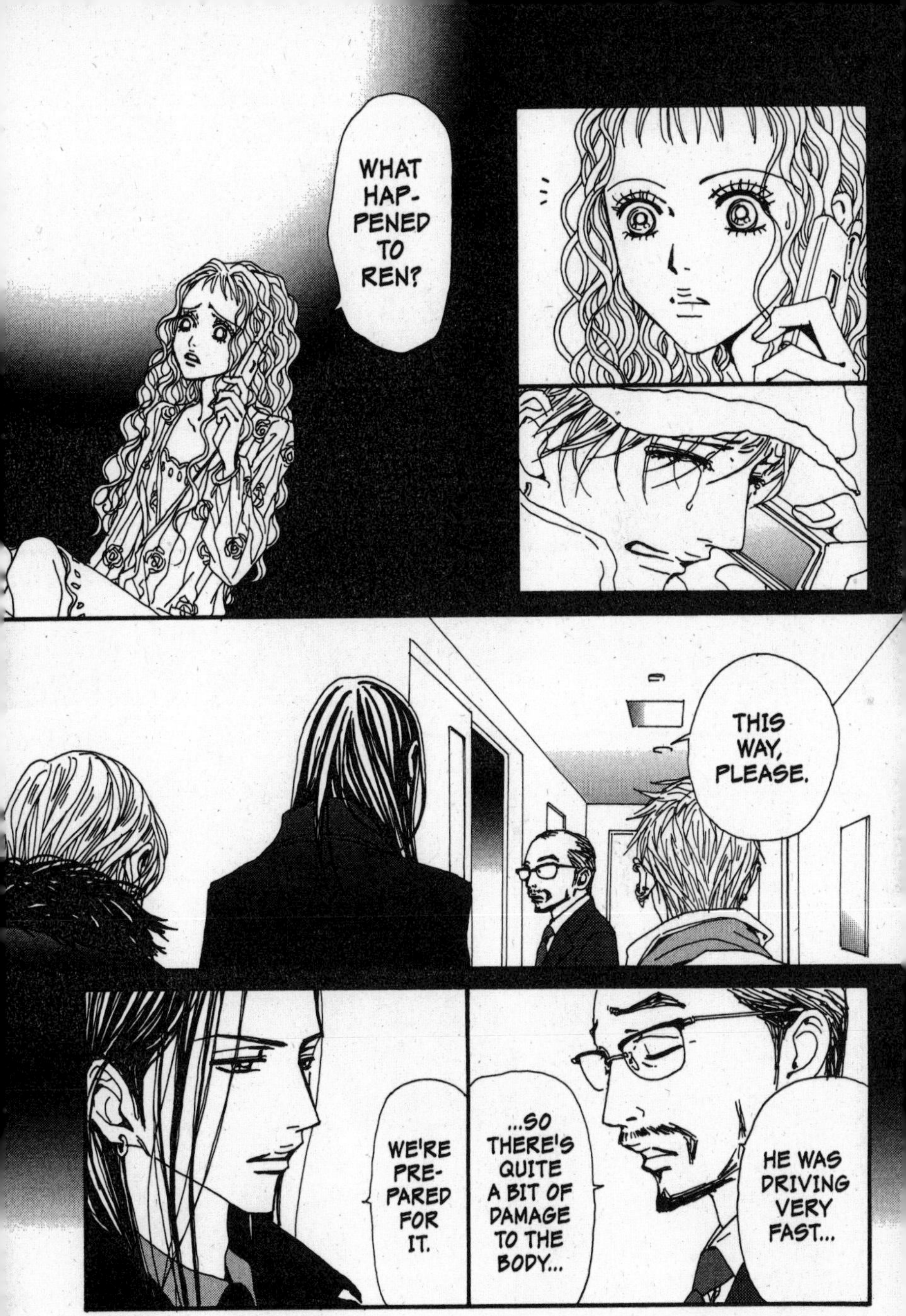
WHAT HAP-PENED TO REN?
THIS WAY, PLEASE.
HE WAS DRIVING VERY FAST...
...SO THERE'S QUITE A BIT OF DAMAGE TO THE BODY...
WE'RE PRE-PARED FOR IT.

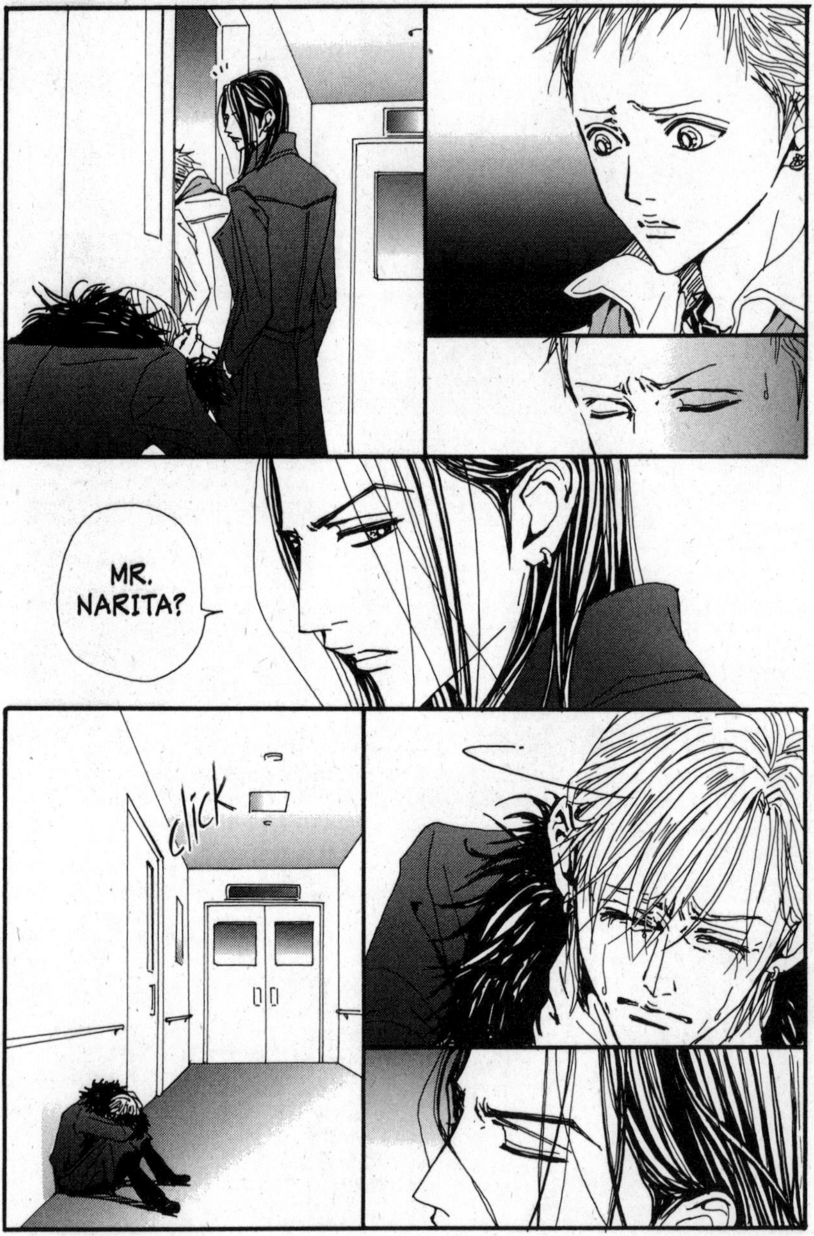
MR. NARITA?
click

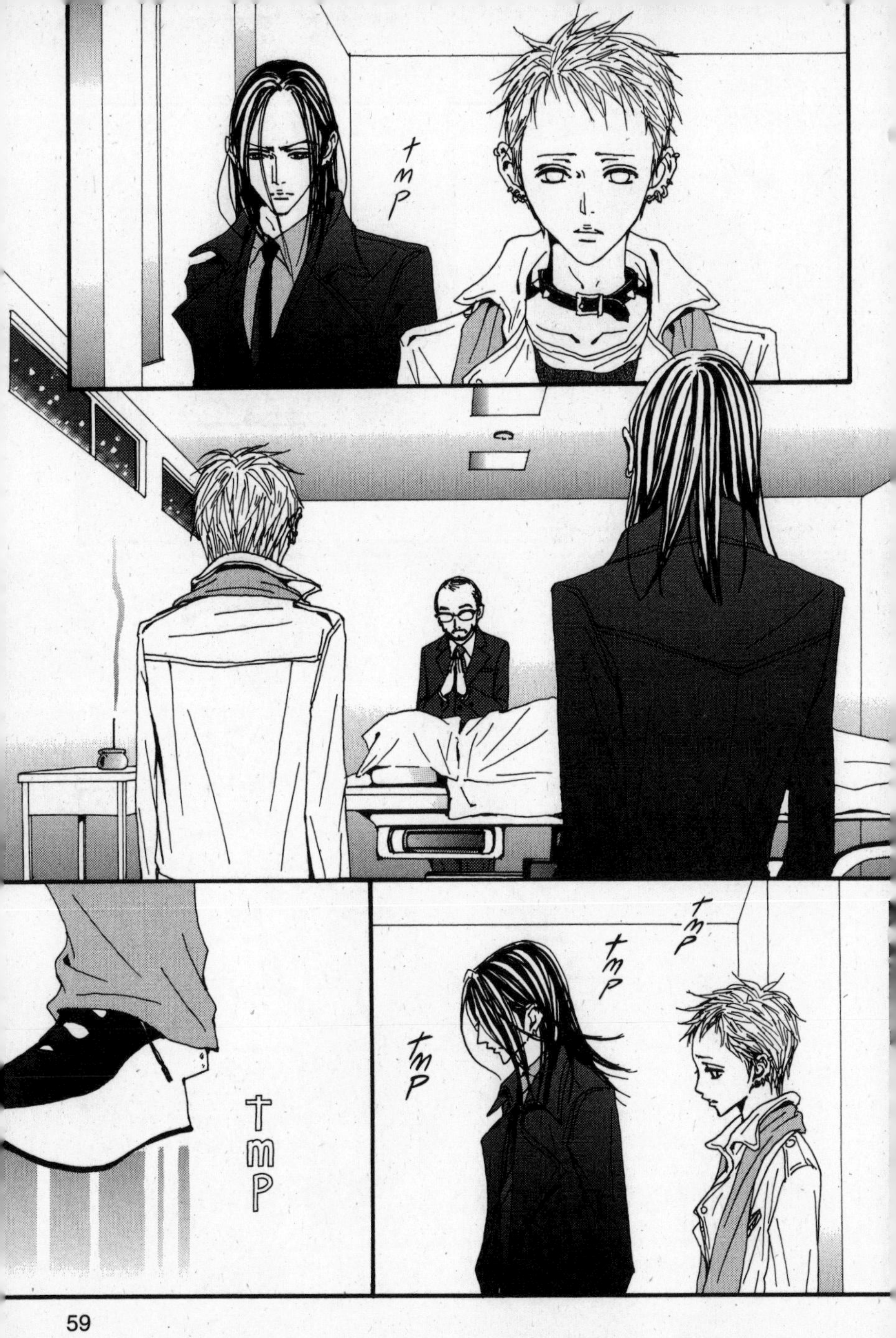
TMP
TMP
TMP
TMP
TMP

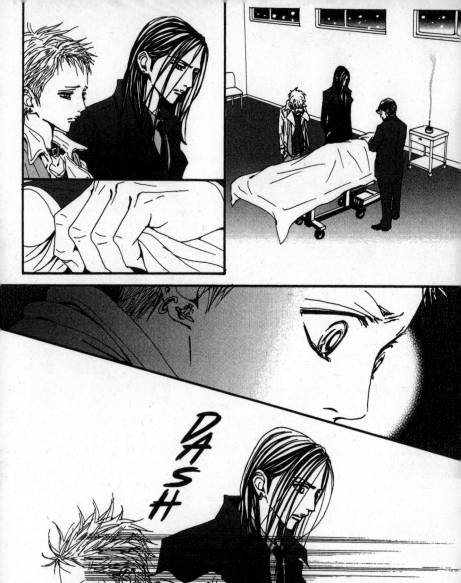

DASH

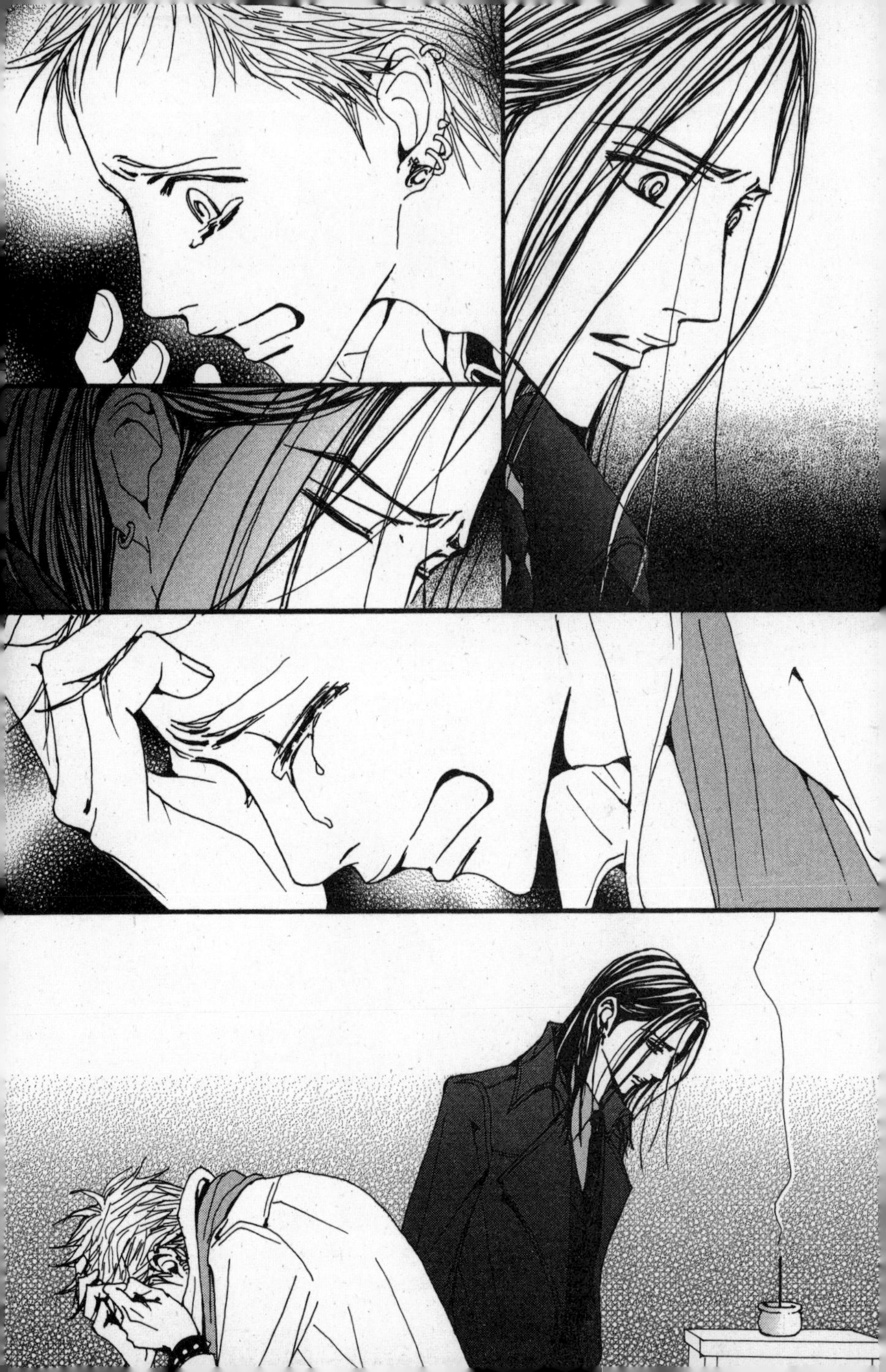

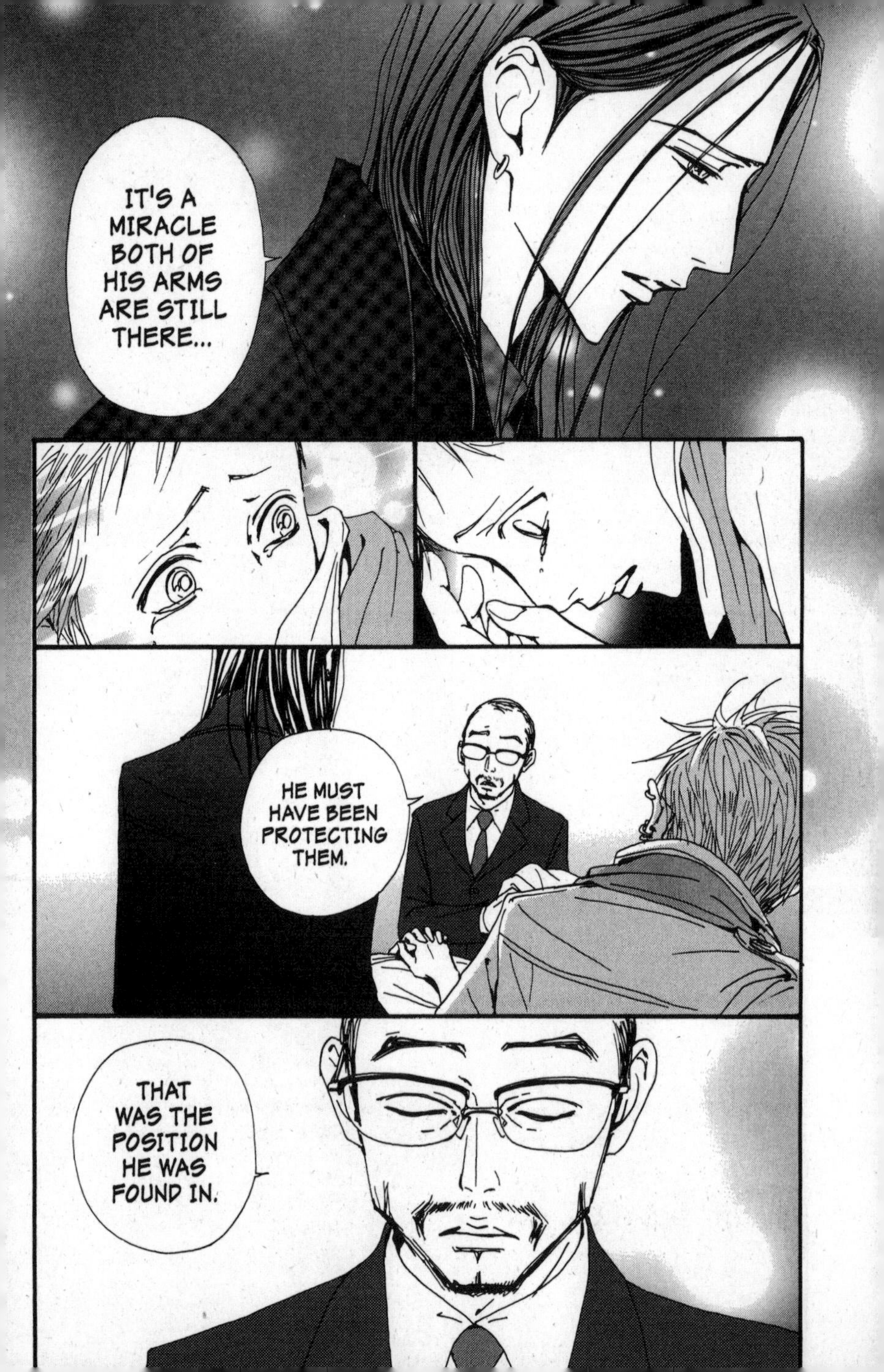
IT'S A MIRACLE BOTH OF HIS ARMS ARE STILL THERE...
HE MUST HAVE BEEN PROTECTING THEM.
THAT WAS THE POSITION HE WAS FOUND IN.

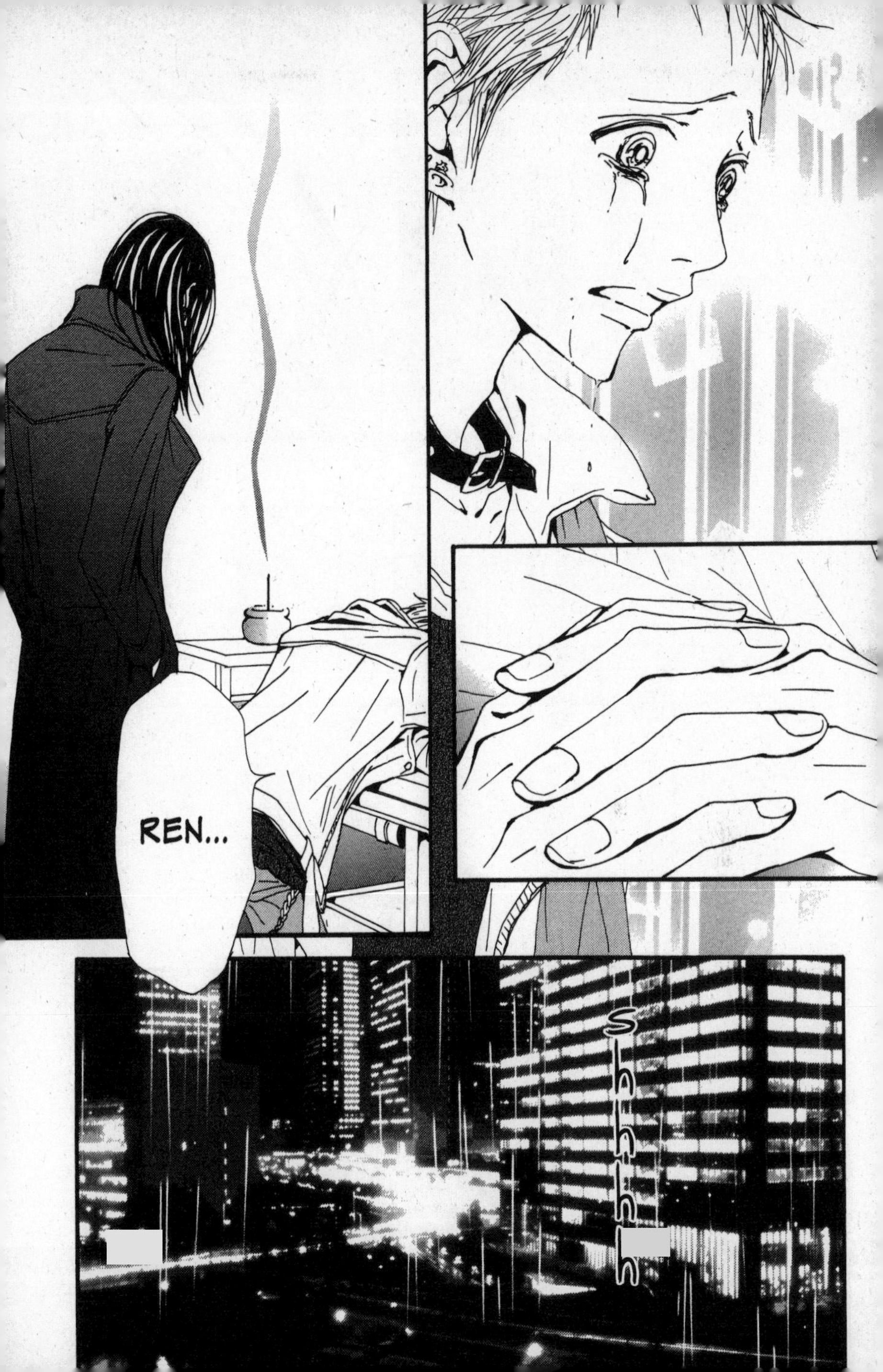
REN...
Shhhh

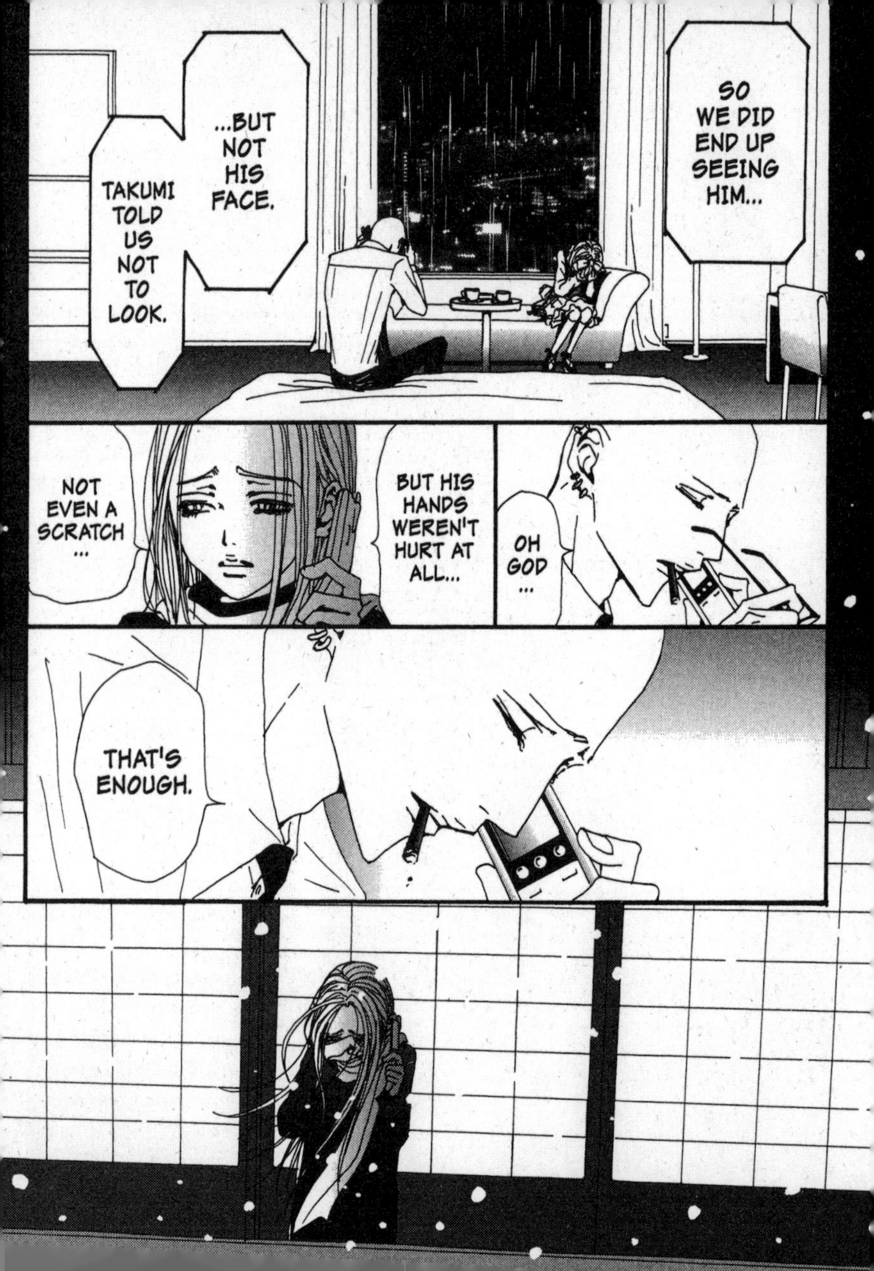
SO WE DID END UP SEEING HIM...
...BUT NOT HIS FACE.
TAKUMI TOLD US NOT TO LOOK.
OH GOD ...
BUT HIS HANDS WEREN'T HURT AT ALL...
NOT EVEN A SCRATCH ...
THAT'S ENOUGH.

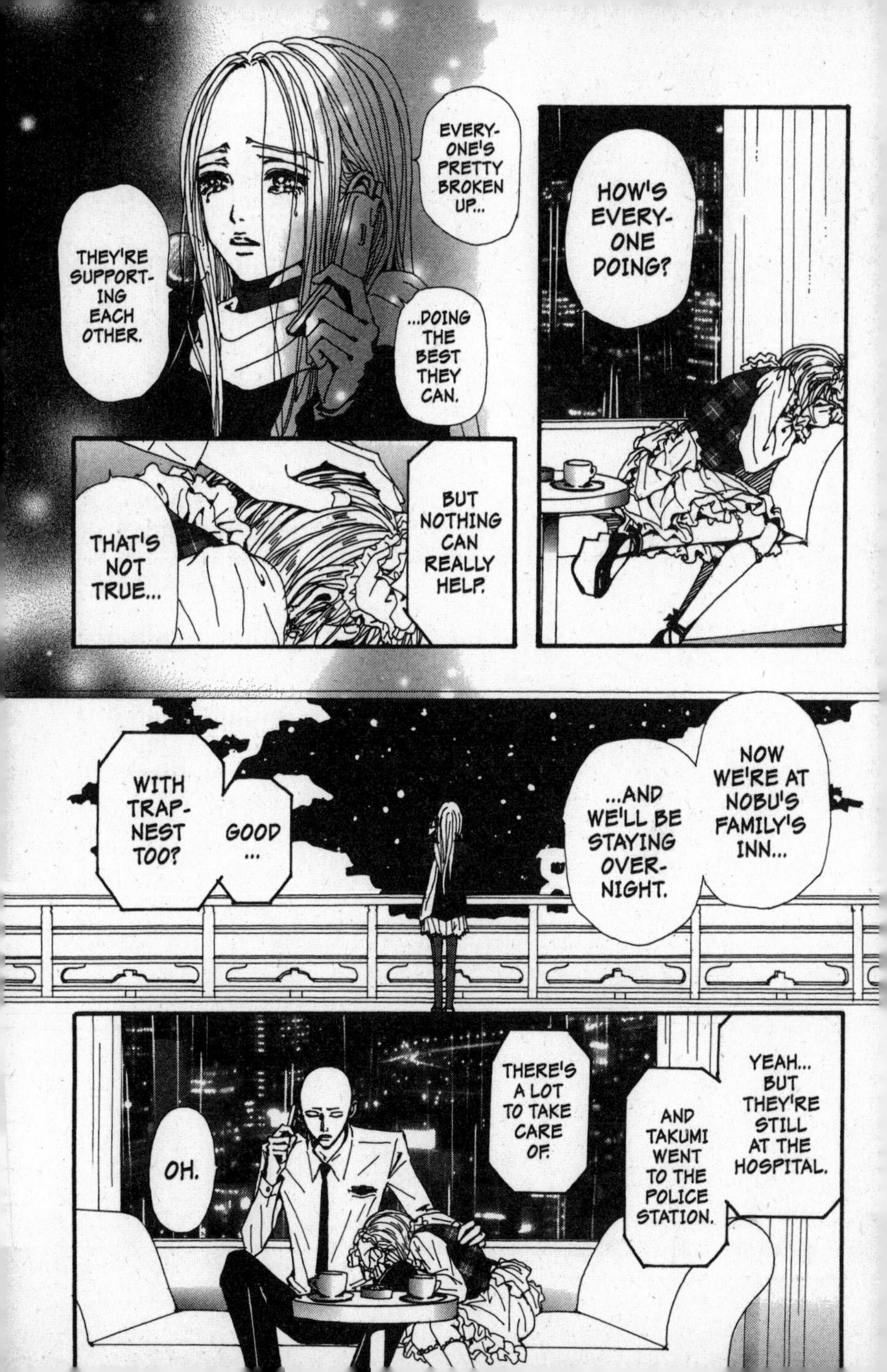
HOW'S EVERY-ONE DOING?
EVERY-ONE'S PRETTY BROKEN UP...
THEY'RE SUPPORT-ING EACH OTHER.
...DOING THE BEST THEY CAN.
BUT NOTHING CAN REALLY HELP.
THAT'S NOT TRUE...
NOW WE'RE AT NOBU'S FAMILY'S INN...
...AND WE'LL BE STAYING OVER-NIGHT.
GOOD ...
WITH TRAP-NEST TOO?
YEAH... BUT THEY'RE STILL AT THE HOSPITAL.
AND TAKUMI WENT TO THE POLICE STATION.
THERE'S A LOT TO TAKE CARE OF.
OH.

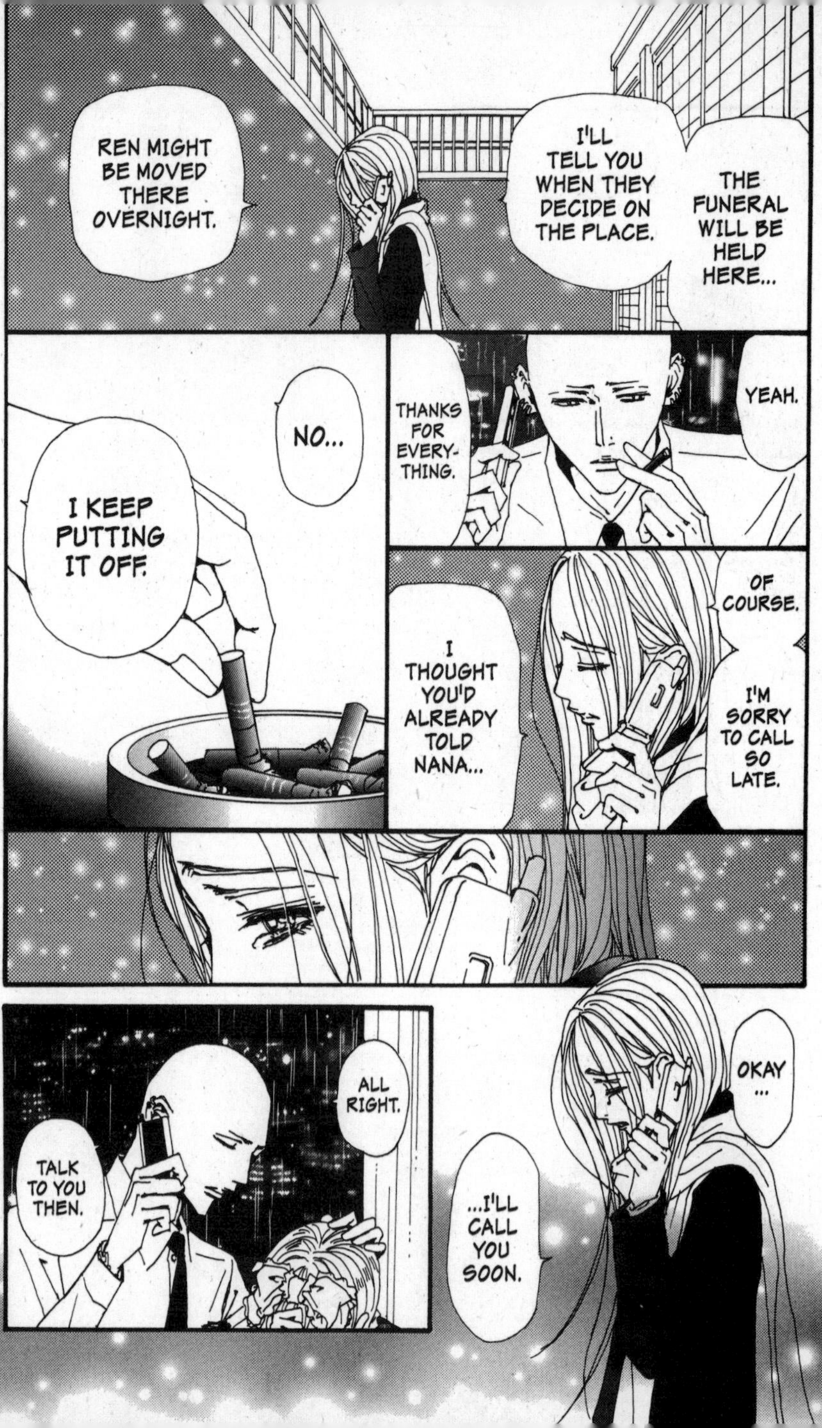
THE FUNERAL WILL BE HELD HERE...
I'LL TELL YOU WHEN THEY DECIDE ON THE PLACE.
REN MIGHT BE MOVED THERE OVERNIGHT.
YEAH.
THANKS FOR EVERY-THING.
OF COURSE.
I'M SORRY TO CALL SO LATE.
I THOUGHT YOU'D ALREADY TOLD NANA...
NO...
I KEEP PUTTING IT OFF.
OKAY ...
...I'LL CALL YOU SOON.
ALL RIGHT.
TALK TO YOU THEN.

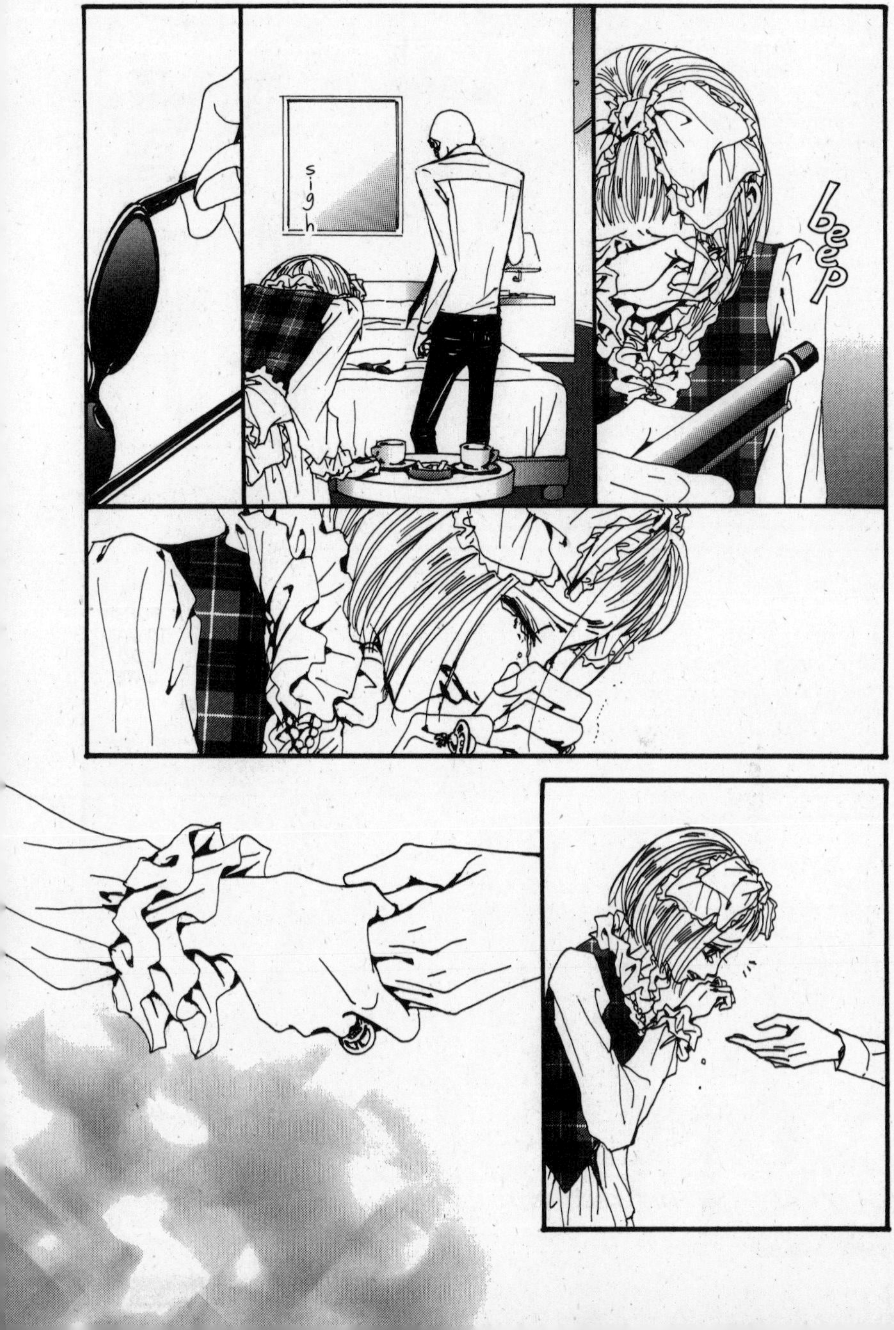
beep
sigh

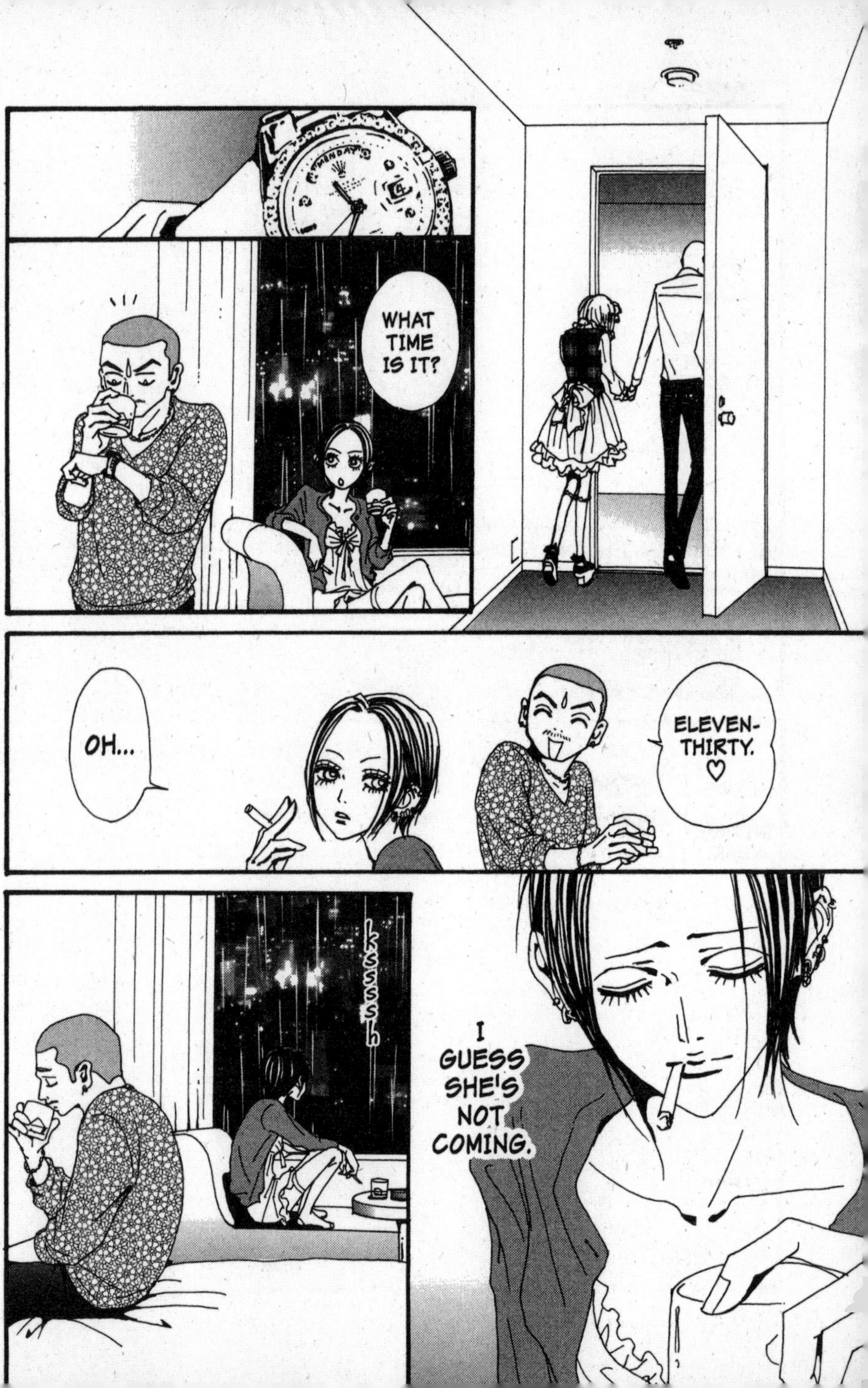
WHAT TIME IS IT?
ELEVEN-THIRTY. ♡
OH...
I GUESS SHE'S NOT COMING.
kssssh

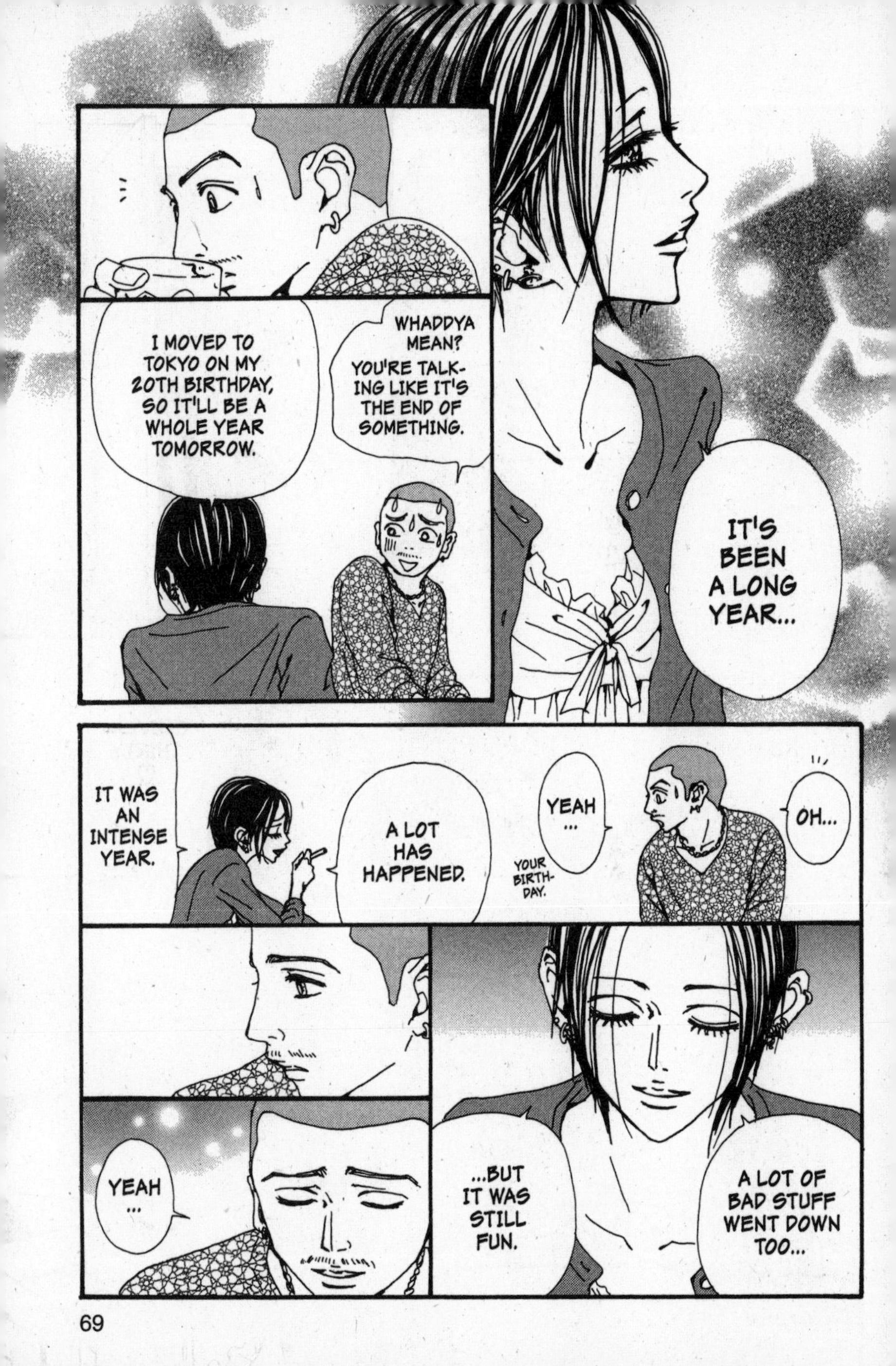
IT'S BEEN A LONG YEAR...
WHADDYA MEAN? YOU'RE TALKING LIKE IT'S THE END OF SOMETHING.
I MOVED TO TOKYO ON MY 20TH BIRTHDAY, SO IT'LL BE A WHOLE YEAR TOMORROW.
OH...
YOUR BIRTHDAY.
YEAH ...
A LOT HAS HAPPENED.
IT WAS AN INTENSE YEAR.
A LOT OF BAD STUFF WENT DOWN TOO...
...BUT IT WAS STILL FUN.
YEAH ...

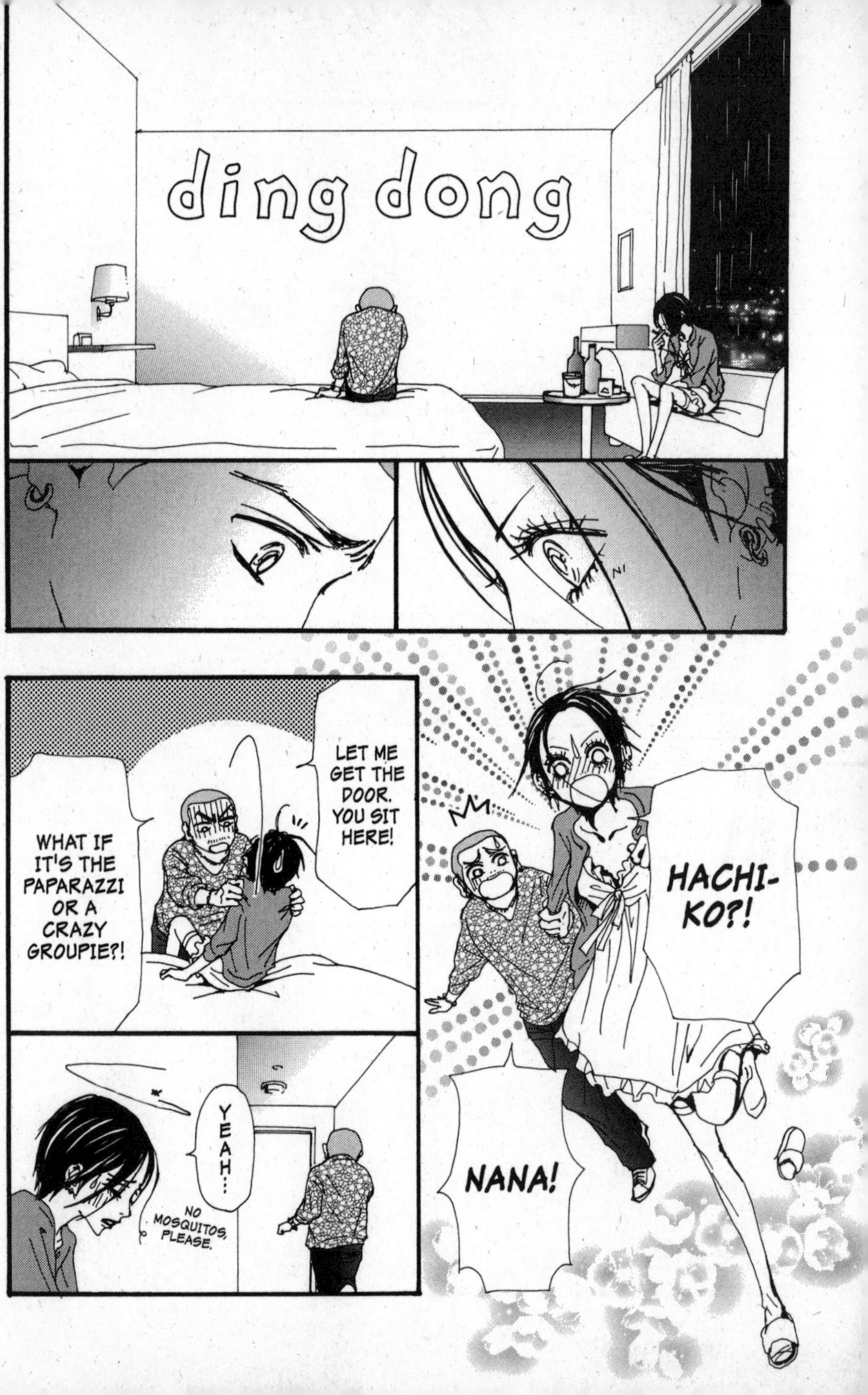
ding dong
NI
HACHI-KO?!
NANA!
LET ME GET THE DOOR. YOU SIT HERE!
WHAT IF IT'S THE PAPARAZZI OR A CRAZY GROUPIE?!
YEAH...
NO MOSQUITOS, PLEASE.

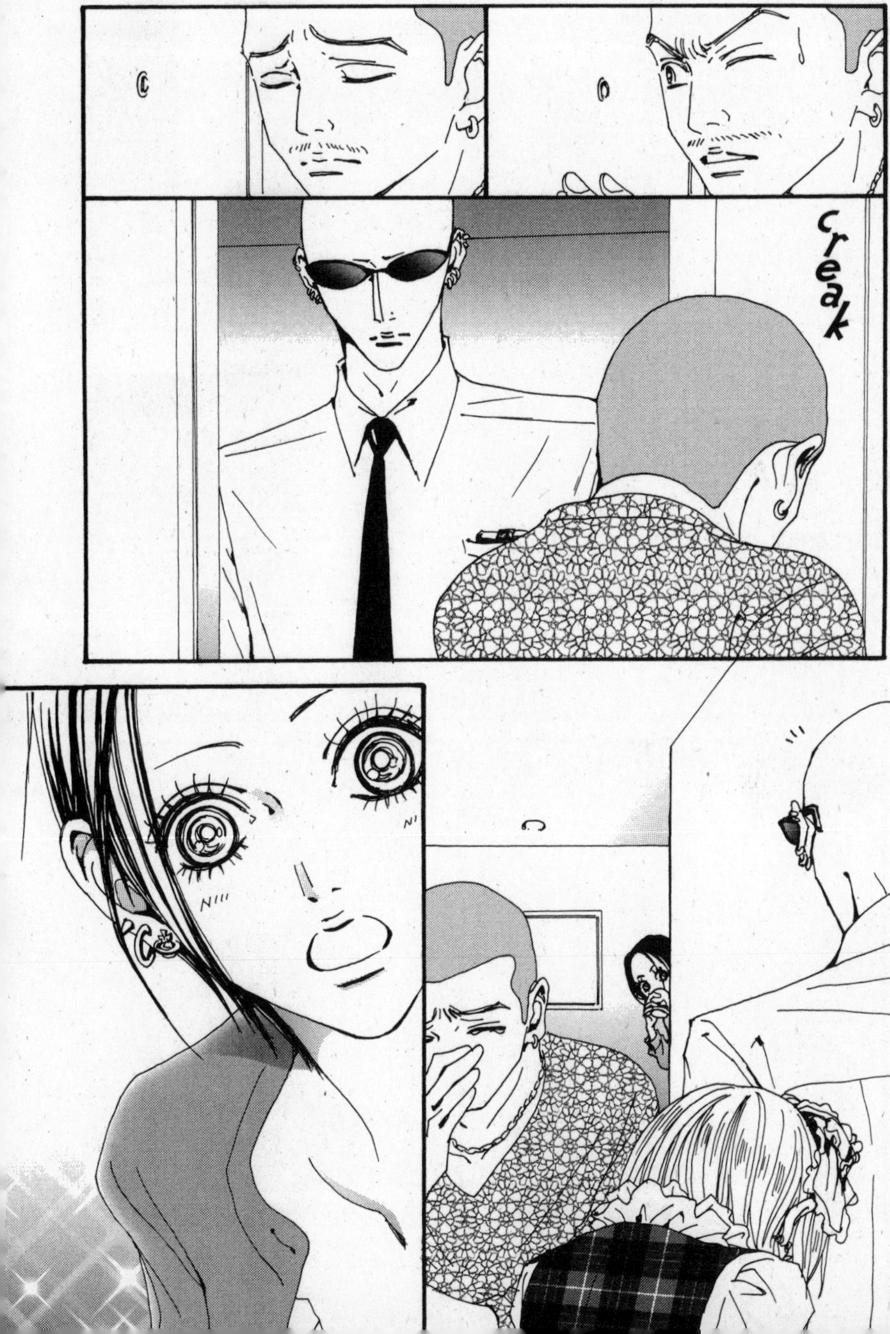
creak

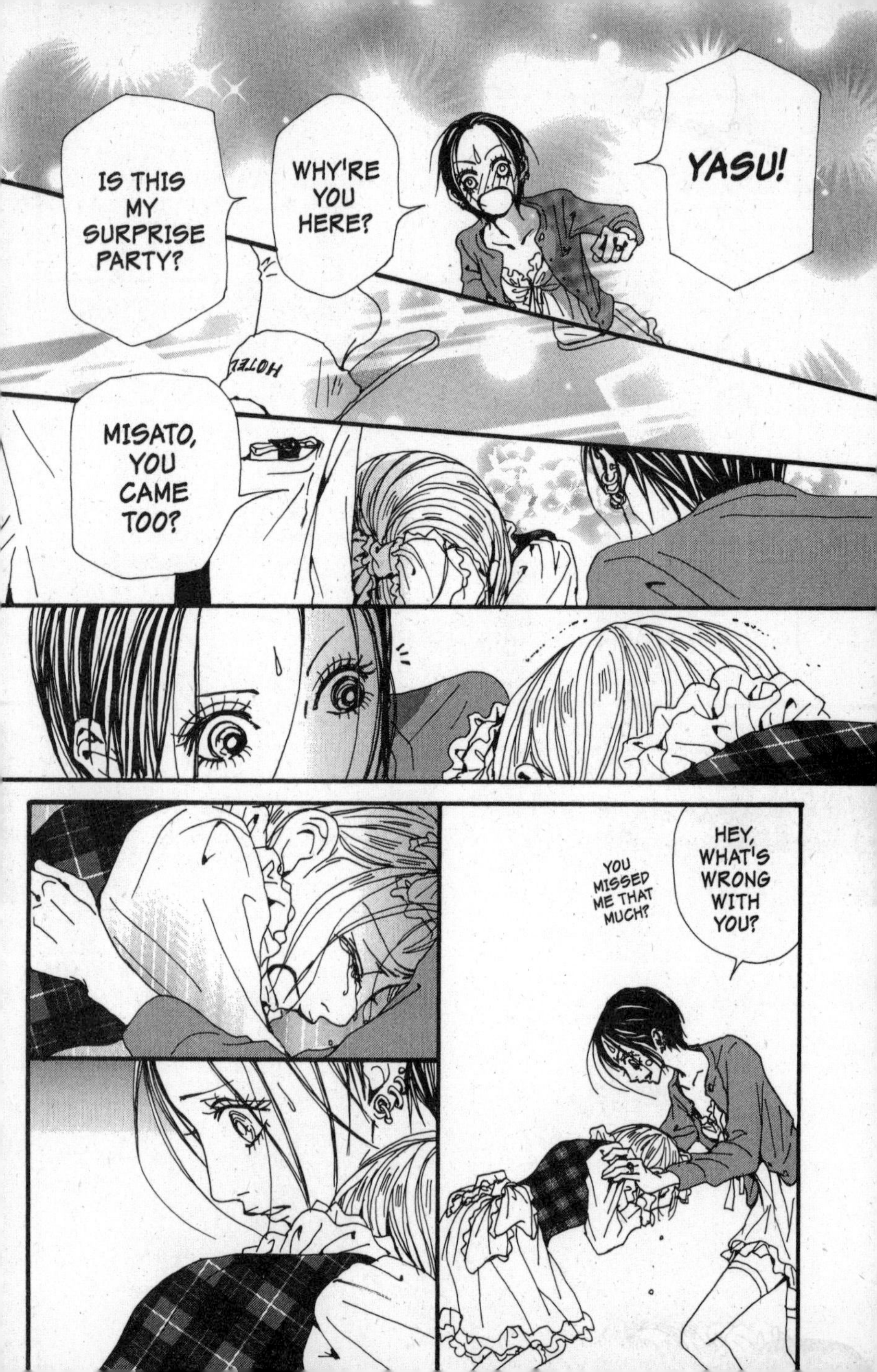
YASU!
WHY'RE YOU HERE?
IS THIS MY SURPRISE PARTY?
MISATO, YOU CAME TOO?
HEY, WHAT'S WRONG WITH YOU?
YOU MISSED ME THAT MUCH?

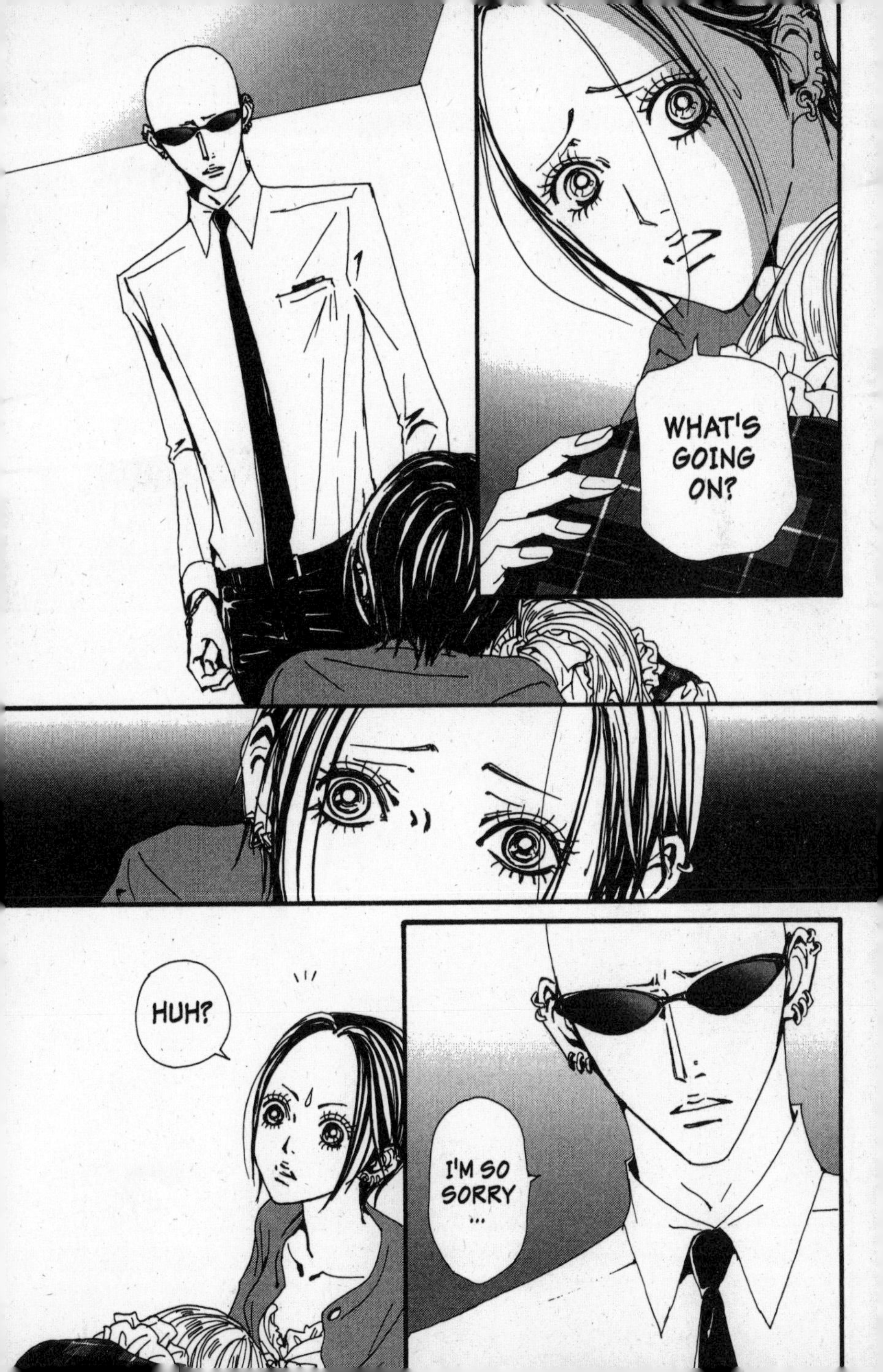
WHAT'S GOING ON?
I'M SO SORRY ...
HUH?

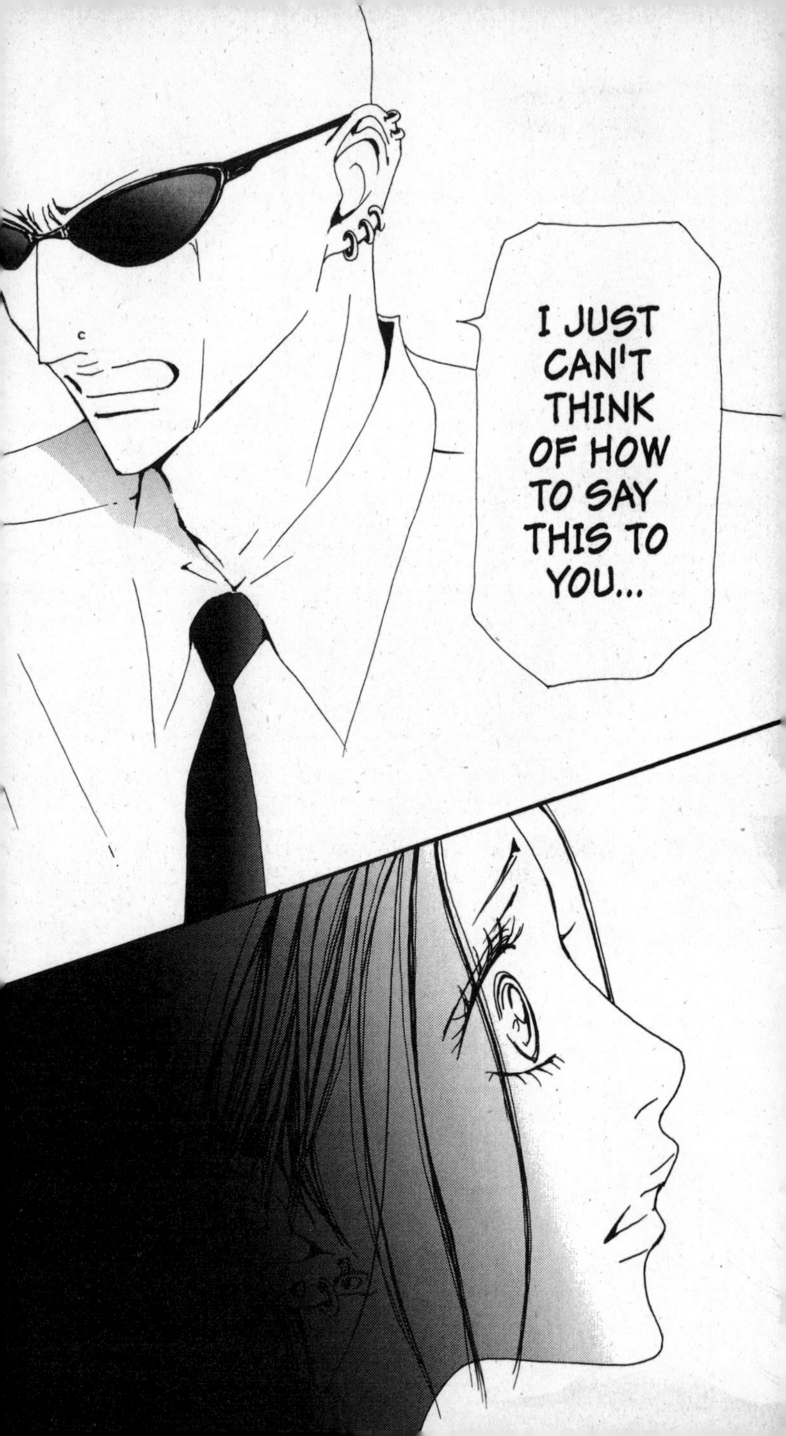
I JUST CAN'T THINK OF HOW TO SAY THIS TO YOU...

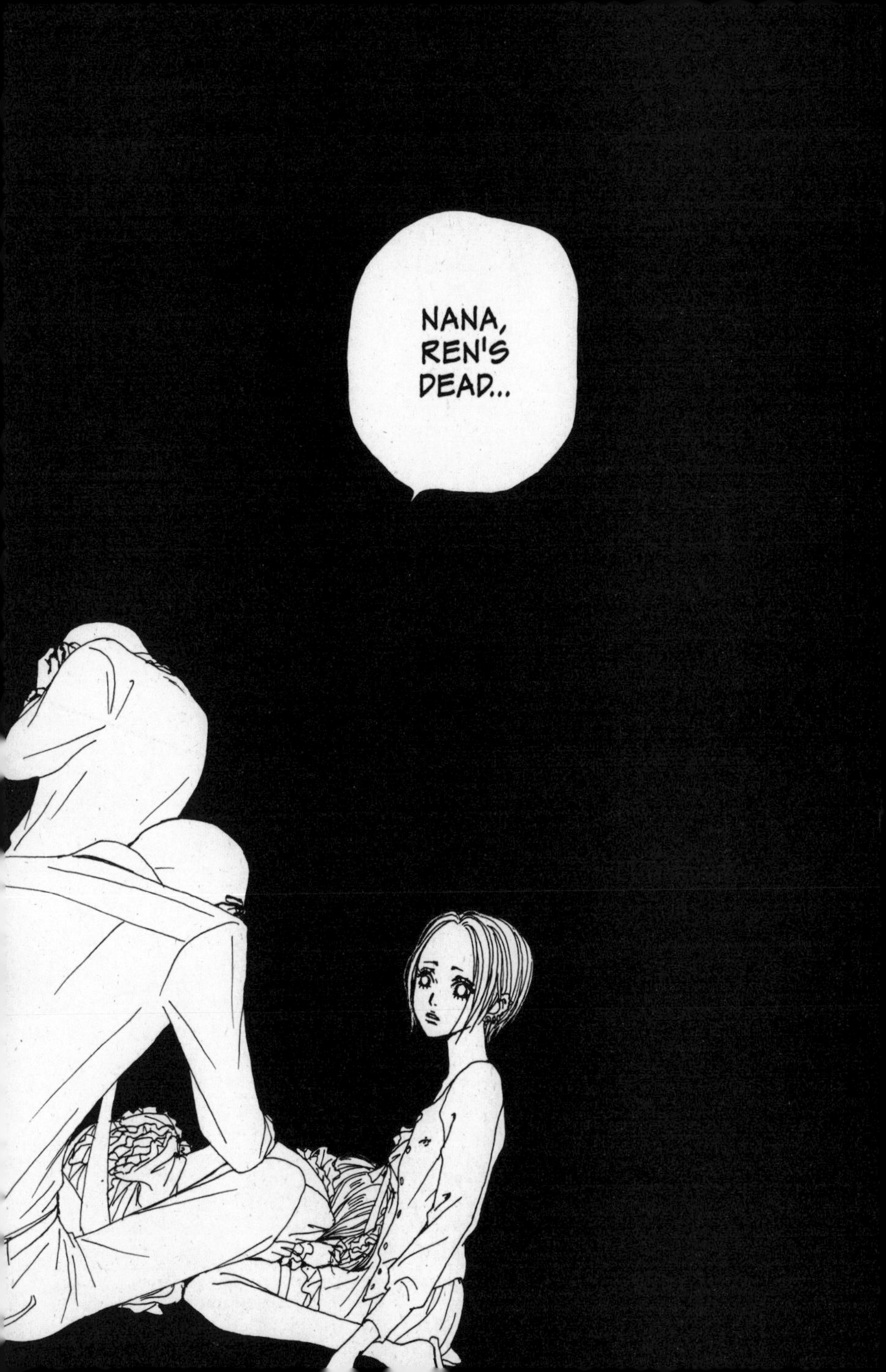
NANA, REN'S DEAD...

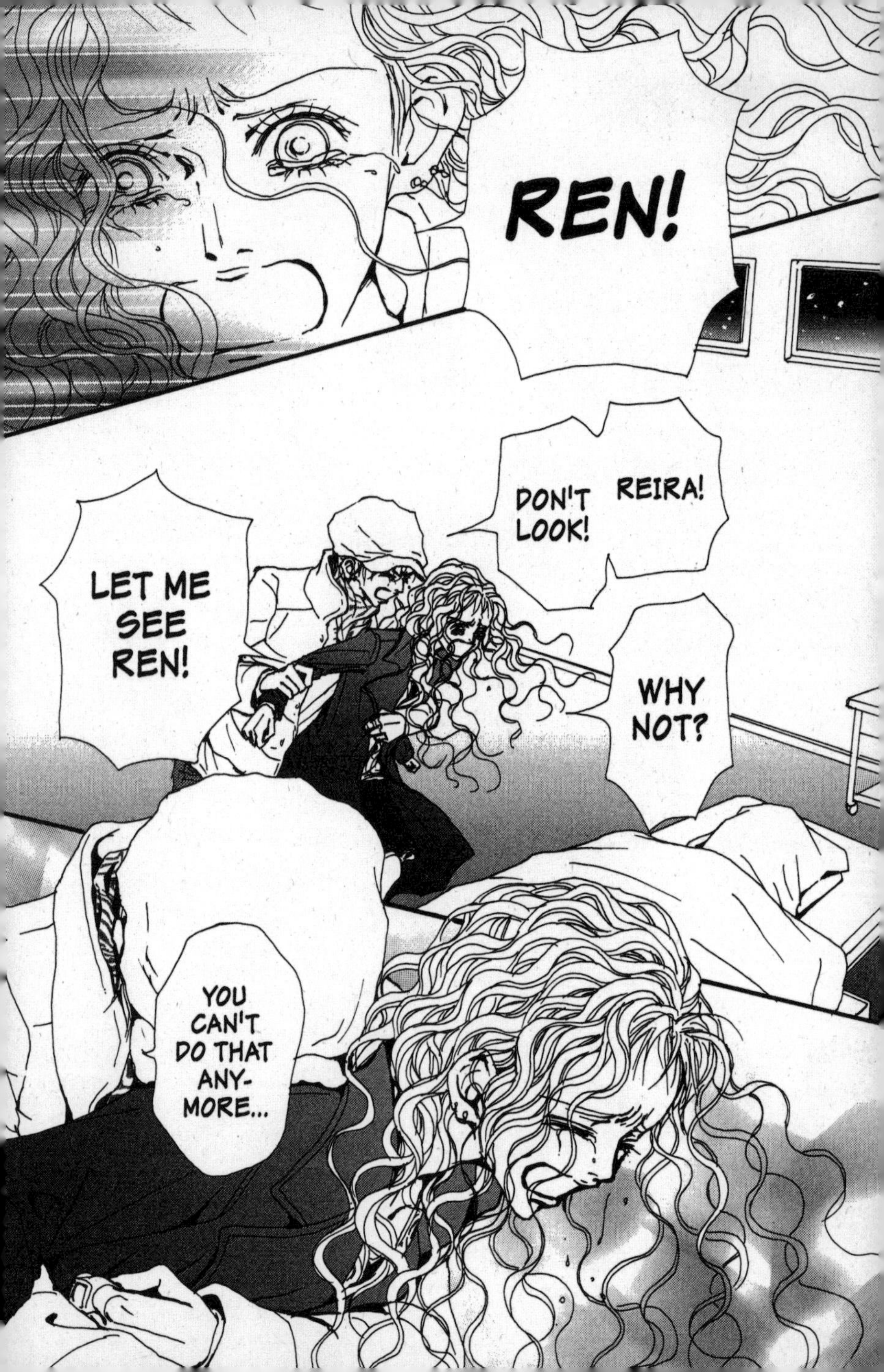
REN!
REIRA!
DON'T LOOK!
WHY NOT?
LET ME SEE REN!
YOU CAN'T DO THAT ANY-MORE...

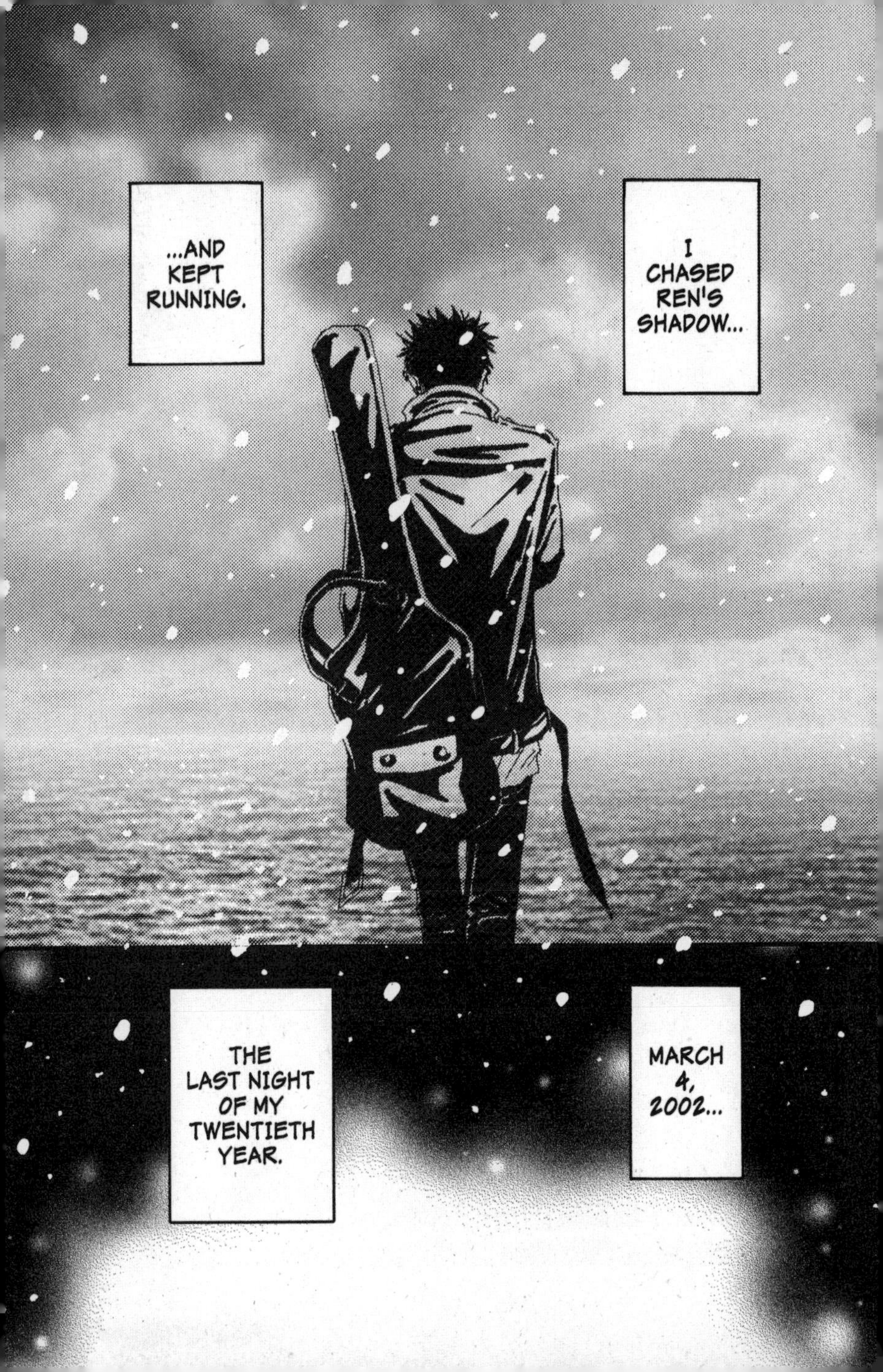
I CHASED REN'S SHADOW...
...AND KEPT RUNNING.
MARCH 4, 2002...
THE LAST NIGHT OF MY TWENTIETH YEAR.

THAT'S
WHEN
MY
WHOLE
WORLD
STOPPED.

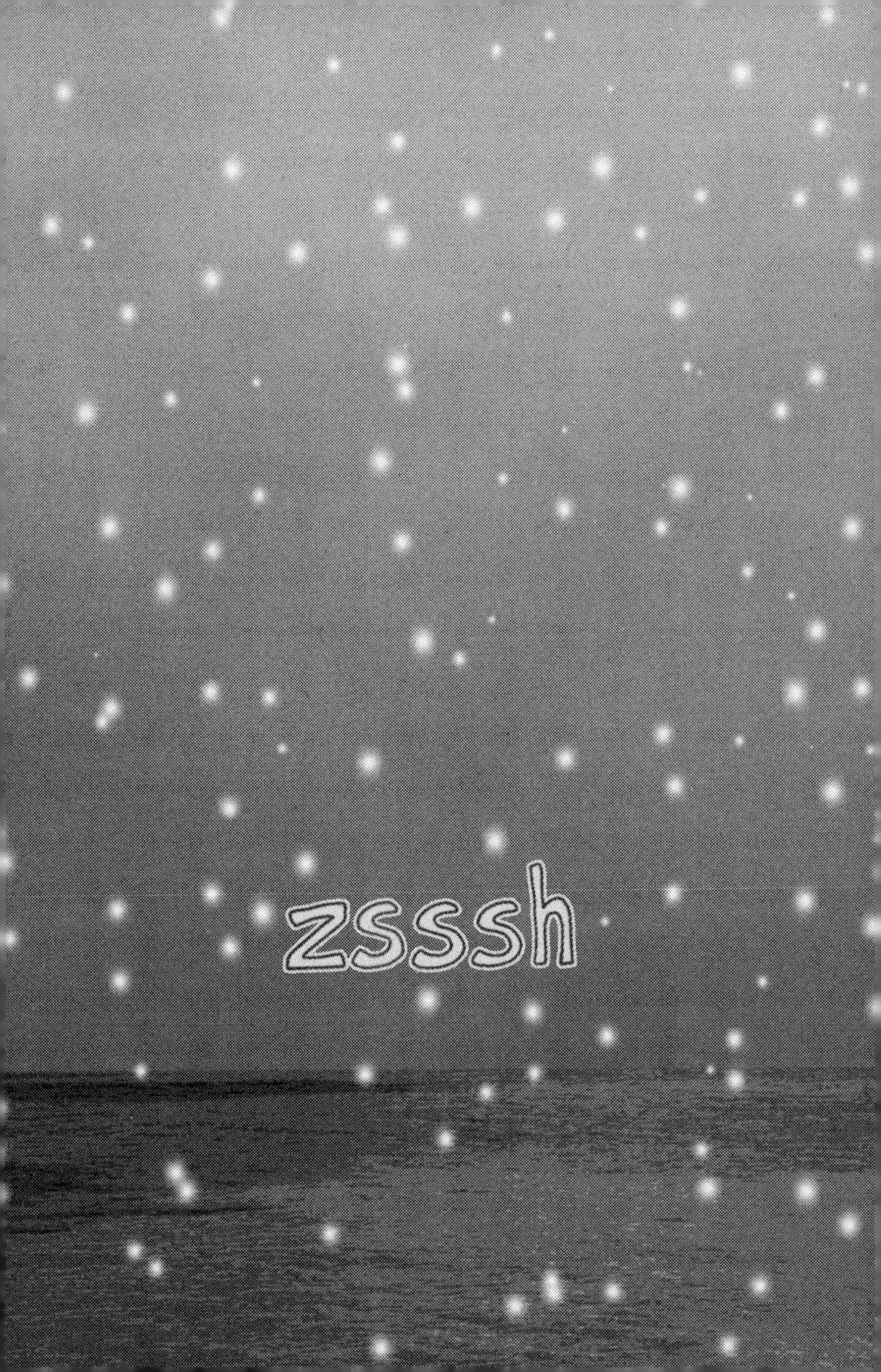
zsssh

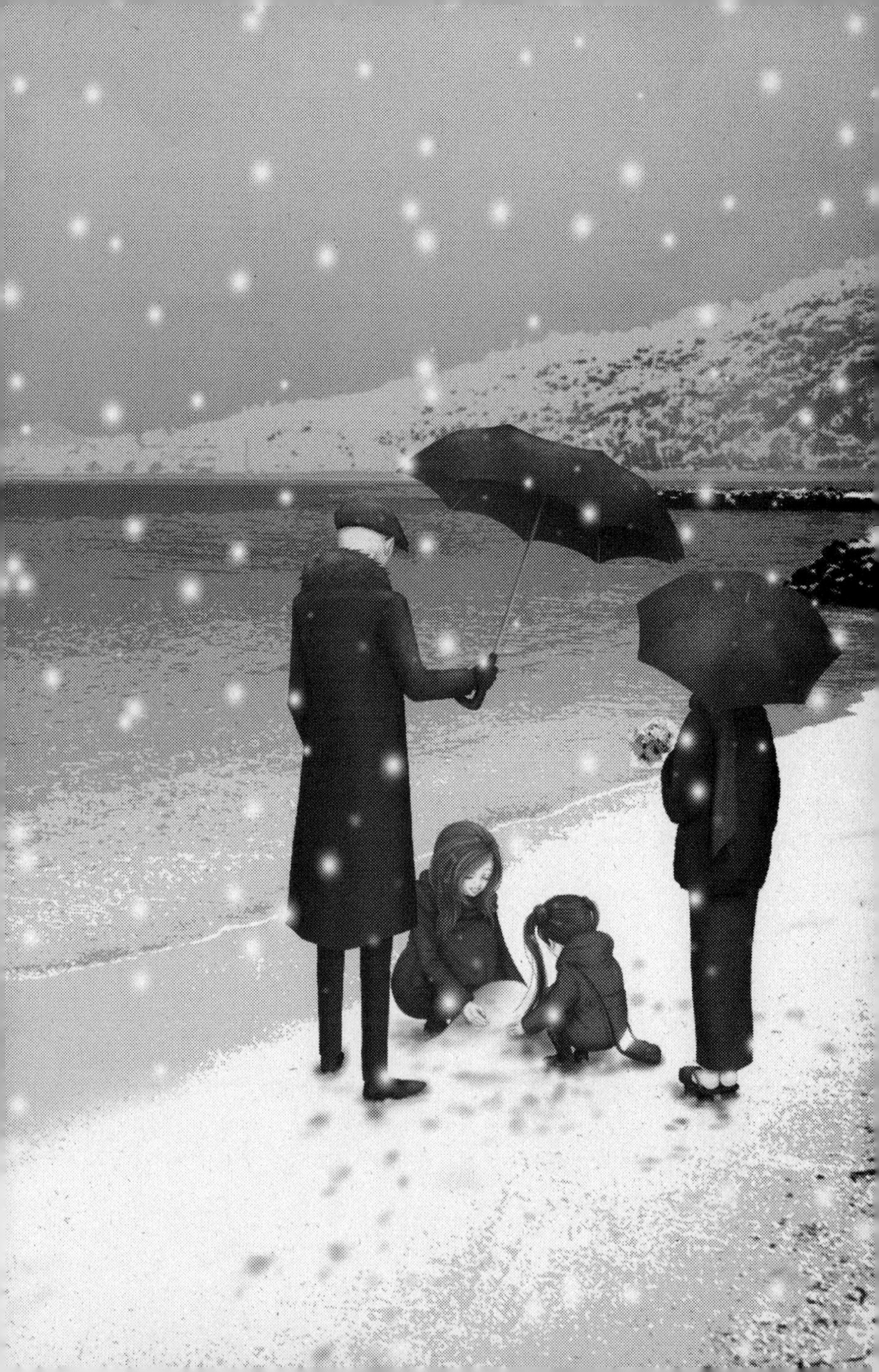

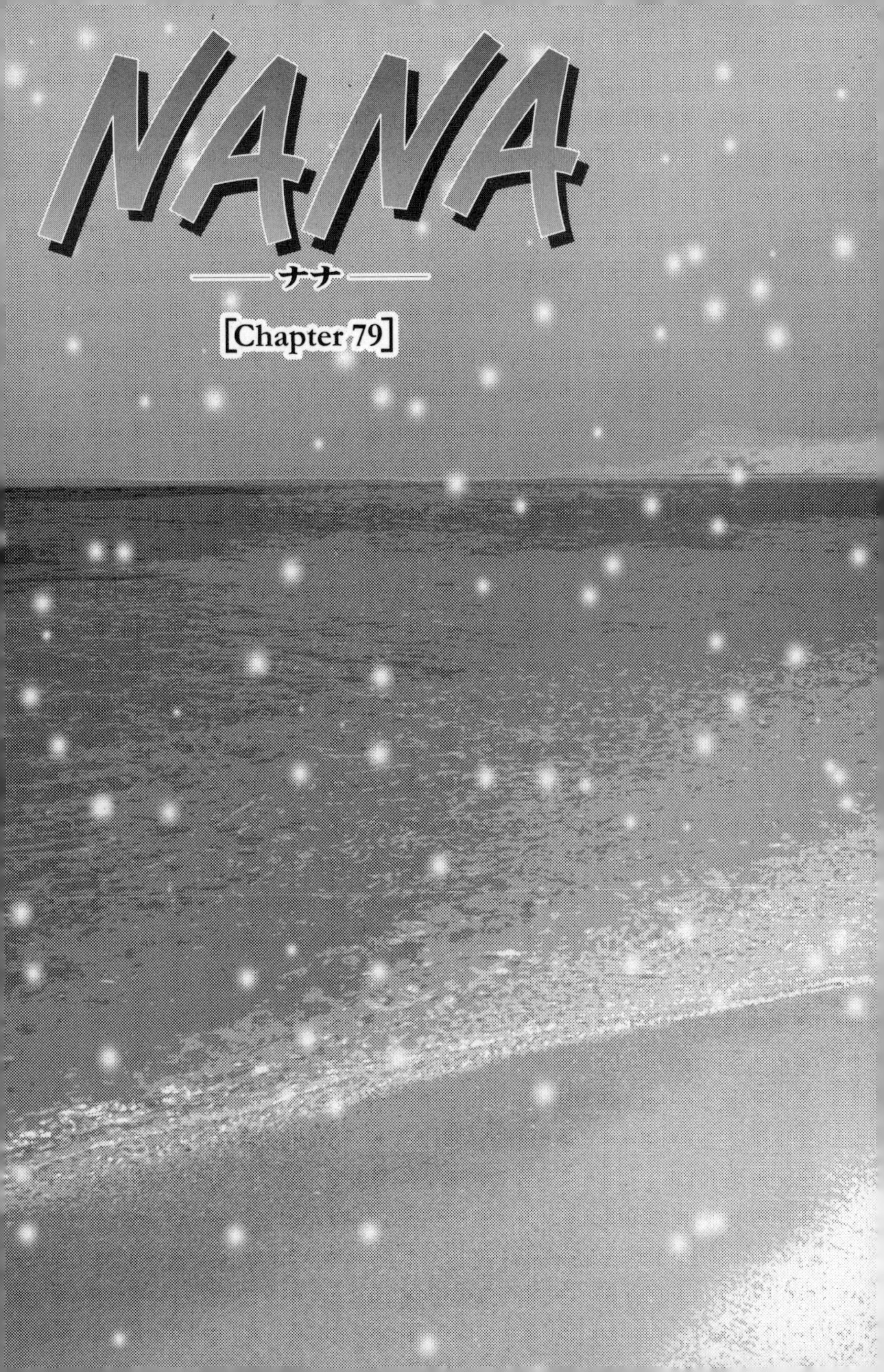
NANA
ナナ
[Chapter 79]

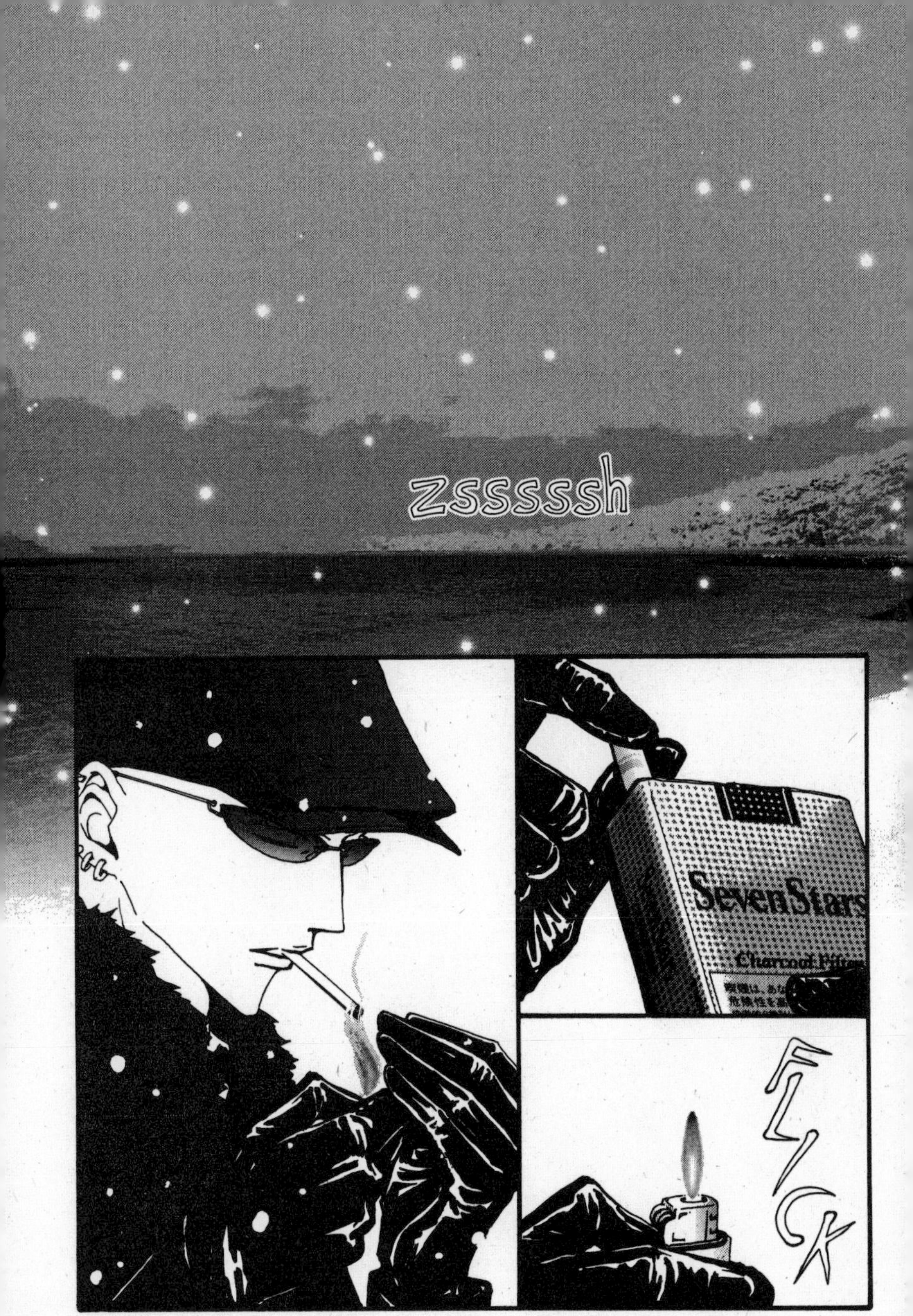
zssssssh
SevenStars
FLICK

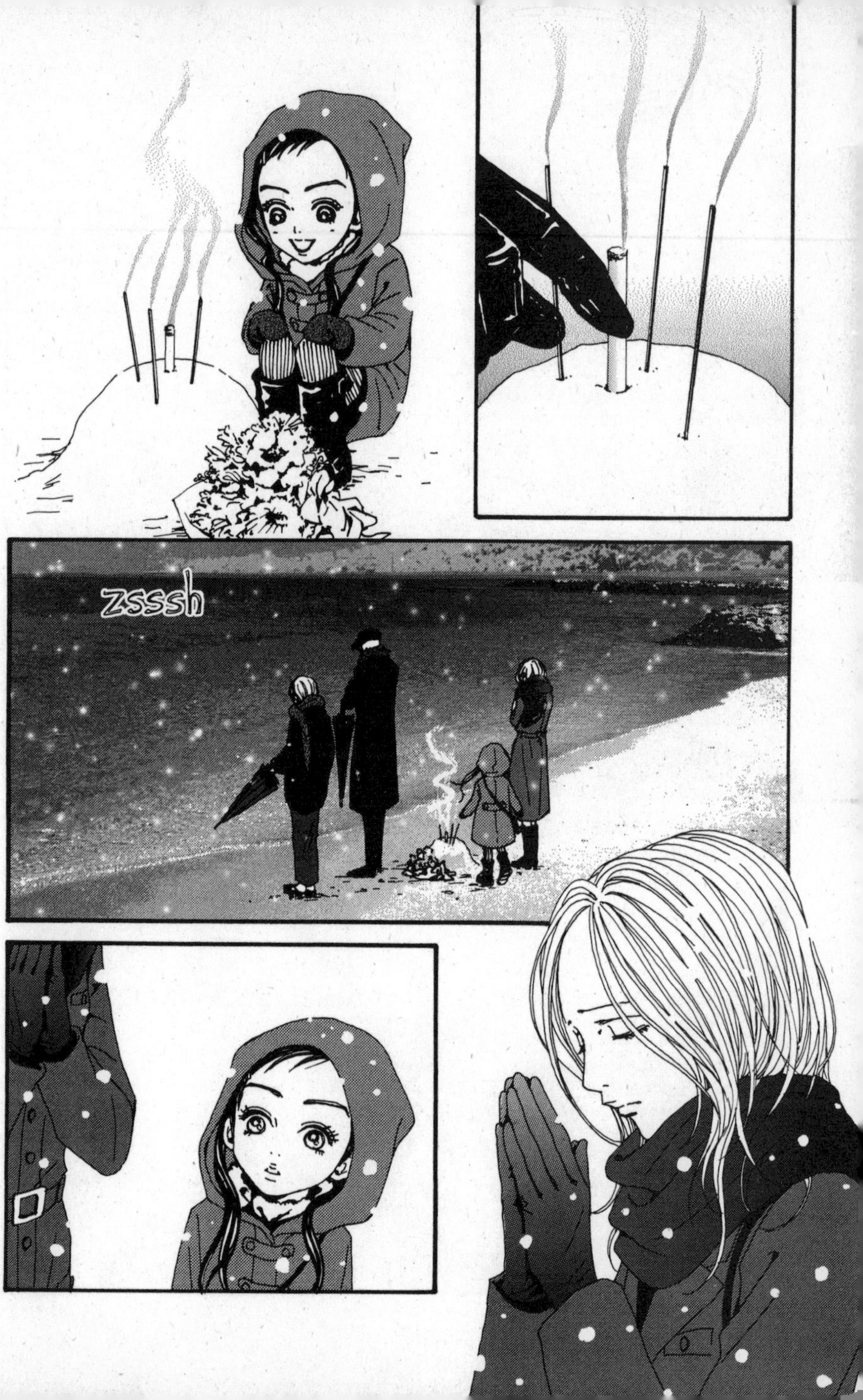
zsssh

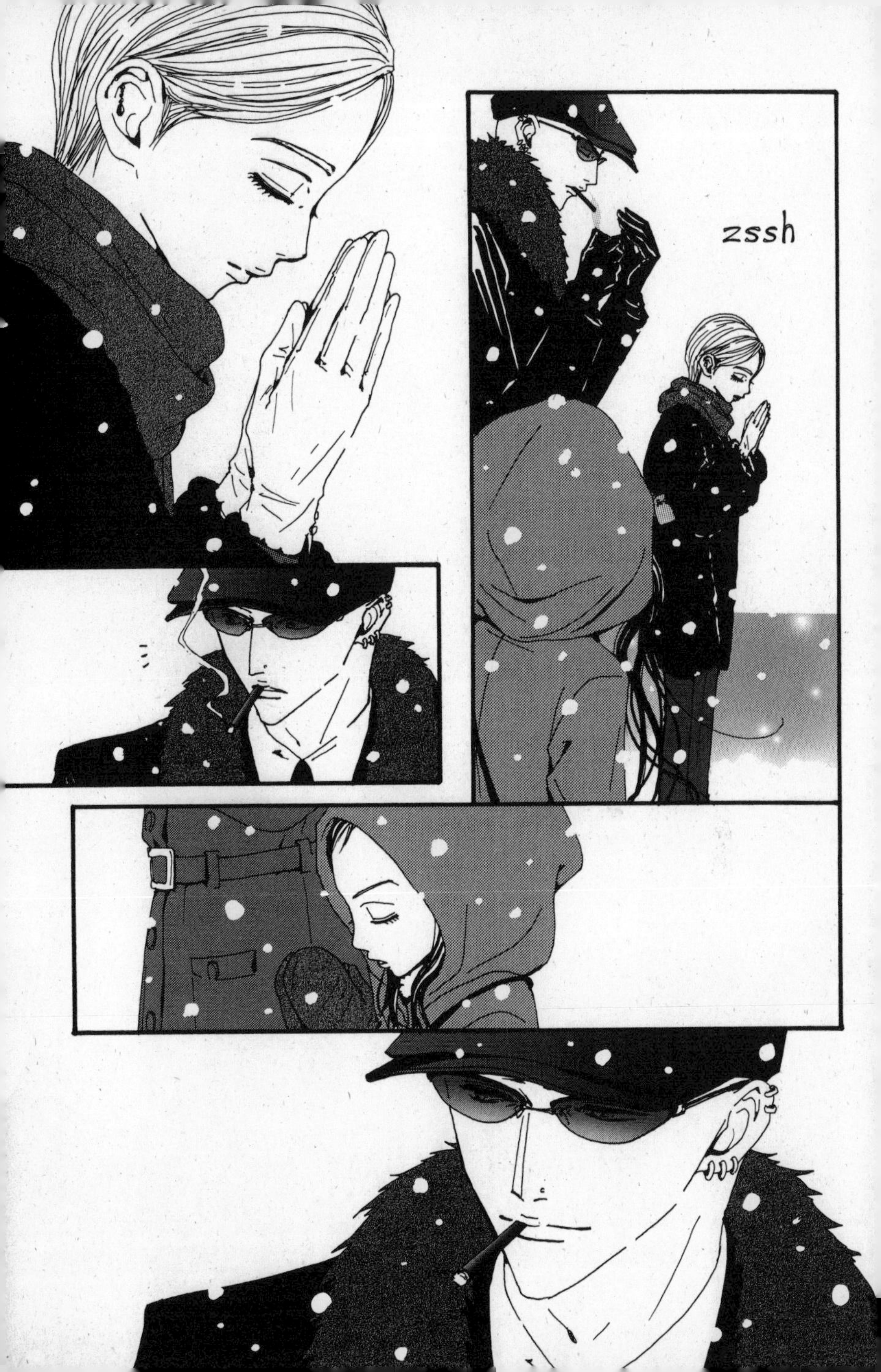
zssh

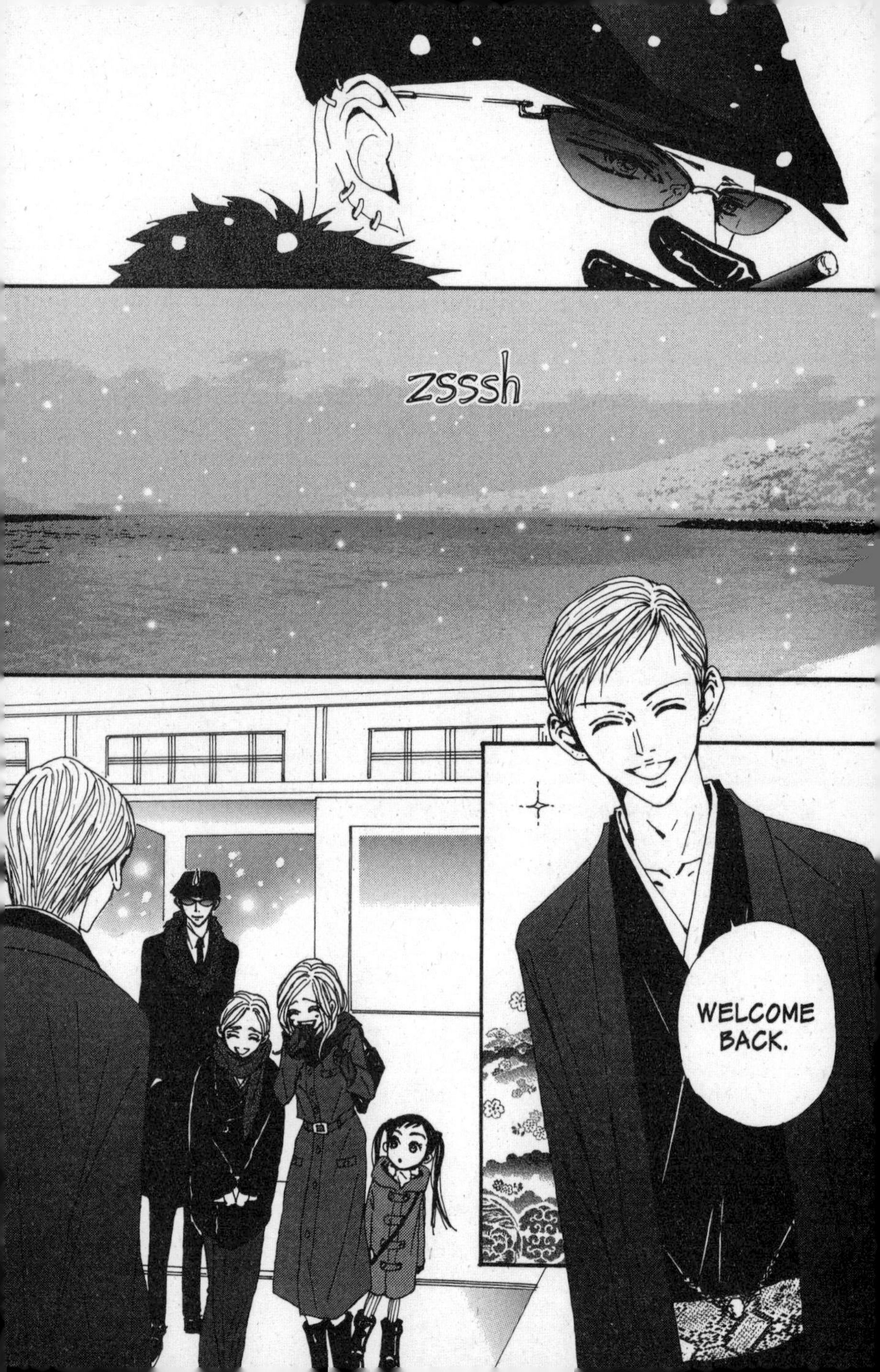
zsssh
WELCOME BACK.

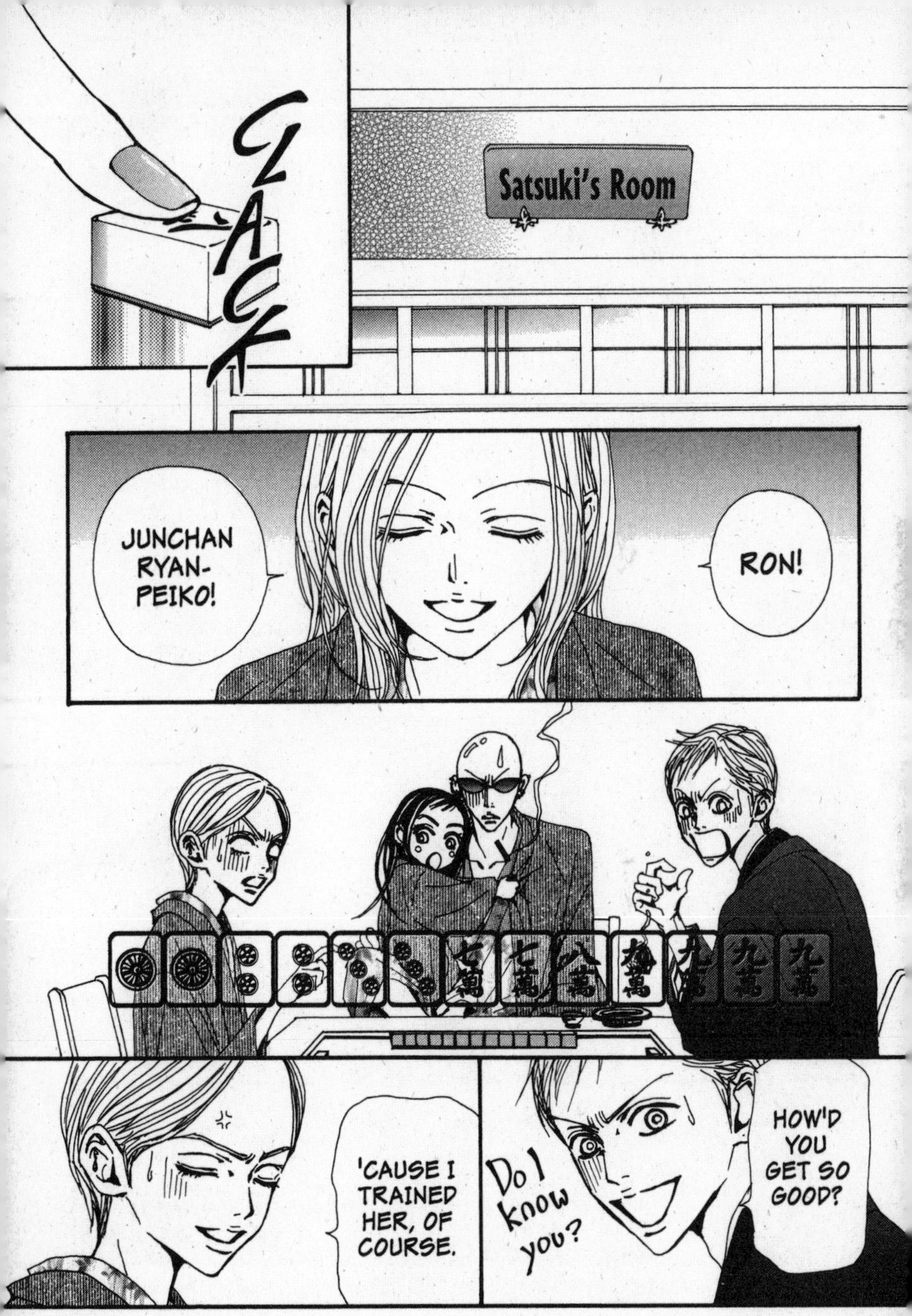
Satsuki's Room
CLACK
RON!
JUNCHAN RYAN-PEIKO!
HOW'D YOU GET SO GOOD?
Do I know you?
'CAUSE I TRAINED HER, OF COURSE.

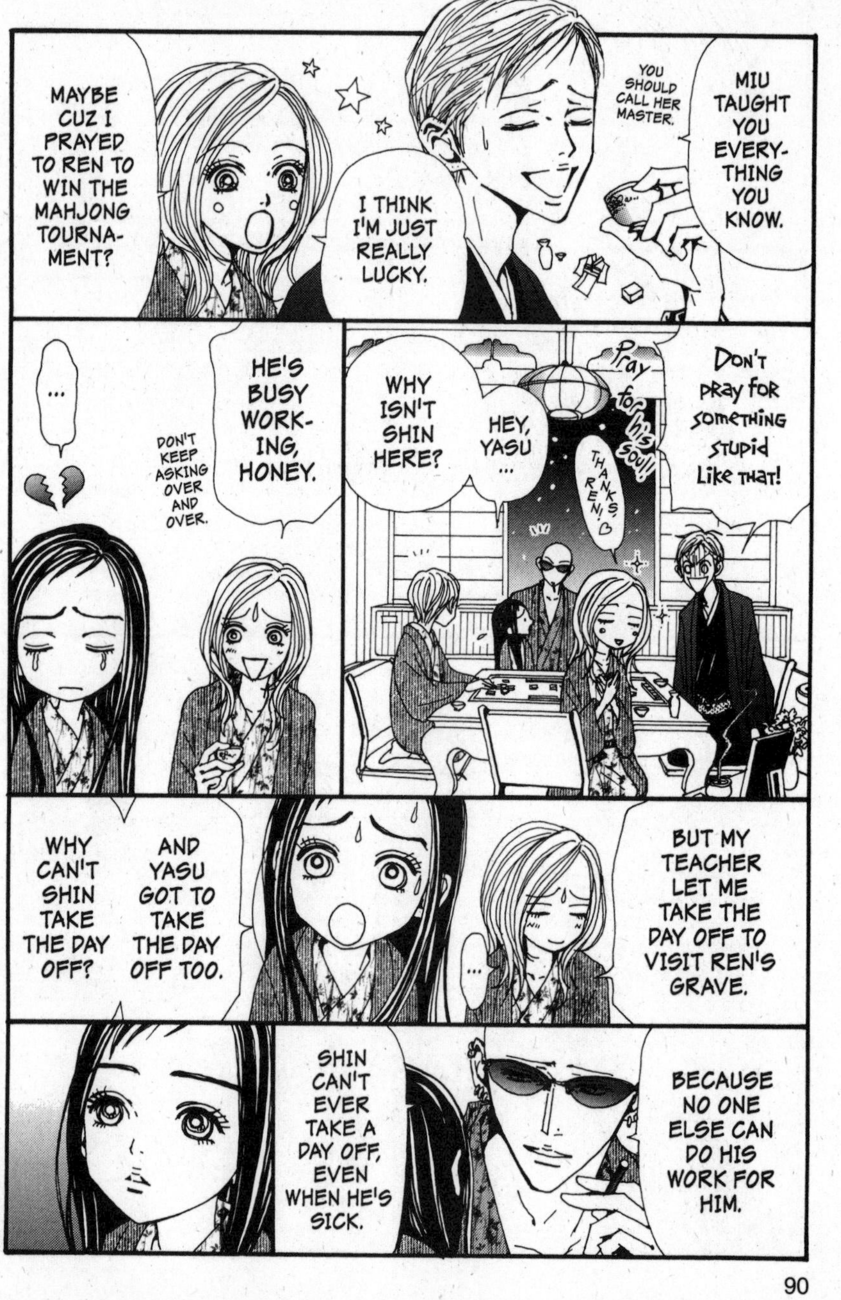
MIU TAUGHT YOU EVERYTHING YOU KNOW.
YOU SHOULD CALL HER MASTER.
I THINK I'M JUST REALLY LUCKY.
MAYBE CUZ I PRAYED TO REN TO WIN THE MAHJONG TOURNAMENT?
Don't pray for something stupid like that!
Pray for his soul!
THANKS, REN! ♡
HEY, YASU ...
WHY ISN'T SHIN HERE?
HE'S BUSY WORKING, HONEY.
DON'T KEEP ASKING OVER AND OVER.
...
BUT MY TEACHER LET ME TAKE THE DAY OFF TO VISIT REN'S GRAVE.
...
AND YASU GOT TO TAKE THE DAY OFF TOO.
WHY CAN'T SHIN TAKE THE DAY OFF?
BECAUSE NO ONE ELSE CAN DO HIS WORK FOR HIM.
SHIN CAN'T EVER TAKE A DAY OFF, EVEN WHEN HE'S SICK.

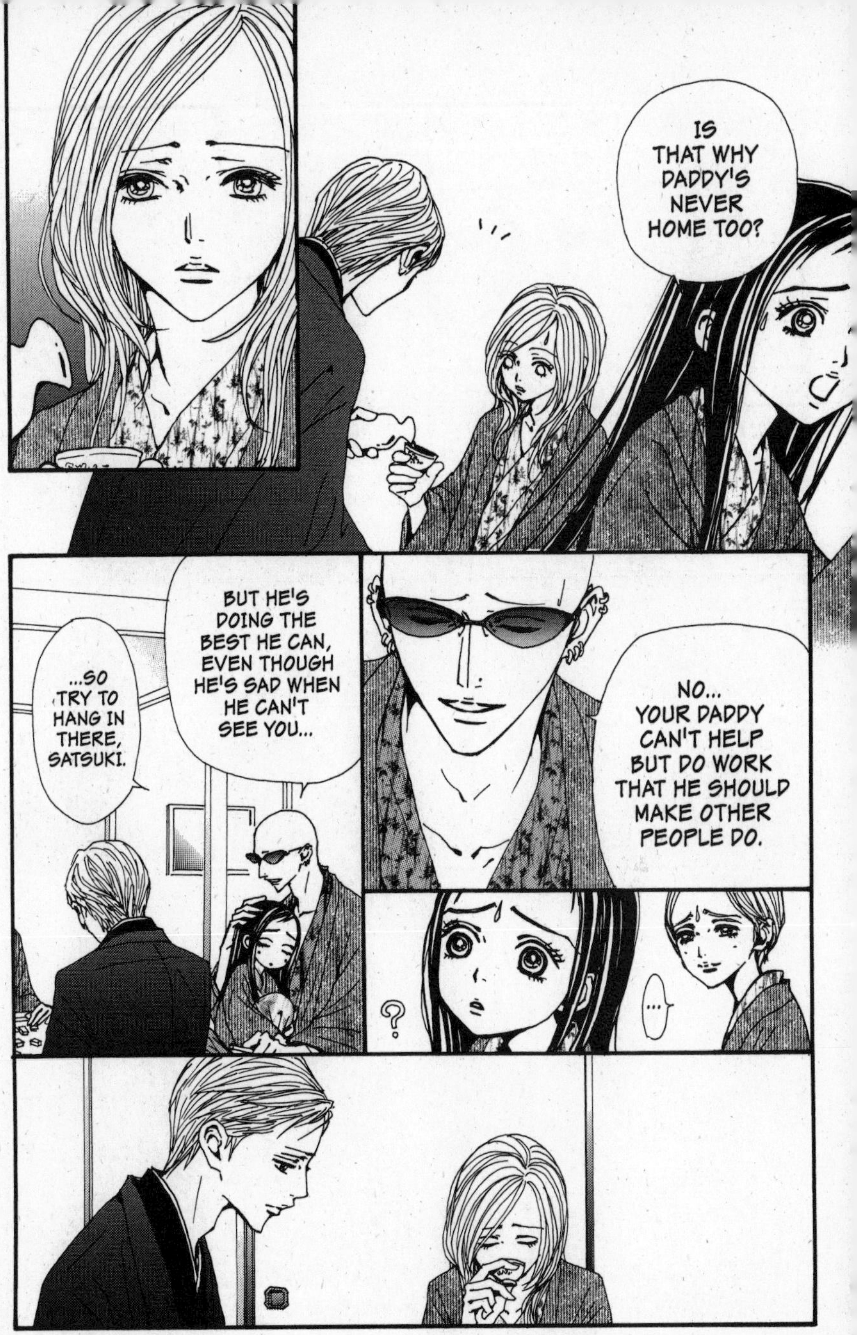
IS THAT WHY DADDY'S NEVER HOME TOO?
NO... YOUR DADDY CAN'T HELP BUT DO WORK THAT HE SHOULD MAKE OTHER PEOPLE DO.
...
?
BUT HE'S DOING THE BEST HE CAN, EVEN THOUGH HE'S SAD WHEN HE CAN'T SEE YOU...
...SO TRY TO HANG IN THERE, SATSUKI.

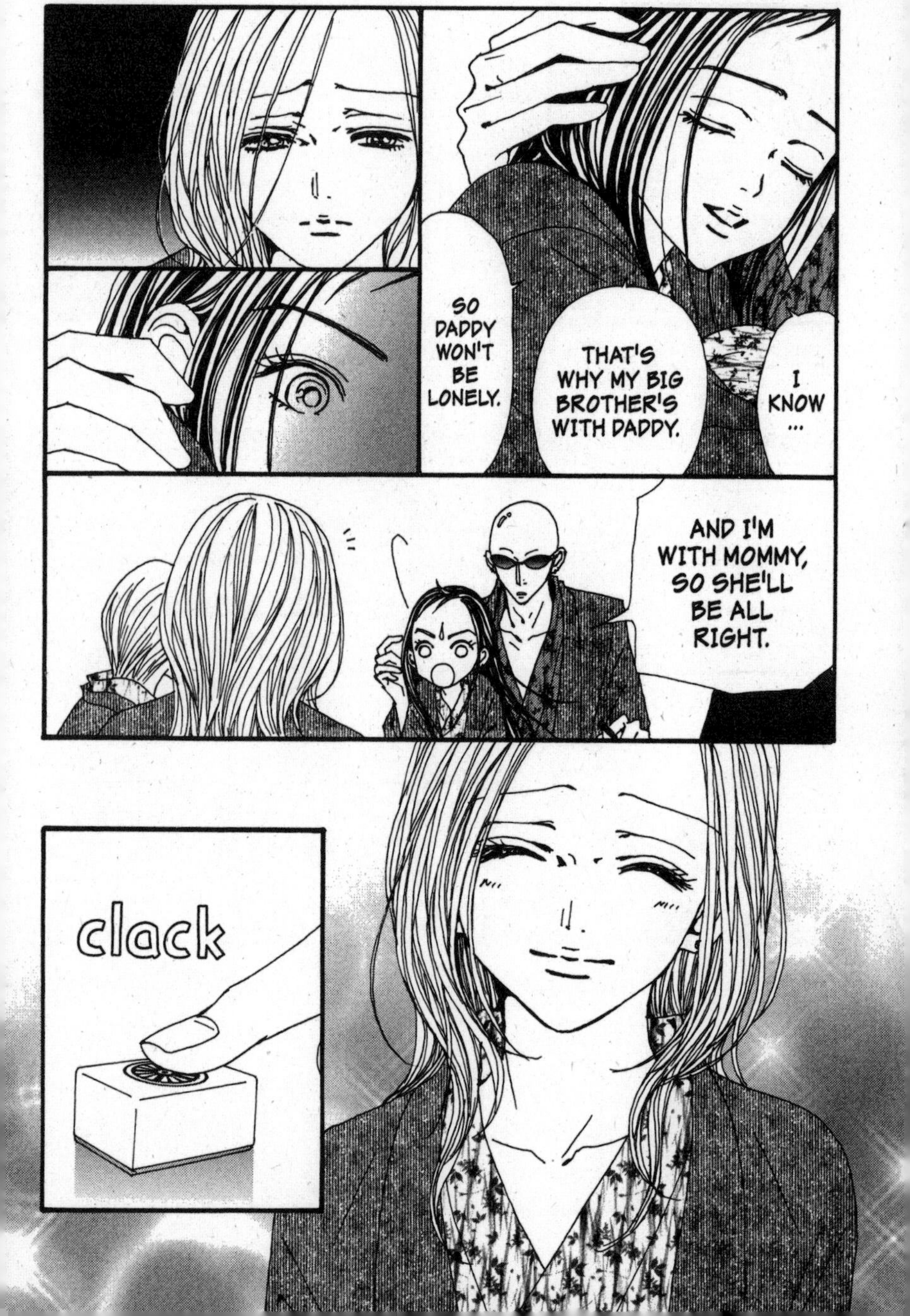
I KNOW...
THAT'S WHY MY BIG BROTHER'S WITH DADDY.
SO DADDY WON'T BE LONELY.
AND I'M WITH MOMMY, SO SHE'LL BE ALL RIGHT.
clack

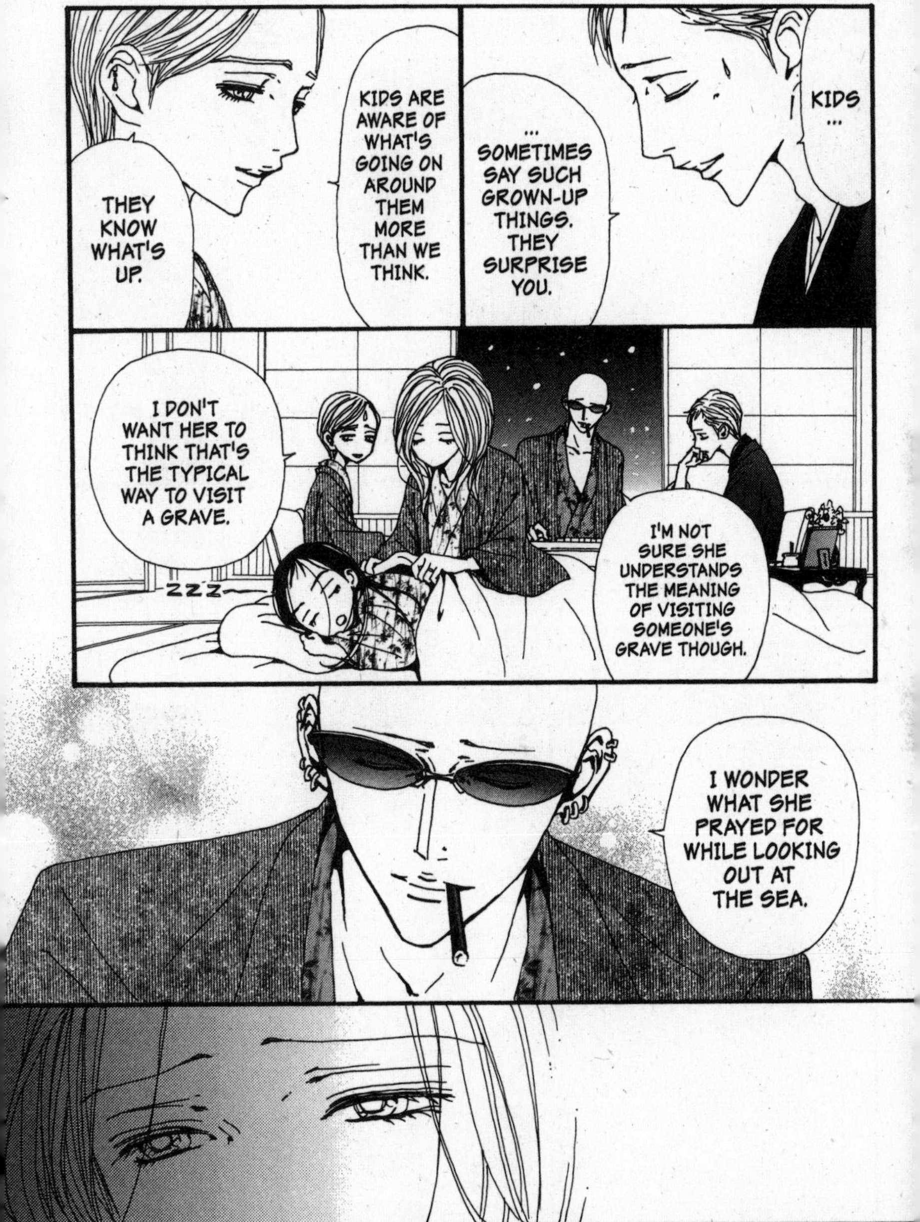
KIDS ...
... SOMETIMES SAY SUCH GROWN-UP THINGS. THEY SURPRISE YOU.
KIDS ARE AWARE OF WHAT'S GOING ON AROUND THEM MORE THAN WE THINK.
THEY KNOW WHAT'S UP.
I'M NOT SURE SHE UNDERSTANDS THE MEANING OF VISITING SOMEONE'S GRAVE THOUGH.
I DON'T WANT HER TO THINK THAT'S THE TYPICAL WAY TO VISIT A GRAVE.
ZZZ~
I WONDER WHAT SHE PRAYED FOR WHILE LOOKING OUT AT THE SEA.

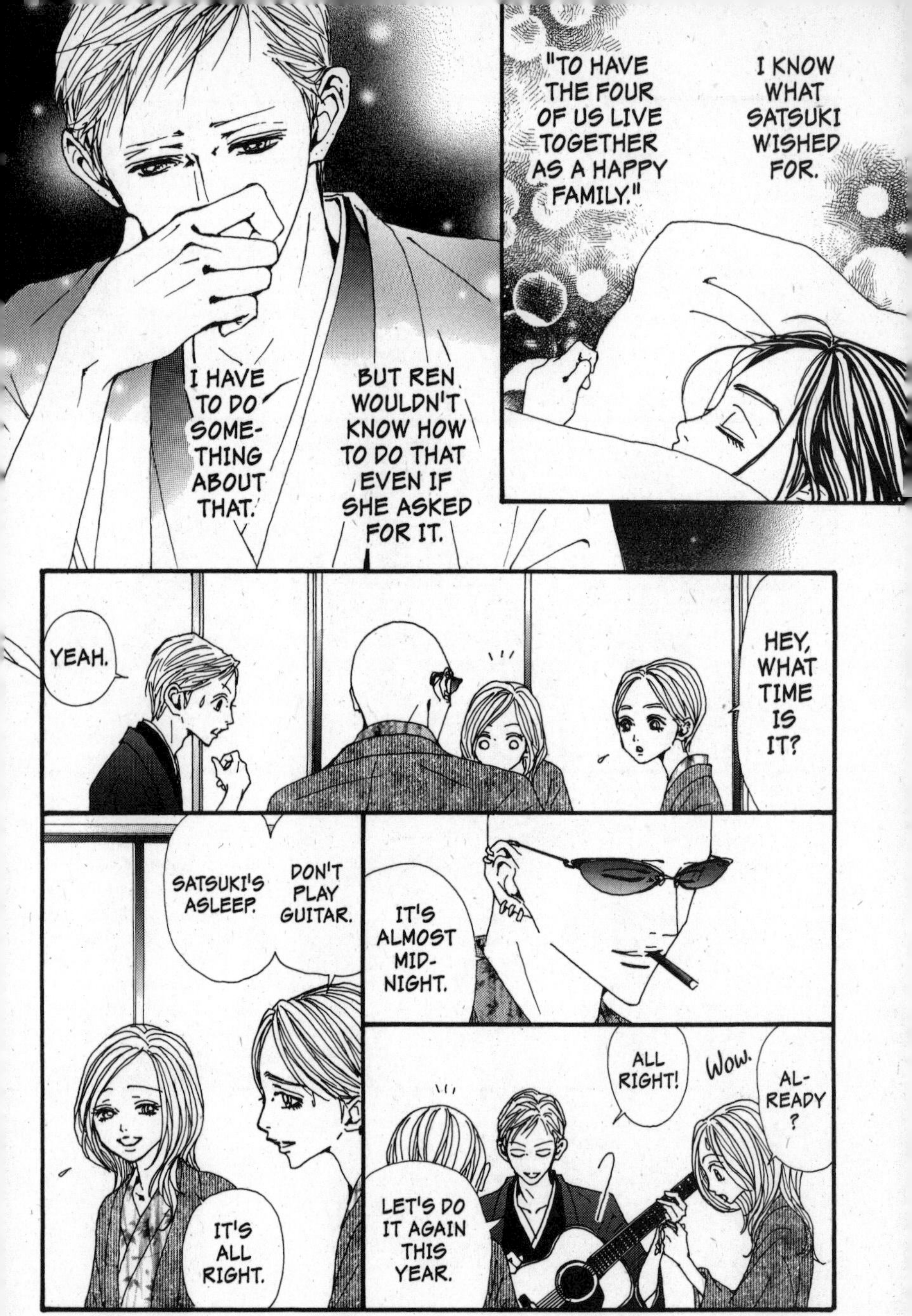
I KNOW WHAT SATSUKI WISHED FOR.
"TO HAVE THE FOUR OF US LIVE TOGETHER AS A HAPPY FAMILY."
BUT REN WOULDN'T KNOW HOW TO DO THAT EVEN IF SHE ASKED FOR IT.
I HAVE TO DO SOMETHING ABOUT THAT.
HEY, WHAT TIME IS IT?
YEAH.
IT'S ALMOST MIDNIGHT.
AL-READY?
WOW.
ALL RIGHT!
LET'S DO IT AGAIN THIS YEAR.
DON'T PLAY GUITAR.
SATSUKI'S ASLEEP.
IT'S ALL RIGHT.

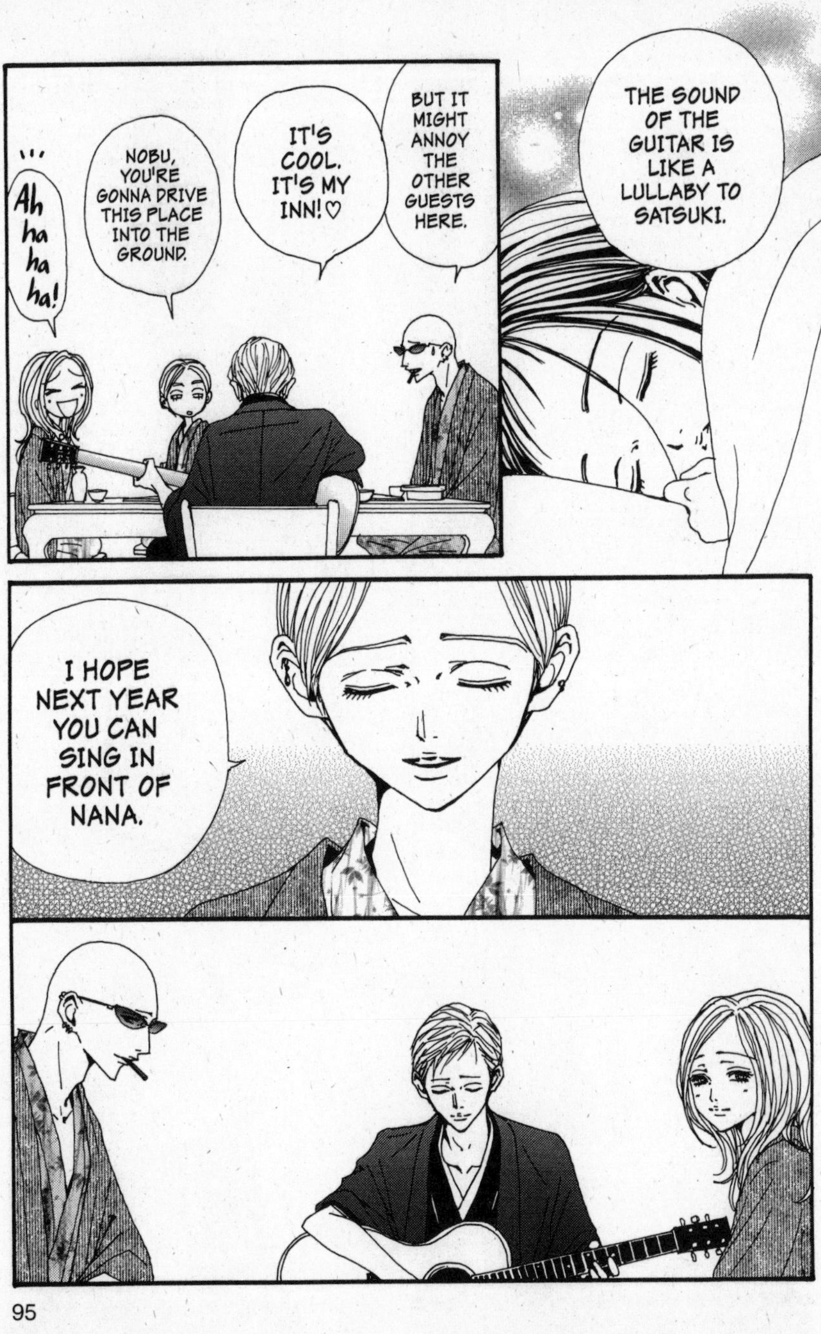
THE SOUND OF THE GUITAR IS LIKE A LULLABY TO SATSUKI.
BUT IT MIGHT ANNOY THE OTHER GUESTS HERE.
IT'S COOL. IT'S MY INN!♡
NOBU, YOU'RE GONNA DRIVE THIS PLACE INTO THE GROUND.
...
Ah ha ha ha!
I HOPE NEXT YEAR YOU CAN SING IN FRONT OF NANA.

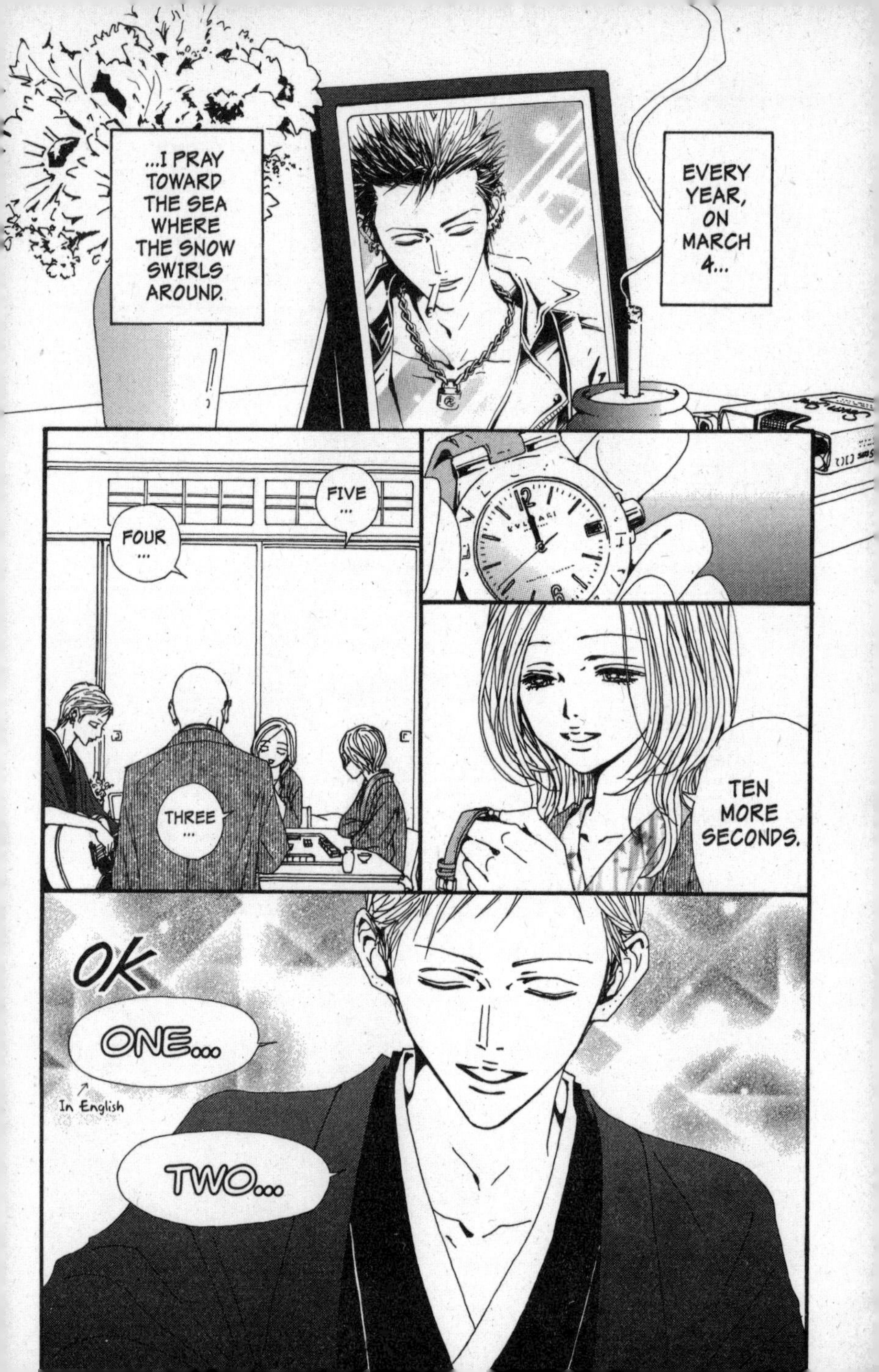
EVERY YEAR, ON MARCH 4...
...I PRAY TOWARD THE SEA WHERE THE SNOW SWIRLS AROUND.
TEN MORE SECONDS.
FIVE ...
FOUR ...
THREE ...
OK
ONE...
In English
TWO...

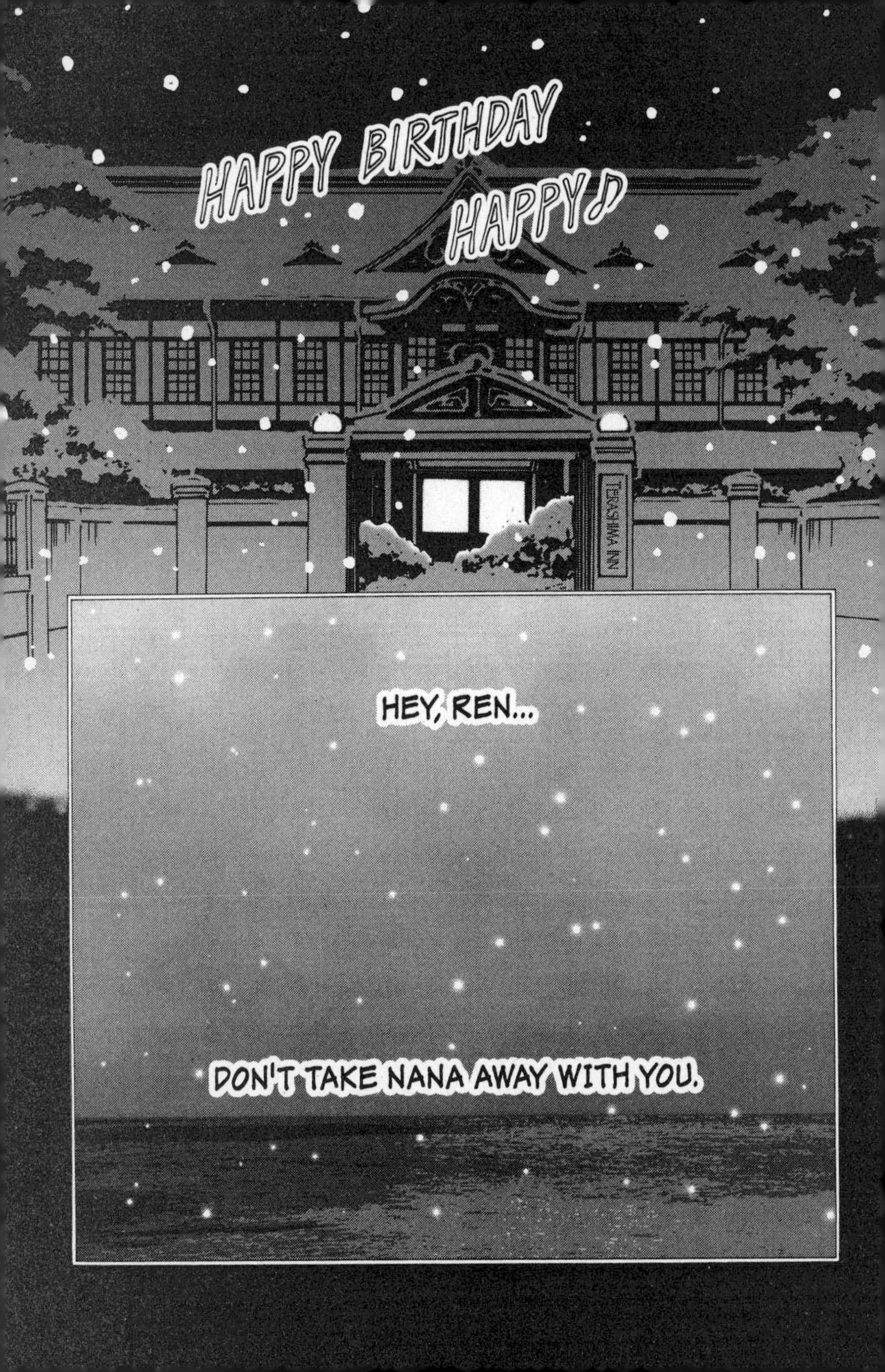
HAPPY BIRTHDAY
HAPPY♪
TERASHIMA INN
HEY, REN...
DON'T TAKE NANA AWAY WITH YOU.

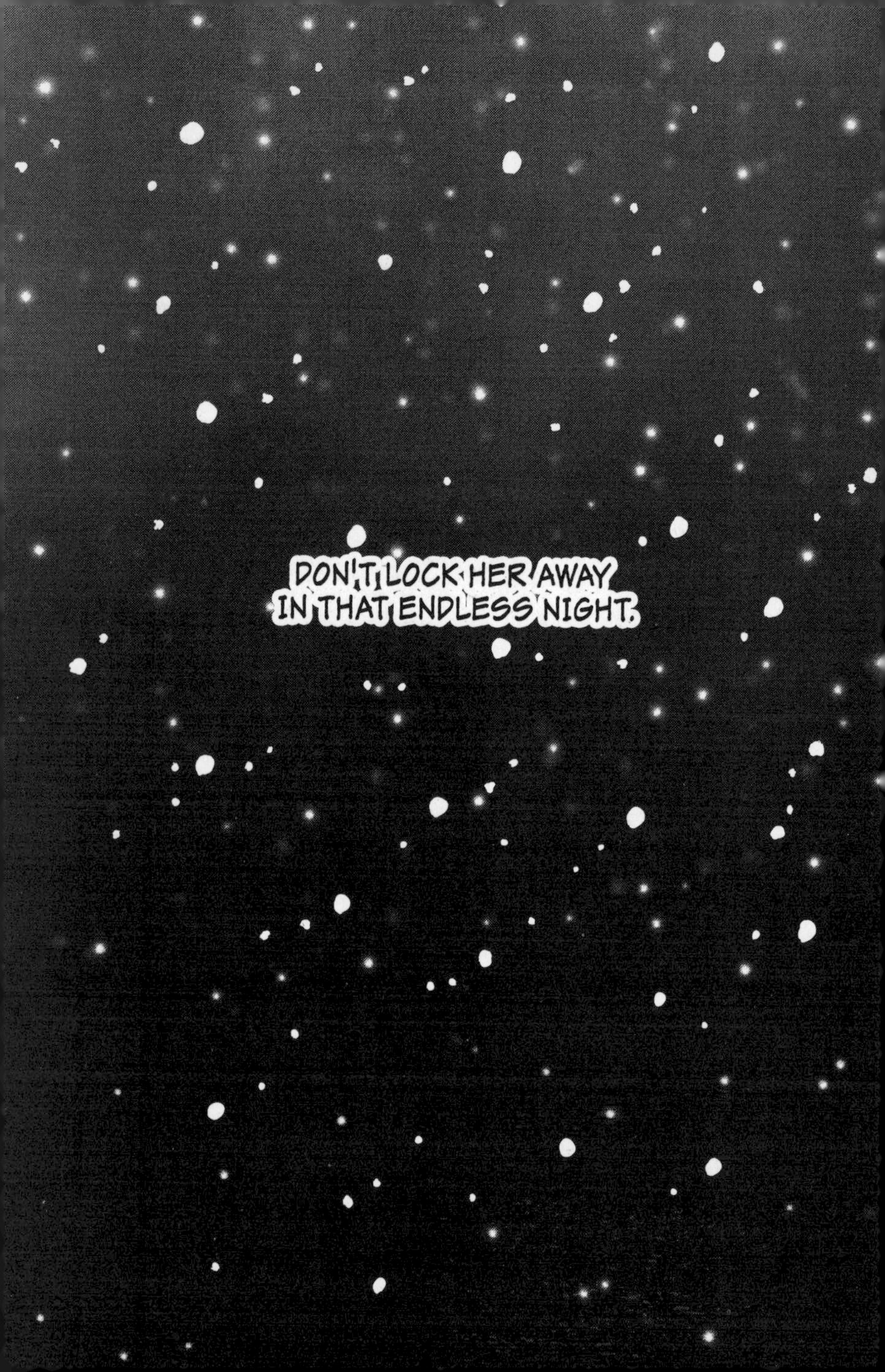
DON'T LOCK HER AWAY IN THAT ENDLESS NIGHT.

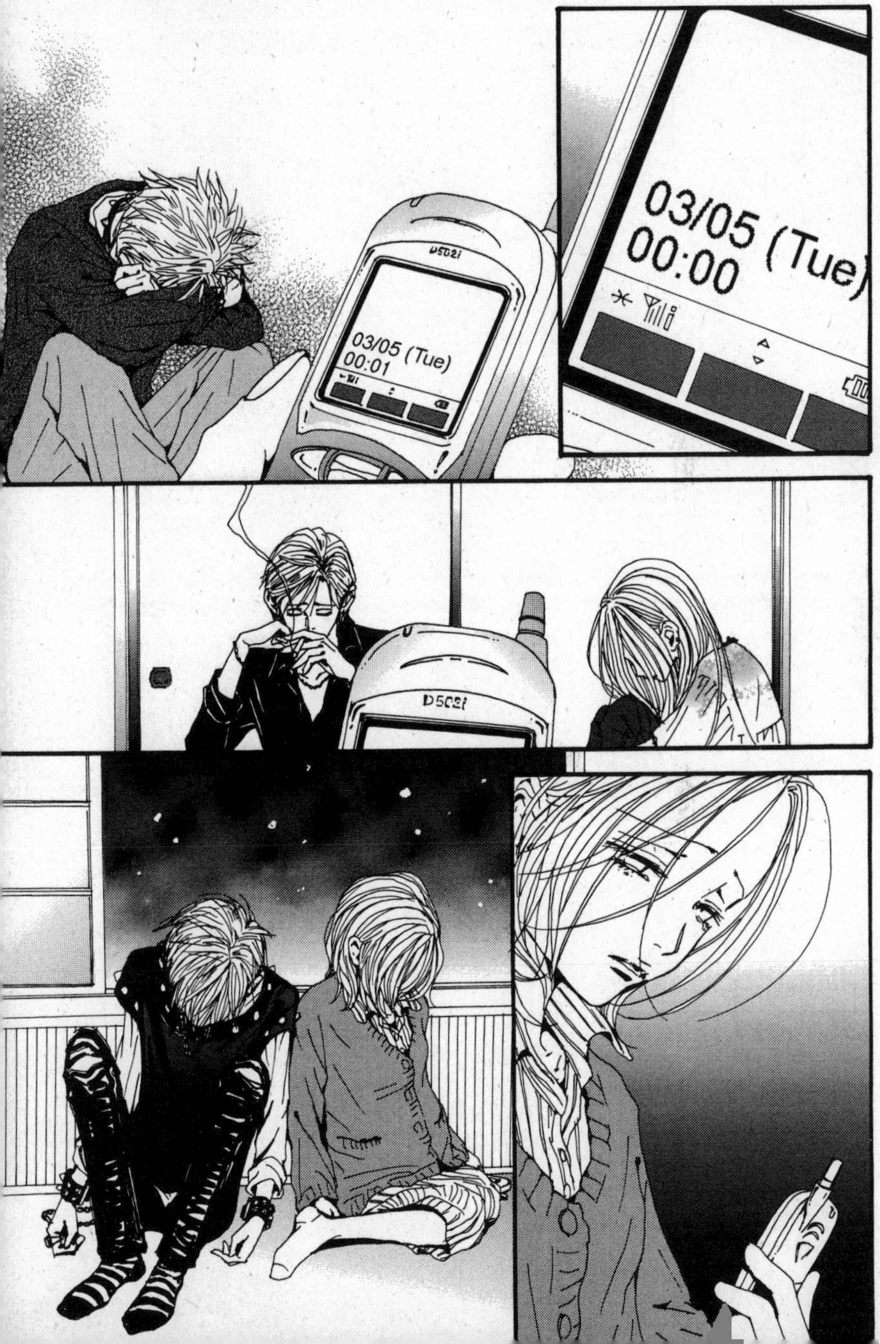
03/05 (Tue)
00:00
D502i
03/05 (Tue)
00:01
D502i

WHY IS TIME JUST CRAWLING BY?

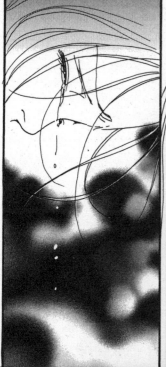

I DON'T KNOW HOW TO WAIT FOR MORNING TO COME.

I CAN'T SEND NANA A BIRTH-DAY EMAIL.

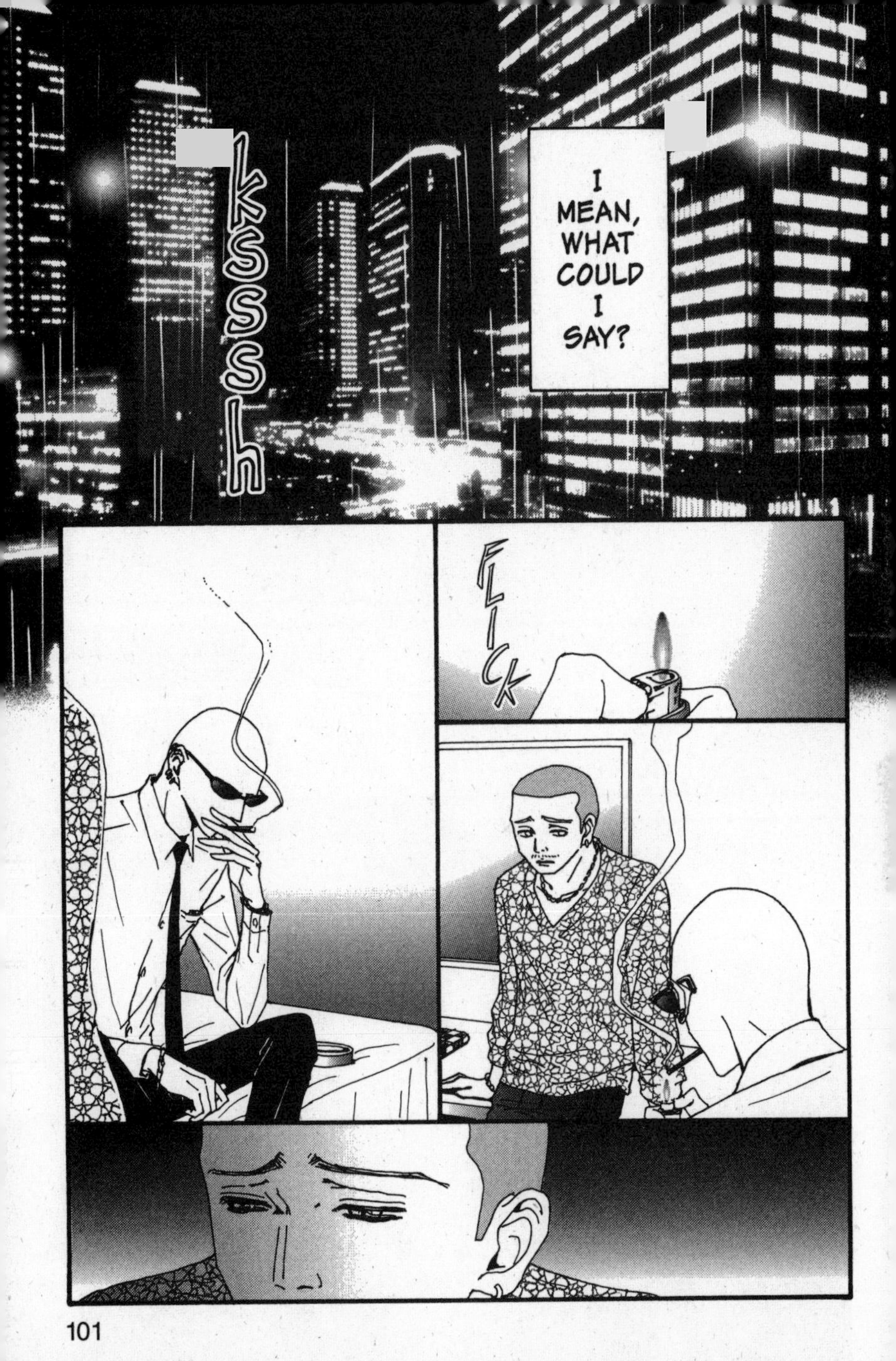
I MEAN, WHAT COULD I SAY?
KSSSH
FLICK

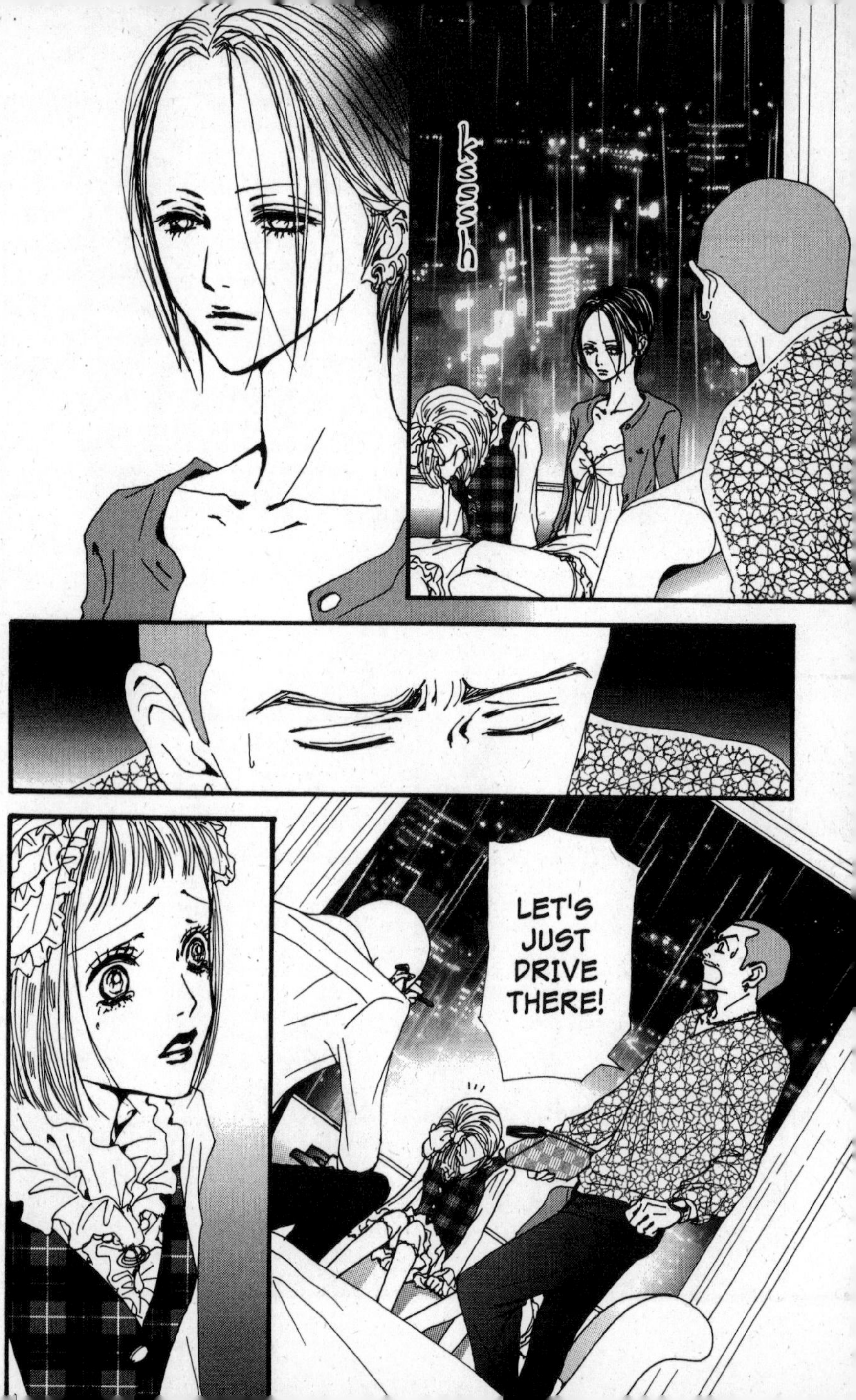
kssssh
LET'S JUST DRIVE THERE!

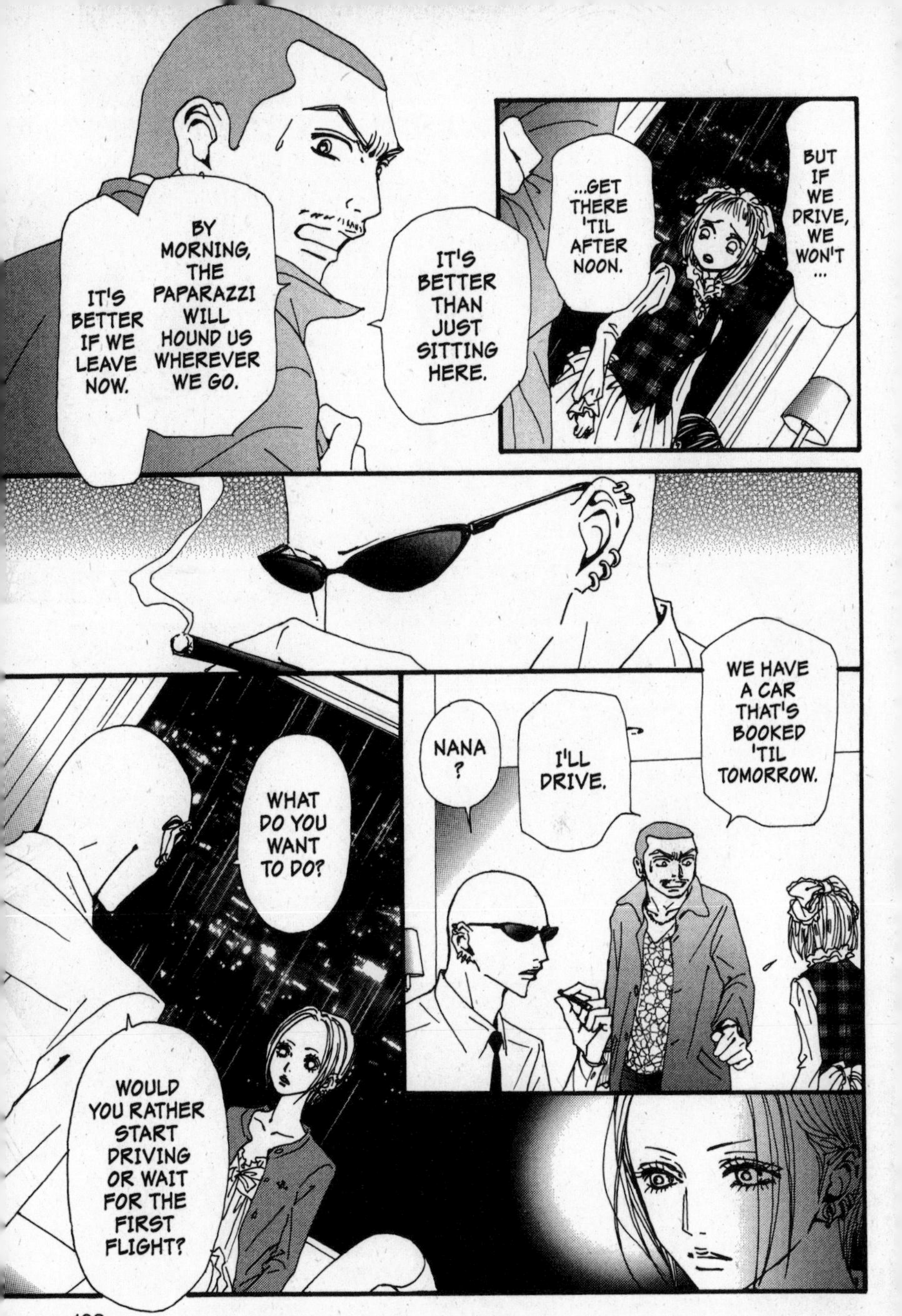
BUT IF WE DRIVE, WE WON'T ...
...GET THERE 'TIL AFTER NOON.
IT'S BETTER THAN JUST SITTING HERE.
BY MORNING, THE PAPARAZZI WILL HOUND US WHEREVER WE GO.
IT'S BETTER IF WE LEAVE NOW.
WE HAVE A CAR THAT'S BOOKED 'TIL TOMORROW.
I'LL DRIVE.
NANA?
WHAT DO YOU WANT TO DO?
WOULD YOU RATHER START DRIVING OR WAIT FOR THE FIRST FLIGHT?

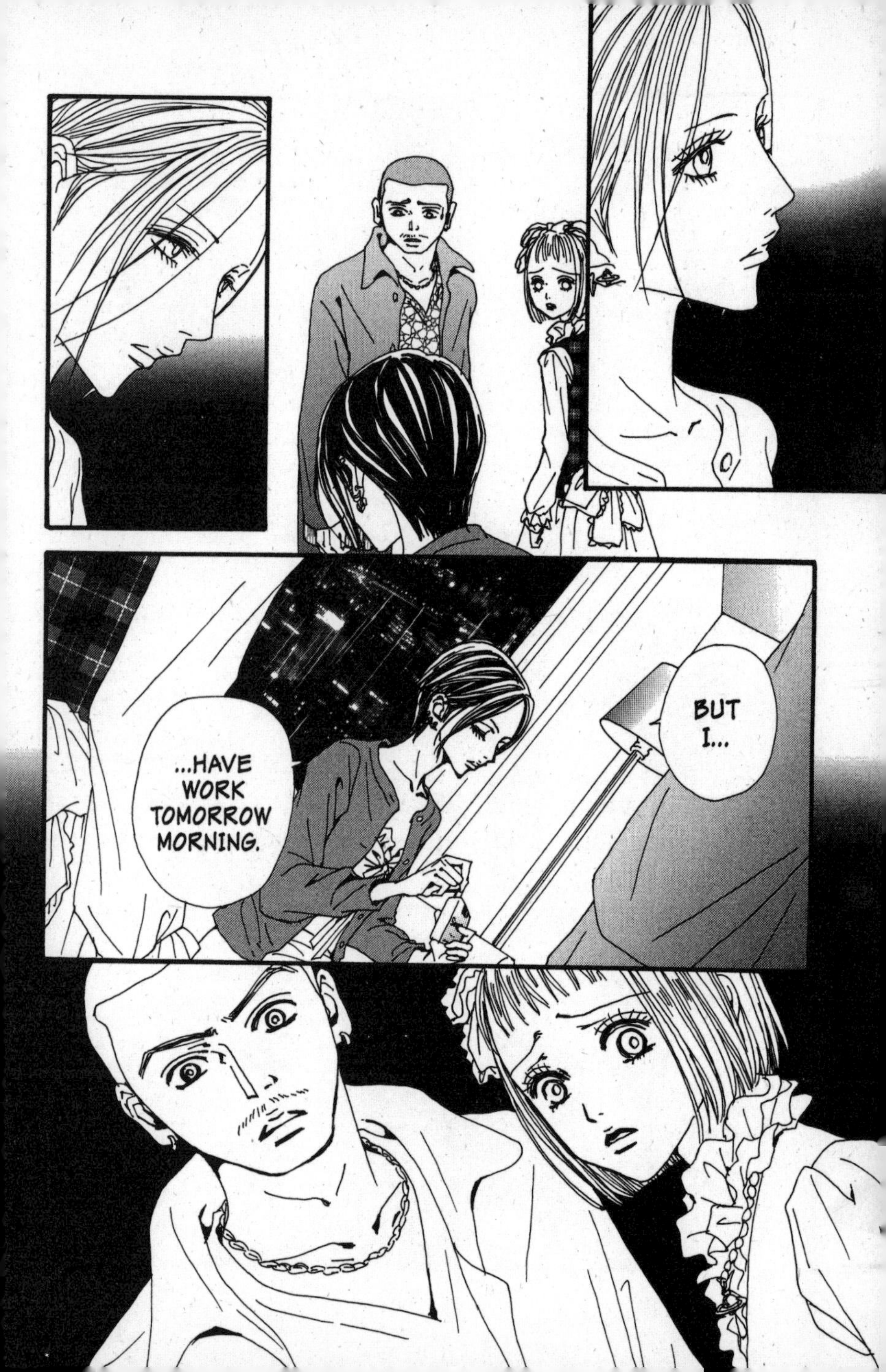
BUT I...
...HAVE WORK TOMORROW MORNING.

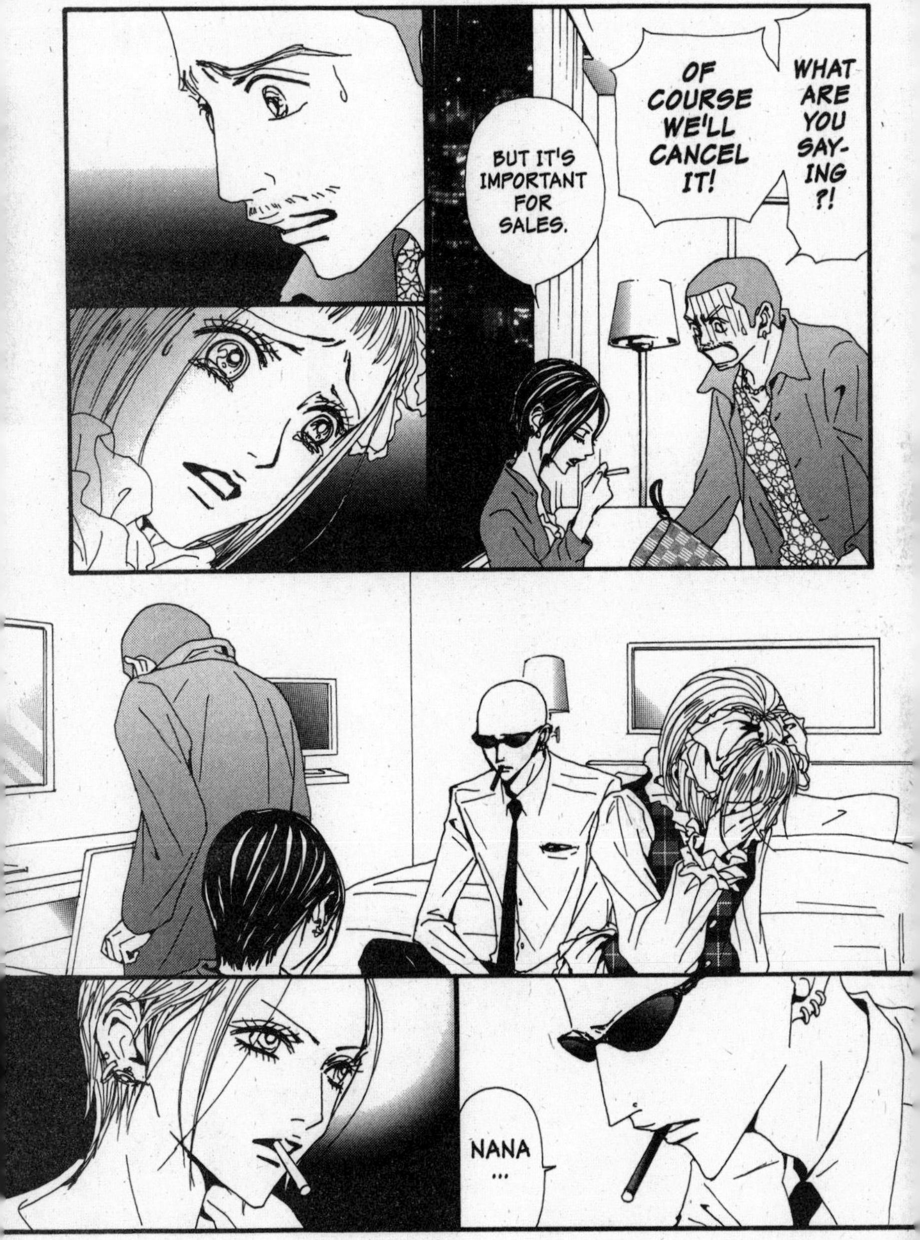
WHAT ARE YOU SAYING?!
OF COURSE WE'LL CANCEL IT!
BUT IT'S IMPORTANT FOR SALES.
NANA ...

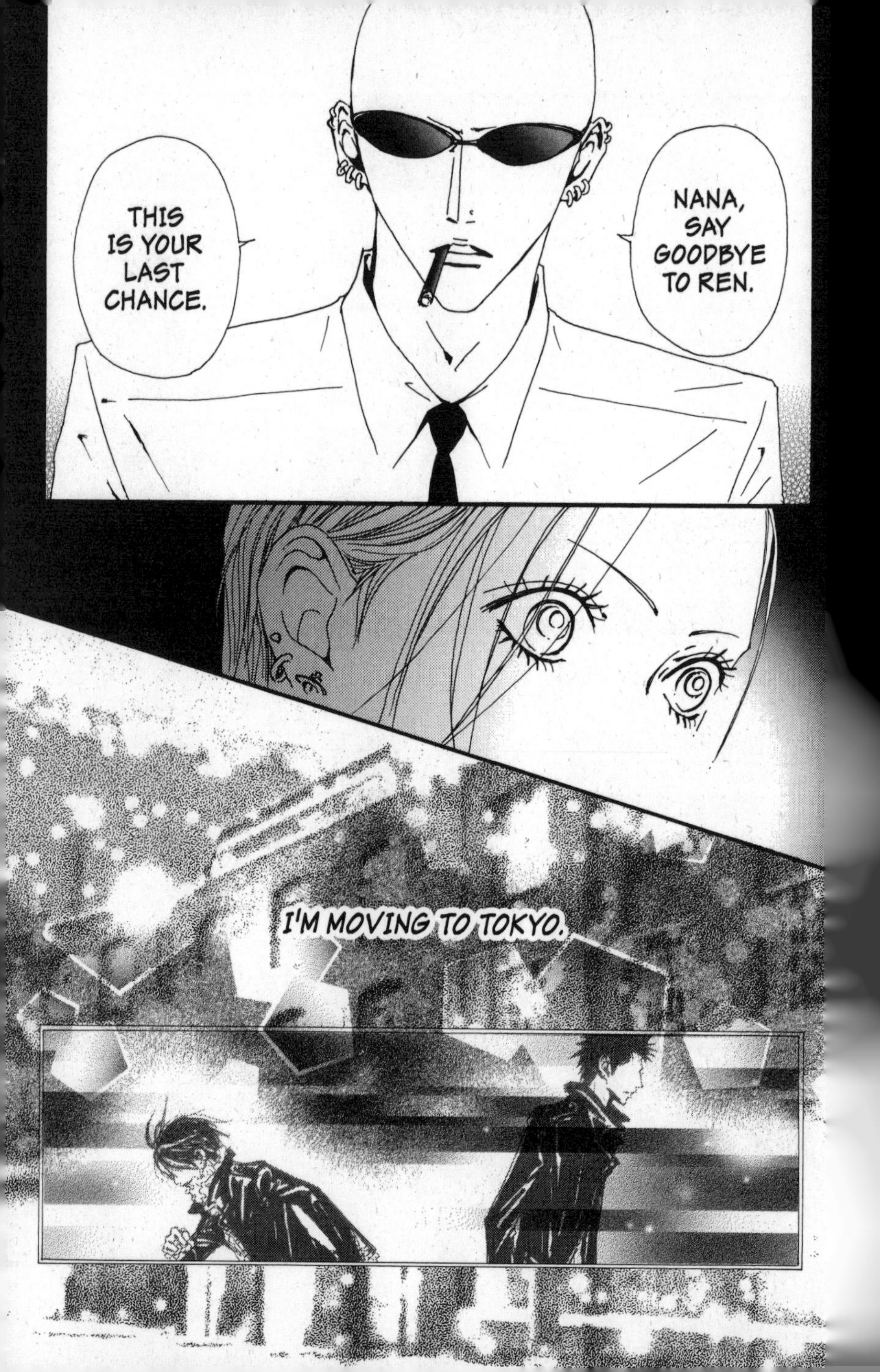
NANA, SAY GOODBYE TO REN.
THIS IS YOUR LAST CHANCE.
I'M MOVING TO TOKYO.

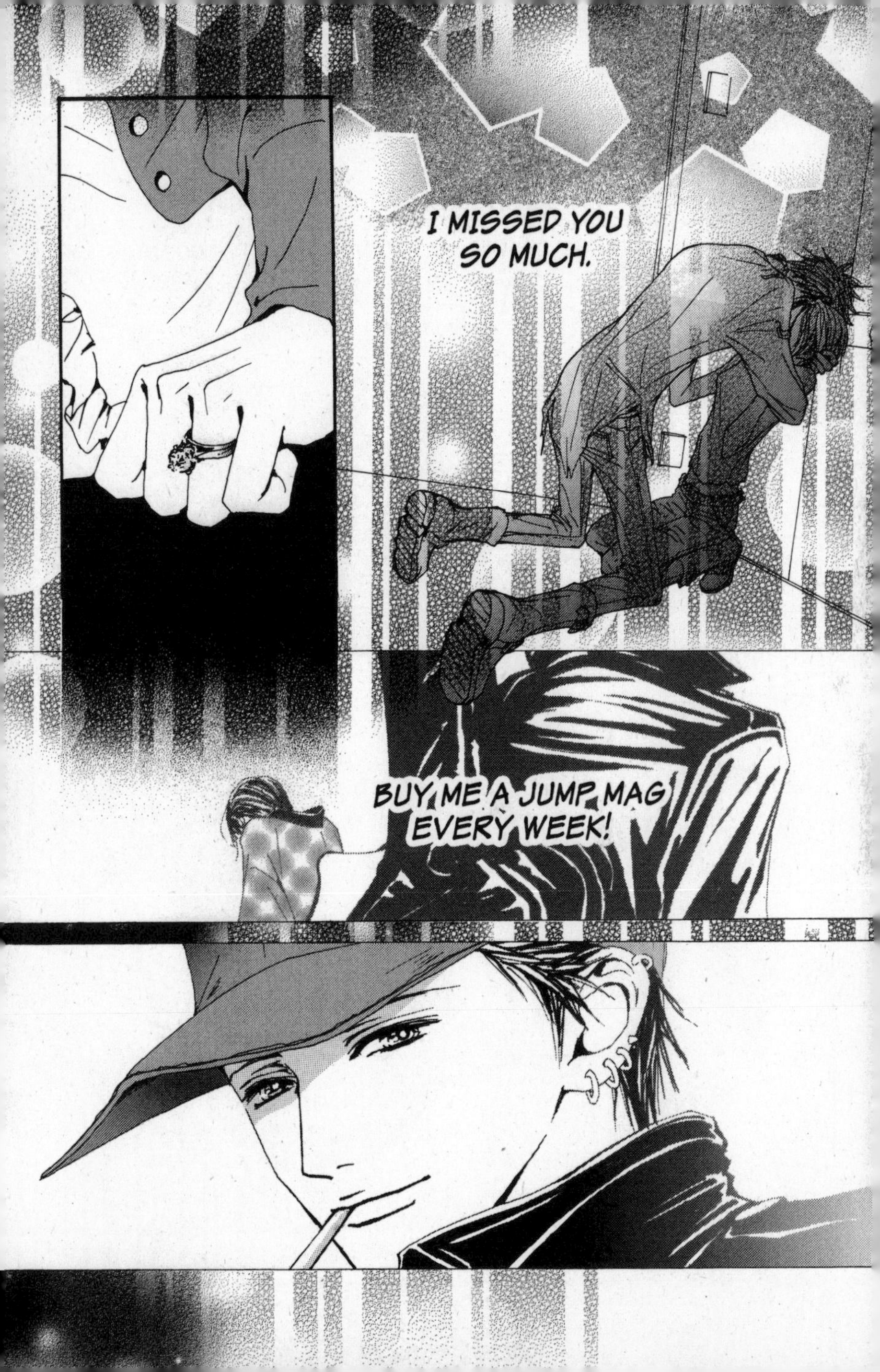
I MISSED YOU SO MUCH.
BUY ME A JUMP MAG EVERY WEEK!

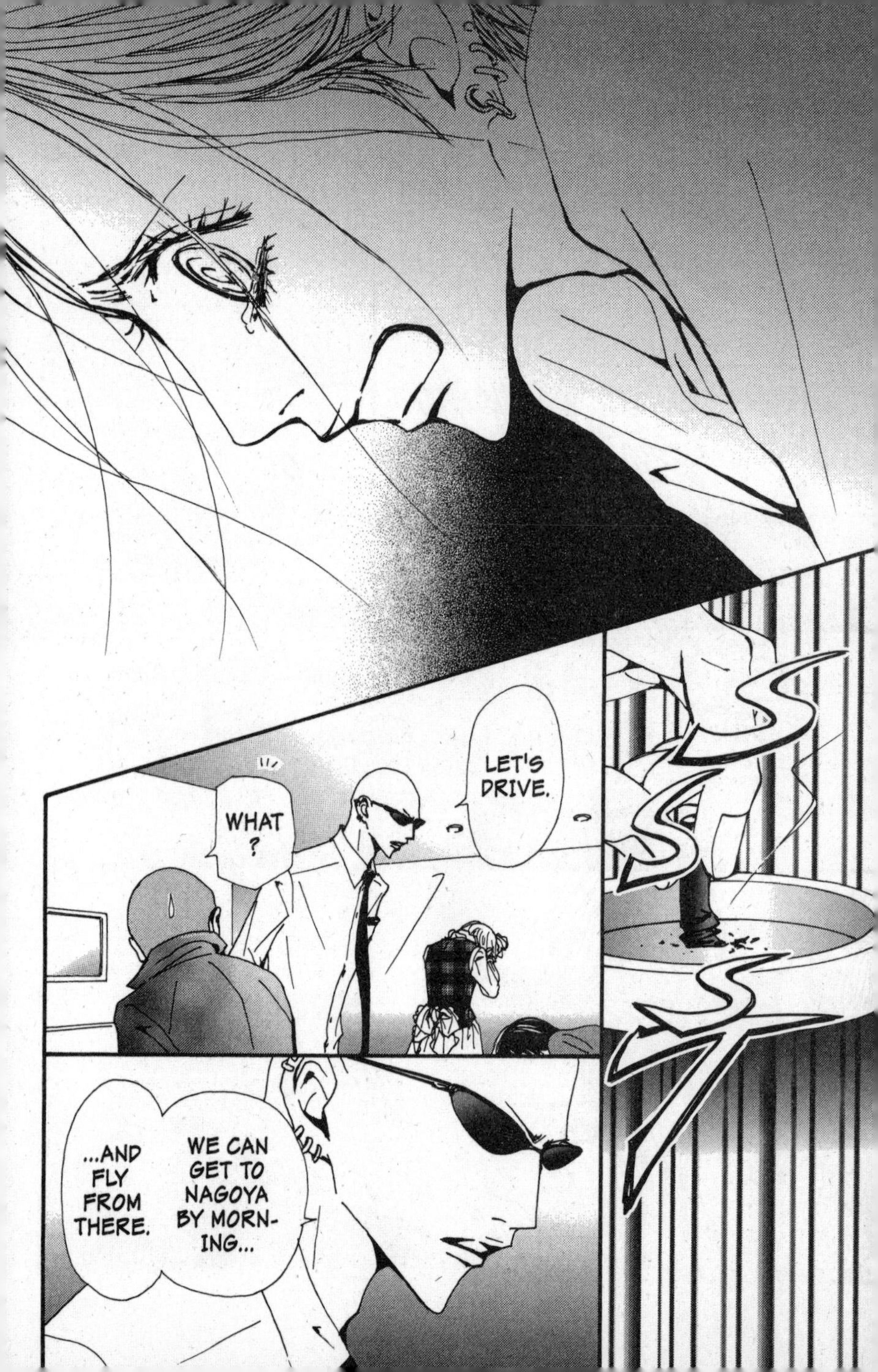
LET'S DRIVE.
WHAT?
WE CAN GET TO NAGOYA BY MORNING...
...AND FLY FROM THERE.

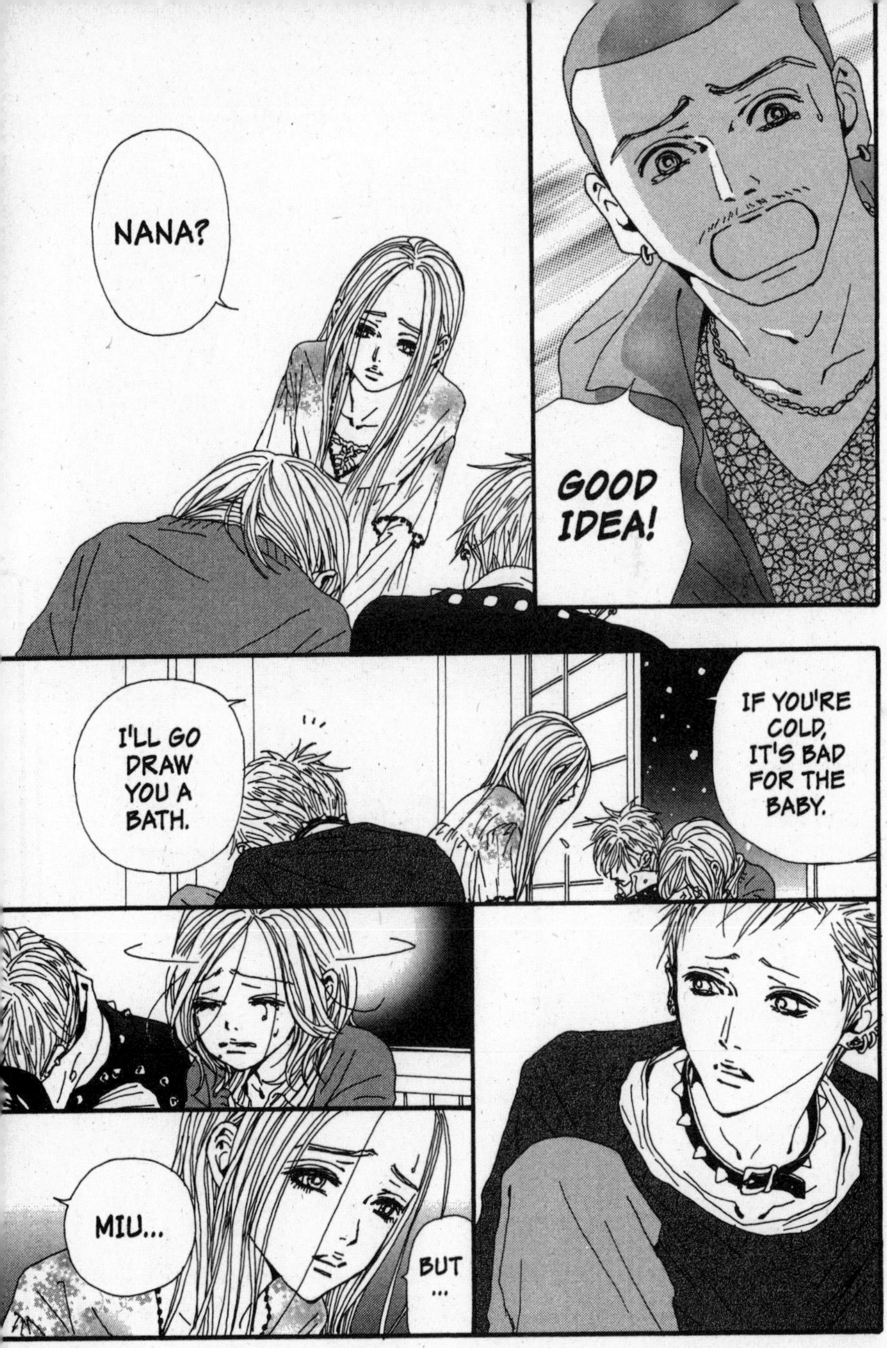
GOOD IDEA!
NANA?
IF YOU'RE COLD, IT'S BAD FOR THE BABY.
I'LL GO DRAW YOU A BATH.
MIU...
BUT ...

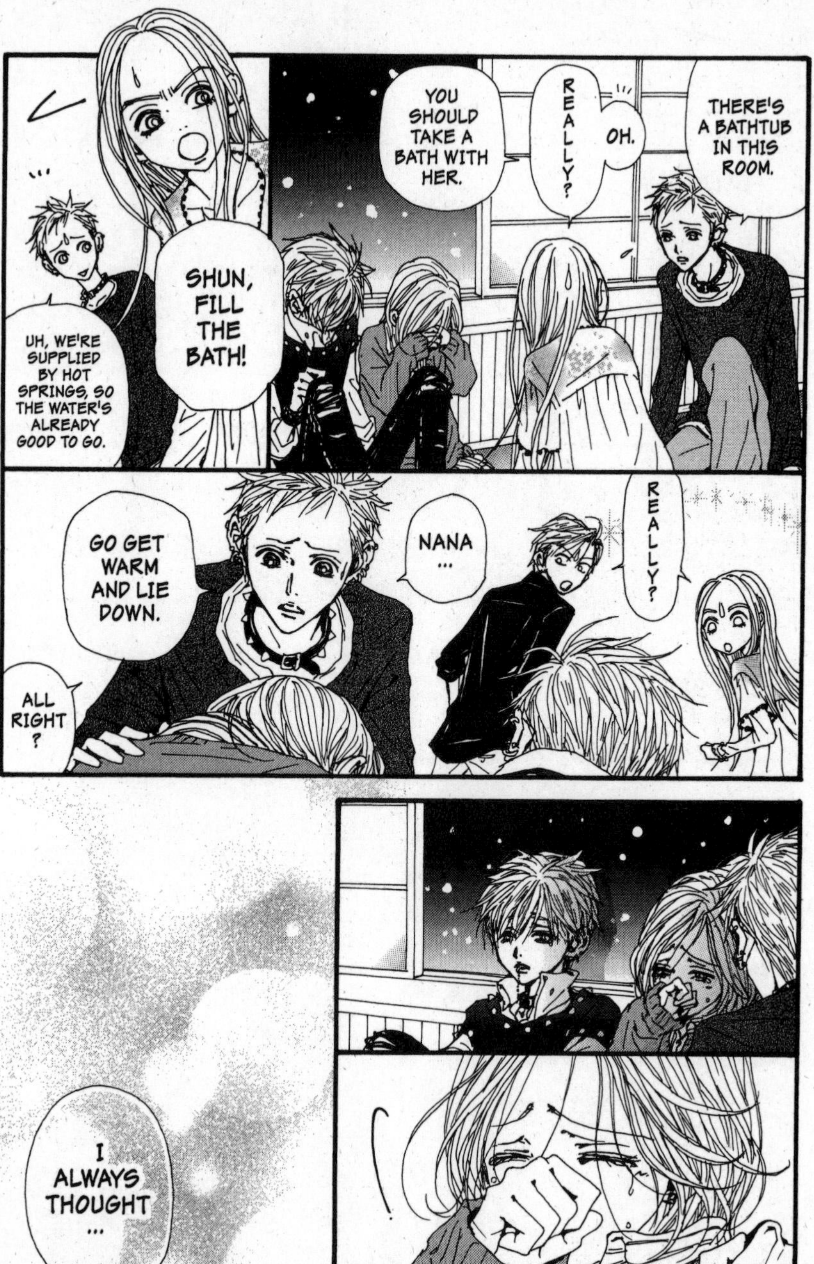
THERE'S A BATHTUB IN THIS ROOM.
OH.
REALLY?
YOU SHOULD TAKE A BATH WITH HER.
SHUN, FILL THE BATH!
UH, WE'RE SUPPLIED BY HOT SPRINGS, SO THE WATER'S ALREADY GOOD TO GO.
REALLY?
NANA ...
GO GET WARM AND LIE DOWN.
ALL RIGHT?
I ALWAYS THOUGHT ...

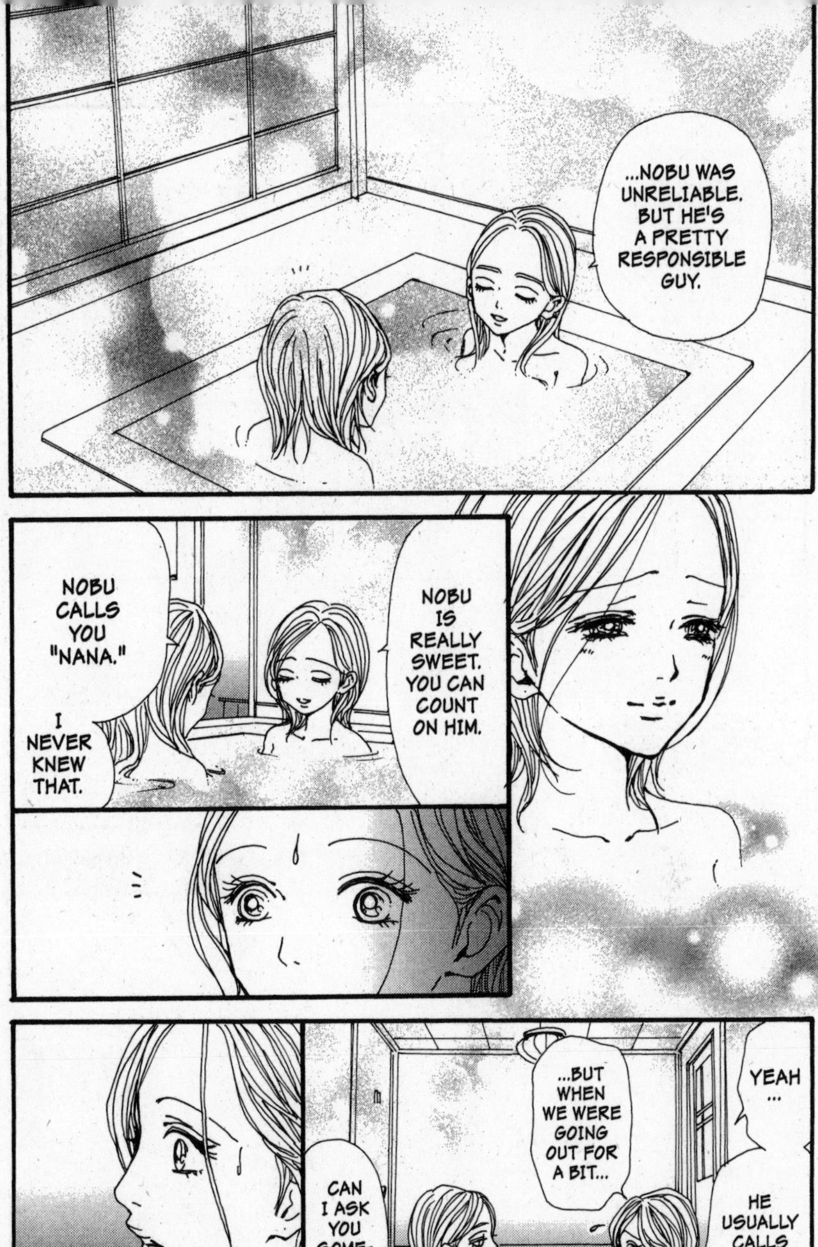
...NOBU WAS UNRELIABLE. BUT HE'S A PRETTY RESPONSIBLE GUY.
NOBU IS REALLY SWEET. YOU CAN COUNT ON HIM.
NOBU CALLS YOU "NANA."
I NEVER KNEW THAT.
YEAH ...
HE USUALLY CALLS ME HACHI...
...BUT WHEN WE WERE GOING OUT FOR A BIT...
CAN I ASK YOU SOME-THING ?

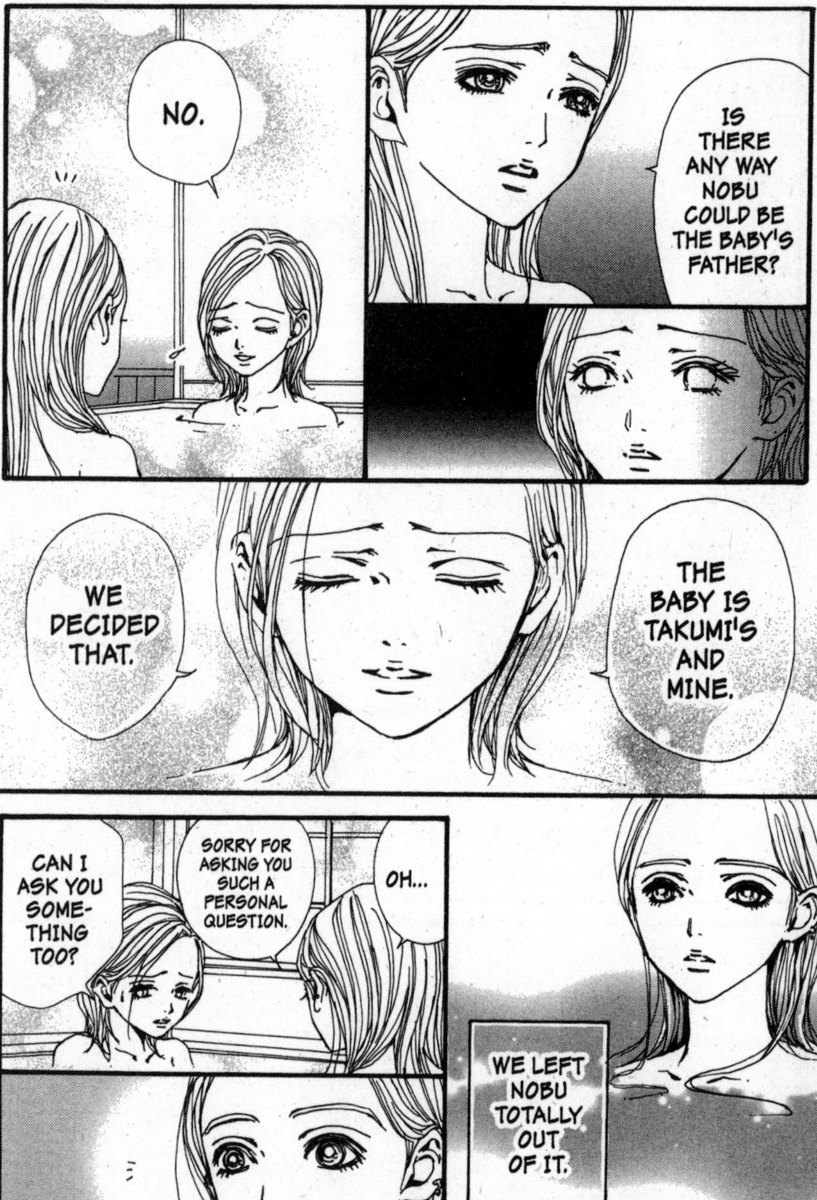
IS THERE ANY WAY NOBU COULD BE THE BABY'S FATHER?
NO.
THE BABY IS TAKUMI'S AND MINE.
WE DECIDED THAT.
WE LEFT NOBU TOTALLY OUT OF IT.
OH...
SORRY FOR ASKING YOU SUCH A PERSONAL QUESTION.
CAN I ASK YOU SOMETHING TOO?

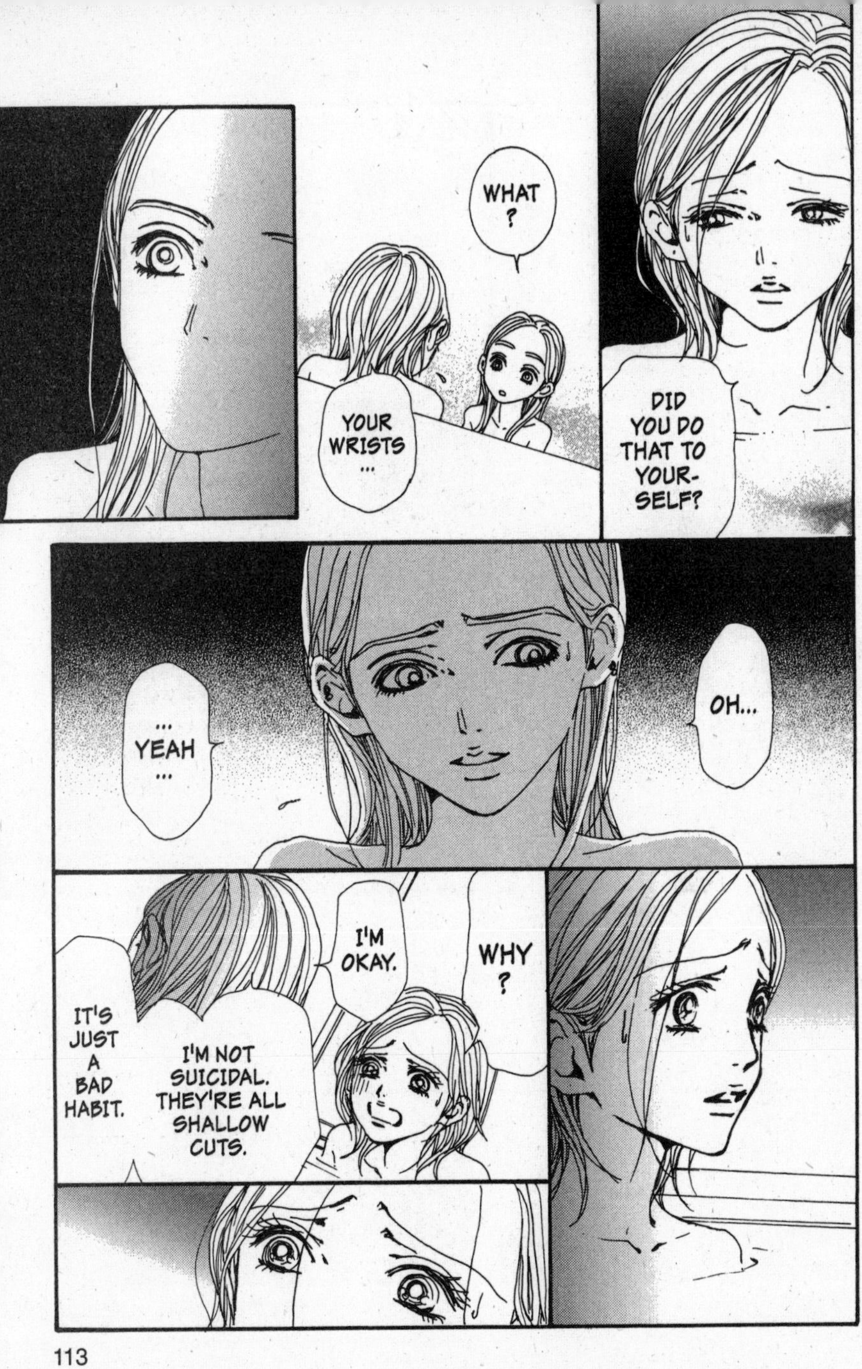
DID YOU DO THAT TO YOURSELF?
WHAT ?
YOUR WRISTS ...
OH...
... YEAH ...
WHY ?
I'M OKAY.
I'M NOT SUICIDAL. THEY'RE ALL SHALLOW CUTS.
IT'S JUST A BAD HABIT.

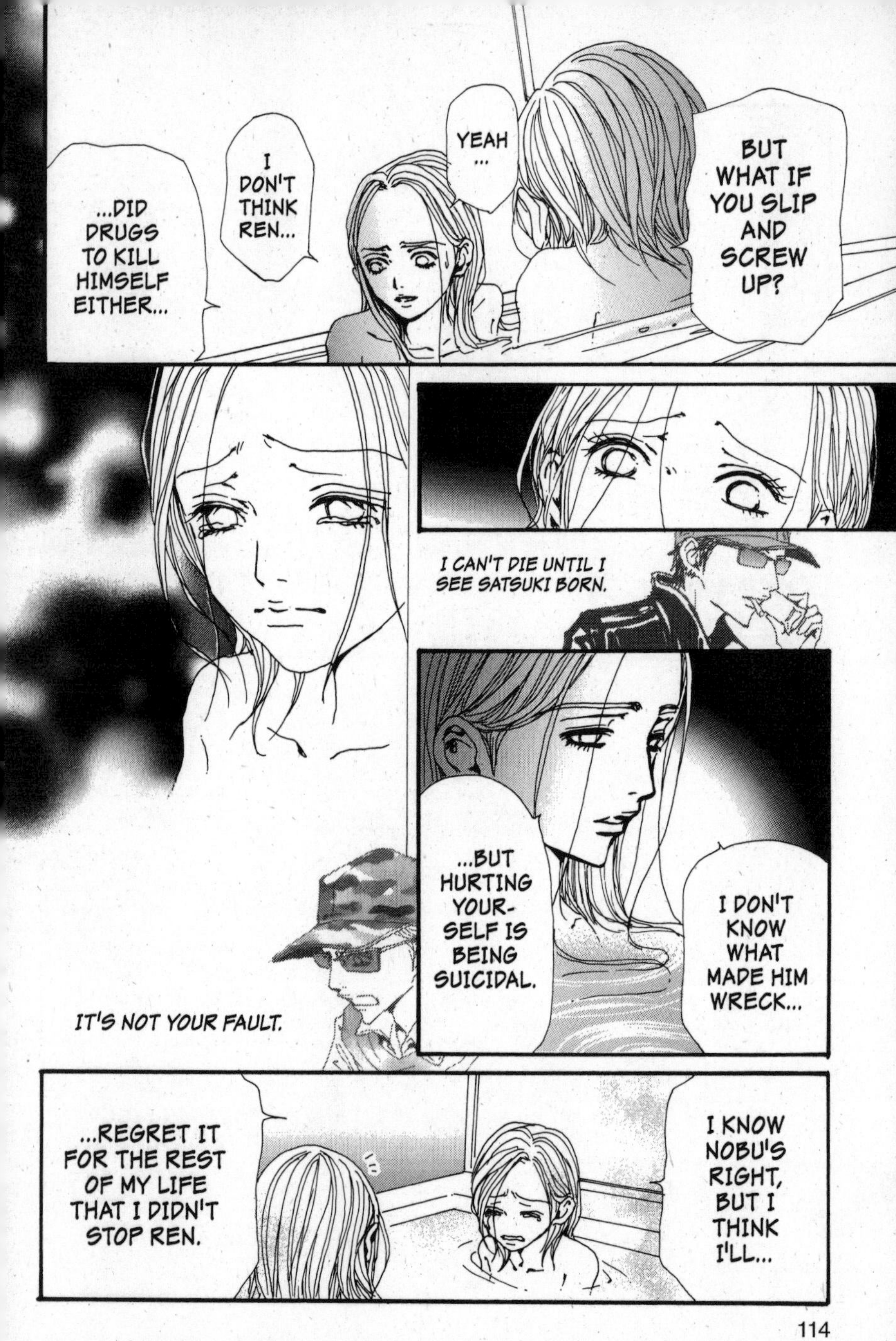
BUT WHAT IF YOU SLIP AND SCREW UP?
YEAH...
I DON'T THINK REN...
...DID DRUGS TO KILL HIMSELF EITHER...
I CAN'T DIE UNTIL I SEE SATSUKI BORN.
I DON'T KNOW WHAT MADE HIM WRECK...
...BUT HURTING YOUR-SELF IS BEING SUICIDAL.
IT'S NOT YOUR FAULT.
I KNOW NOBU'S RIGHT, BUT I THINK I'LL...
...REGRET IT FOR THE REST OF MY LIFE THAT I DIDN'T STOP REN.

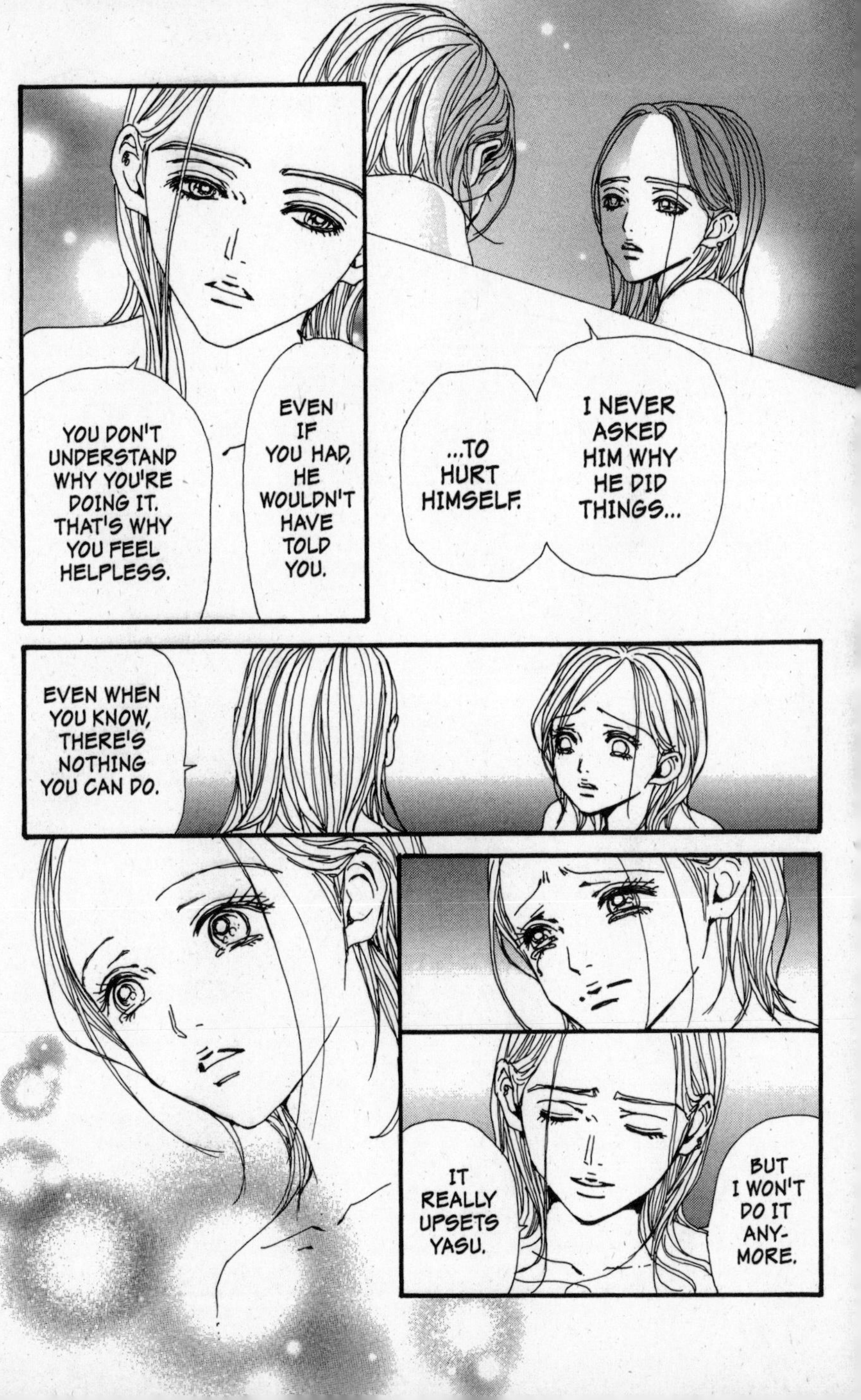
I NEVER ASKED HIM WHY HE DID THINGS...
...TO HURT HIMSELF.
EVEN IF YOU HAD, HE WOULDN'T HAVE TOLD YOU.
YOU DON'T UNDERSTAND WHY YOU'RE DOING IT. THAT'S WHY YOU FEEL HELPLESS.
EVEN WHEN YOU KNOW, THERE'S NOTHING YOU CAN DO.
BUT I WON'T DO IT ANY-MORE.
IT REALLY UPSETS YASU.

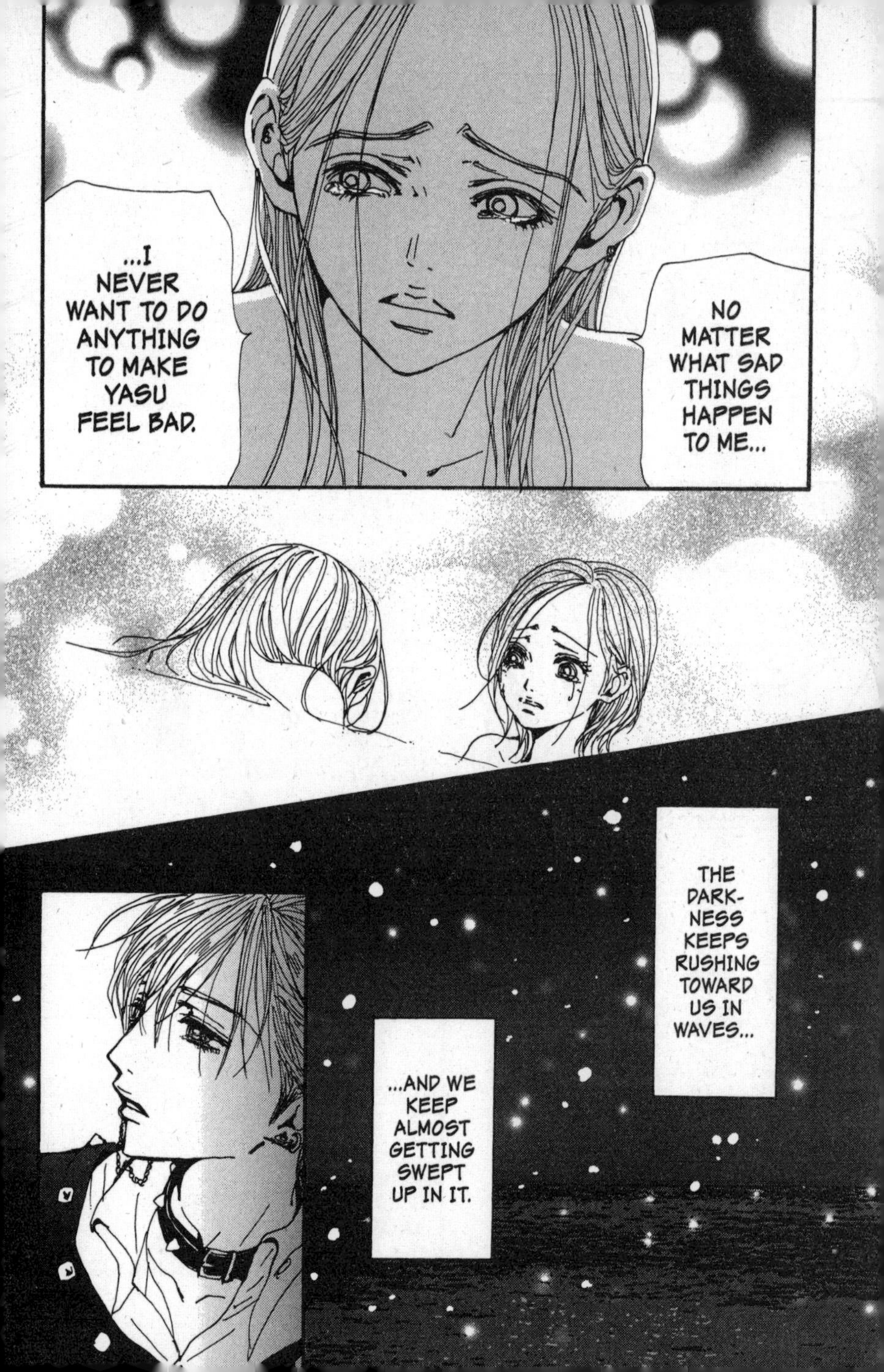
NO MATTER WHAT SAD THINGS HAPPEN TO ME...
...I NEVER WANT TO DO ANYTHING TO MAKE YASU FEEL BAD.
THE DARKNESS KEEPS RUSHING TOWARD US IN WAVES...
...AND WE KEEP ALMOST GETTING SWEPT UP IN IT.

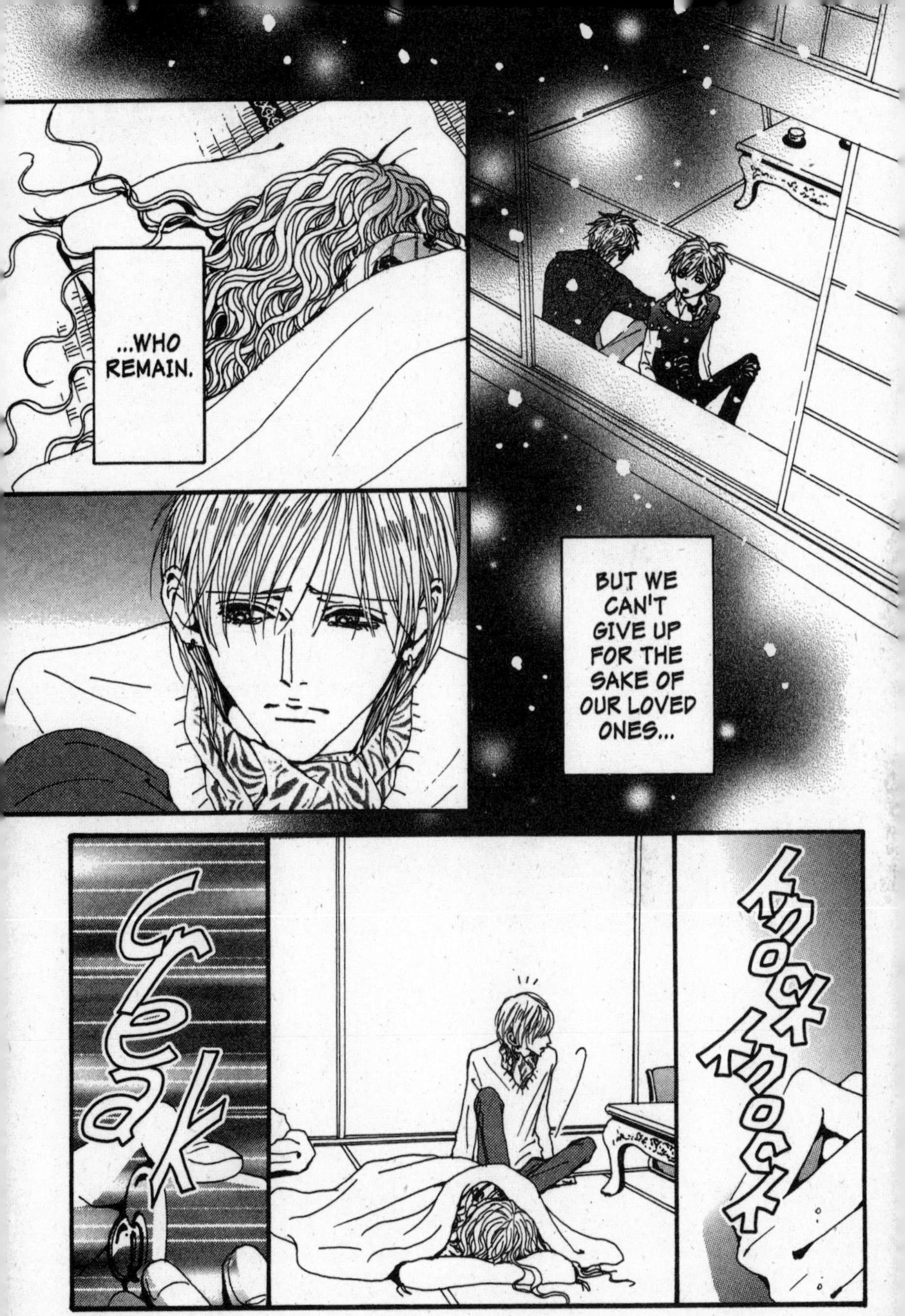
BUT WE CAN'T GIVE UP FOR THE SAKE OF OUR LOVED ONES...
...WHO REMAIN.
knock knock
creak

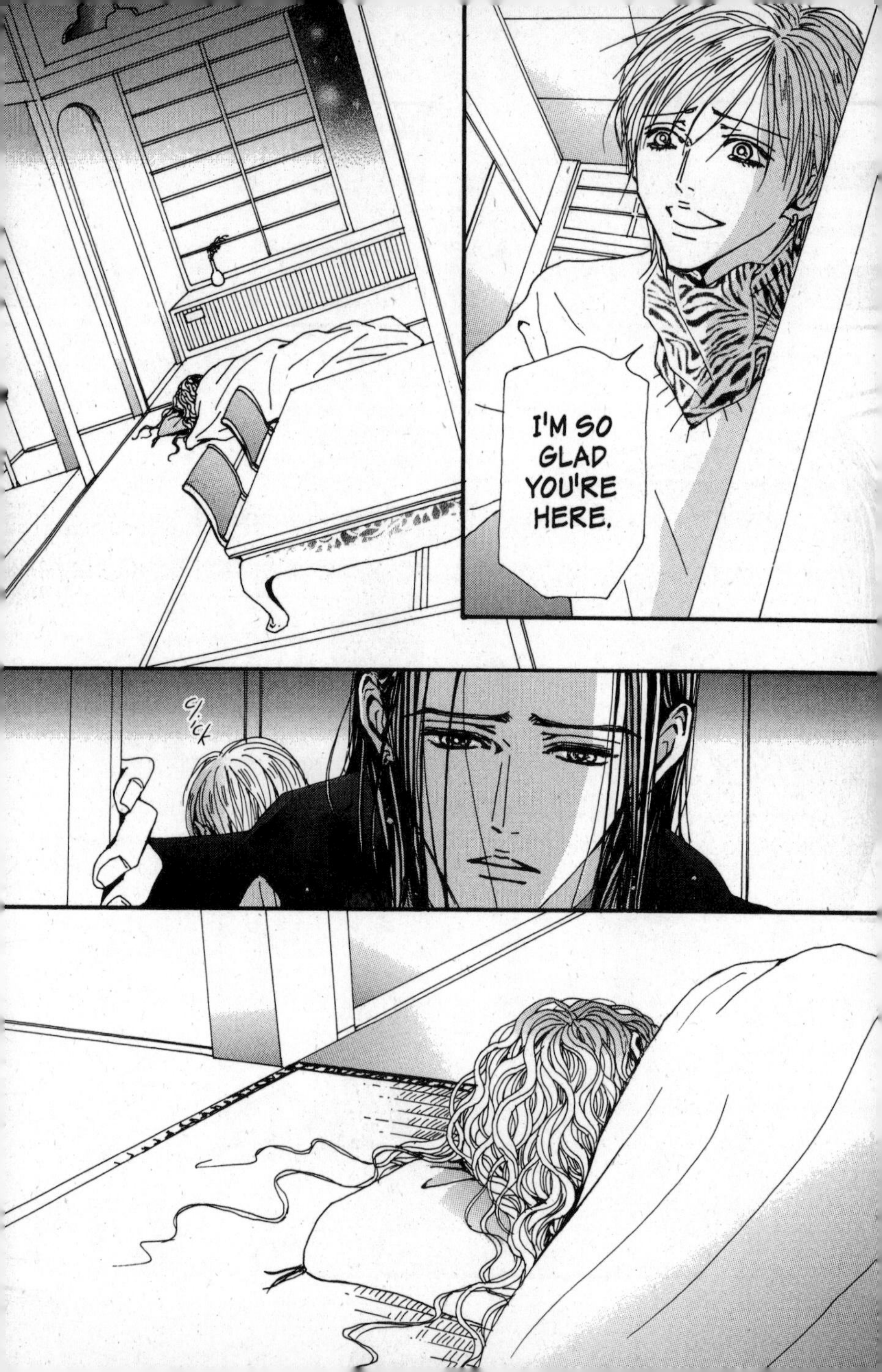
I'M SO GLAD YOU'RE HERE.
click

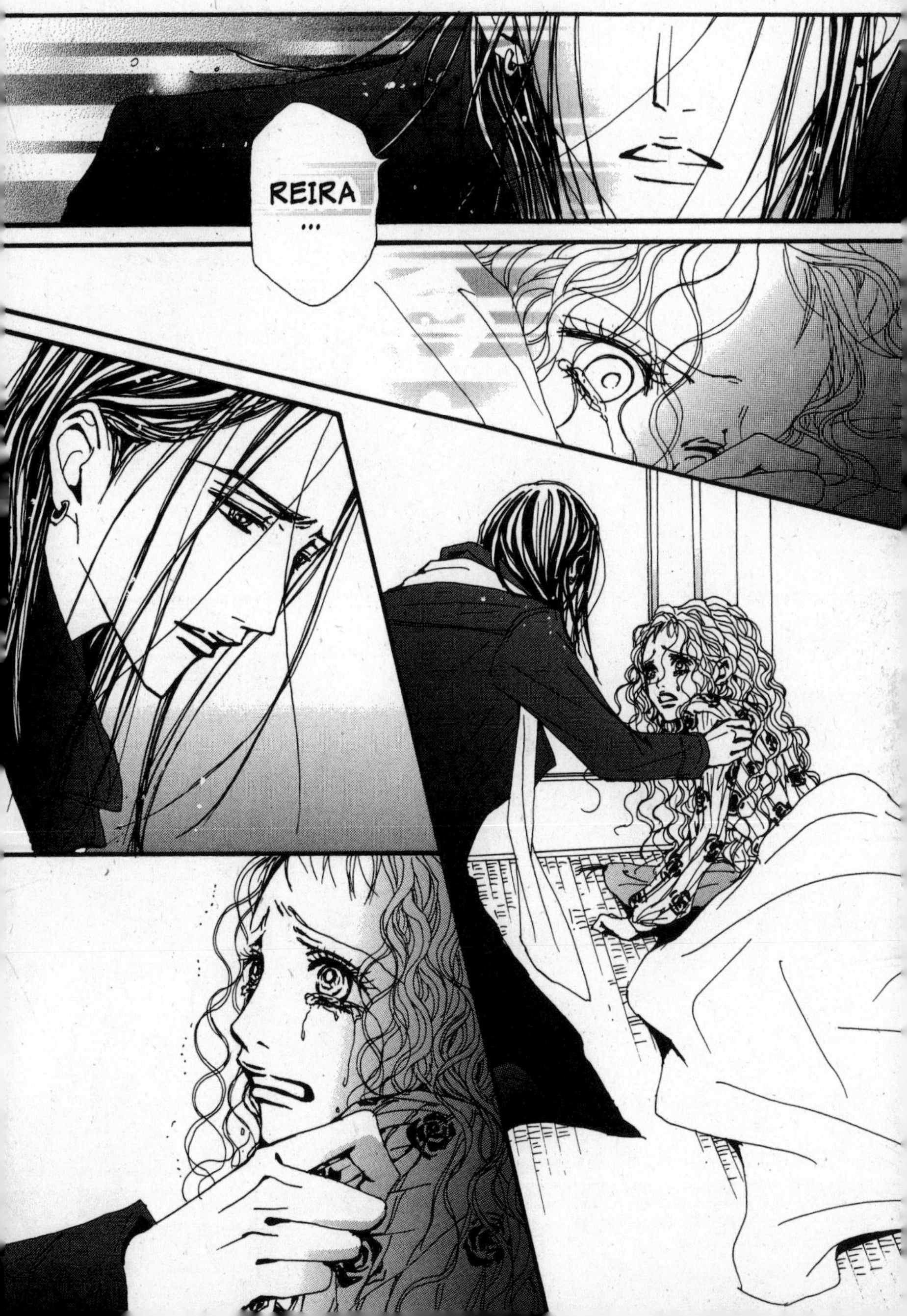
REIRA ...

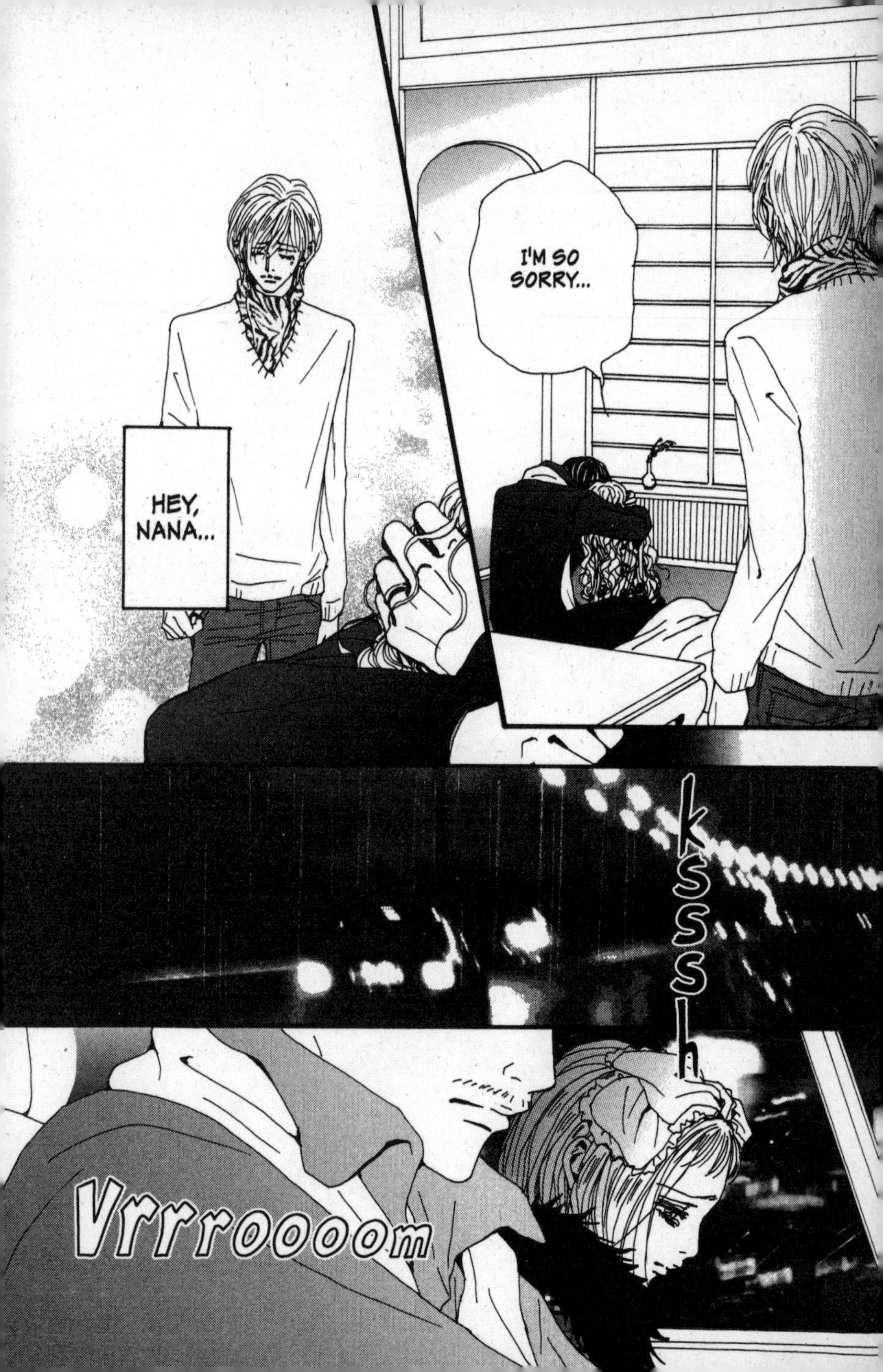
I'M SO SORRY...
HEY, NANA...
ksssh
Vrrroooom

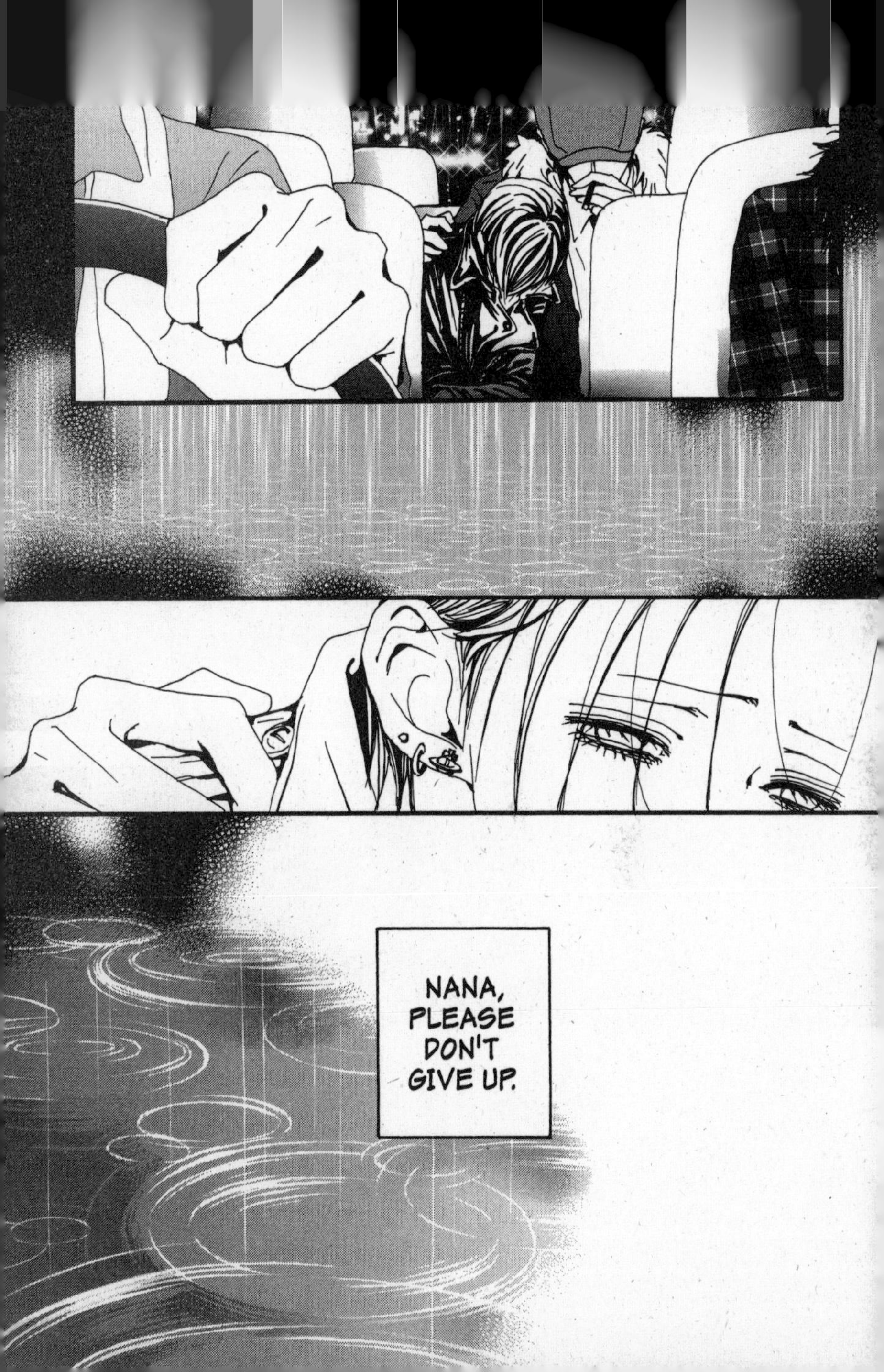
NANA, PLEASE DON'T GIVE UP.

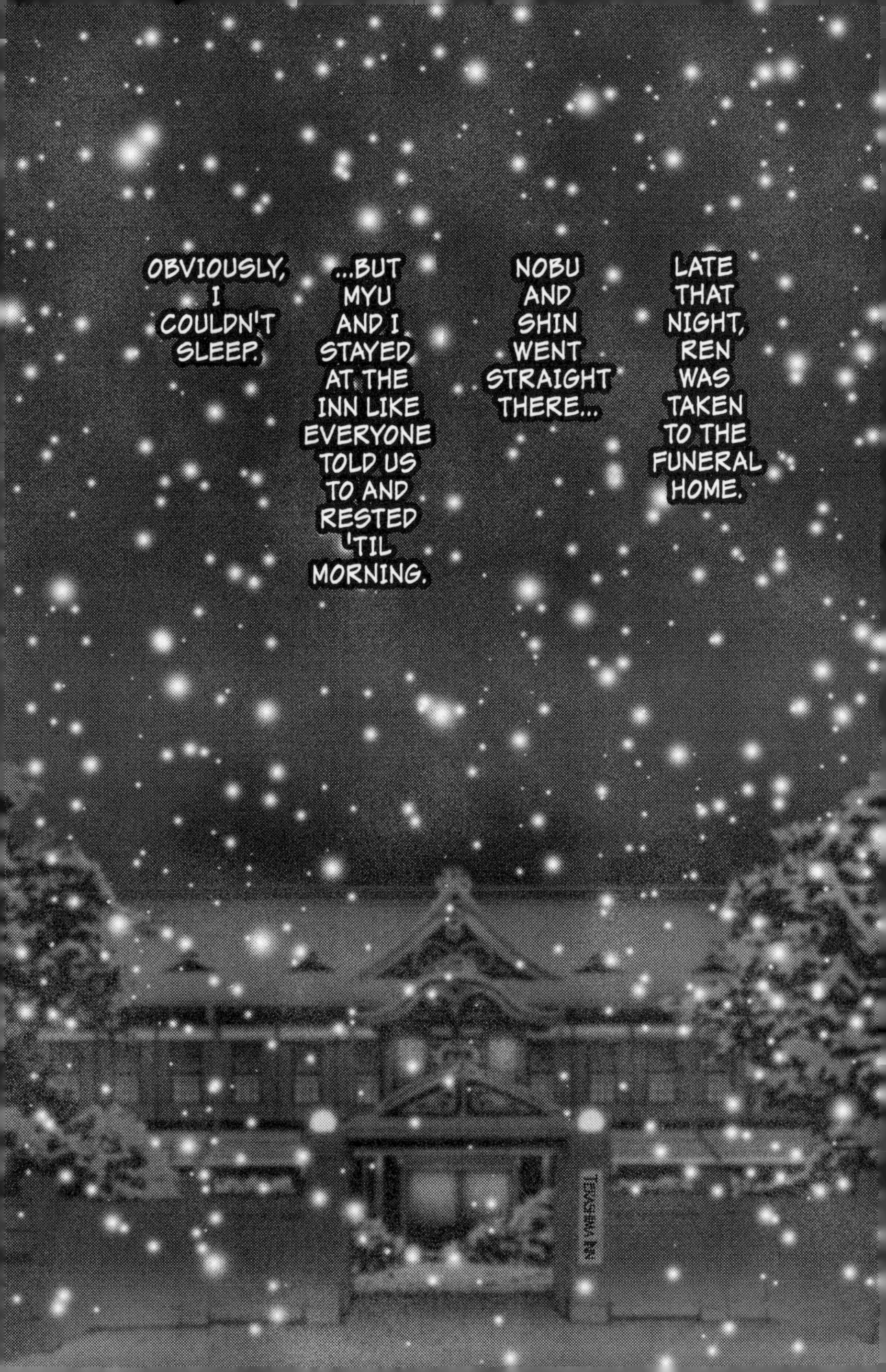
LATE THAT NIGHT, REN WAS TAKEN TO THE FUNERAL HOME.
NOBU AND SHIN WENT STRAIGHT THERE...
...BUT MYU AND I STAYED AT THE INN LIKE EVERYONE TOLD US TO AND RESTED 'TIL MORNING.
OBVIOUSLY, I COULDN'T SLEEP.

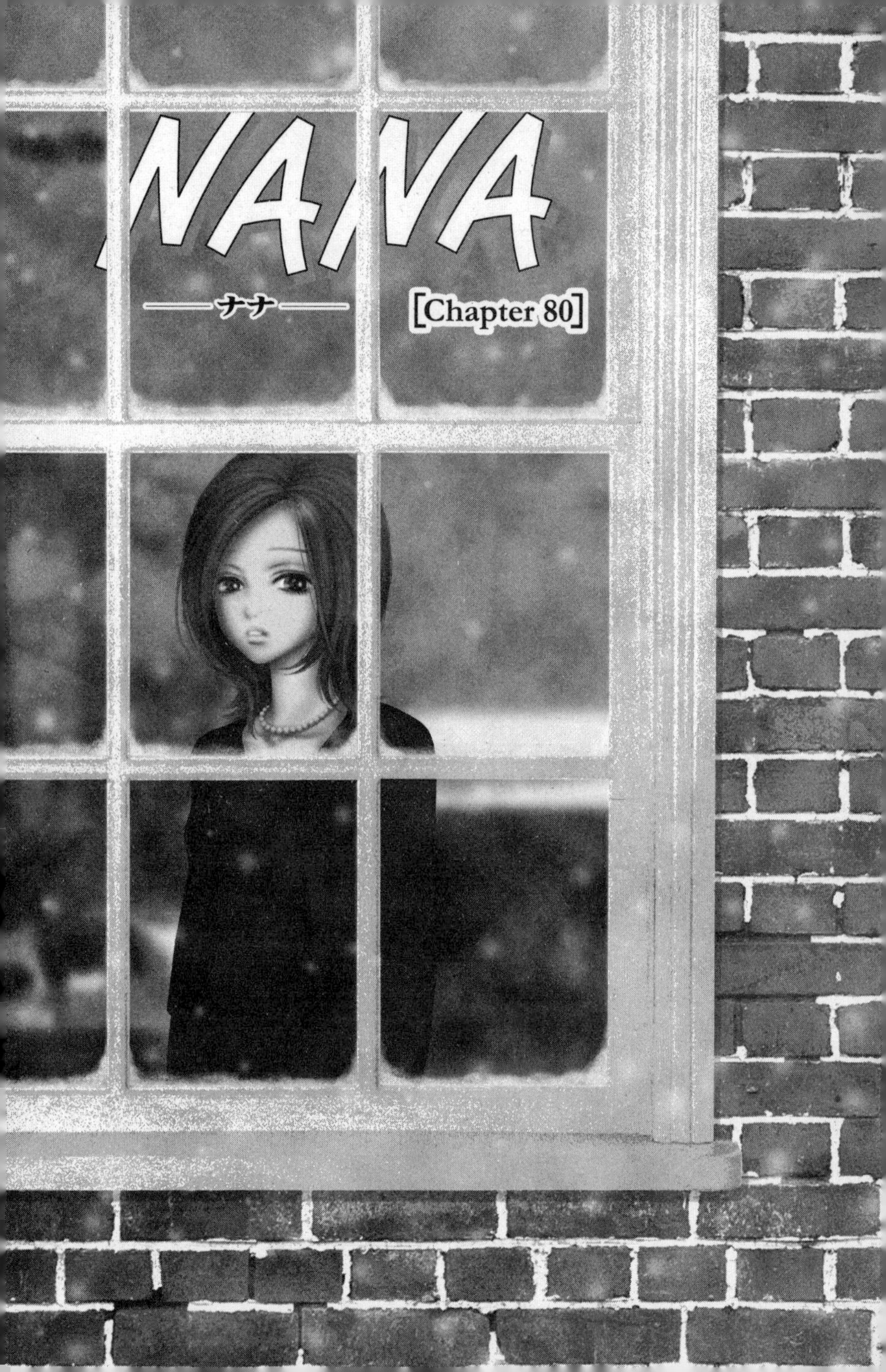
NANA
ナナ
[Chapter 80]

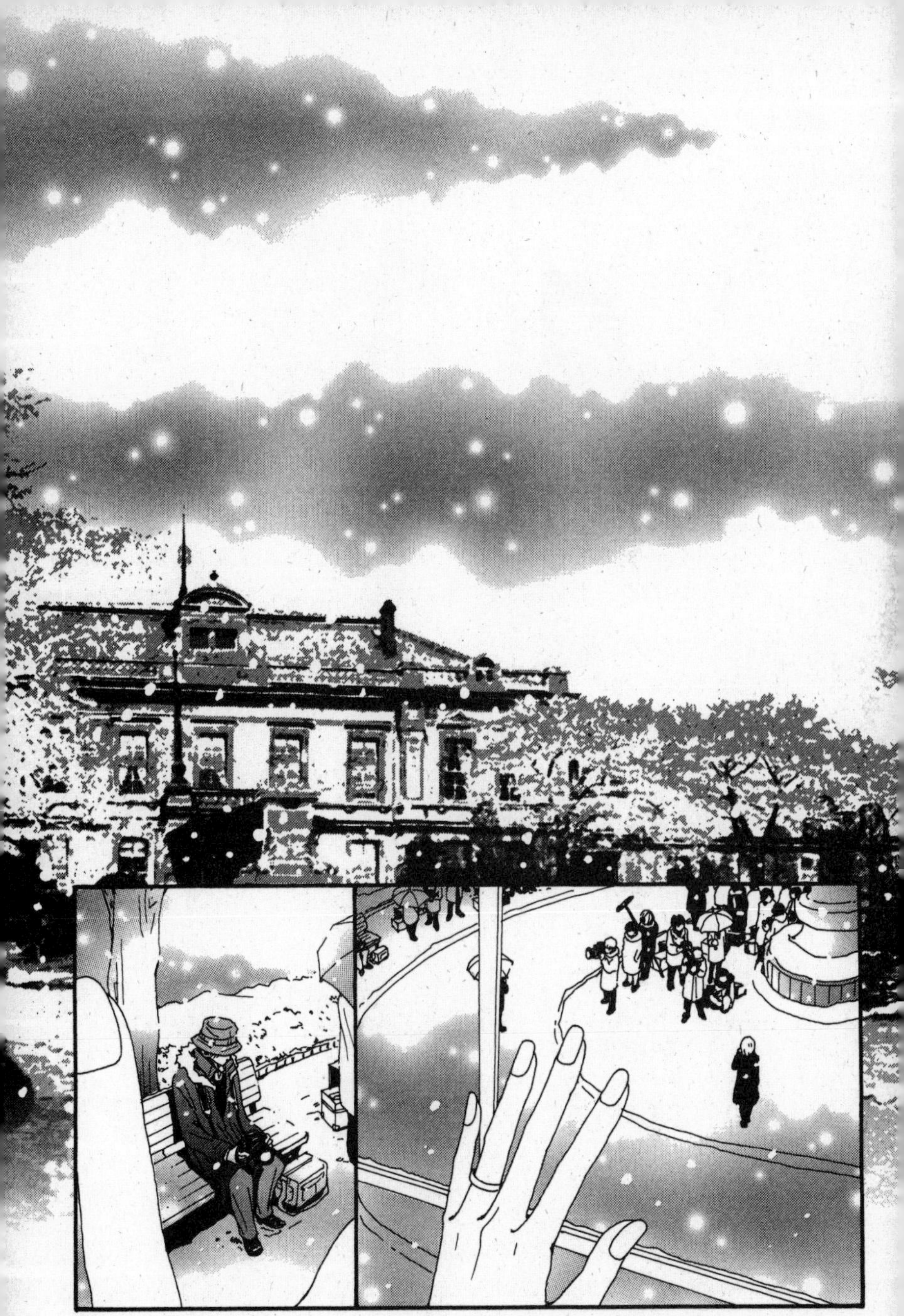

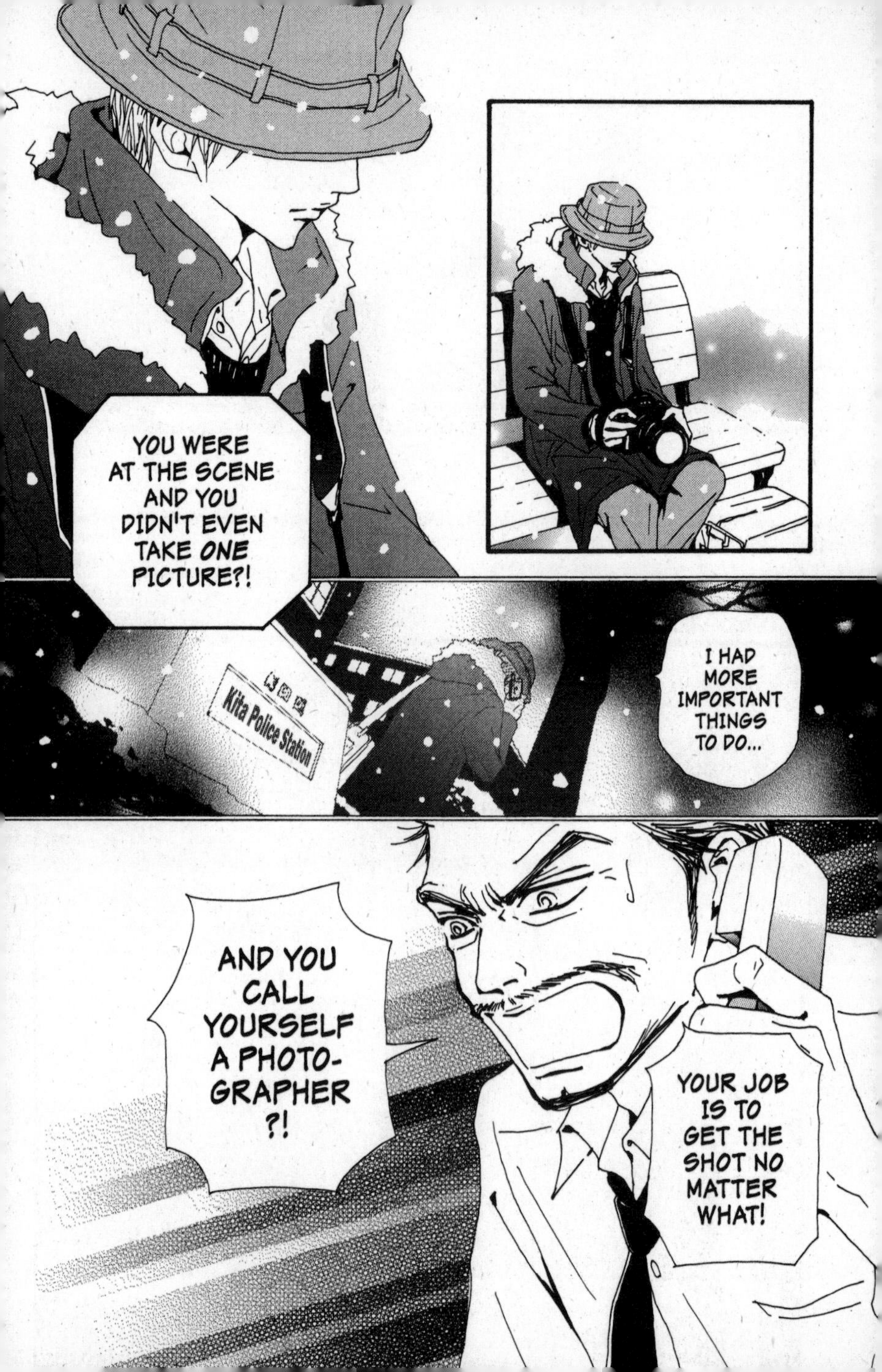
YOU WERE AT THE SCENE AND YOU DIDN'T EVEN TAKE ONE PICTURE?!
Kita Police Station
I HAD MORE IMPORTANT THINGS TO DO...
YOUR JOB IS TO GET THE SHOT NO MATTER WHAT!
AND YOU CALL YOURSELF A PHOTO-GRAPHER?!

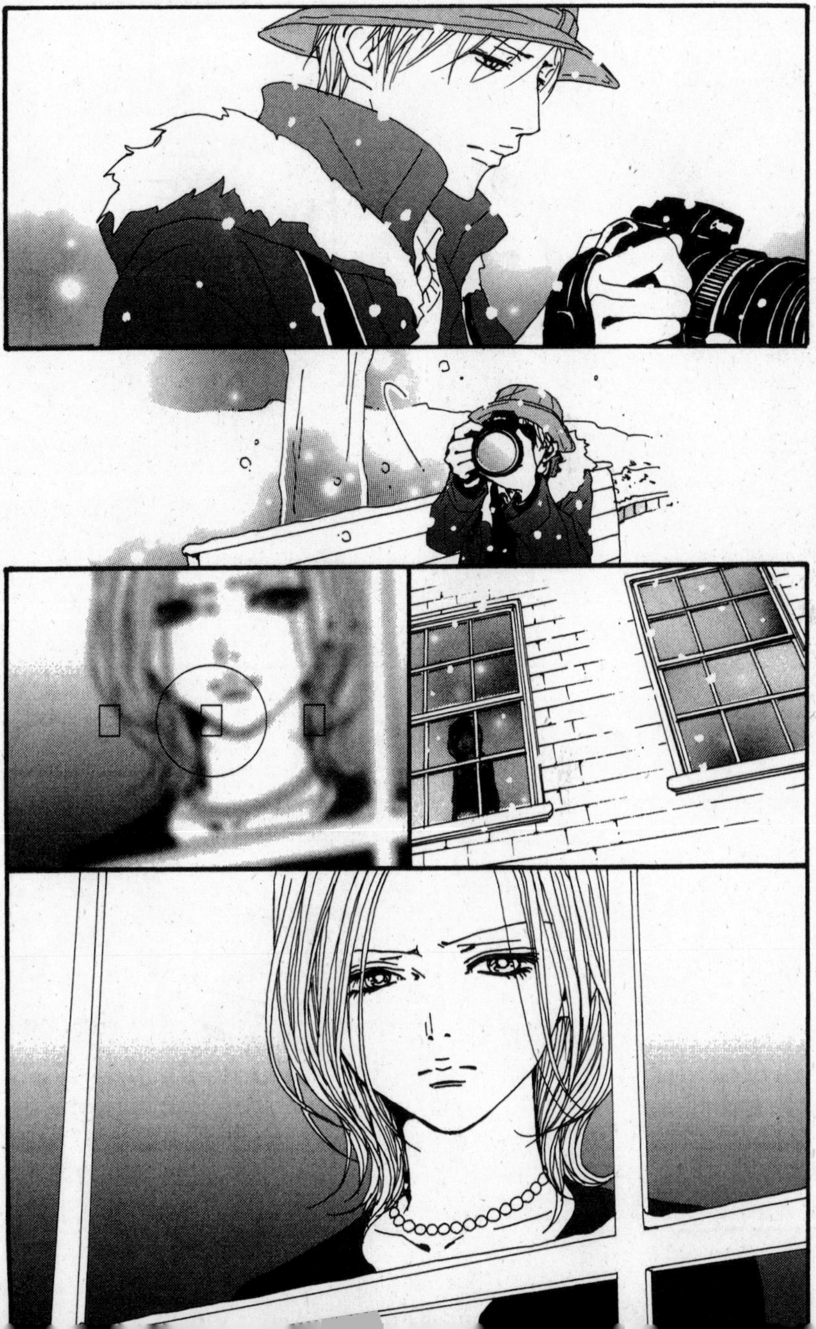

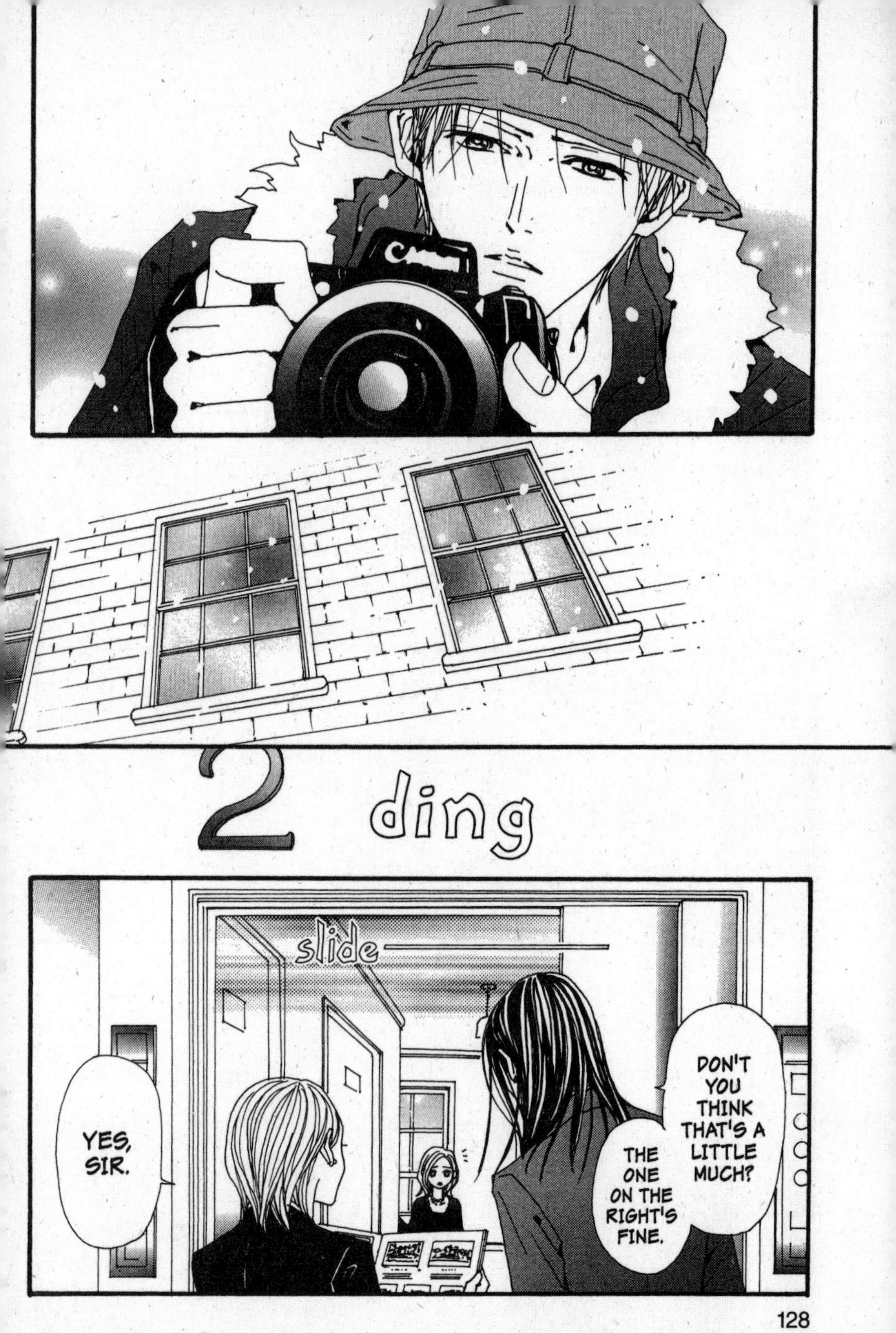
2
ding
slide
DON'T YOU THINK THAT'S A LITTLE MUCH?
THE ONE ON THE RIGHT'S FINE.
YES, SIR.

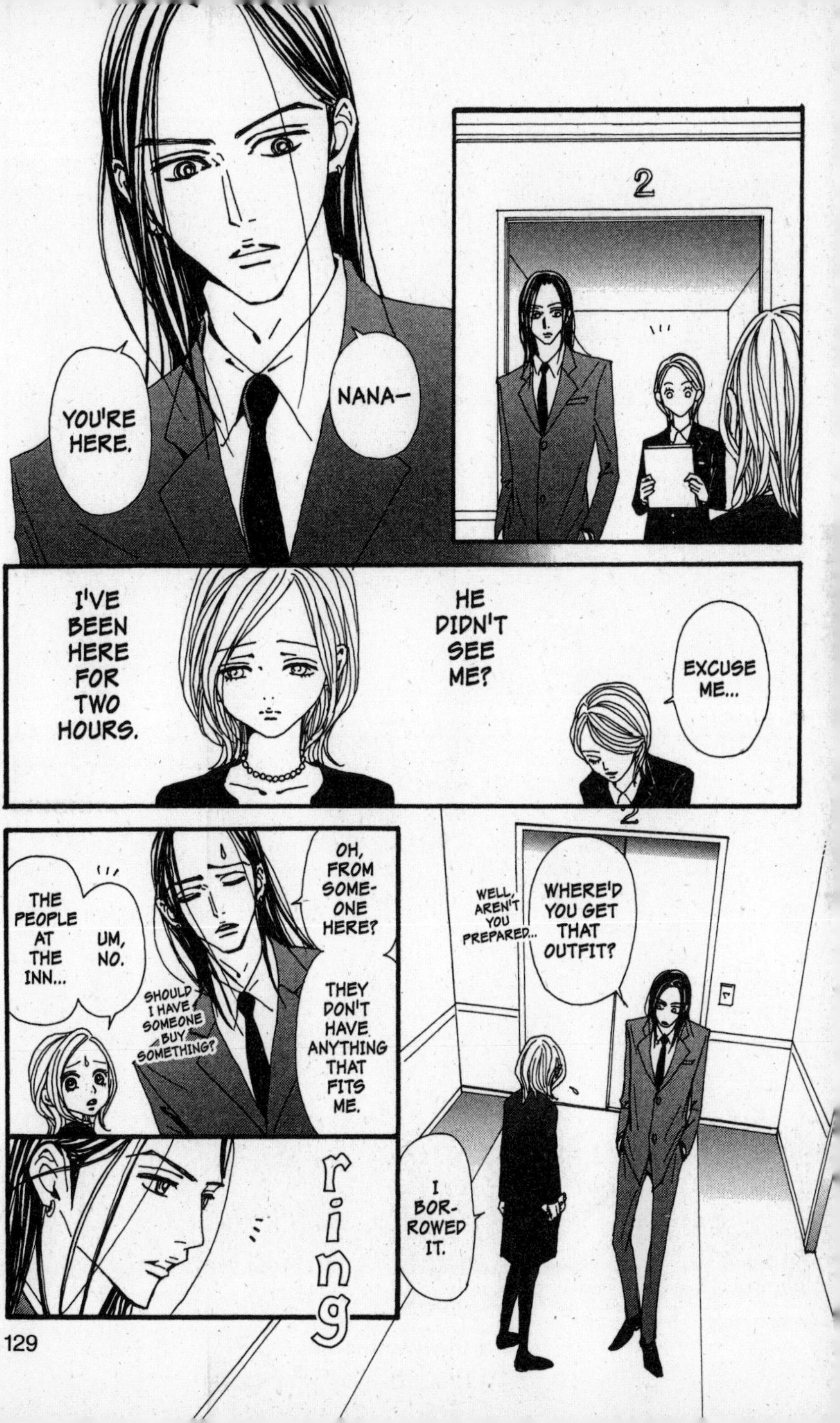
2
NANA—
YOU'RE HERE.
EXCUSE ME...
HE DIDN'T SEE ME?
I'VE BEEN HERE FOR TWO HOURS.
2
WHERE'D YOU GET THAT OUTFIT?
WELL, AREN'T YOU PREPARED...
I BORROWED IT.
OH, FROM SOMEONE HERE?
UM, NO.
THE PEOPLE AT THE INN...
THEY DON'T HAVE ANYTHING THAT FITS ME.
SHOULD I HAVE SOMEONE BUY SOMETHING?
ring

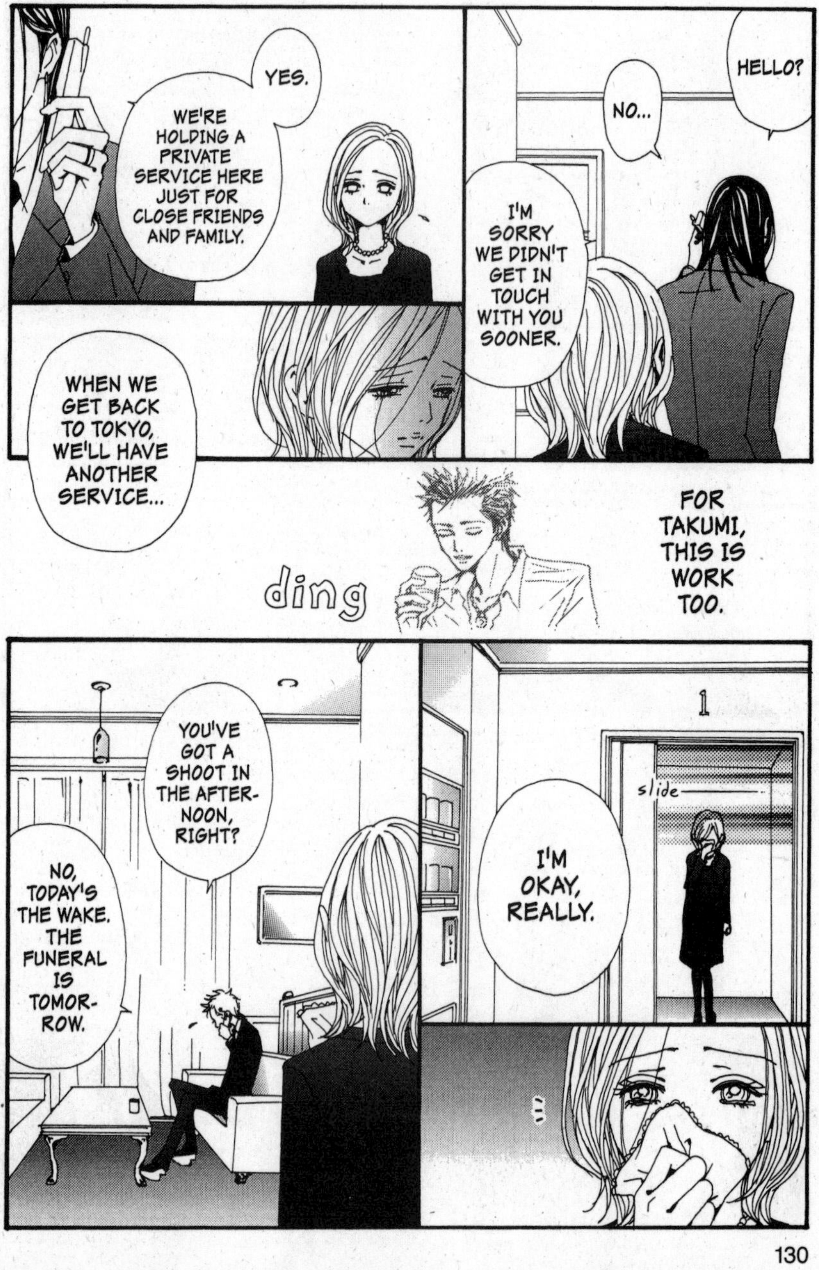
HELLO?
NO...
I'M SORRY WE DIDN'T GET IN TOUCH WITH YOU SOONER.
YES.
WE'RE HOLDING A PRIVATE SERVICE HERE JUST FOR CLOSE FRIENDS AND FAMILY.
WHEN WE GET BACK TO TOKYO, WE'LL HAVE ANOTHER SERVICE...
FOR TAKUMI, THIS IS WORK TOO.
ding
slide
I'M OKAY, REALLY.
...
YOU'VE GOT A SHOOT IN THE AFTER-NOON, RIGHT?
NO, TODAY'S THE WAKE. THE FUNERAL IS TOMOR-ROW.

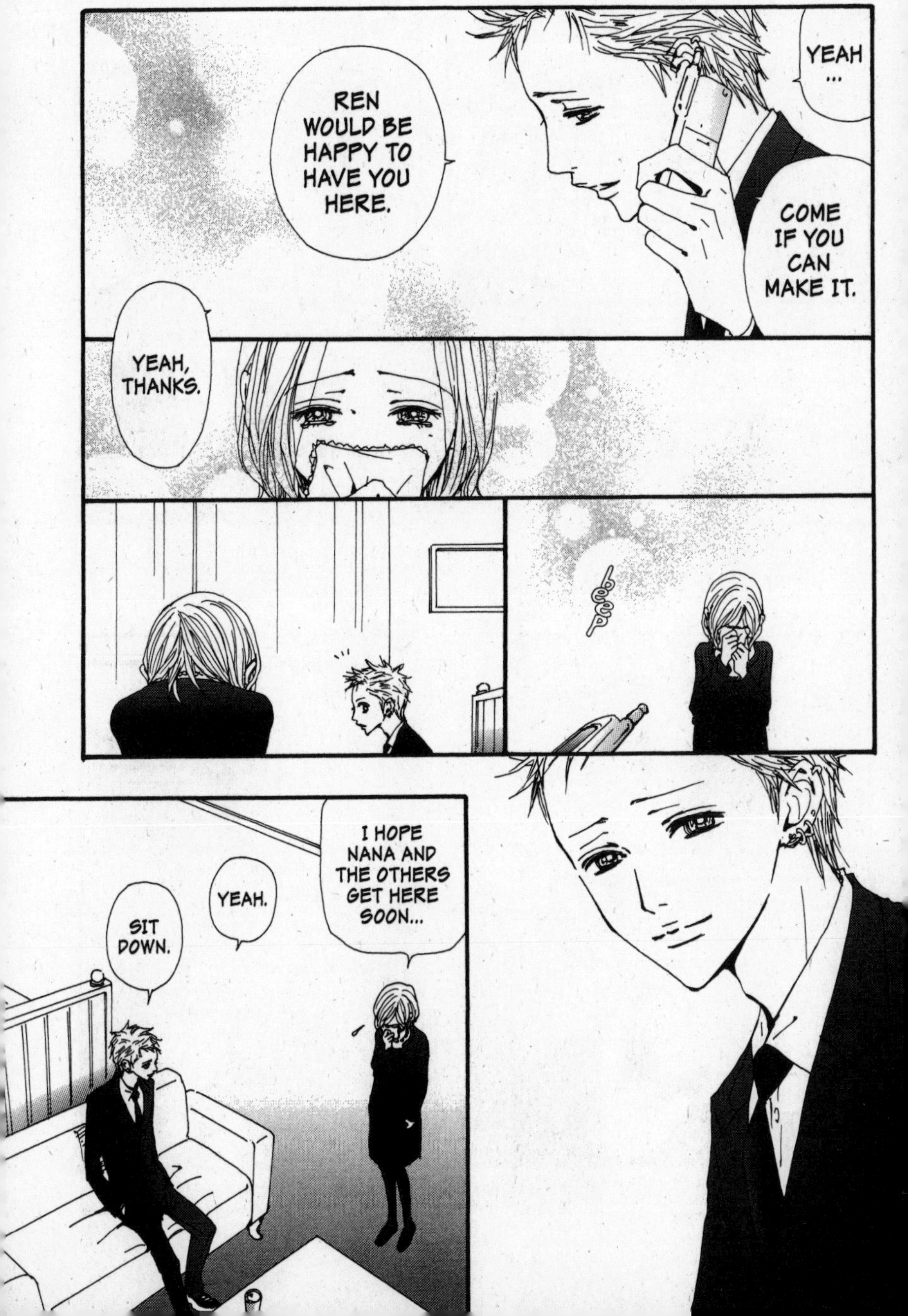
YEAH ...
COME IF YOU CAN MAKE IT.
REN WOULD BE HAPPY TO HAVE YOU HERE.
YEAH, THANKS.
beep
I HOPE NANA AND THE OTHERS GET HERE SOON...
YEAH.
SIT DOWN.

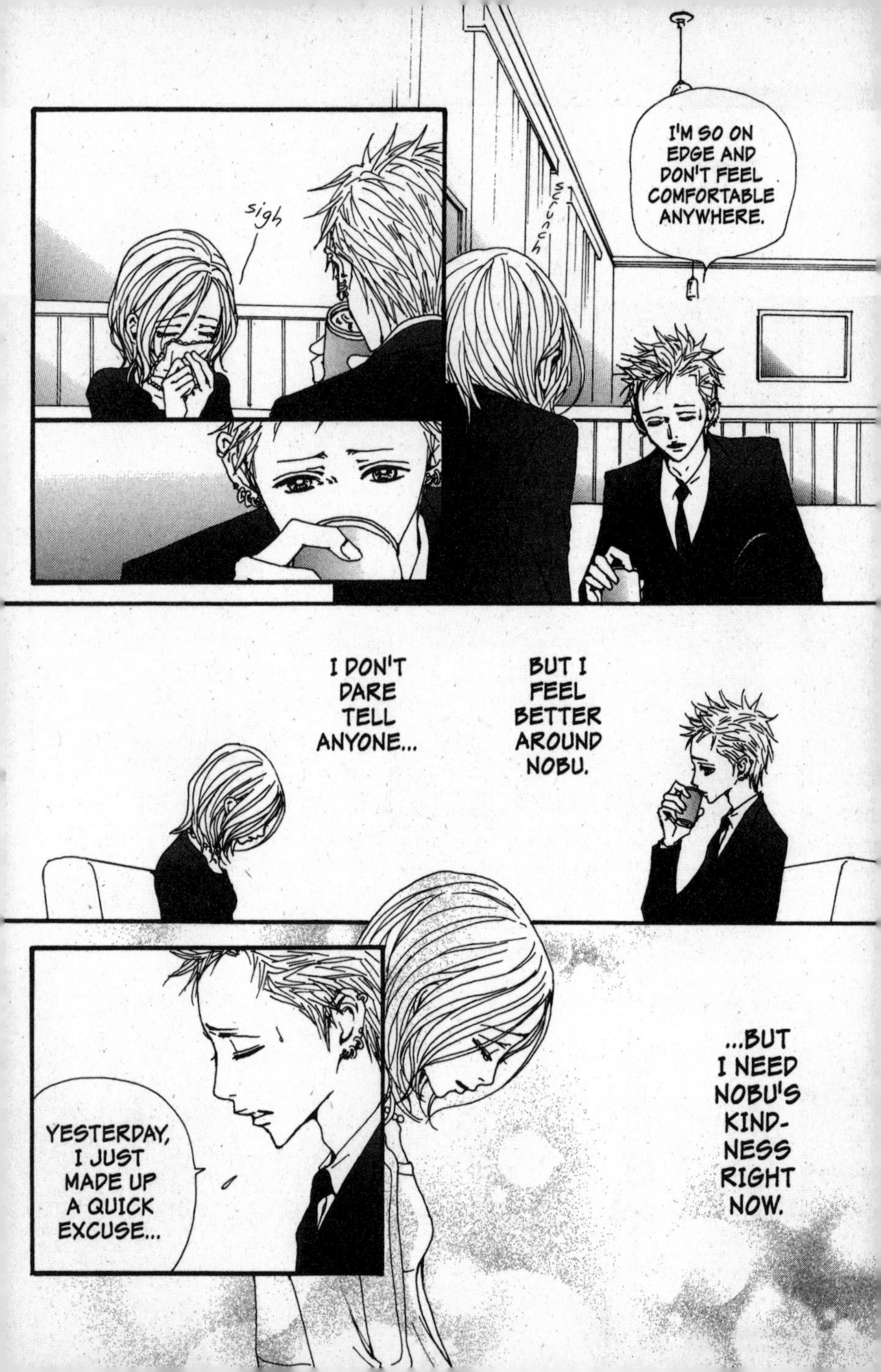
I'M SO ON EDGE AND DON'T FEEL COMFORTABLE ANYWHERE.
scrunch
sigh
I DON'T DARE TELL ANYONE...
BUT I FEEL BETTER AROUND NOBU.
...BUT I NEED NOBU'S KIND-NESS RIGHT NOW.
YESTERDAY, I JUST MADE UP A QUICK EXCUSE...

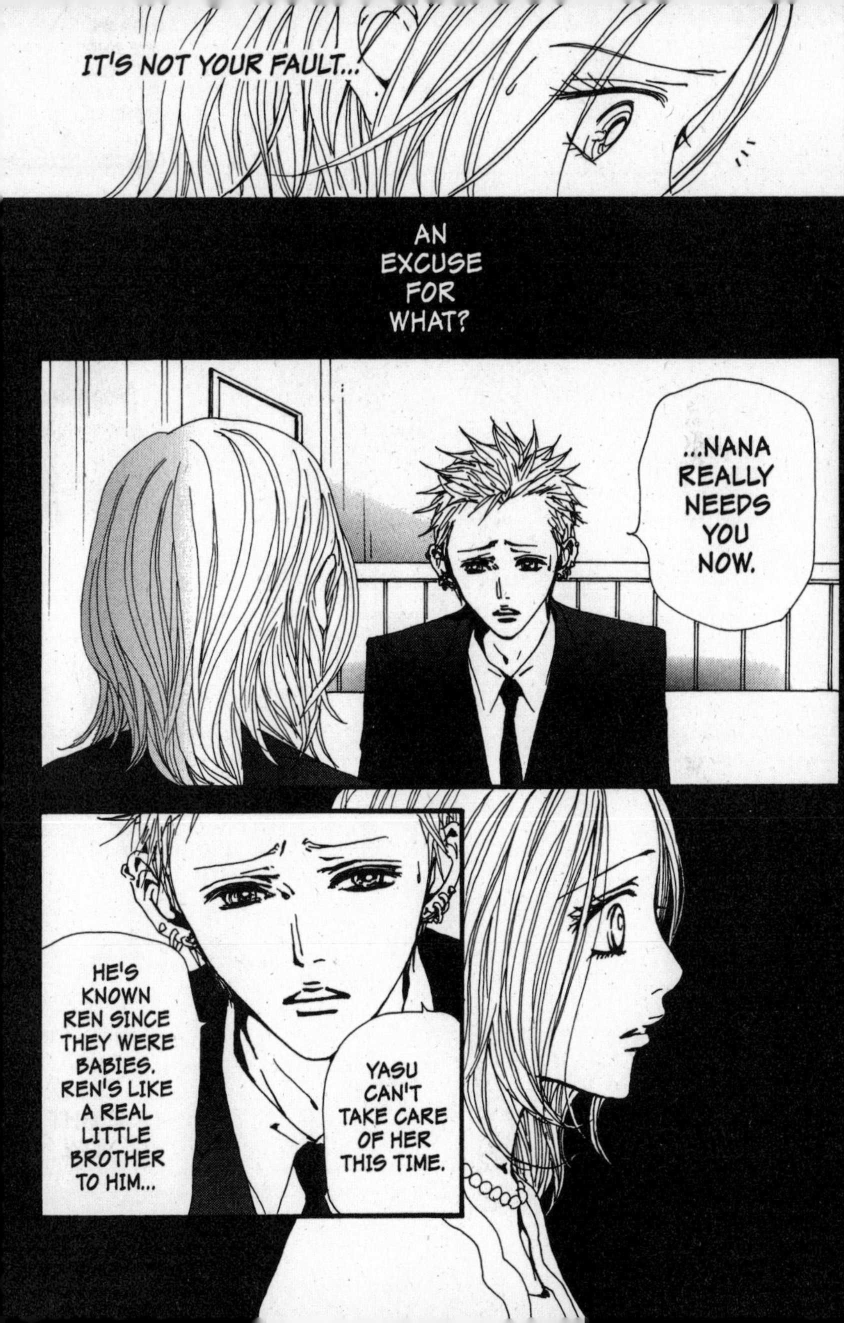
IT'S NOT YOUR FAULT...
AN EXCUSE FOR WHAT?
...NANA REALLY NEEDS YOU NOW.
YASU CAN'T TAKE CARE OF HER THIS TIME.
HE'S KNOWN REN SINCE THEY WERE BABIES. REN'S LIKE A REAL LITTLE BROTHER TO HIM...

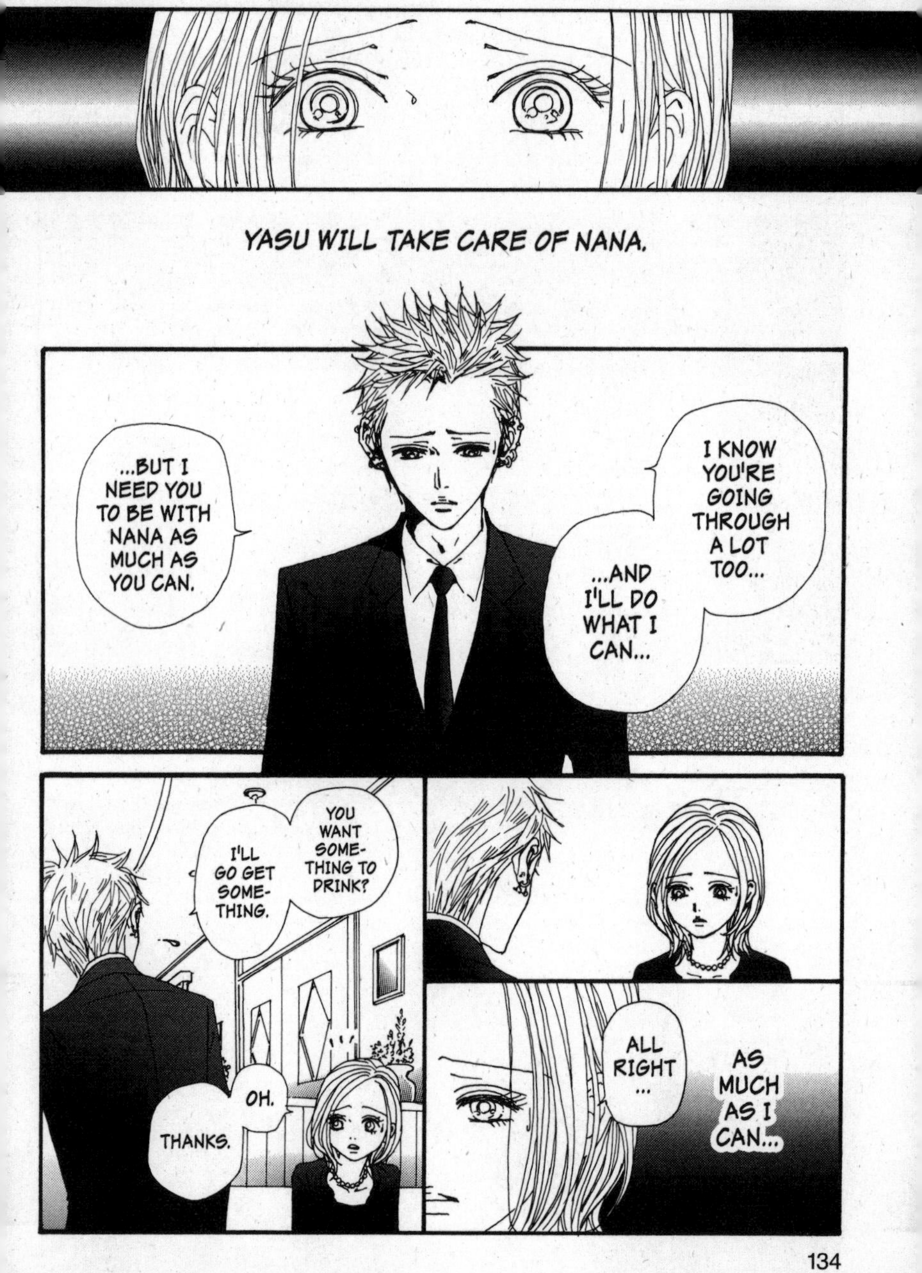
YASU WILL TAKE CARE OF NANA.
I KNOW YOU'RE GOING THROUGH A LOT TOO...
...AND I'LL DO WHAT I CAN...
...BUT I NEED YOU TO BE WITH NANA AS MUCH AS YOU CAN.
ALL RIGHT...
AS MUCH AS I CAN...
YOU WANT SOME-THING TO DRINK?
I'LL GO GET SOME-THING.
OH.
THANKS.

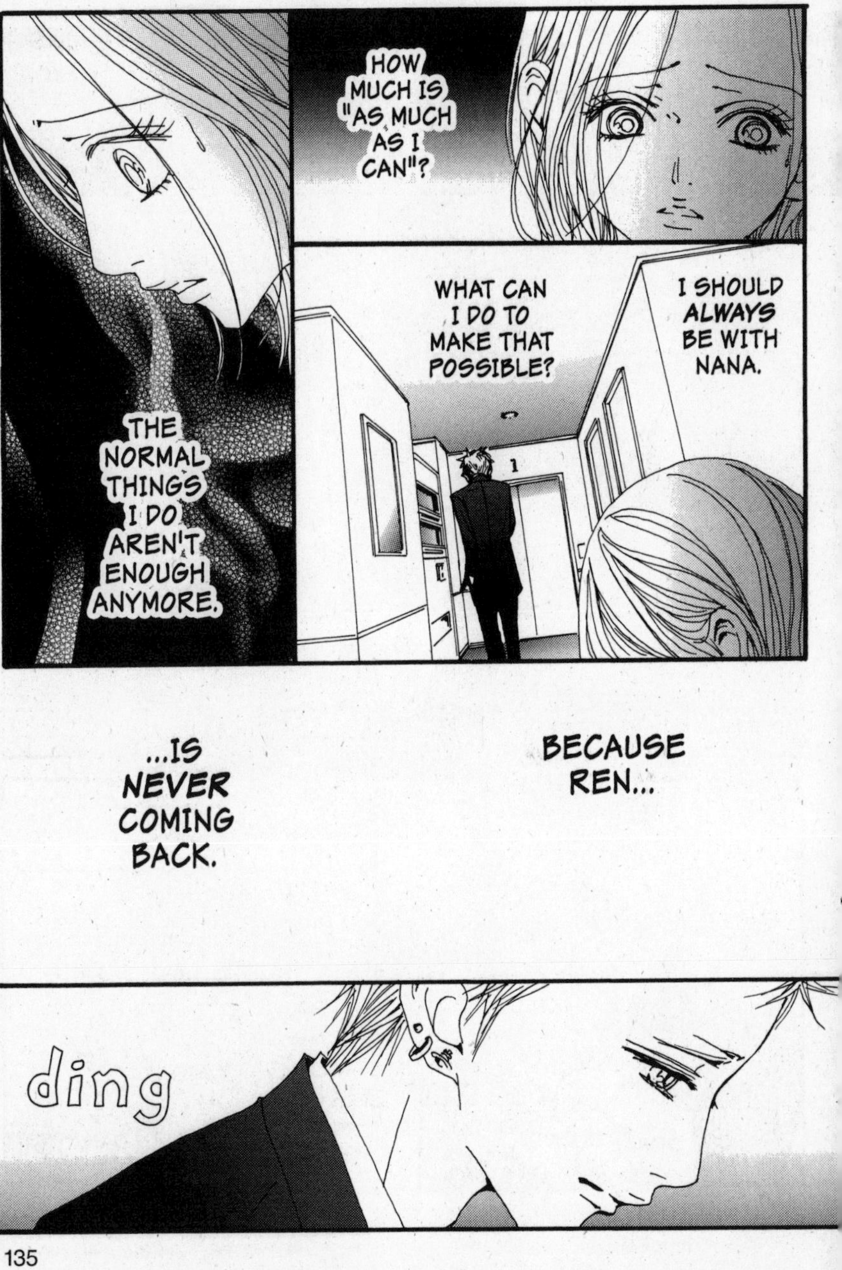
HOW MUCH IS "AS MUCH AS I CAN"?
I SHOULD ALWAYS BE WITH NANA.
WHAT CAN I DO TO MAKE THAT POSSIBLE?
THE NORMAL THINGS I DO AREN'T ENOUGH ANYMORE.
BECAUSE REN...
...IS NEVER COMING BACK.
ding

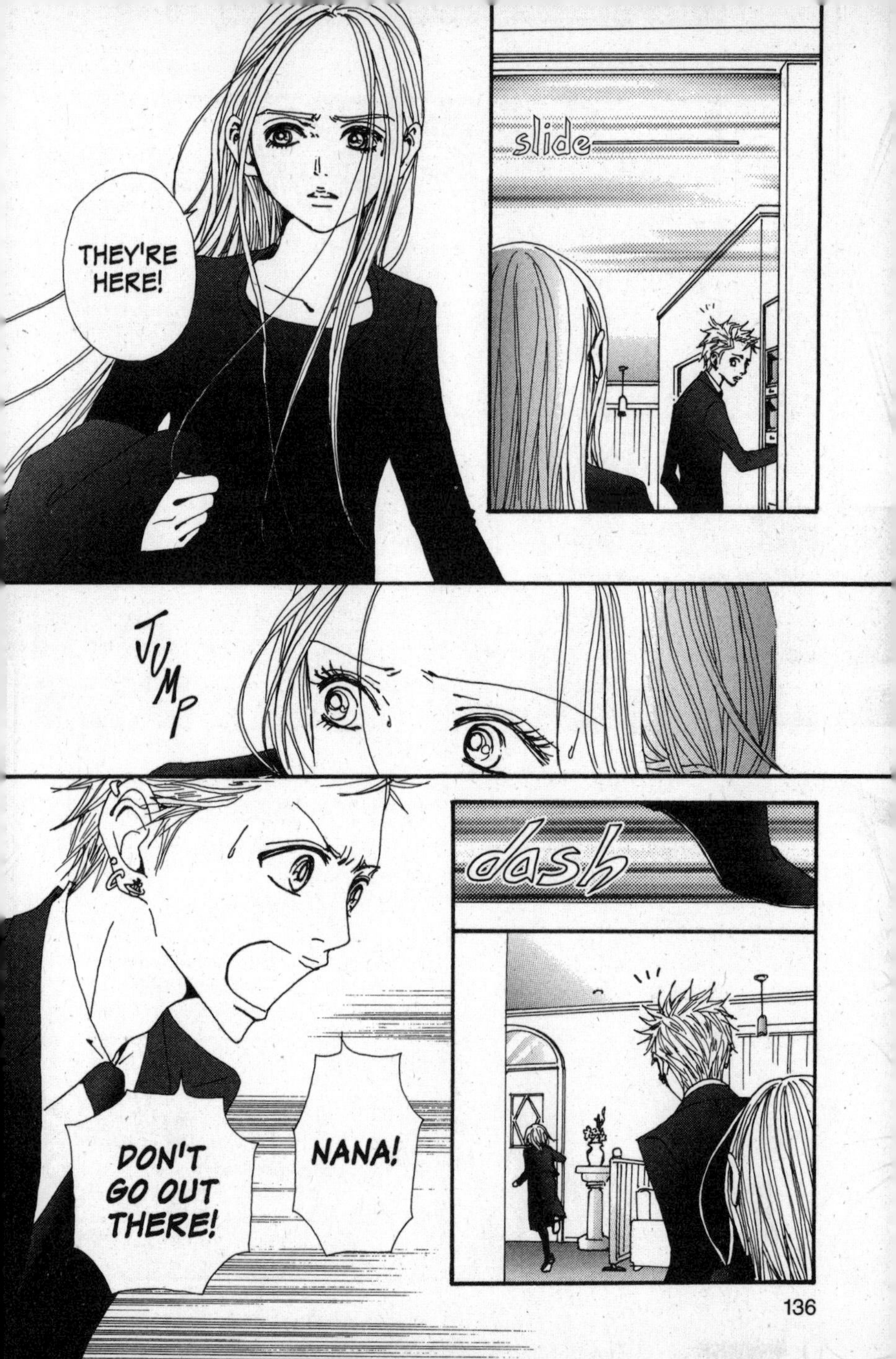
slide
THEY'RE HERE!
JUMP
dash
NANA!
DON'T GO OUT THERE!

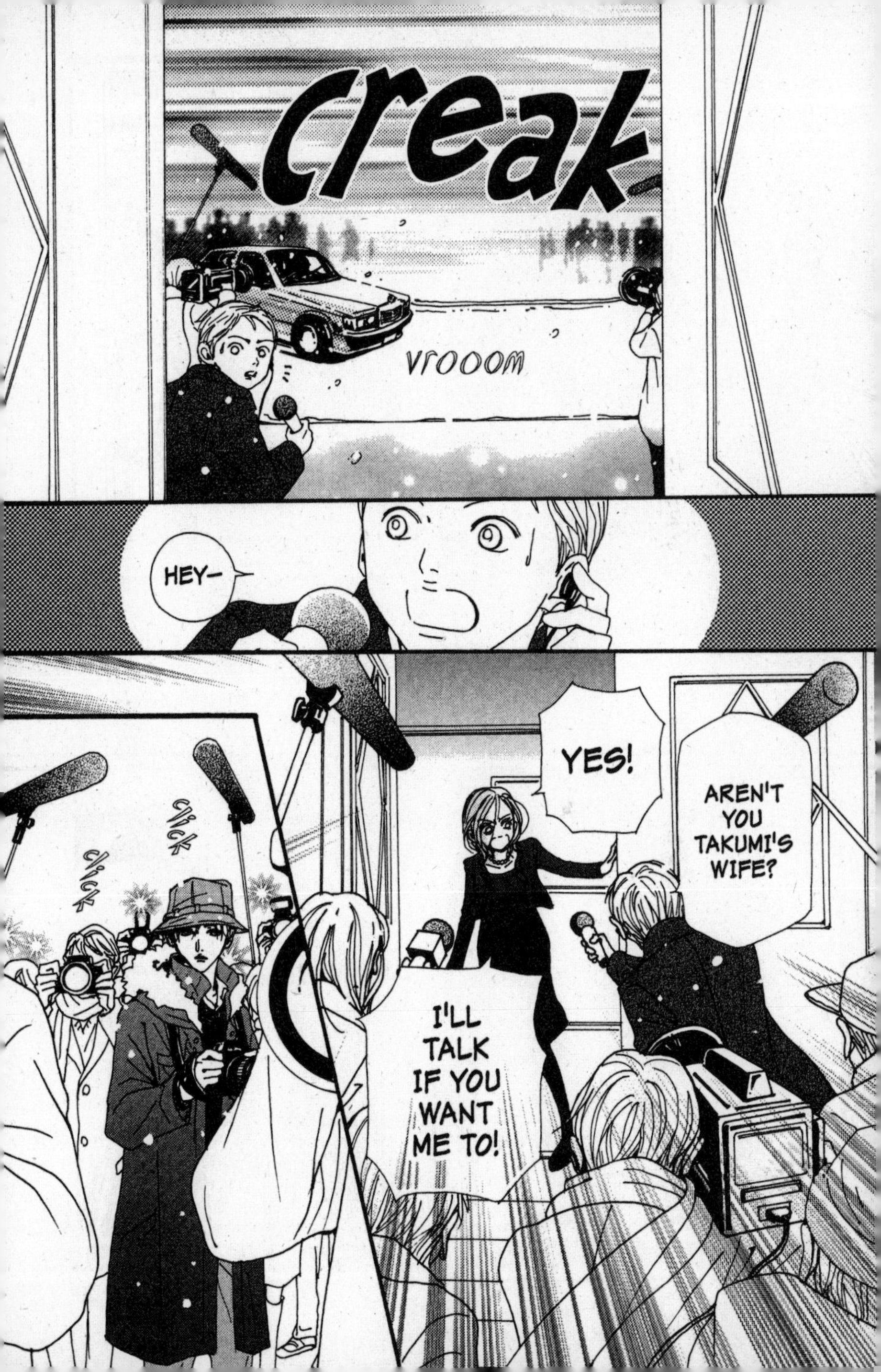
creak
vrooom
HEY–
AREN'T YOU TAKUMI'S WIFE?
YES!
I'LL TALK IF YOU WANT ME TO!
click
click

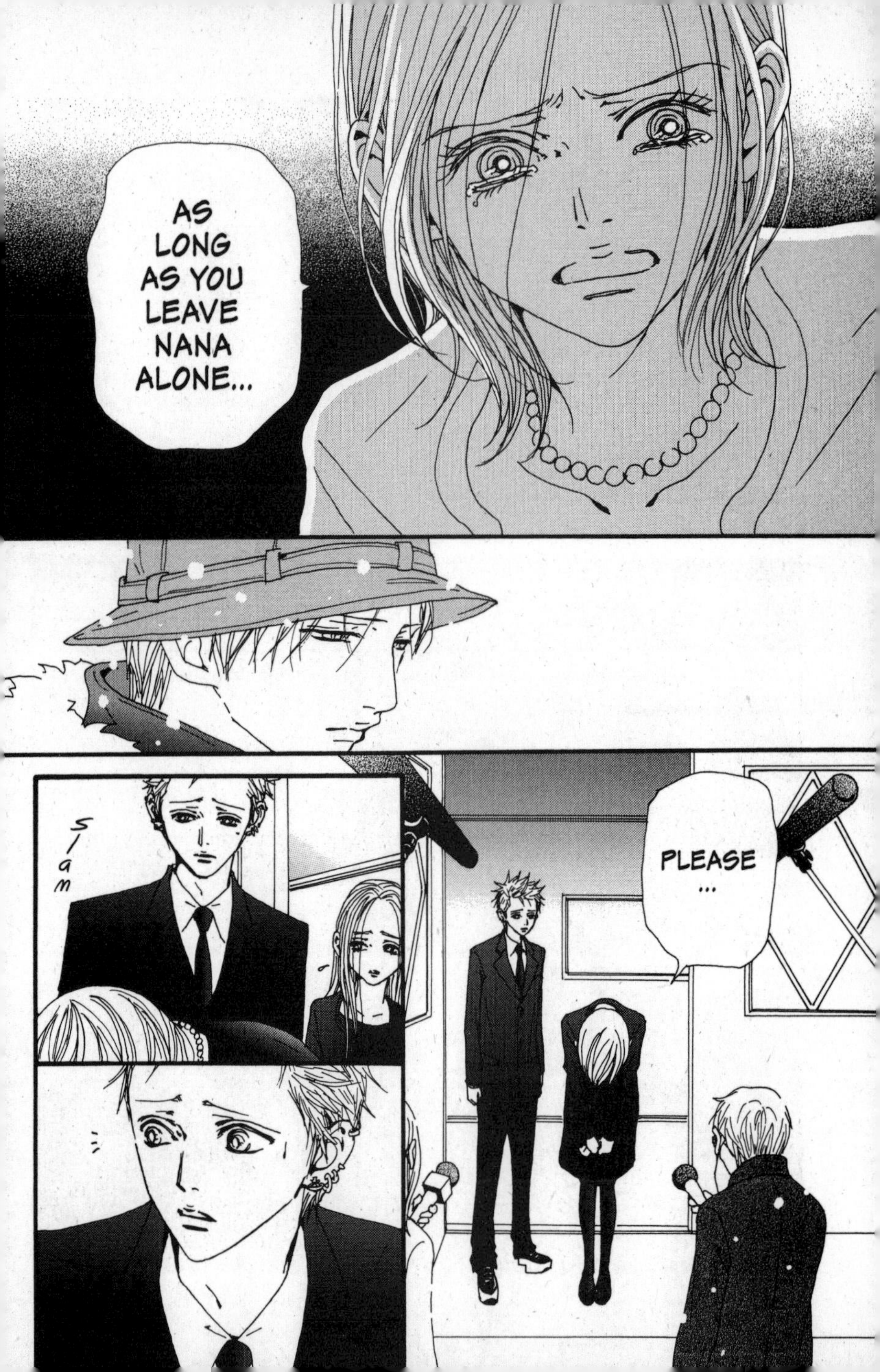
AS LONG AS YOU LEAVE NANA ALONE...
PLEASE ...
slam

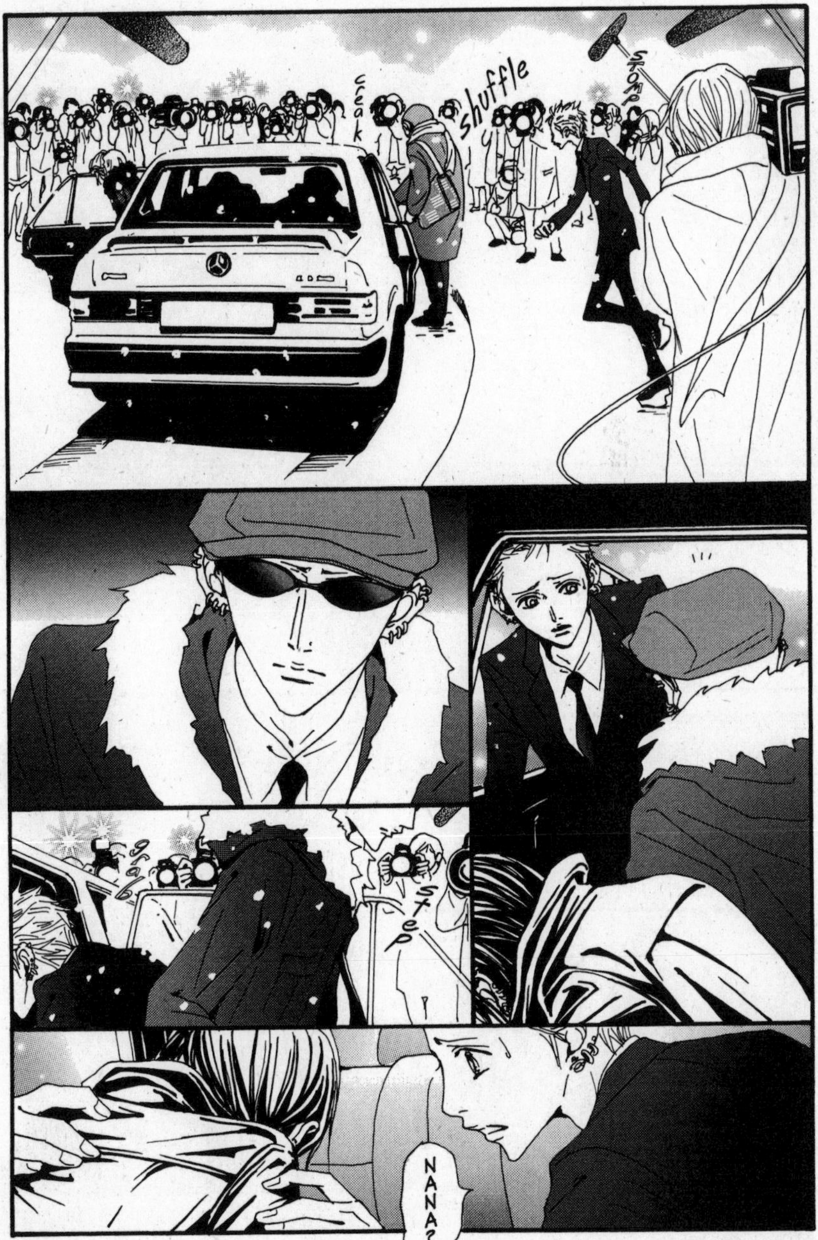
STOMP
shuffle
creak
step
grab
NANA?

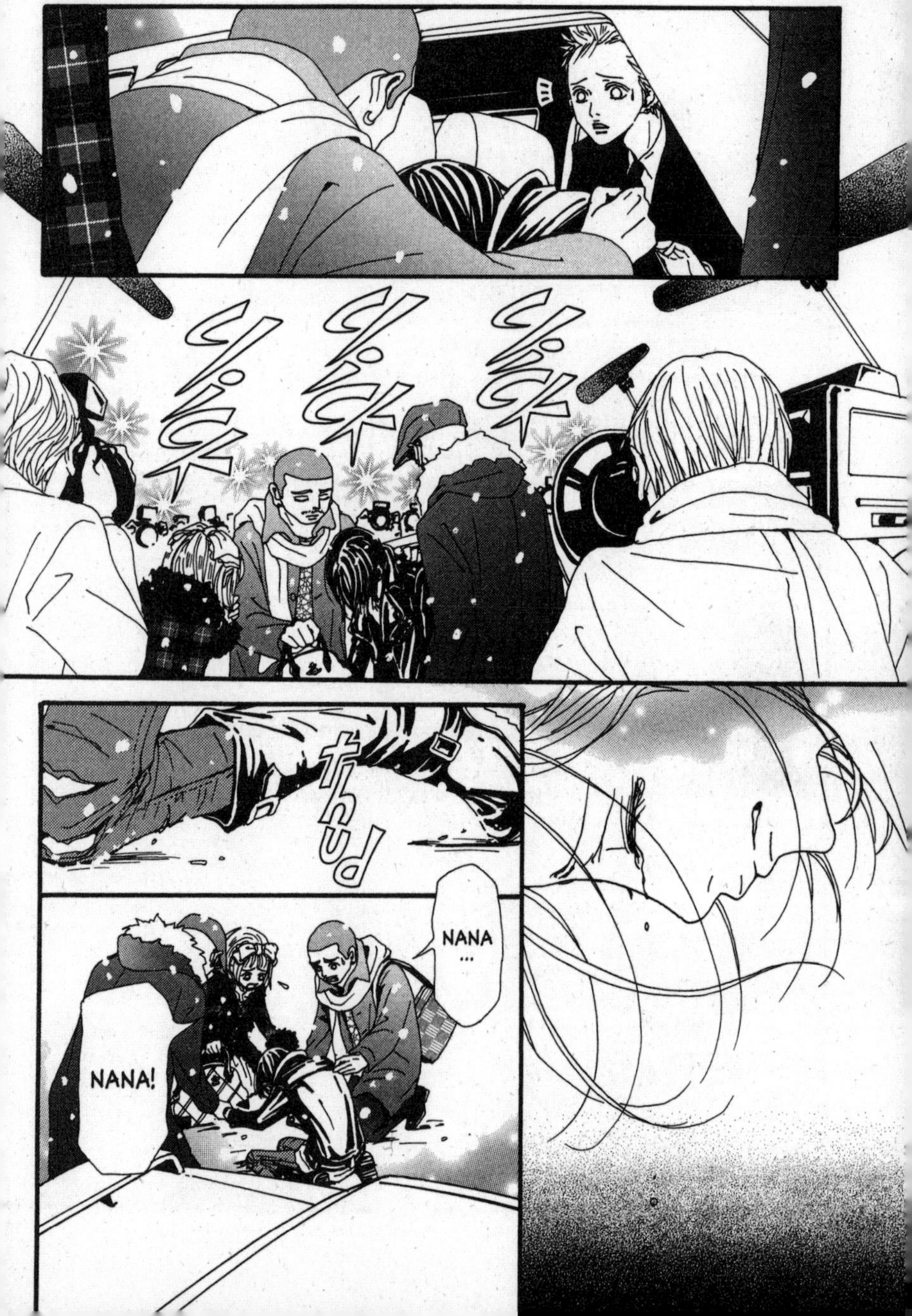
click
click
click
thud
NANA ...
NANA!

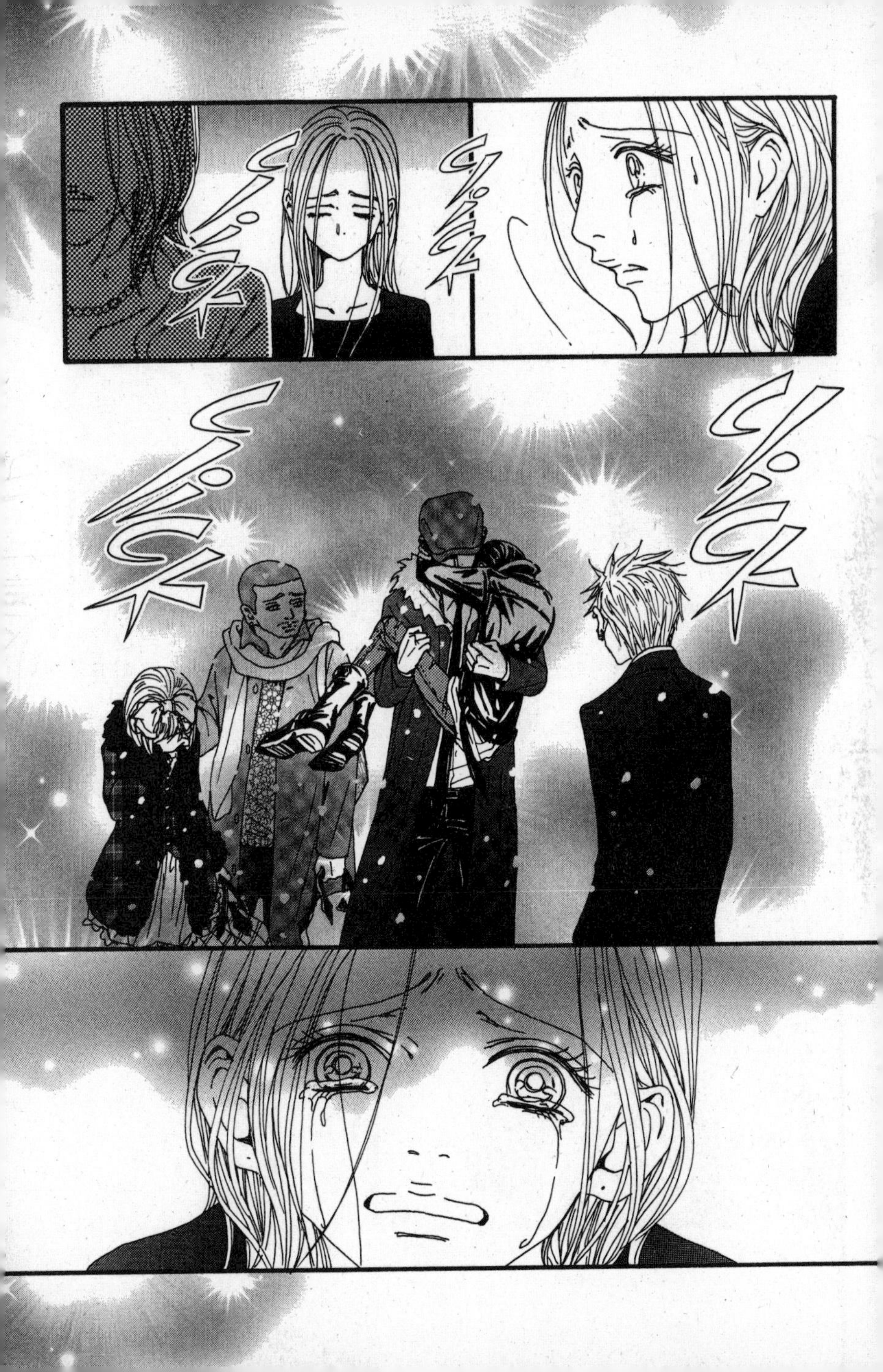

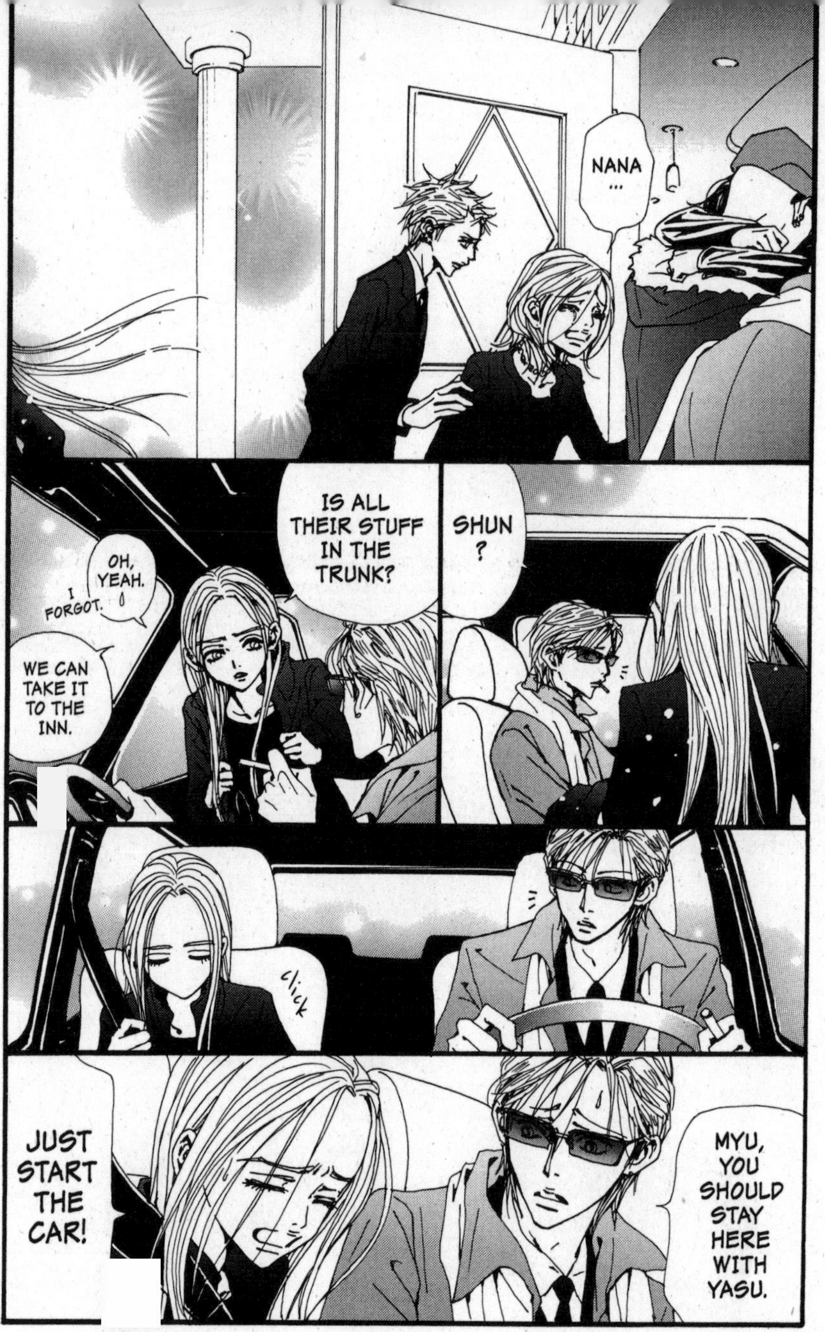
NANA ...
SHUN ?
IS ALL THEIR STUFF IN THE TRUNK?
OH, YEAH.
I FORGOT.
WE CAN TAKE IT TO THE INN.
click
MYU, YOU SHOULD STAY HERE WITH YASU.
JUST START THE CAR!

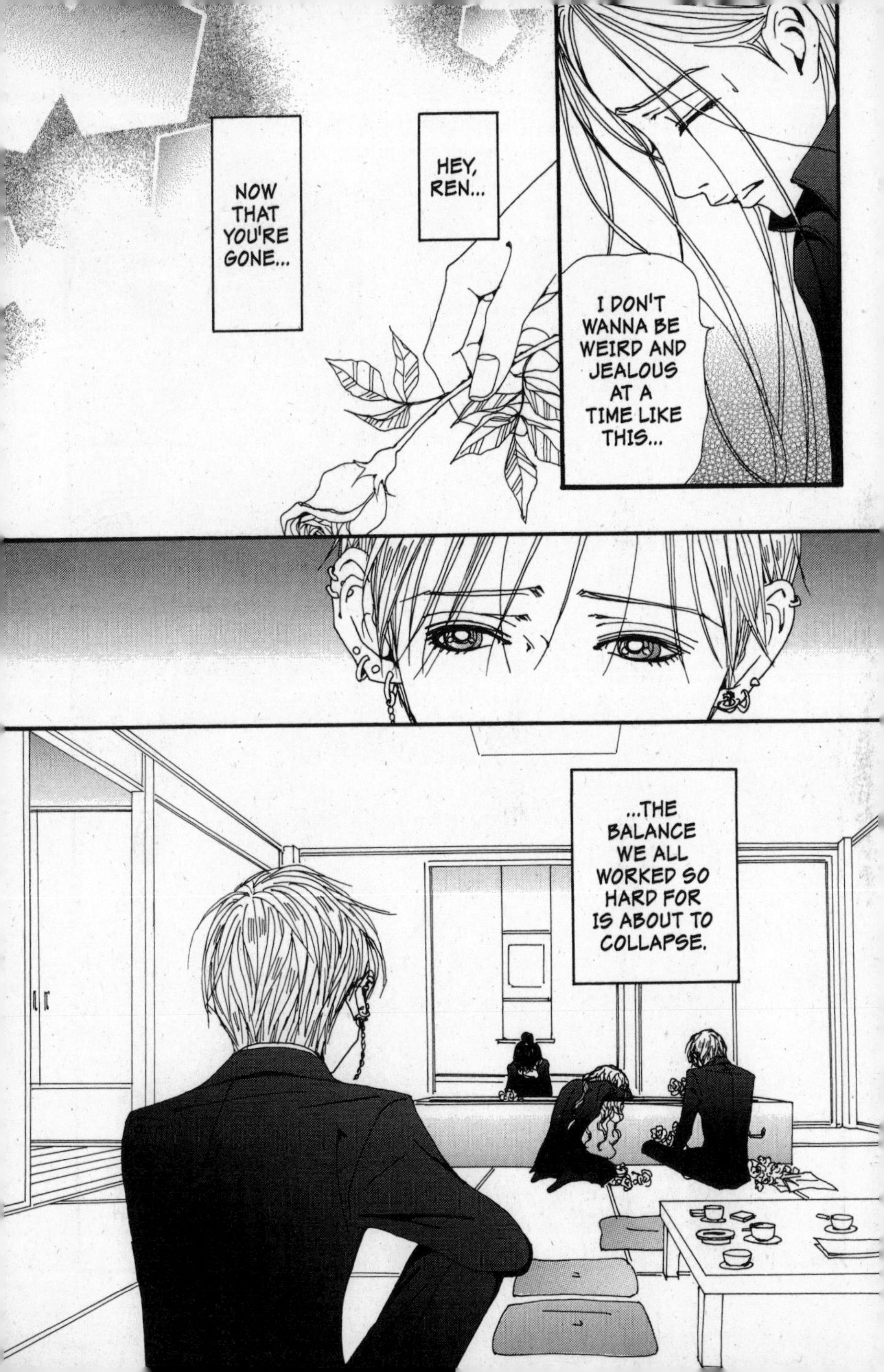
I DON'T WANNA BE WEIRD AND JEALOUS AT A TIME LIKE THIS...
HEY, REN...
NOW THAT YOU'RE GONE...
...THE BALANCE WE ALL WORKED SO HARD FOR IS ABOUT TO COLLAPSE.

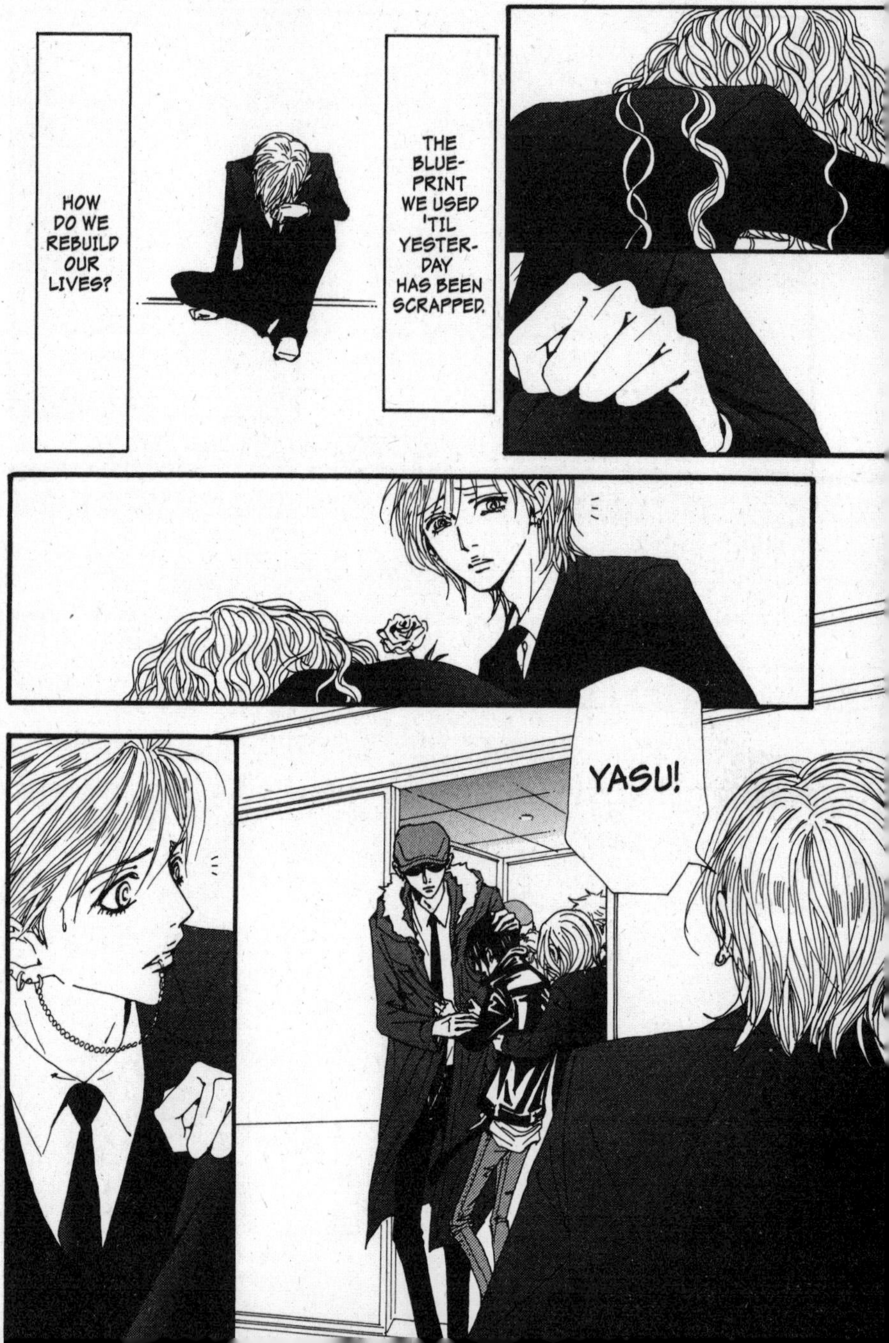
THE BLUE-PRINT WE USED 'TIL YESTER-DAY HAS BEEN SCRAPPED.
HOW DO WE REBUILD OUR LIVES?
YASU!

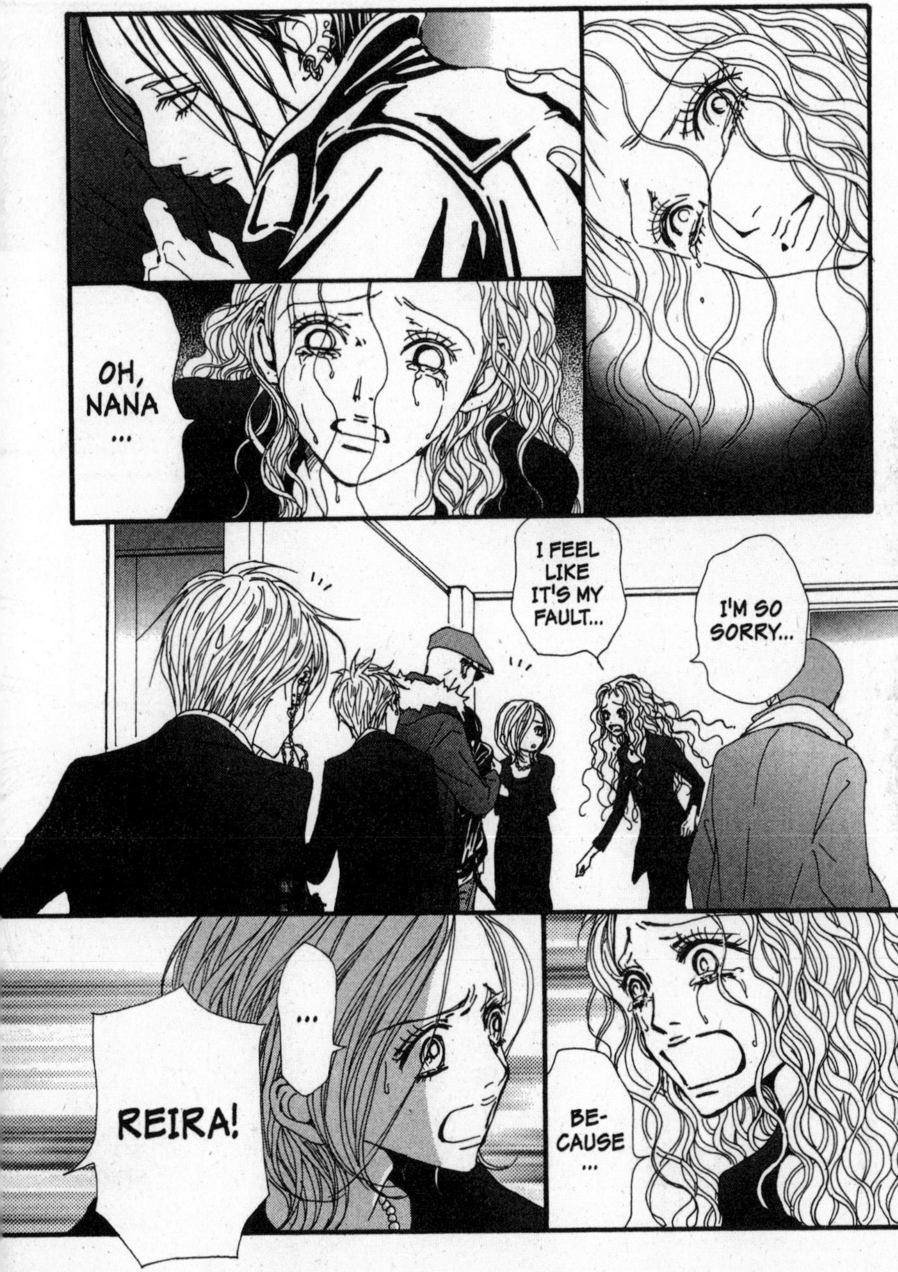
OH, NANA ...
I'M SO SORRY...
I FEEL LIKE IT'S MY FAULT...
BE-CAUSE ...
...
REIRA!

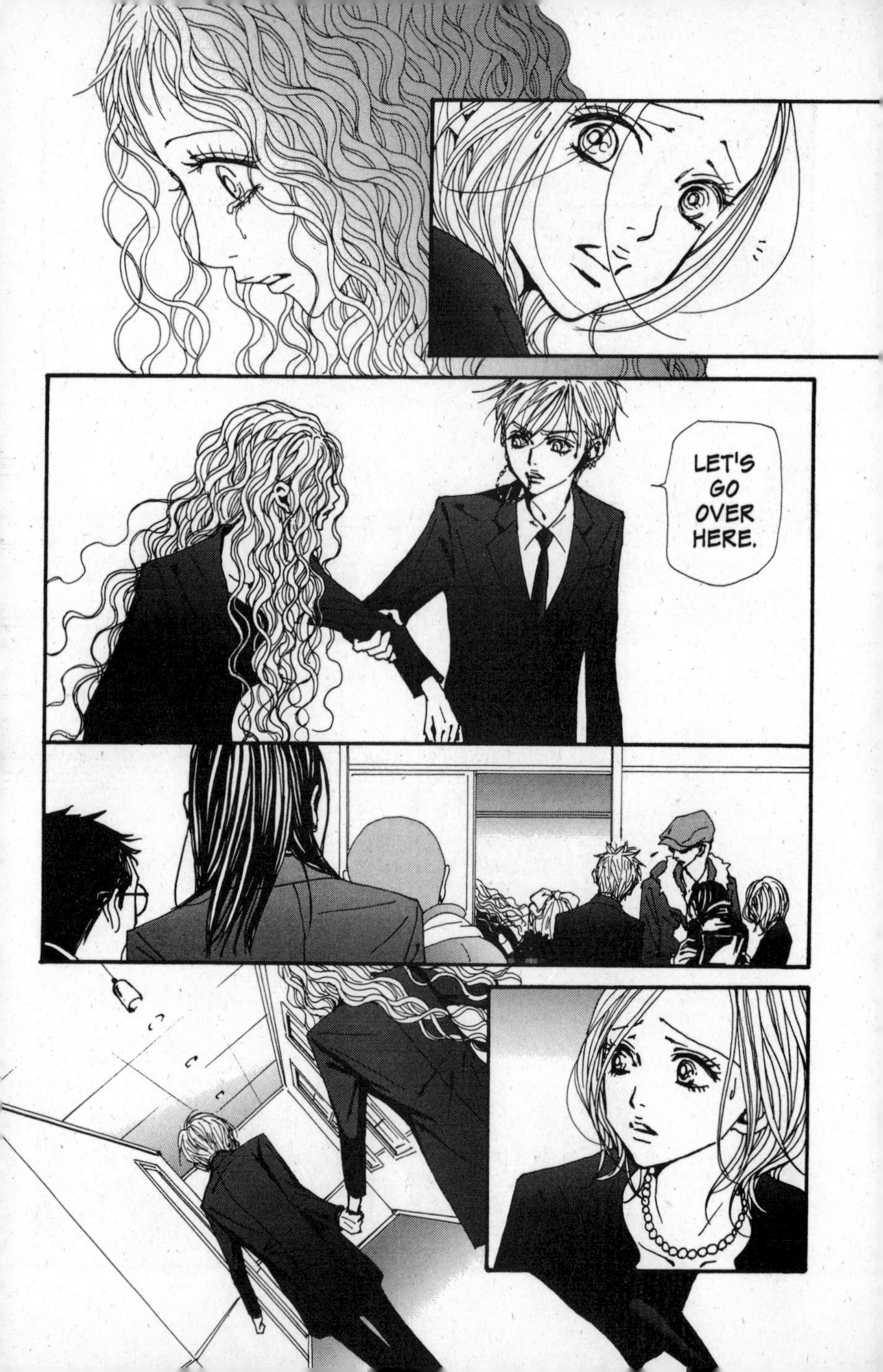
LET'S GO OVER HERE.

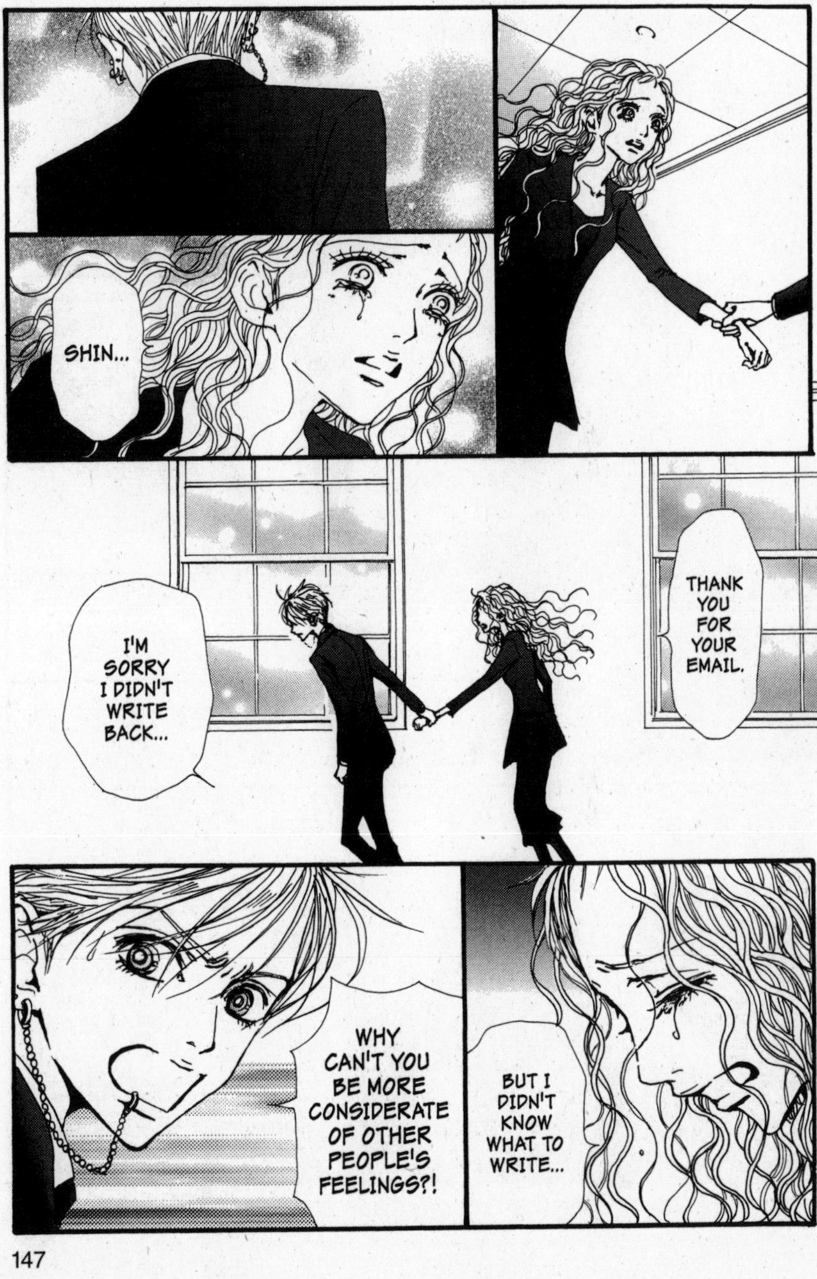
SHIN...
THANK YOU FOR YOUR EMAIL.
I'M SORRY I DIDN'T WRITE BACK...
BUT I DIDN'T KNOW WHAT TO WRITE...
WHY CAN'T YOU BE MORE CONSIDERATE OF OTHER PEOPLE'S FEELINGS?!

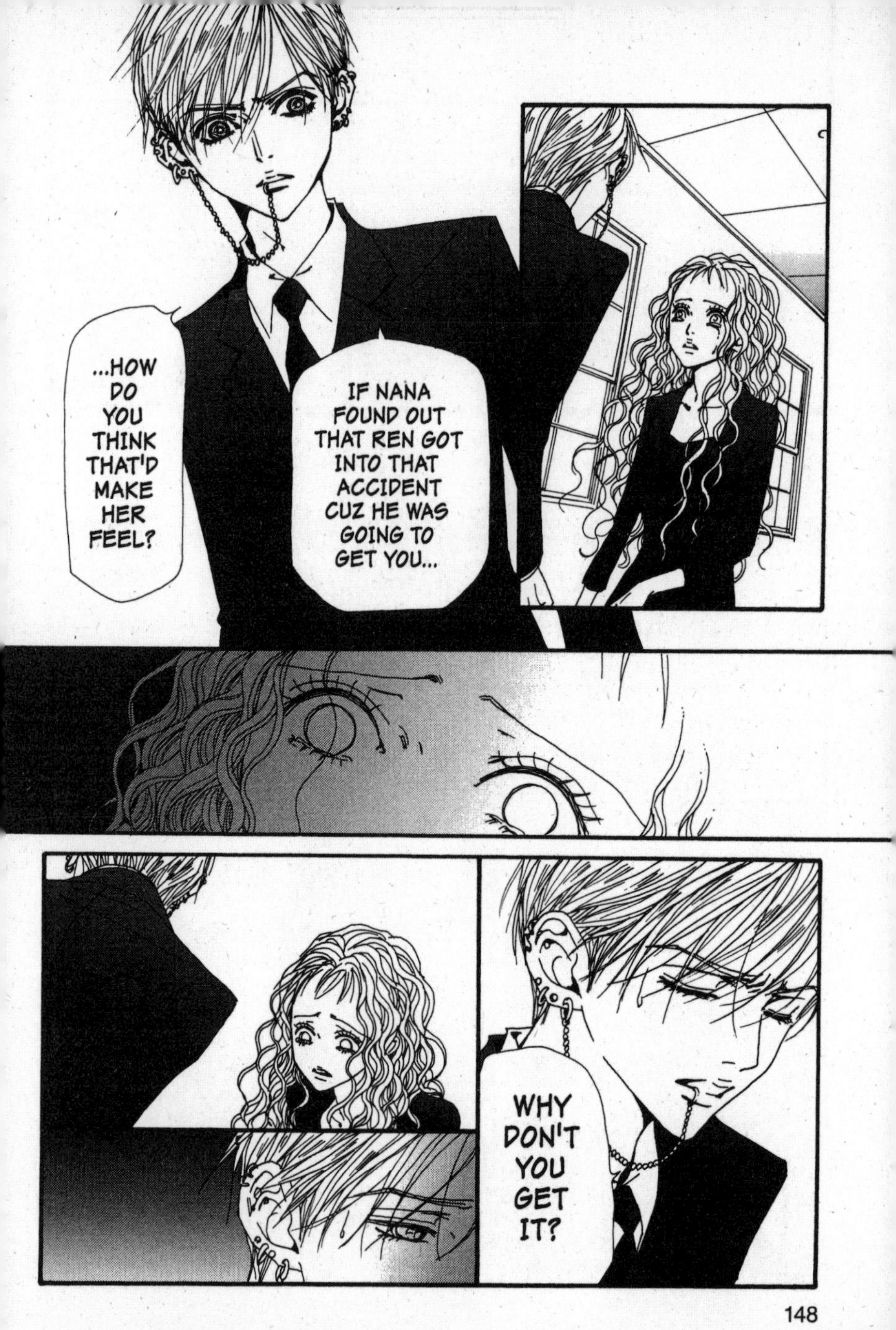
IF NANA FOUND OUT THAT REN GOT INTO THAT ACCIDENT CUZ HE WAS GOING TO GET YOU...
...HOW DO YOU THINK THAT'D MAKE HER FEEL?
WHY DON'T YOU GET IT?

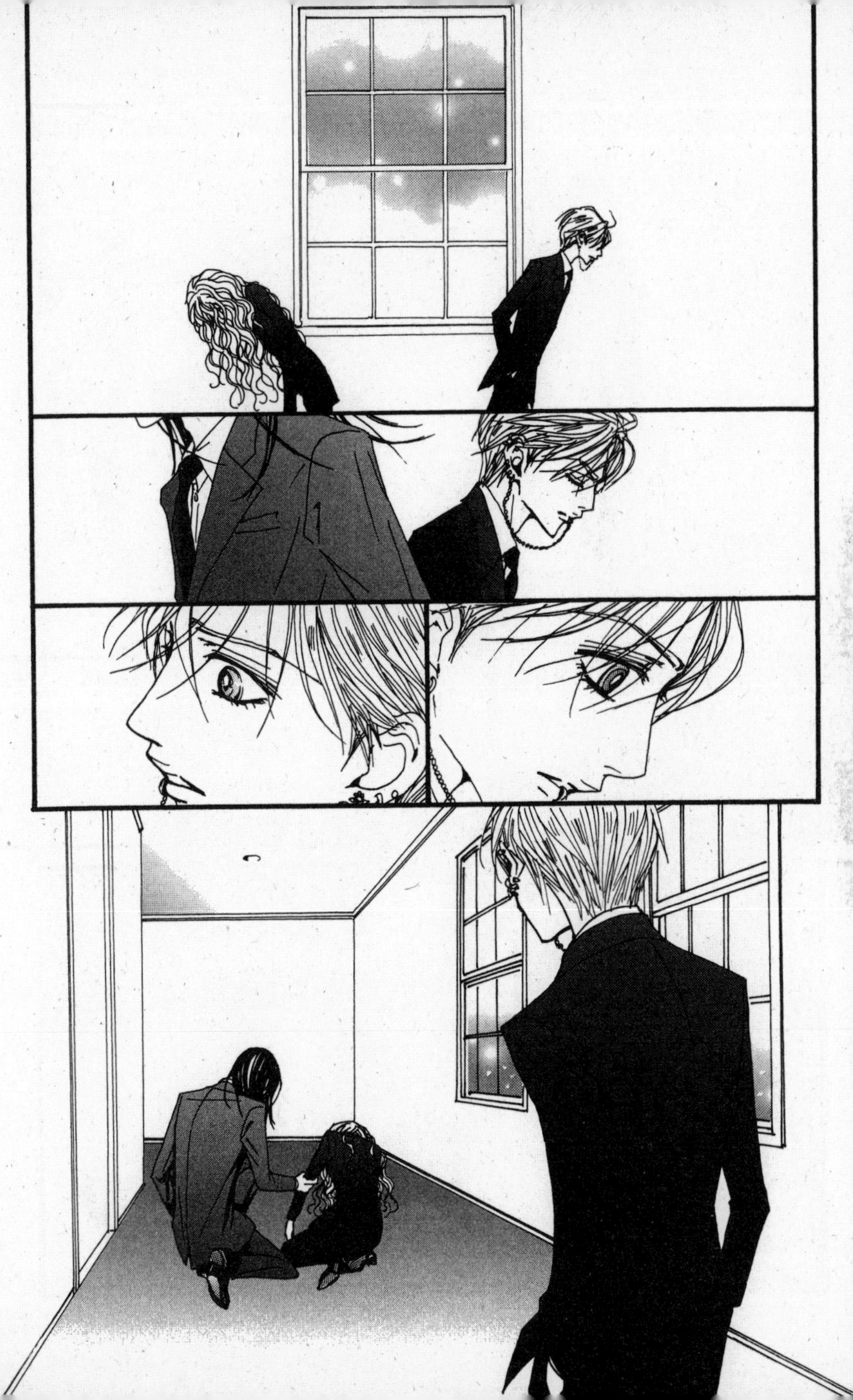

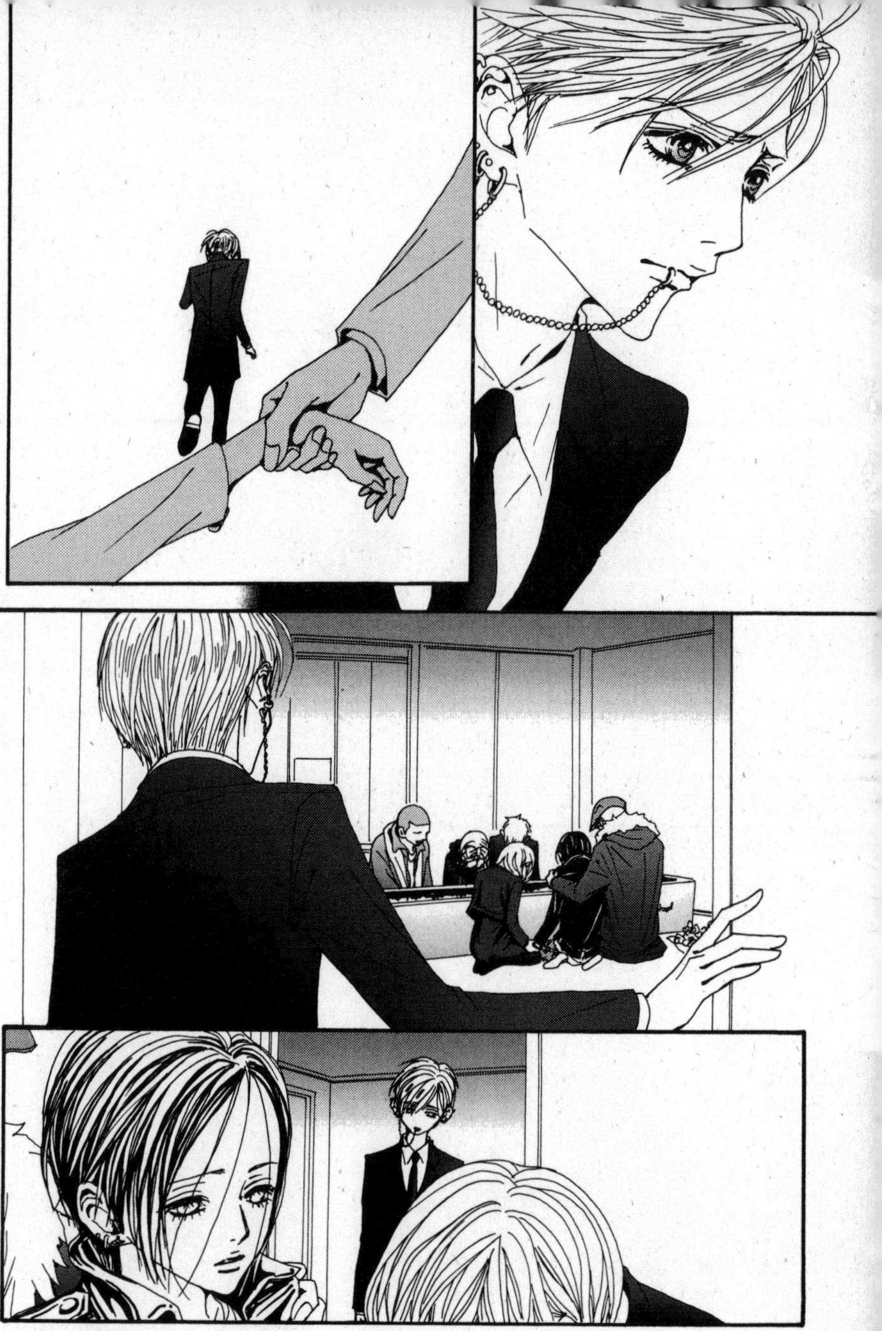

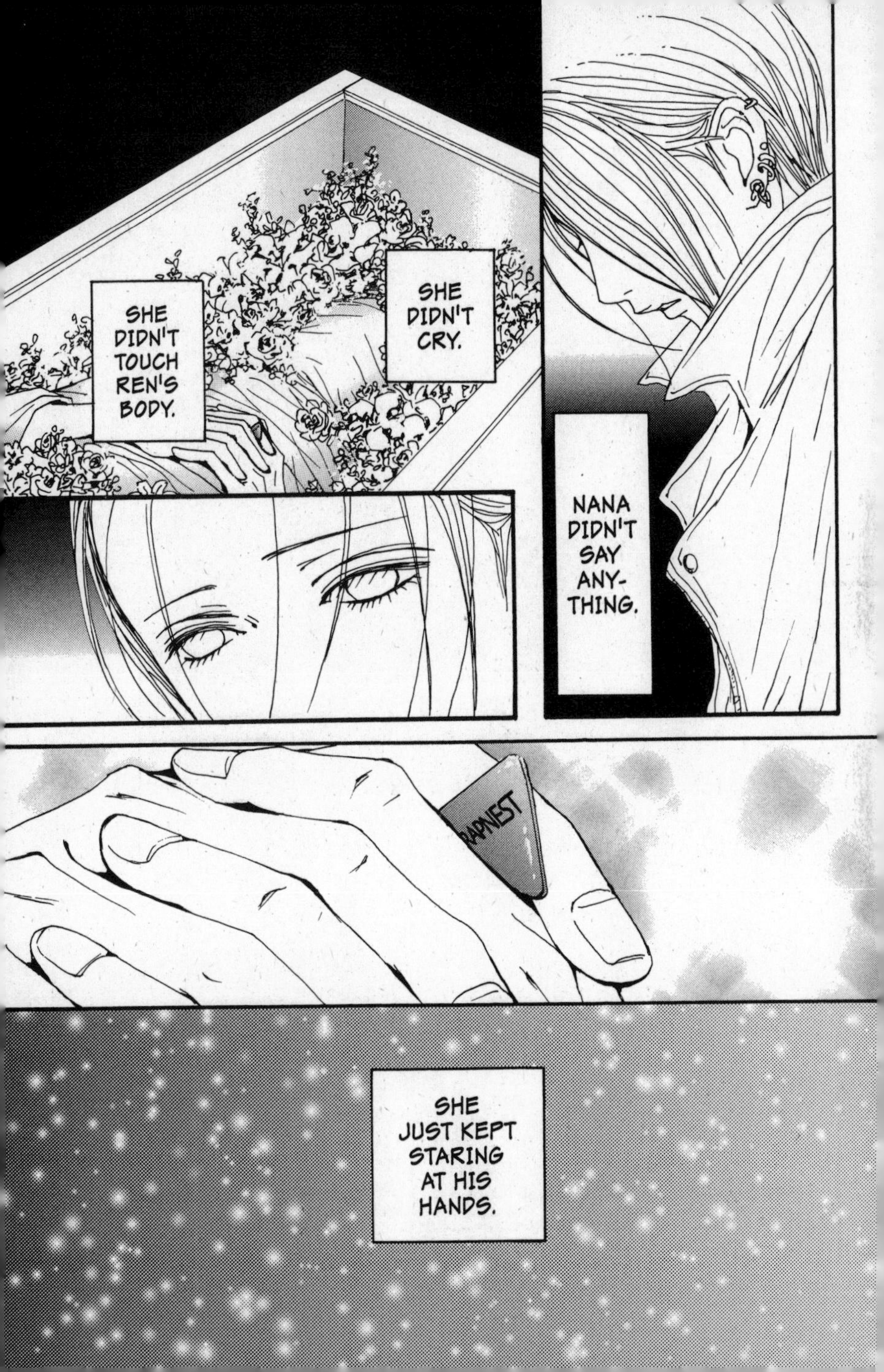
NANA DIDN'T SAY ANYTHING.
SHE DIDN'T CRY.
SHE DIDN'T TOUCH REN'S BODY.
RAPNEST
SHE JUST KEPT STARING AT HIS HANDS.

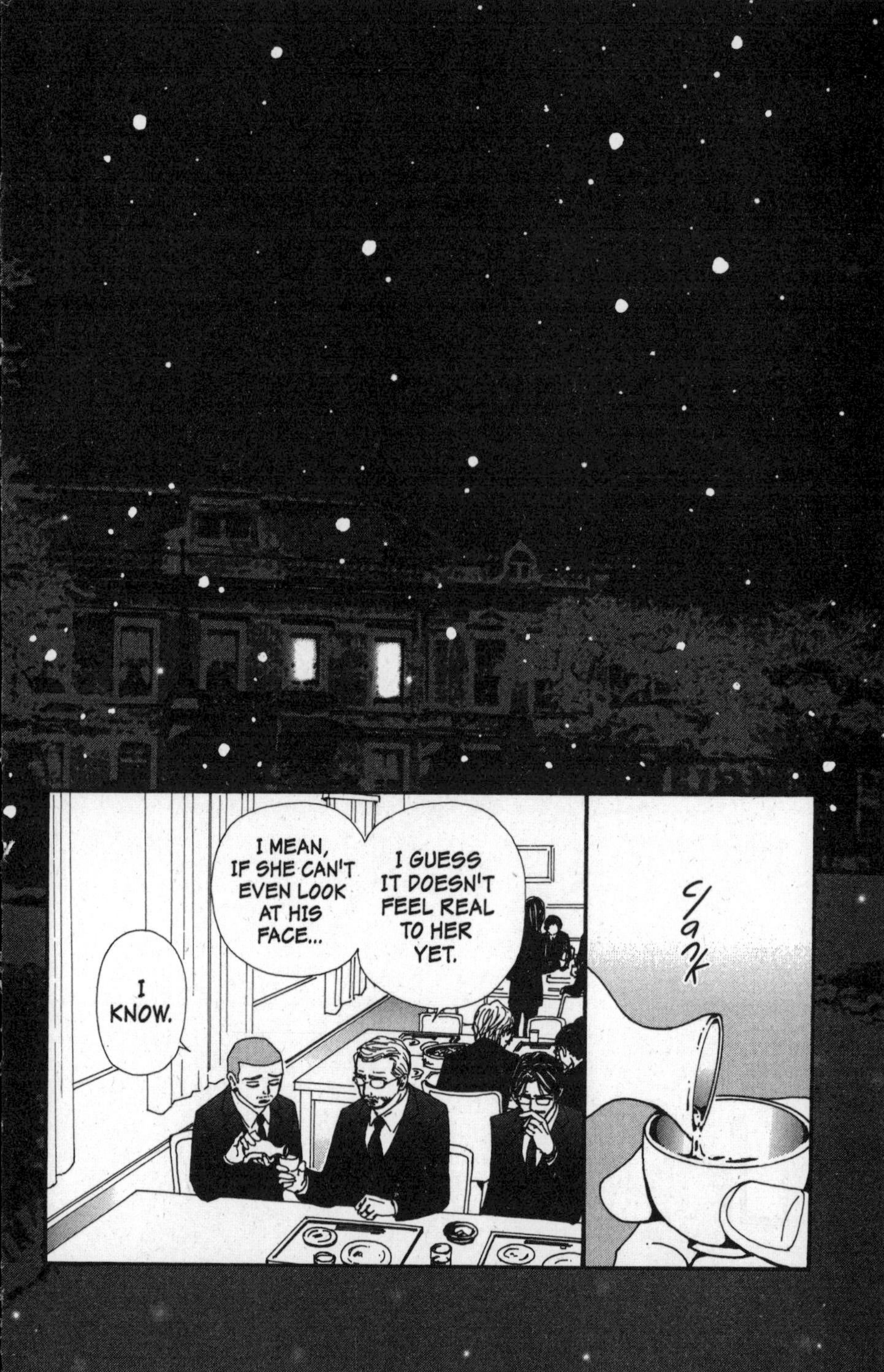
Clank
I GUESS IT DOESN'T FEEL REAL TO HER YET.
I MEAN, IF SHE CAN'T EVEN LOOK AT HIS FACE...
I KNOW.

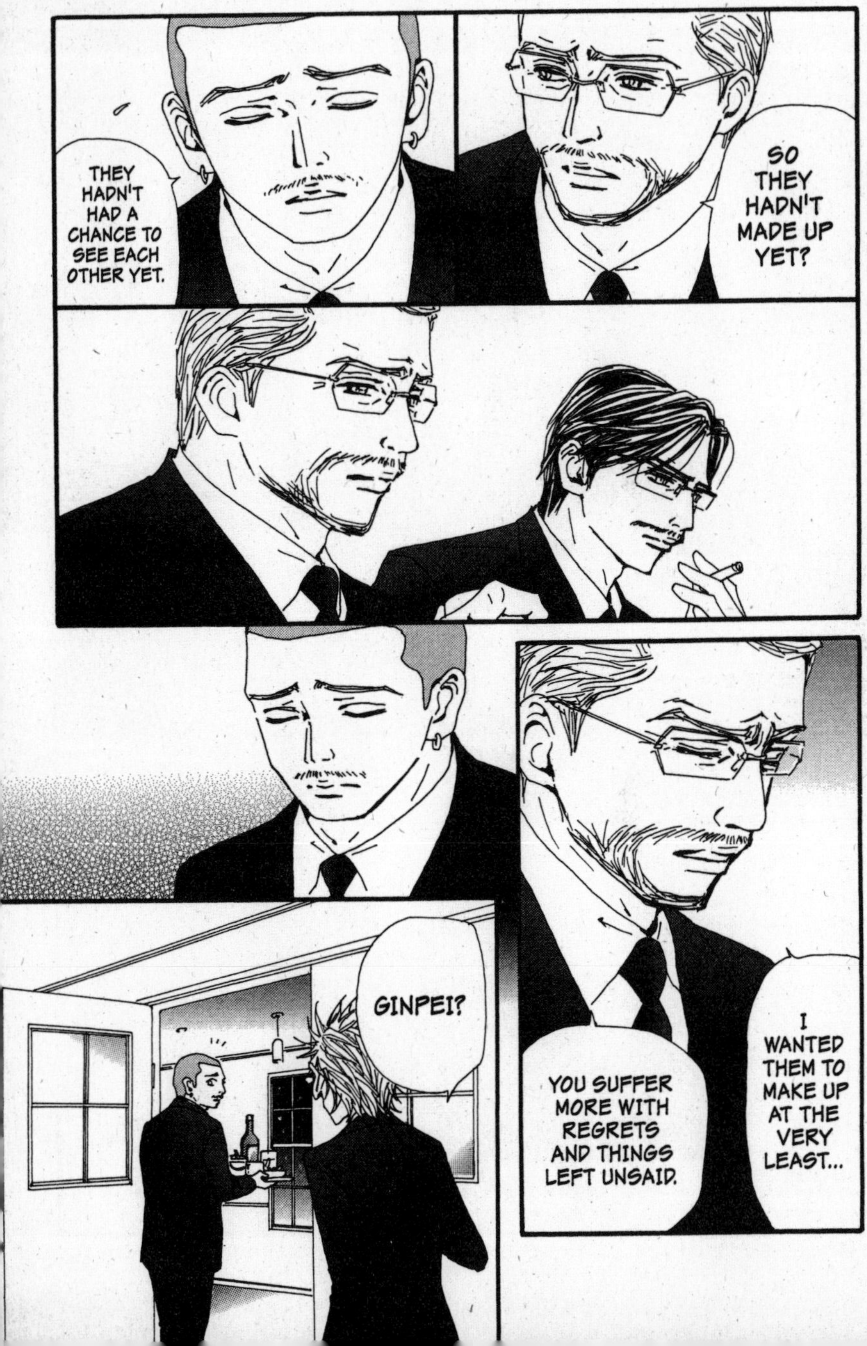
SO THEY HADN'T MADE UP YET?
THEY HADN'T HAD A CHANCE TO SEE EACH OTHER YET.
I WANTED THEM TO MAKE UP AT THE VERY LEAST...
YOU SUFFER MORE WITH REGRETS AND THINGS LEFT UNSAID.
GINPEI?

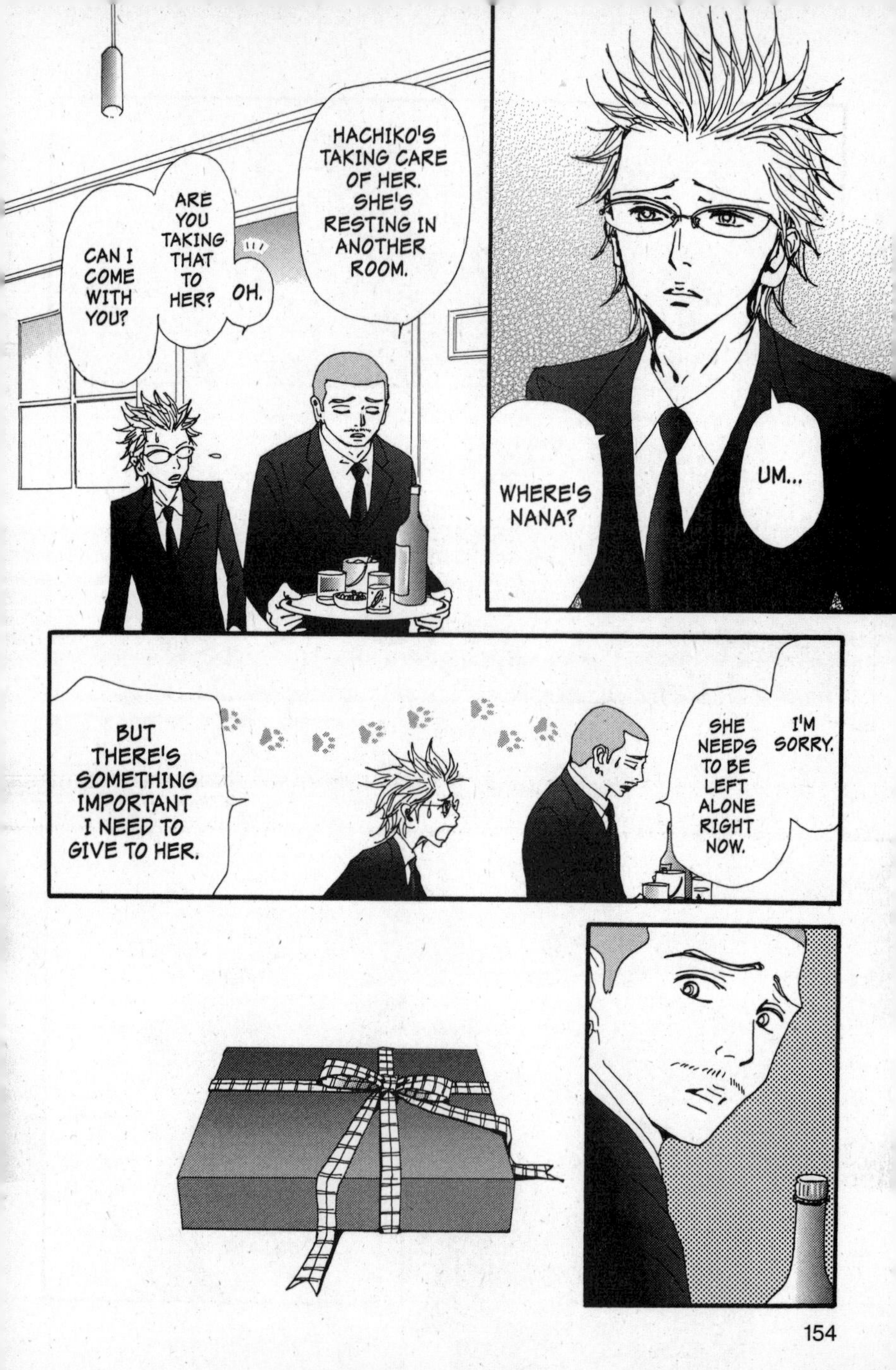
UM...
WHERE'S NANA?
HACHIKO'S TAKING CARE OF HER. SHE'S RESTING IN ANOTHER ROOM.
OH.
ARE YOU TAKING THAT TO HER?
CAN I COME WITH YOU?
I'M SORRY.
SHE NEEDS TO BE LEFT ALONE RIGHT NOW.
BUT THERE'S SOMETHING IMPORTANT I NEED TO GIVE TO HER.

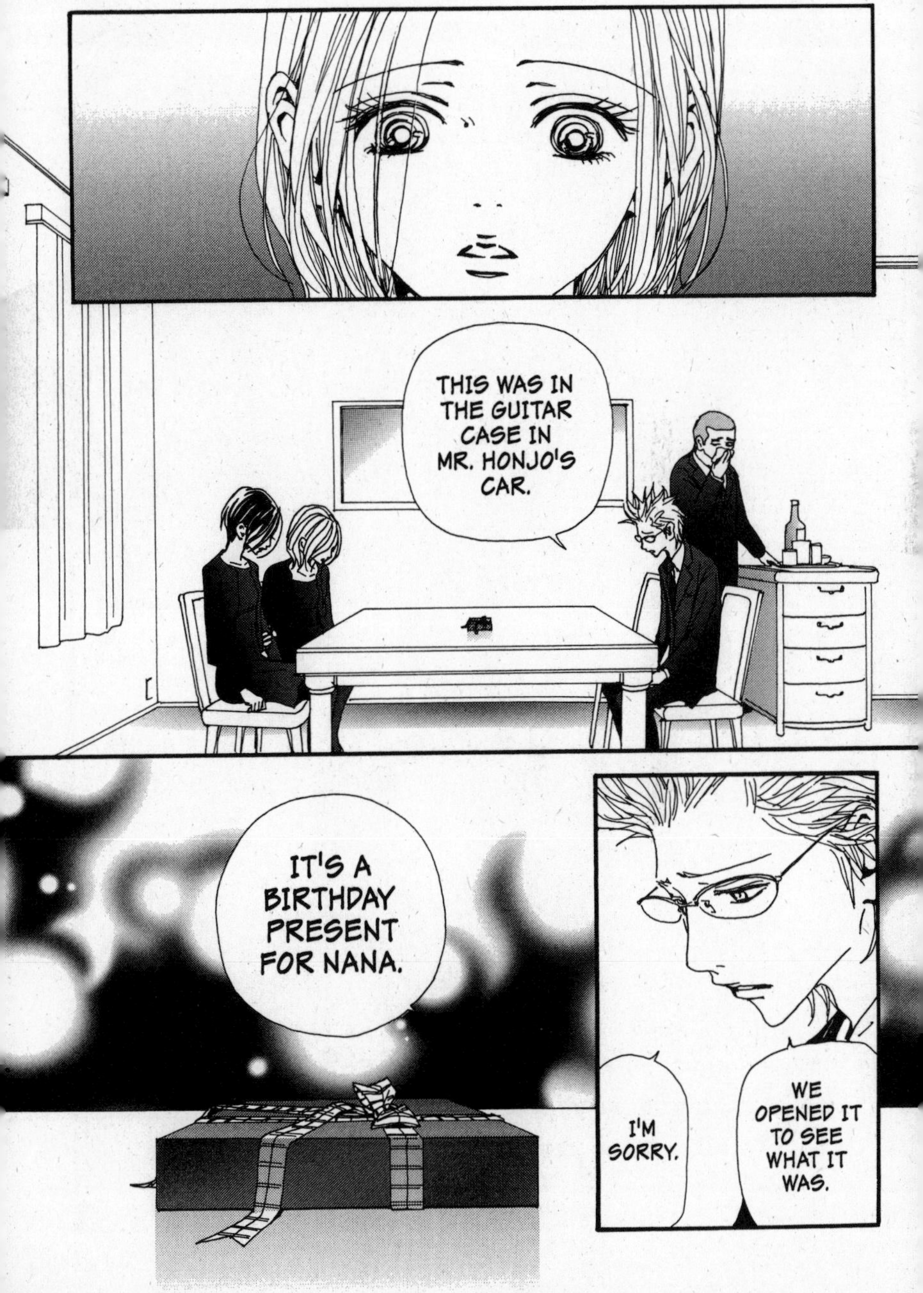
THIS WAS IN THE GUITAR CASE IN MR. HONJO'S CAR.
WE OPENED IT TO SEE WHAT IT WAS.
I'M SORRY.
IT'S A BIRTHDAY PRESENT FOR NANA.

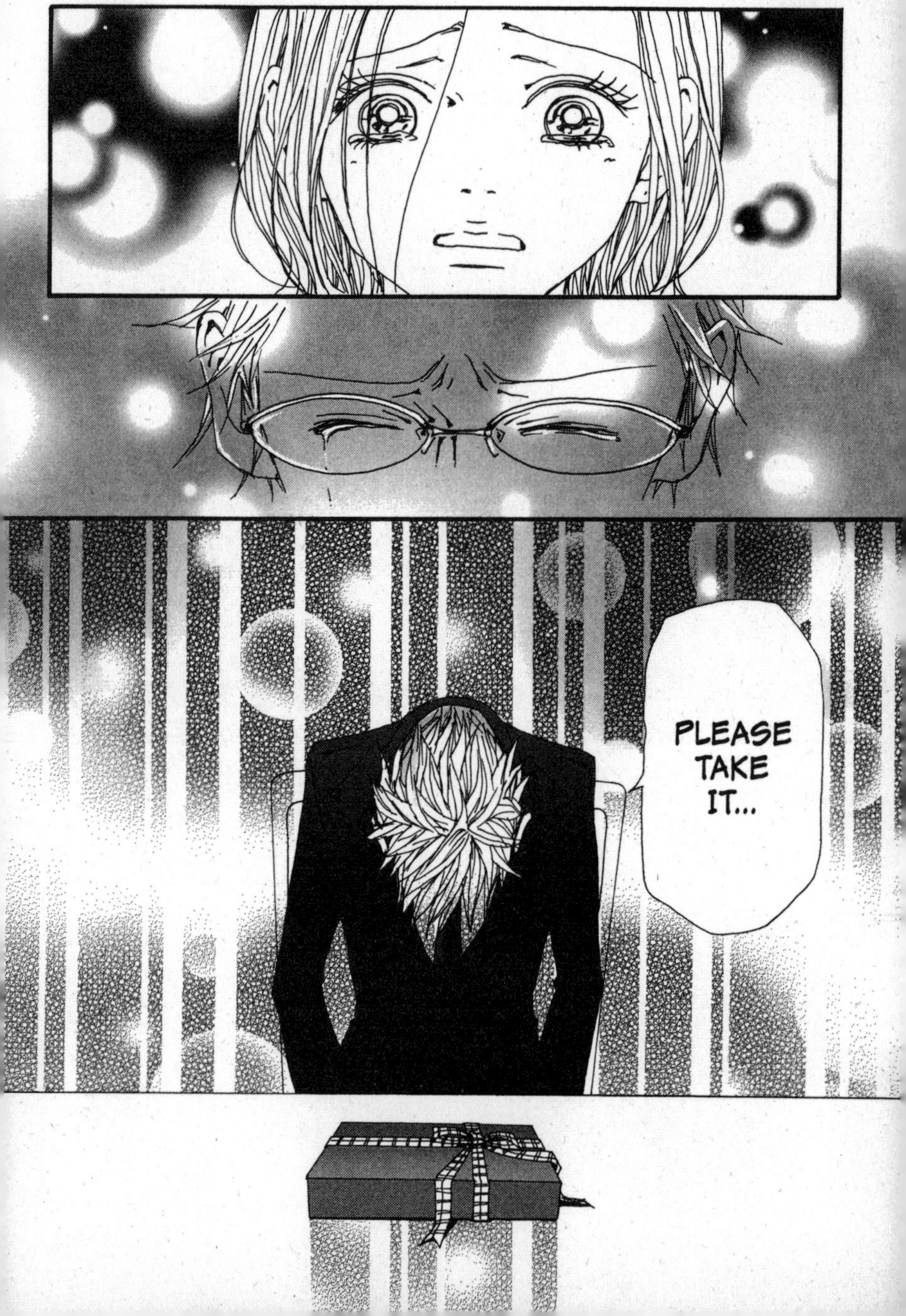
PLEASE TAKE IT...

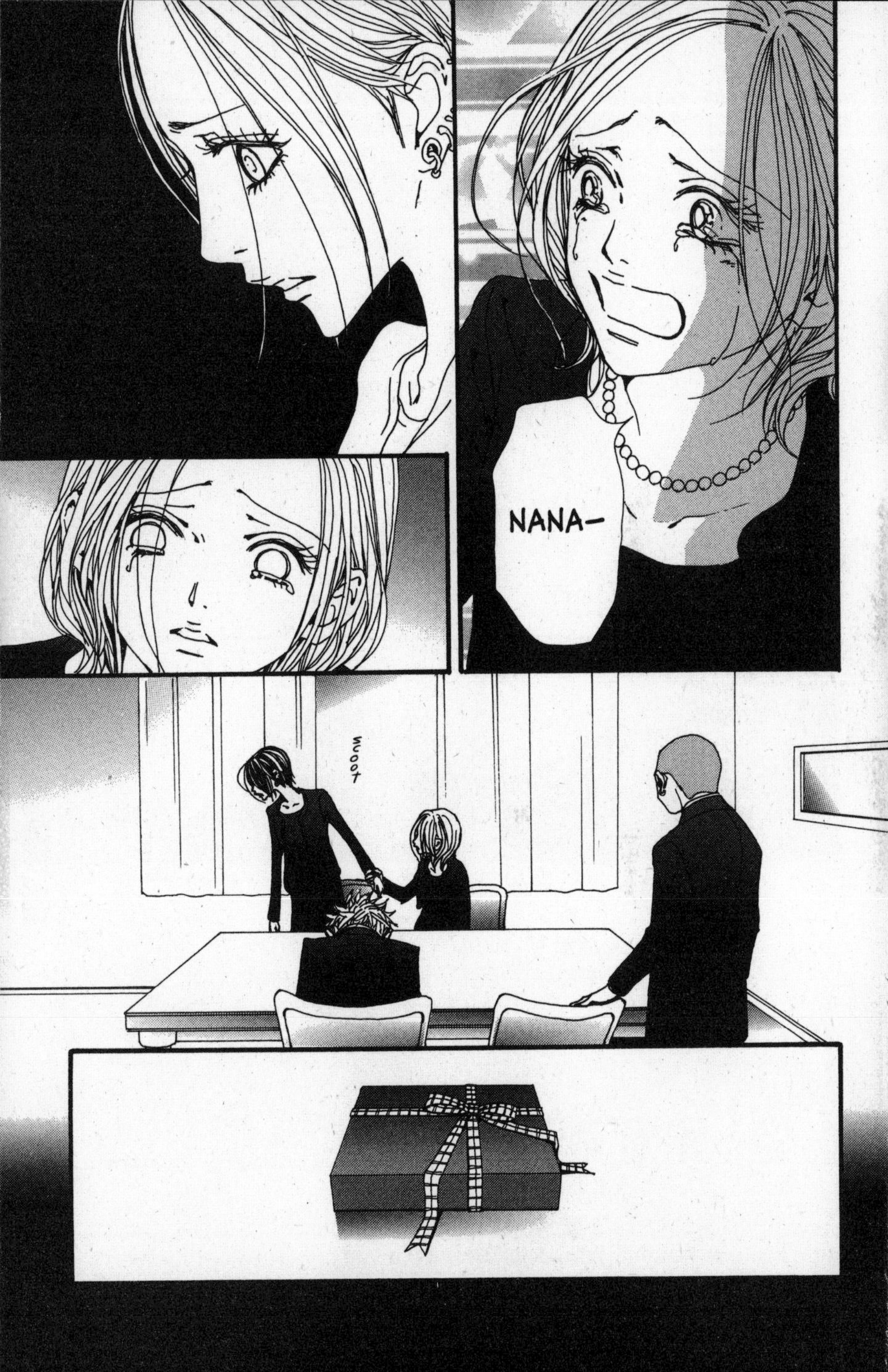
NANA–
scoot

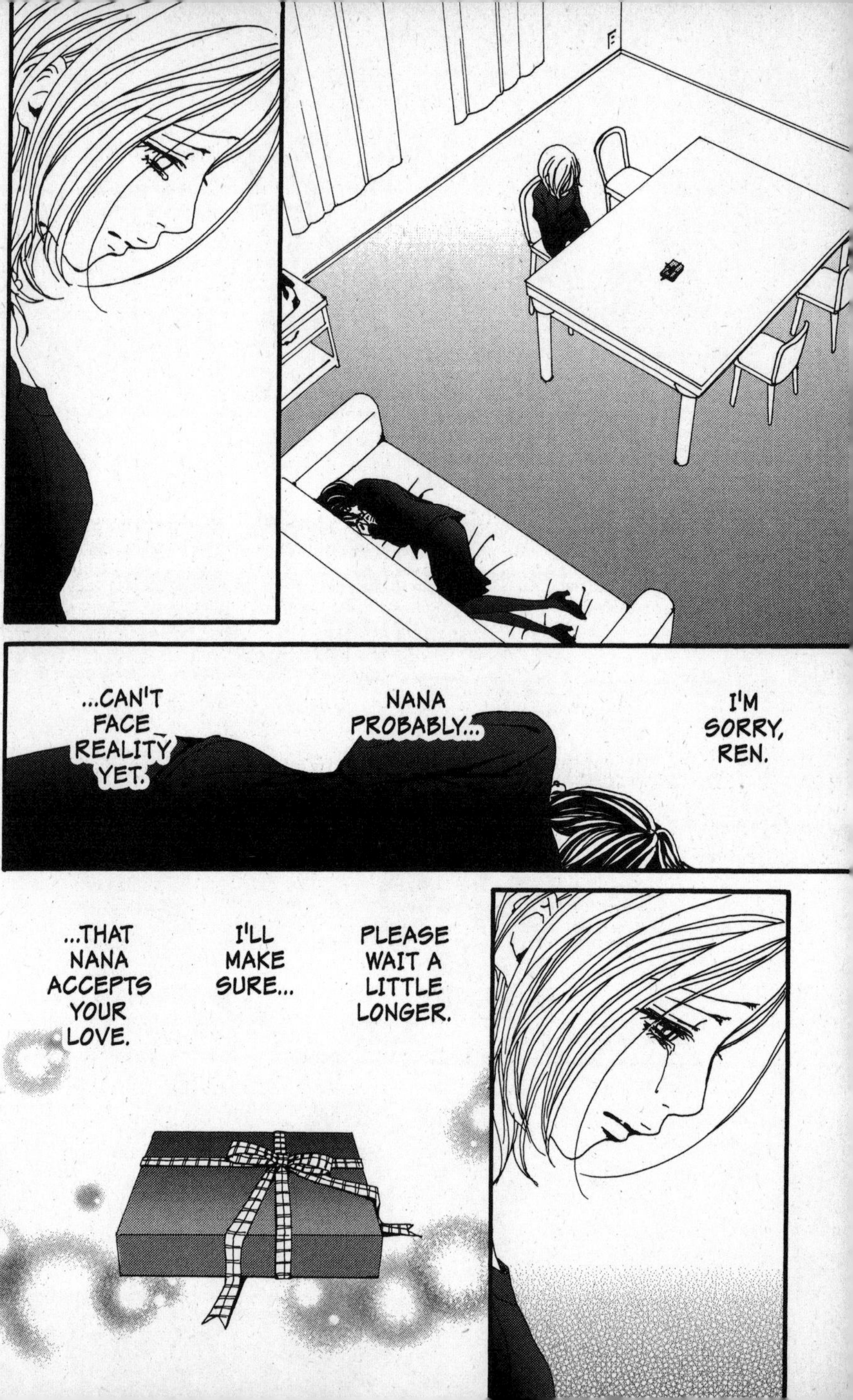
I'M SORRY, REN.
NANA PROBABLY...
...CAN'T FACE REALITY YET.
PLEASE WAIT A LITTLE LONGER.
I'LL MAKE SURE...
...THAT NANA ACCEPTS YOUR LOVE.

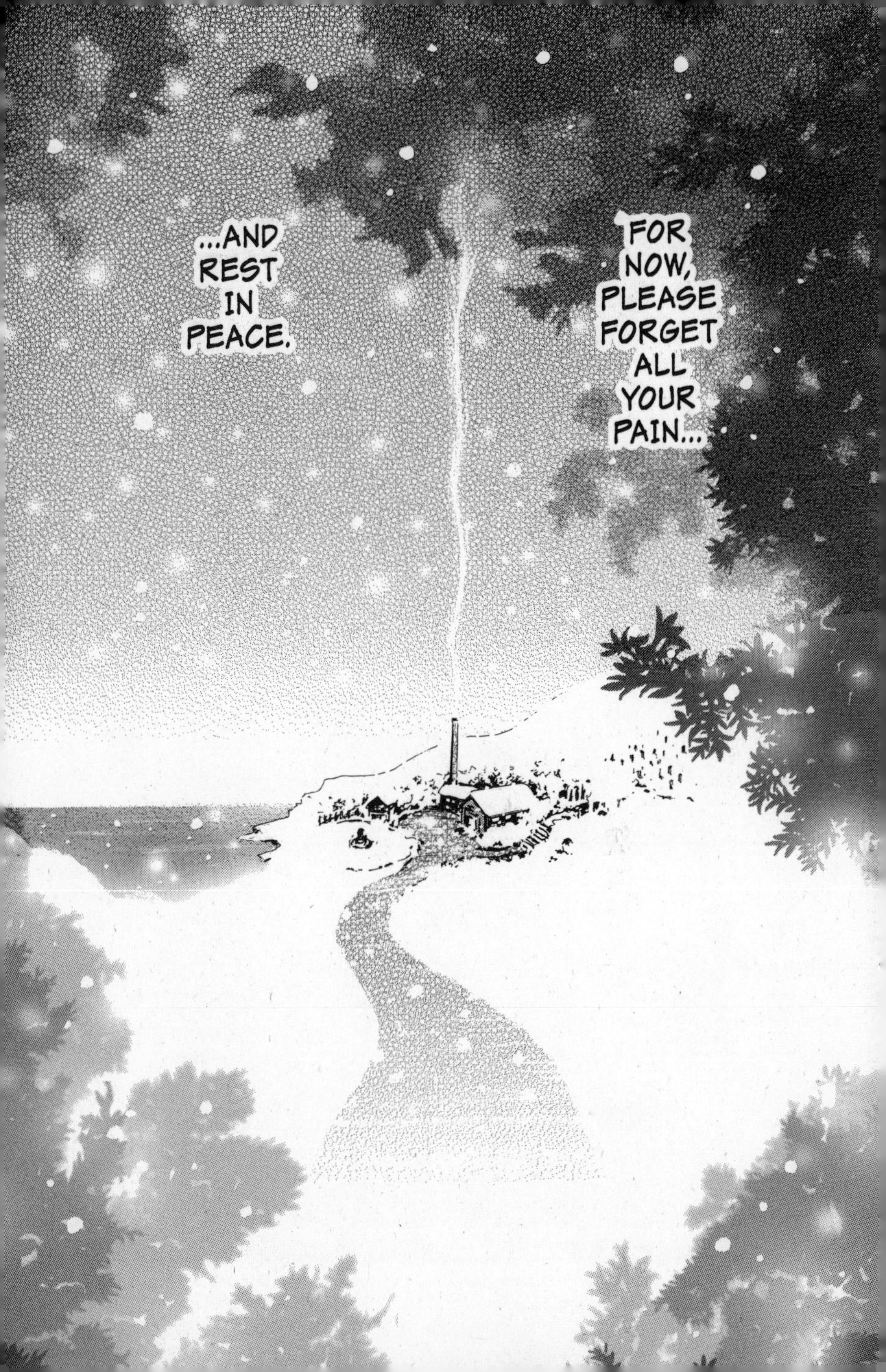
FOR NOW, PLEASE FORGET ALL YOUR PAIN...
...AND REST IN PEACE.

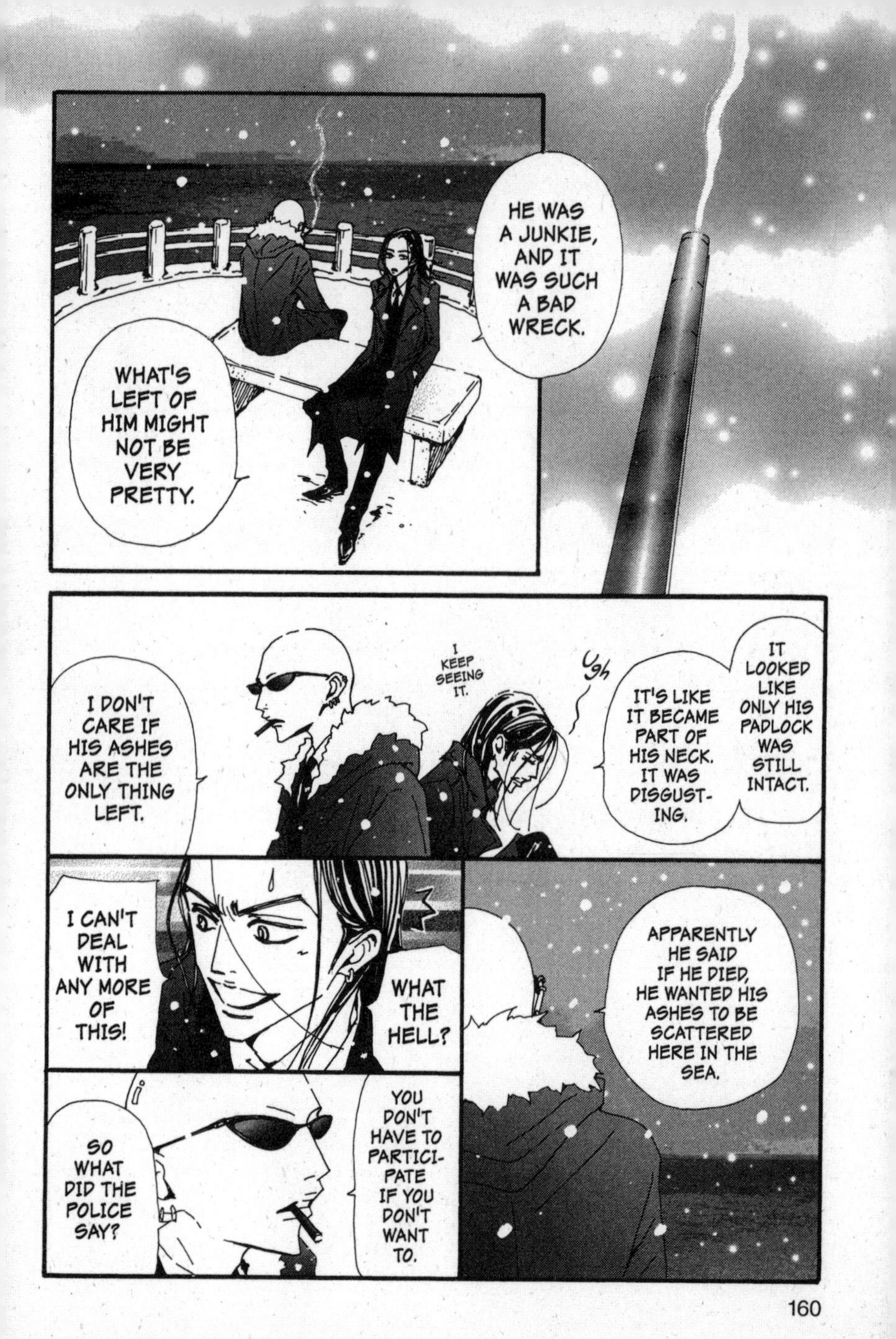
HE WAS A JUNKIE, AND IT WAS SUCH A BAD WRECK.
WHAT'S LEFT OF HIM MIGHT NOT BE VERY PRETTY.
IT LOOKED LIKE ONLY HIS PADLOCK WAS STILL INTACT.
IT'S LIKE IT BECAME PART OF HIS NECK. IT WAS DISGUST-ING.
Ugh
I KEEP SEEING IT.
I DON'T CARE IF HIS ASHES ARE THE ONLY THING LEFT.
APPARENTLY HE SAID IF HE DIED, HE WANTED HIS ASHES TO BE SCATTERED HERE IN THE SEA.
WHAT THE HELL?
I CAN'T DEAL WITH ANY MORE OF THIS!
YOU DON'T HAVE TO PARTICI-PATE IF YOU DON'T WANT TO.
SO WHAT DID THE POLICE SAY?

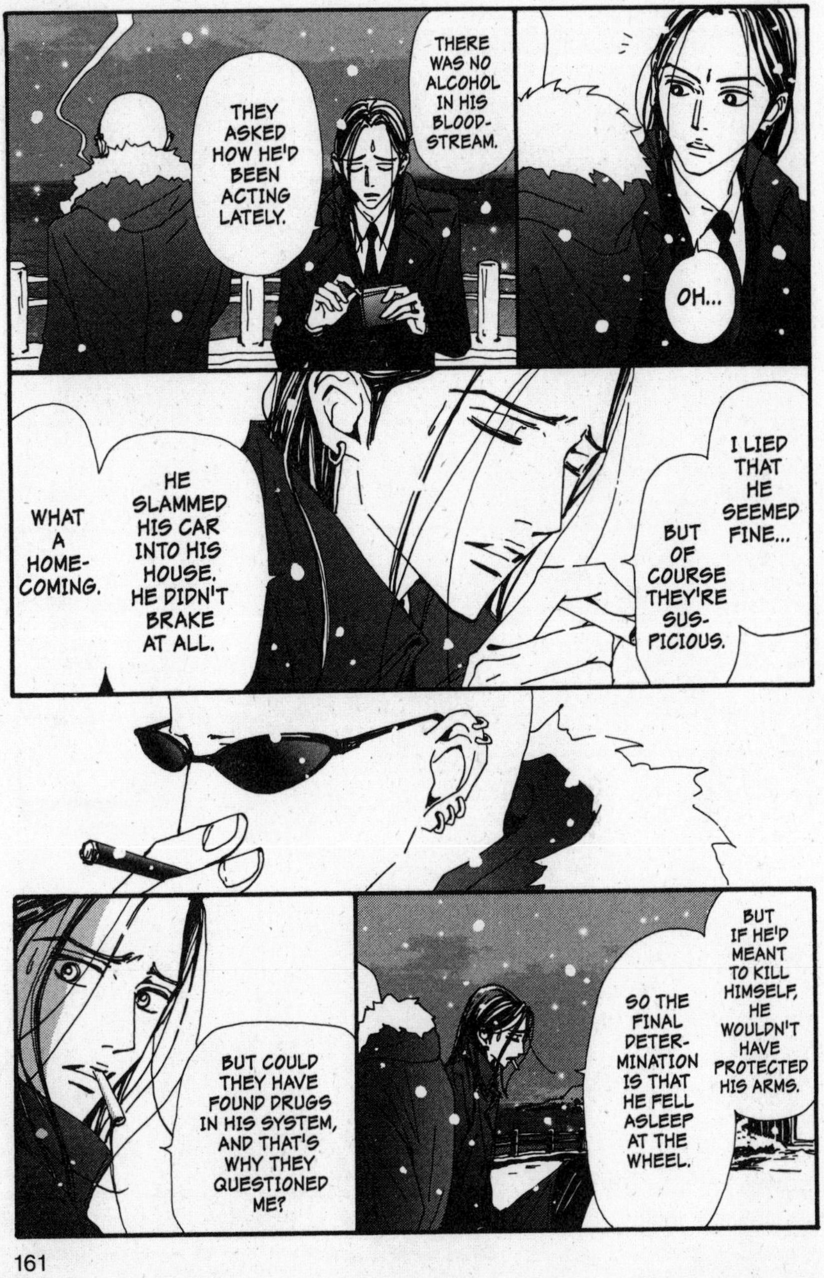
OH...
THERE WAS NO ALCOHOL IN HIS BLOOD-STREAM.
THEY ASKED HOW HE'D BEEN ACTING LATELY.
I LIED THAT HE SEEMED FINE...
BUT OF COURSE THEY'RE SUS-PICIOUS.
HE SLAMMED HIS CAR INTO HIS HOUSE. HE DIDN'T BRAKE AT ALL.
WHAT A HOME-COMING.
BUT IF HE'D MEANT TO KILL HIMSELF, HE WOULDN'T HAVE PROTECTED HIS ARMS.
SO THE FINAL DETER-MINATION IS THAT HE FELL ASLEEP AT THE WHEEL.
BUT COULD THEY HAVE FOUND DRUGS IN HIS SYSTEM, AND THAT'S WHY THEY QUESTIONED ME?

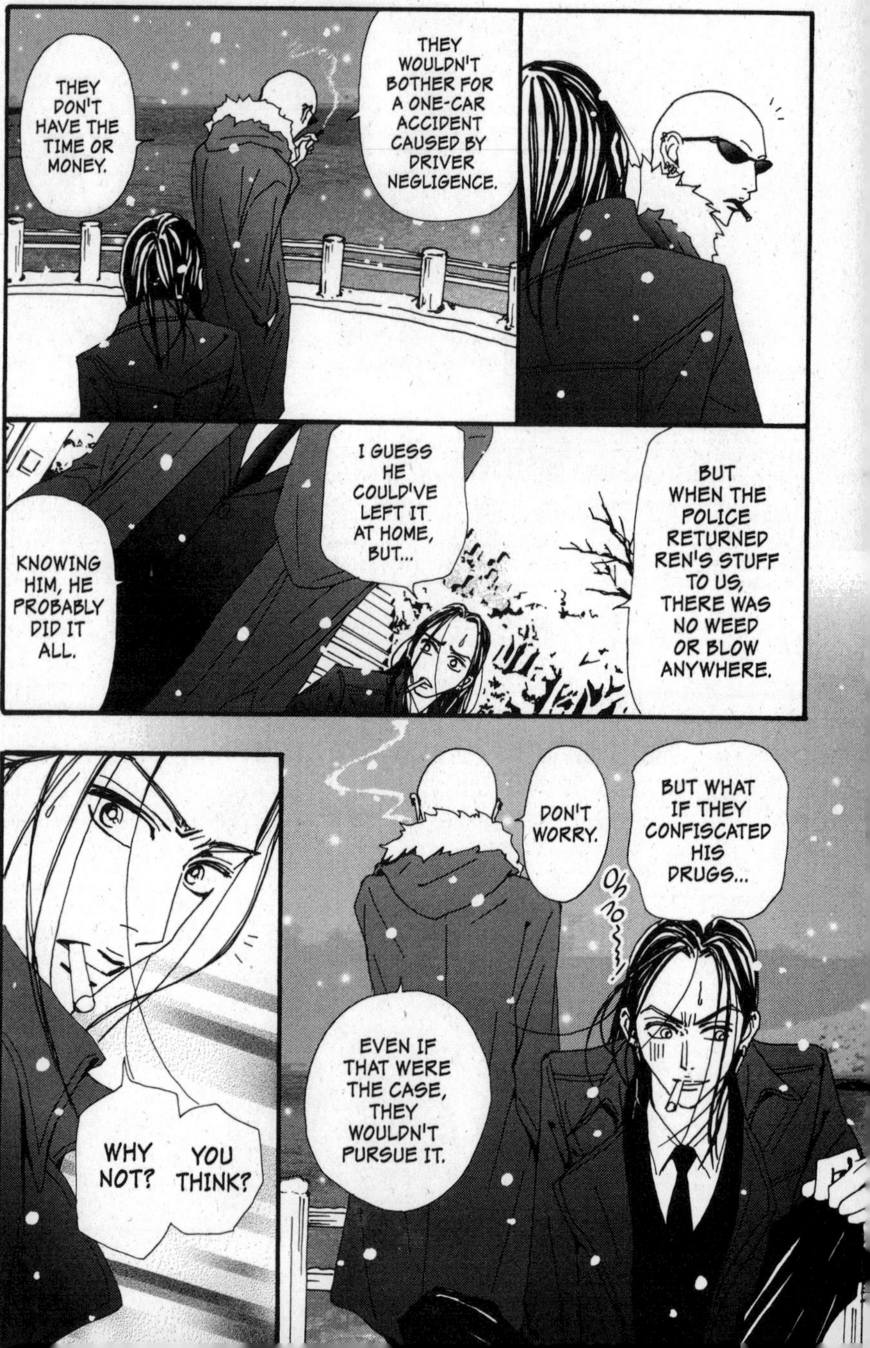
THEY WOULDN'T BOTHER FOR A ONE-CAR ACCIDENT CAUSED BY DRIVER NEGLIGENCE.
THEY DON'T HAVE THE TIME OR MONEY.
BUT WHEN THE POLICE RETURNED REN'S STUFF TO US, THERE WAS NO WEED OR BLOW ANYWHERE.
I GUESS HE COULD'VE LEFT IT AT HOME, BUT...
KNOWING HIM, HE PROBABLY DID IT ALL.
BUT WHAT IF THEY CONFISCATED HIS DRUGS...
OH NO~!
DON'T WORRY.
EVEN IF THAT WERE THE CASE, THEY WOULDN'T PURSUE IT.
YOU THINK?
WHY NOT?

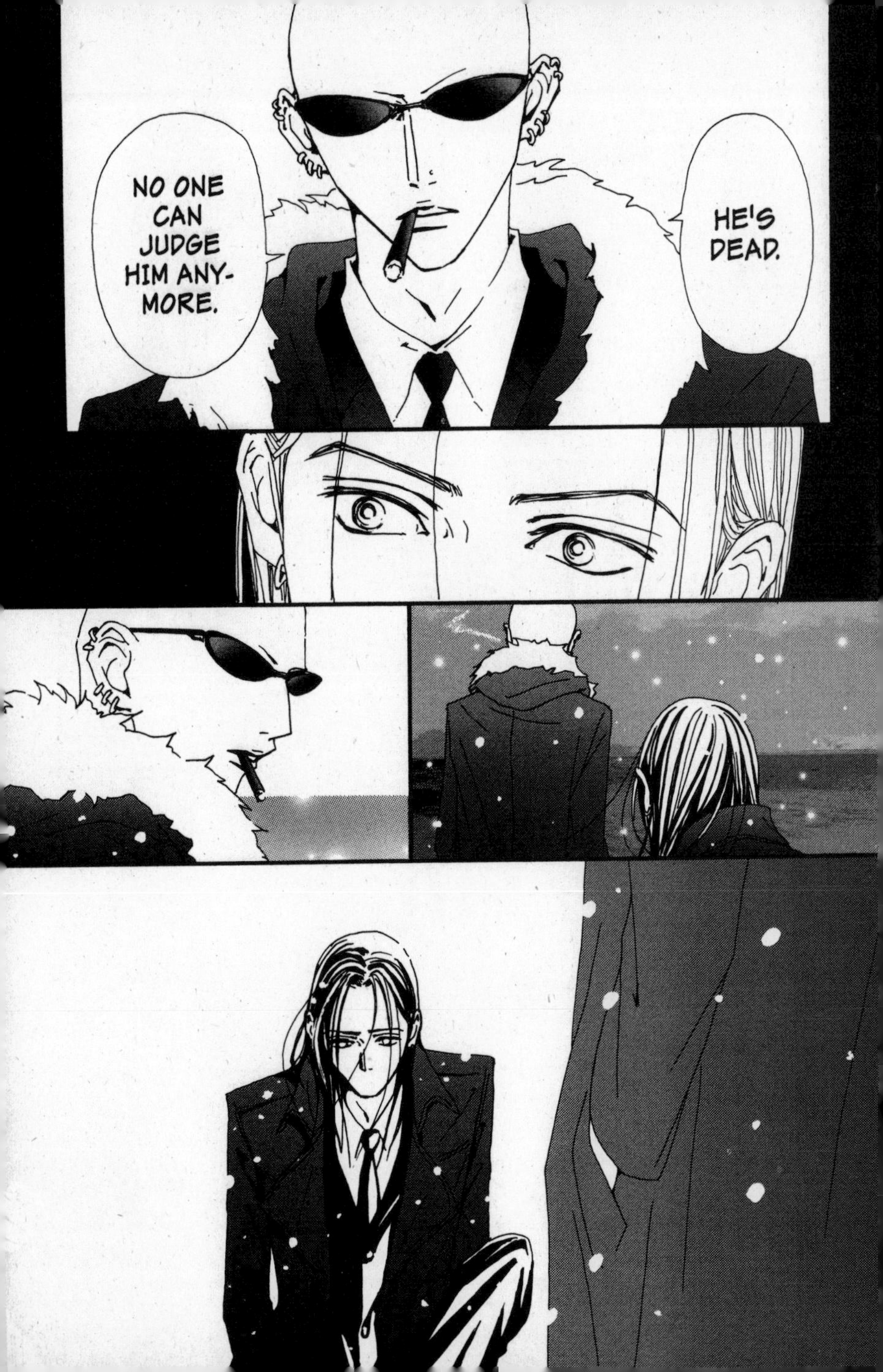
HE'S DEAD.
NO ONE CAN JUDGE HIM ANY-MORE.

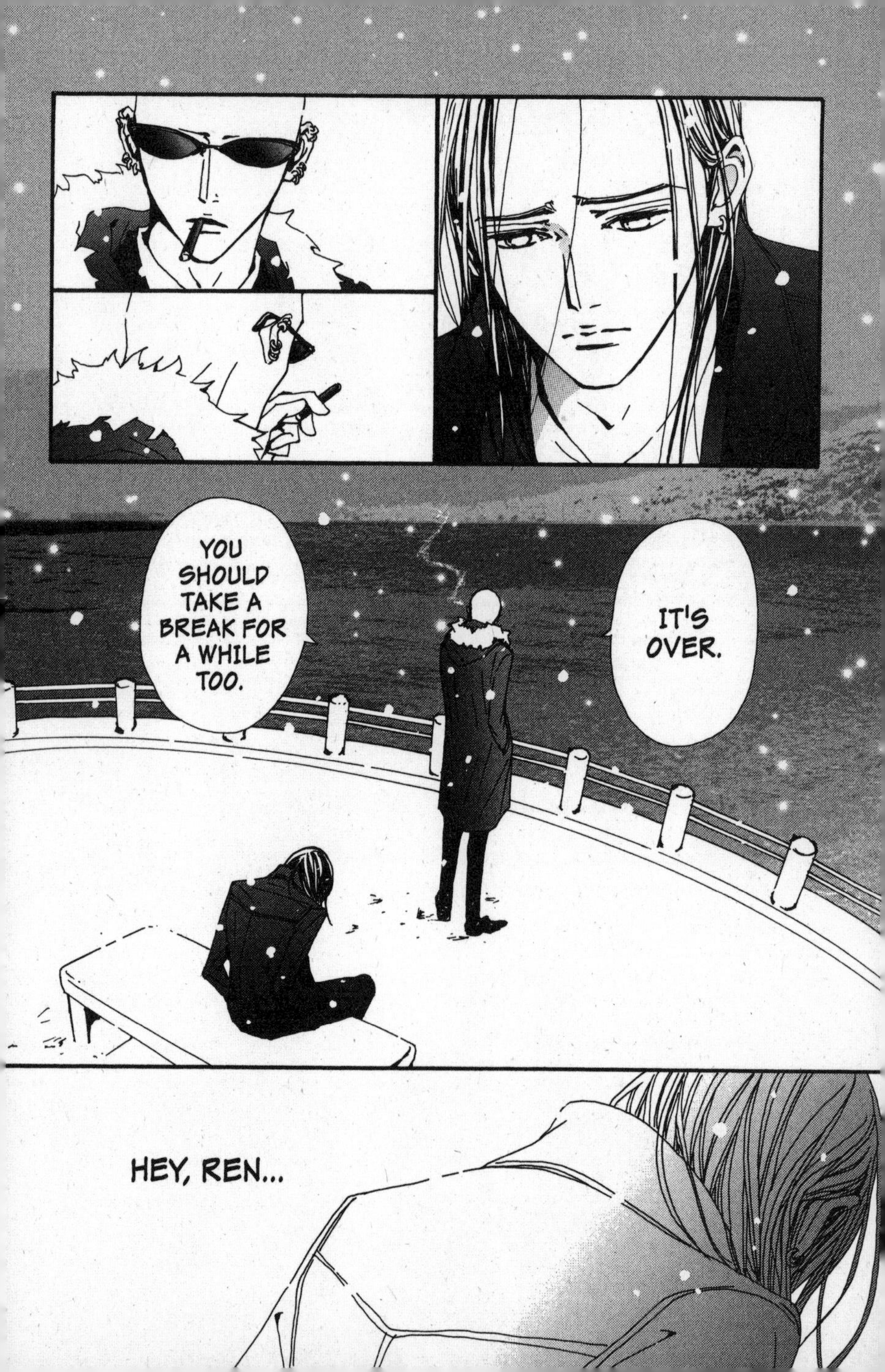
IT'S OVER.
YOU SHOULD TAKE A BREAK FOR A WHILE TOO.
HEY, REN...

AFTER YOU DIED...

...THE FUTURE WE ALL HOPED
FOR WAS WIPED CLEAN.

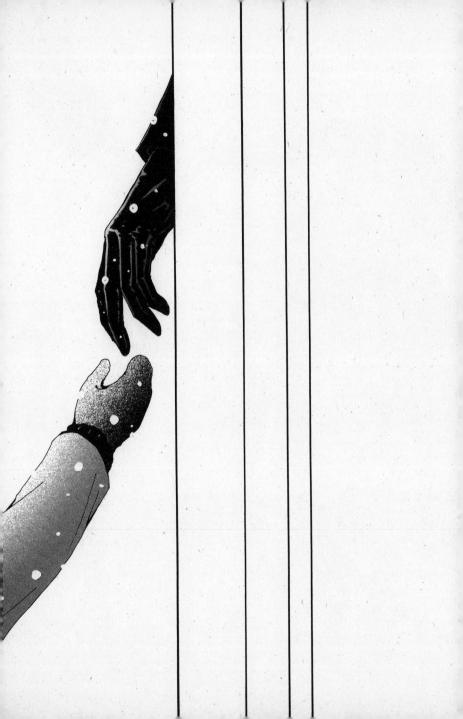

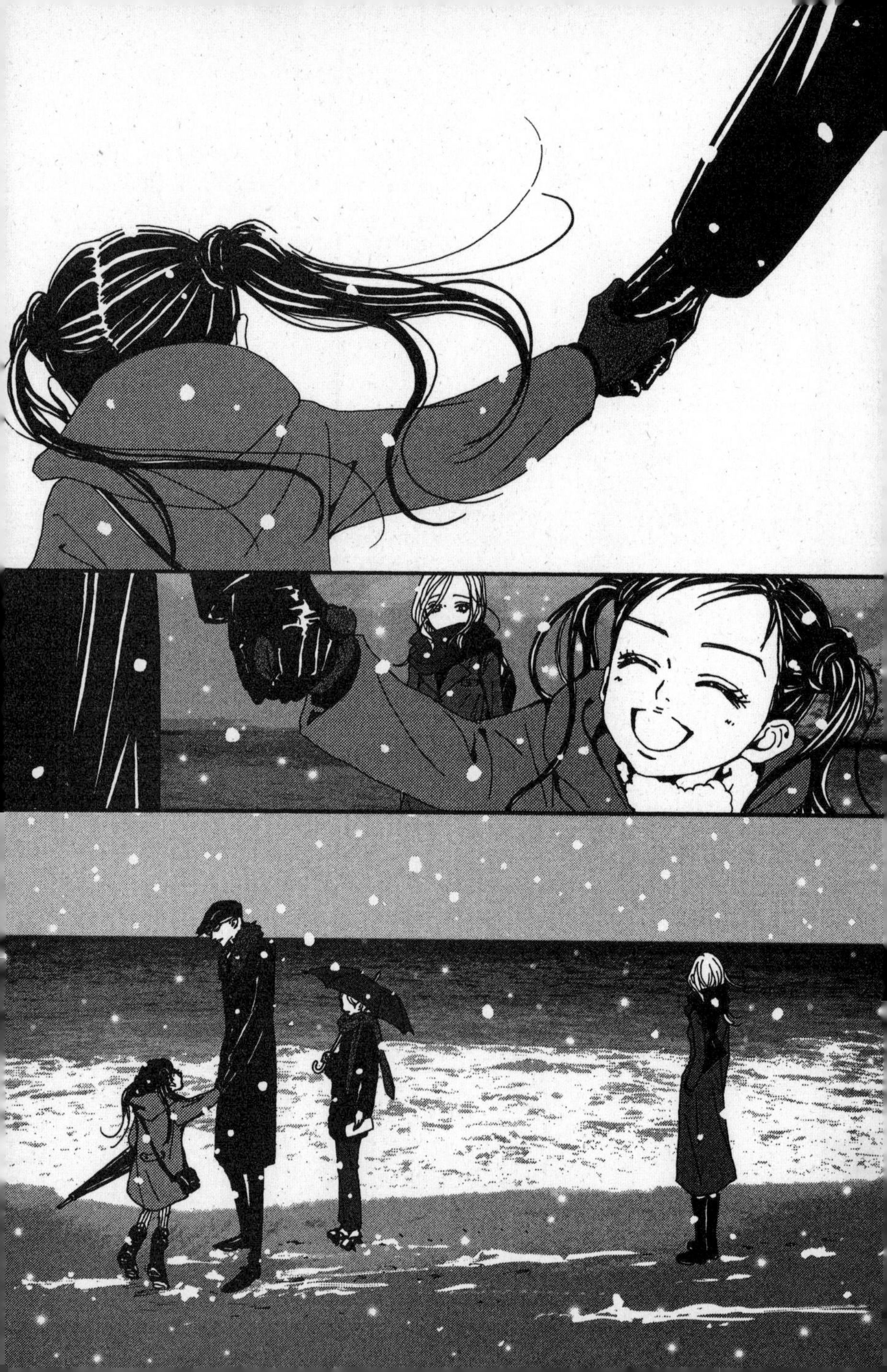

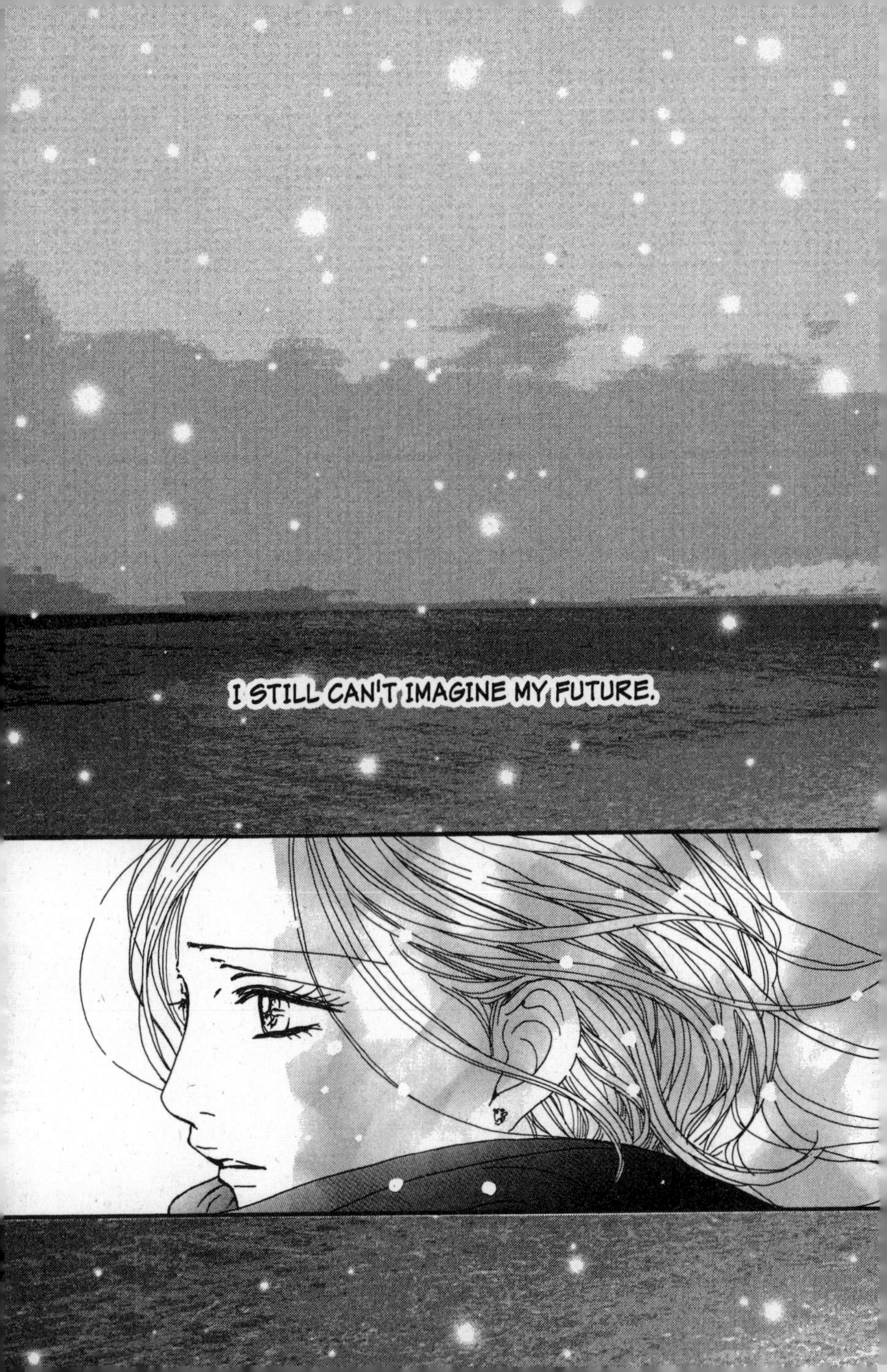
I STILL CAN'T IMAGINE MY FUTURE.

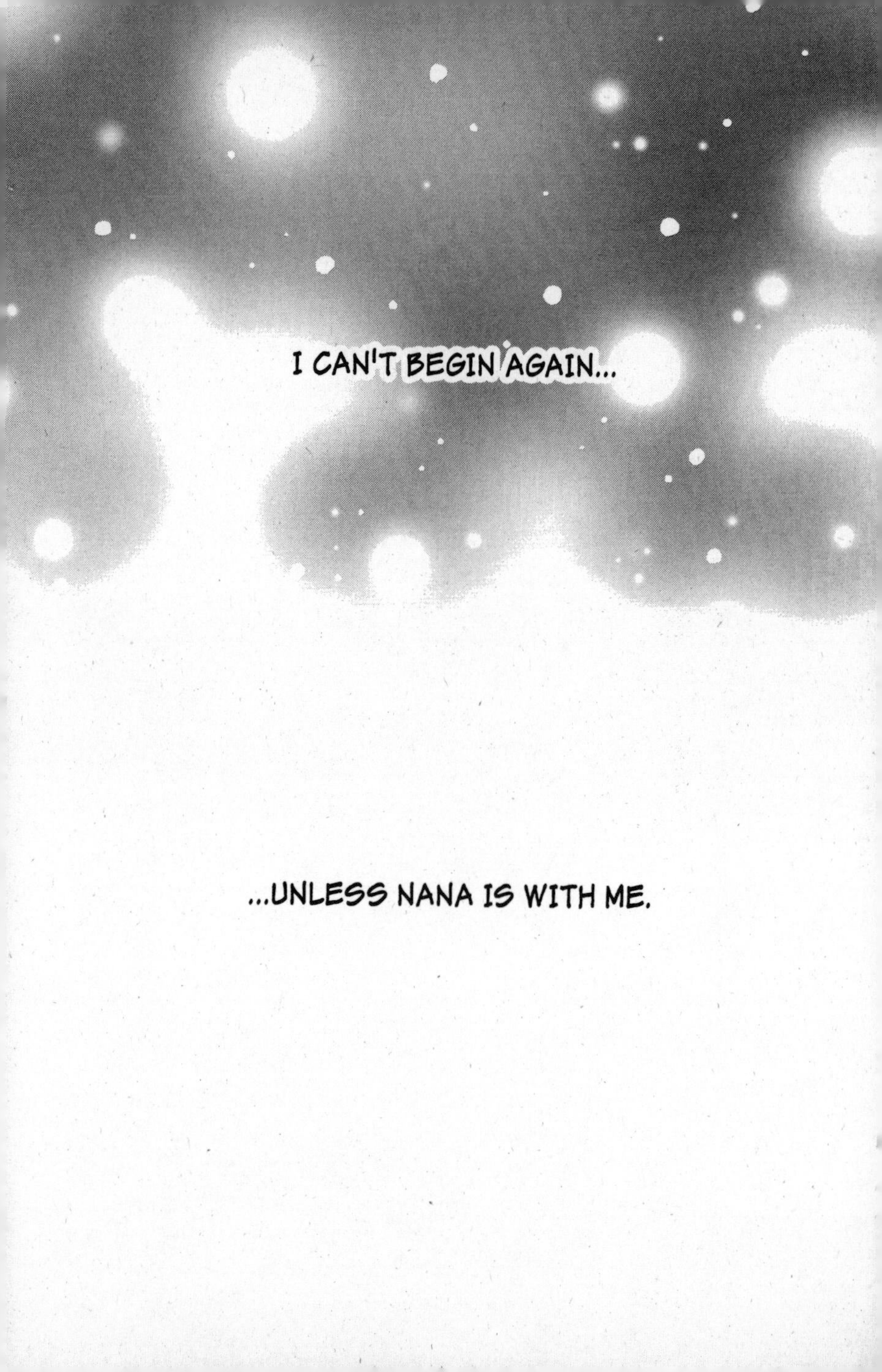
I CAN'T BEGIN AGAIN...
...UNLESS NANA IS WITH ME.

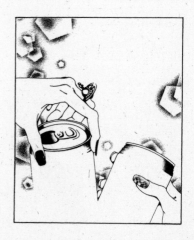

Bonus Page

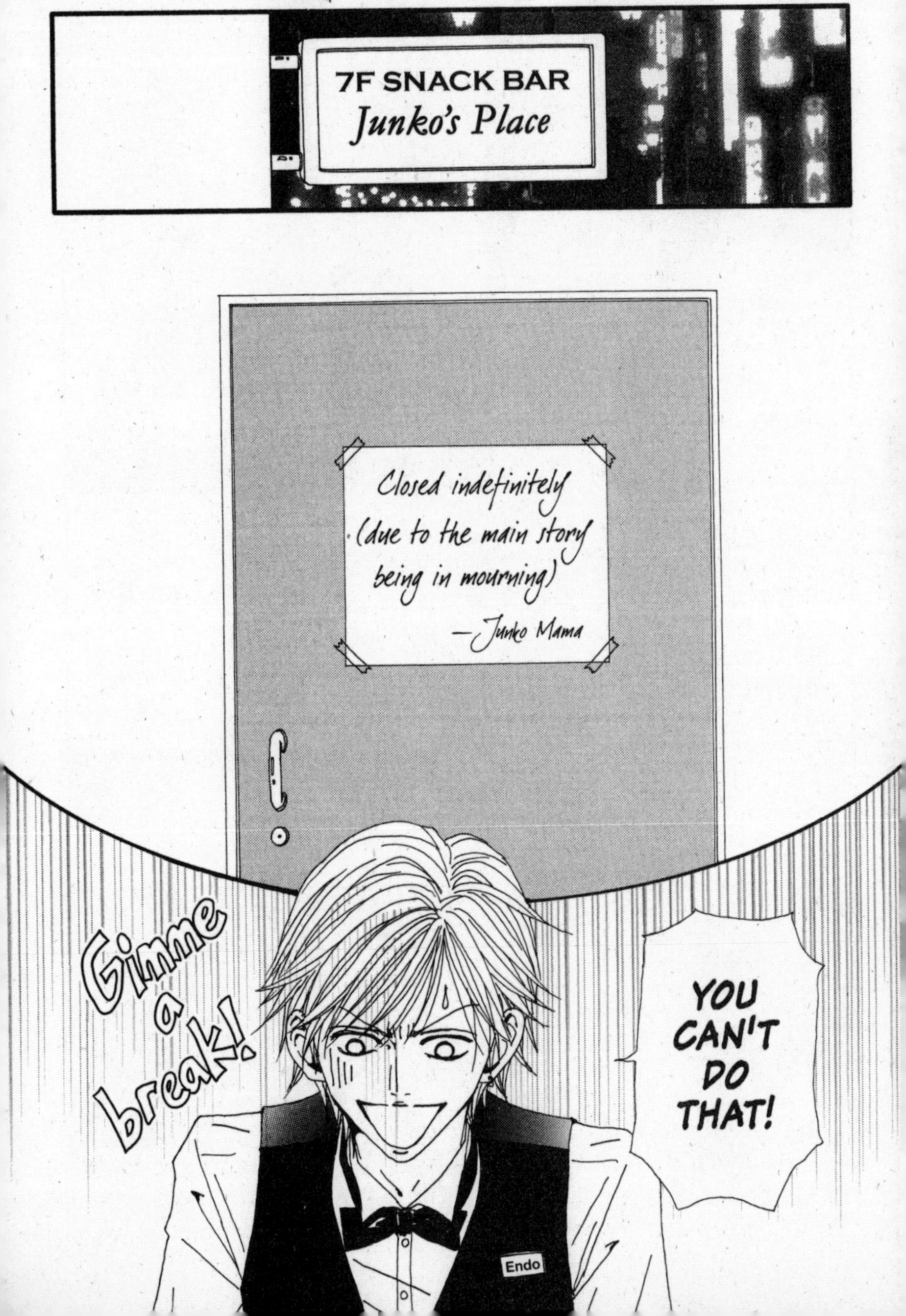
7F SNACK BAR
Junko's Place
Closed indefinitely (due to the main story being in mourning)
—Junko Mama
YOU CAN'T DO THAT!
Gimme a break!
Endo

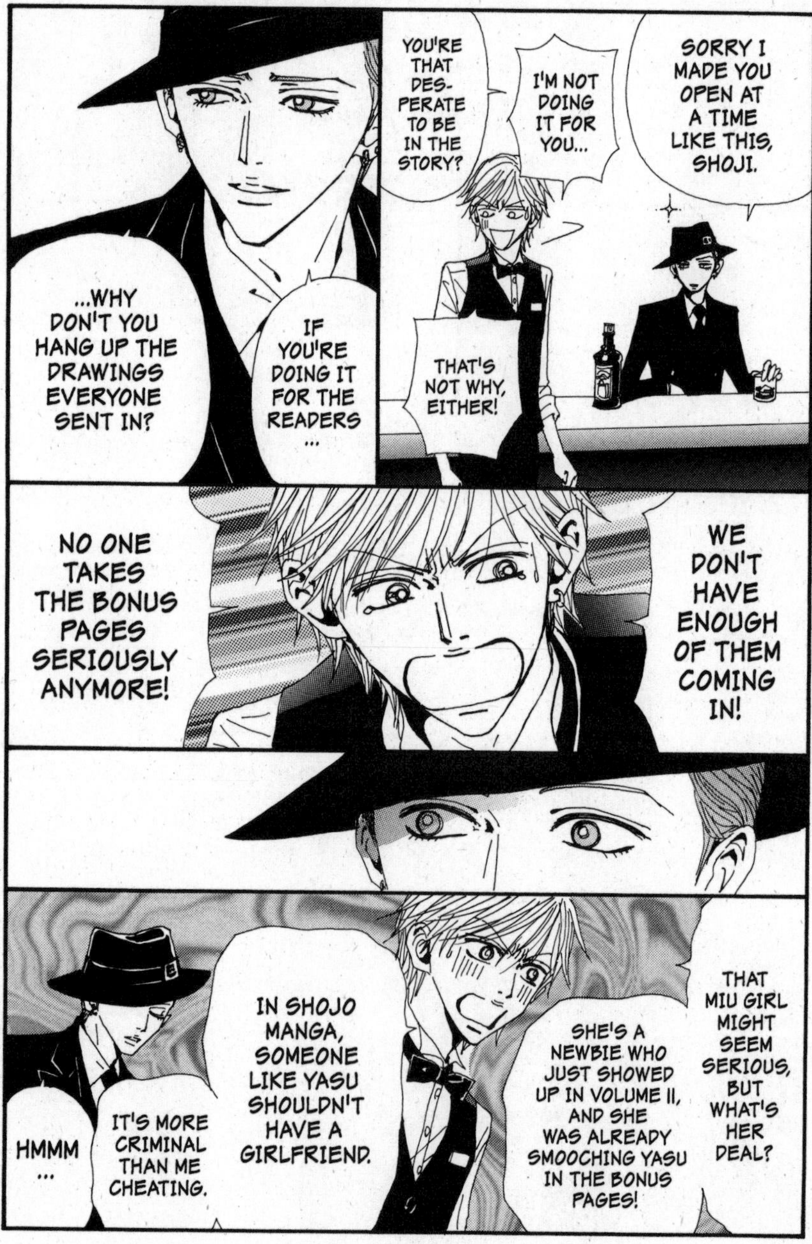
SORRY I MADE YOU OPEN AT A TIME LIKE THIS, SHOJI.
I'M NOT DOING IT FOR YOU...
YOU'RE THAT DES-PERATE TO BE IN THE STORY?
THAT'S NOT WHY, EITHER!
IF YOU'RE DOING IT FOR THE READERS...
...WHY DON'T YOU HANG UP THE DRAWINGS EVERYONE SENT IN?
WE DON'T HAVE ENOUGH OF THEM COMING IN!
NO ONE TAKES THE BONUS PAGES SERIOUSLY ANYMORE!
THAT MIU GIRL MIGHT SEEM SERIOUS, BUT WHAT'S HER DEAL?
SHE'S A NEWBIE WHO JUST SHOWED UP IN VOLUME 11, AND SHE WAS ALREADY SMOOCHING YASU IN THE BONUS PAGES!
IN SHOJO MANGA, SOMEONE LIKE YASU SHOULDN'T HAVE A GIRLFRIEND.
IT'S MORE CRIMINAL THAN ME CHEATING.
HMMM...

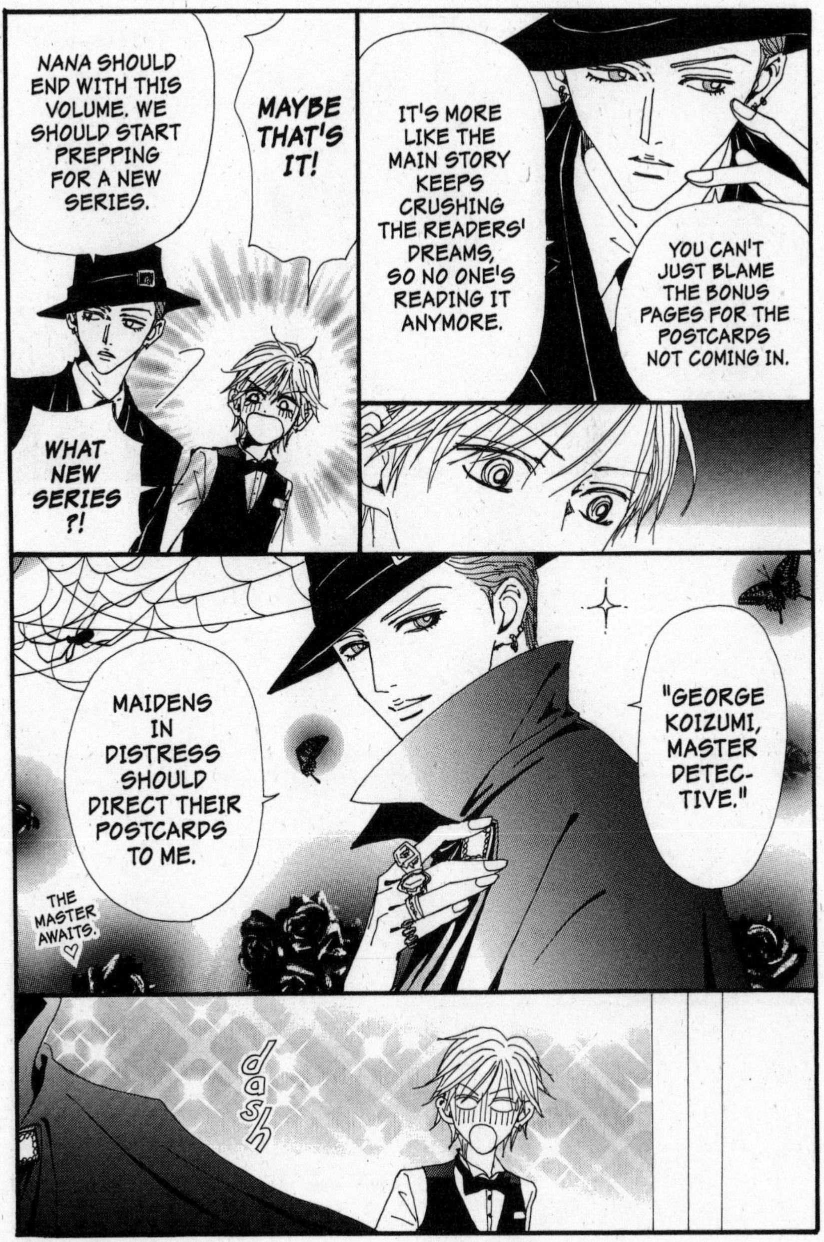
YOU CAN'T JUST BLAME THE BONUS PAGES FOR THE POSTCARDS NOT COMING IN.
IT'S MORE LIKE THE MAIN STORY KEEPS CRUSHING THE READERS' DREAMS, SO NO ONE'S READING IT ANYMORE.
MAYBE THAT'S IT!
NANA SHOULD END WITH THIS VOLUME. WE SHOULD START PREPPING FOR A NEW SERIES.
WHAT NEW SERIES ?!
"GEORGE KOIZUMI, MASTER DETECTIVE."
MAIDENS IN DISTRESS SHOULD DIRECT THEIR POSTCARDS TO ME.
THE MASTER AWAITS. ♡
dash

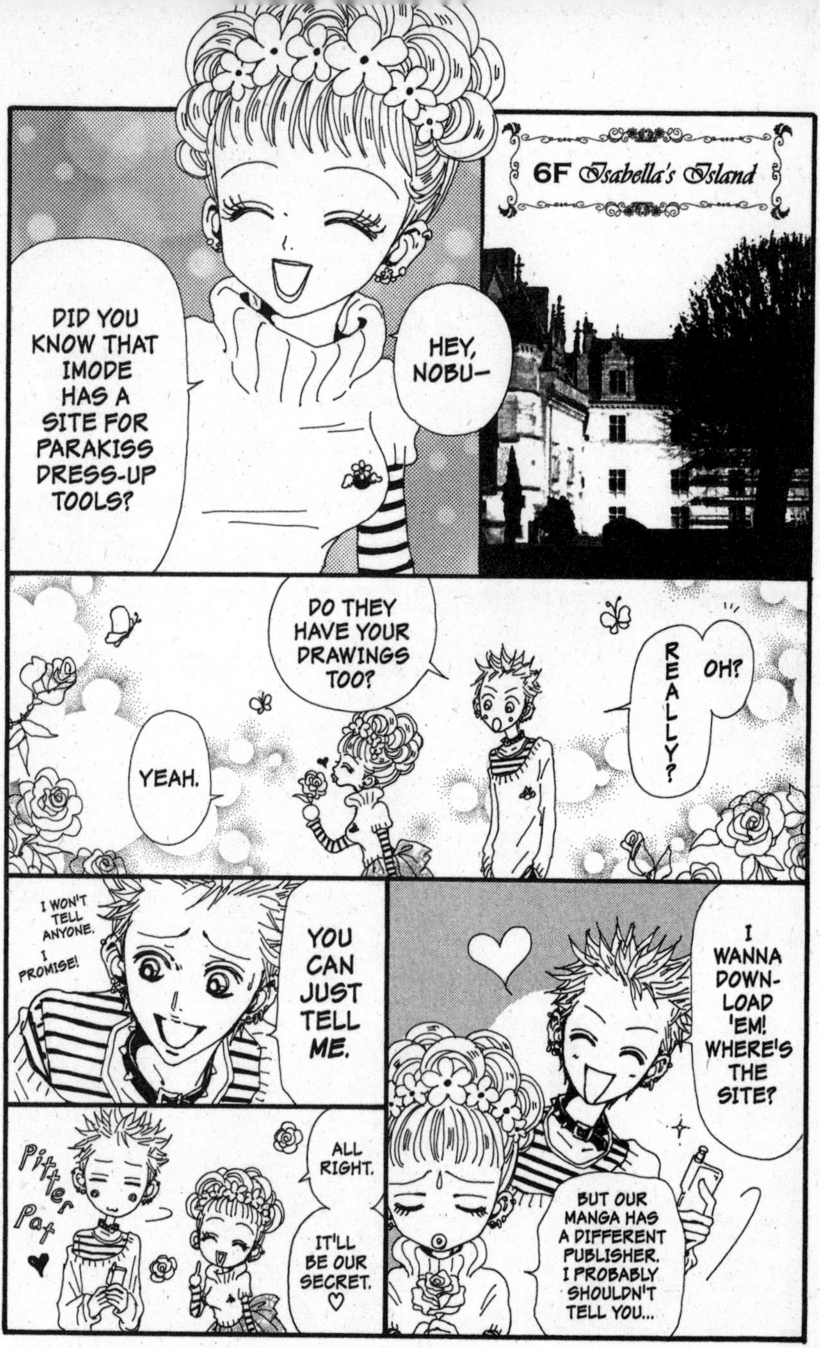
6F Isabella's Island
HEY, NOBU—
DID YOU KNOW THAT IMODE HAS A SITE FOR PARAKISS DRESS-UP TOOLS?
OH? REALLY?
DO THEY HAVE YOUR DRAWINGS TOO?
YEAH.
I WANNA DOWN-LOAD 'EM! WHERE'S THE SITE?
BUT OUR MANGA HAS A DIFFERENT PUBLISHER. I PROBABLY SHOULDN'T TELL YOU...
YOU CAN JUST TELL ME.
I WON'T TELL ANYONE. I PROMISE!
ALL RIGHT.
IT'LL BE OUR SECRET. ♡
Pitter Pat ♥

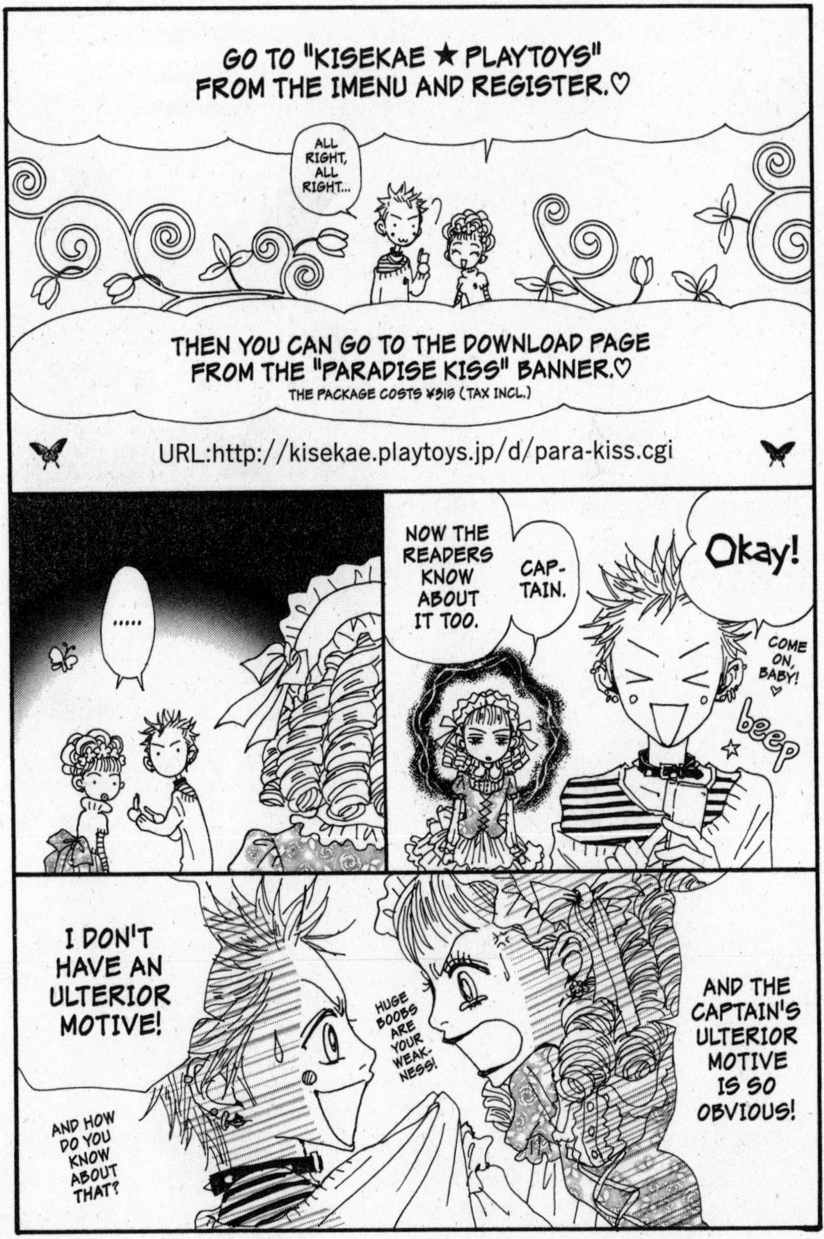
GO TO "KISEKAE ★ PLAYTOYS" FROM THE IMENU AND REGISTER.♡
ALL RIGHT, ALL RIGHT...
THEN YOU CAN GO TO THE DOWNLOAD PAGE FROM THE "PARADISE KISS" BANNER.♡
THE PACKAGE COSTS ¥315 (TAX INCL.)
URL:http://kisekae.playtoys.jp/d/para-kiss.cgi
Okay!
CAP-TAIN.
NOW THE READERS KNOW ABOUT IT TOO.
COME ON, BABY! ♡
beep
......
AND THE CAPTAIN'S ULTERIOR MOTIVE IS SO OBVIOUS!
HUGE BOOBS ARE YOUR WEAK-NESS!
I DON'T HAVE AN ULTERIOR MOTIVE!
AND HOW DO YOU KNOW ABOUT THAT?

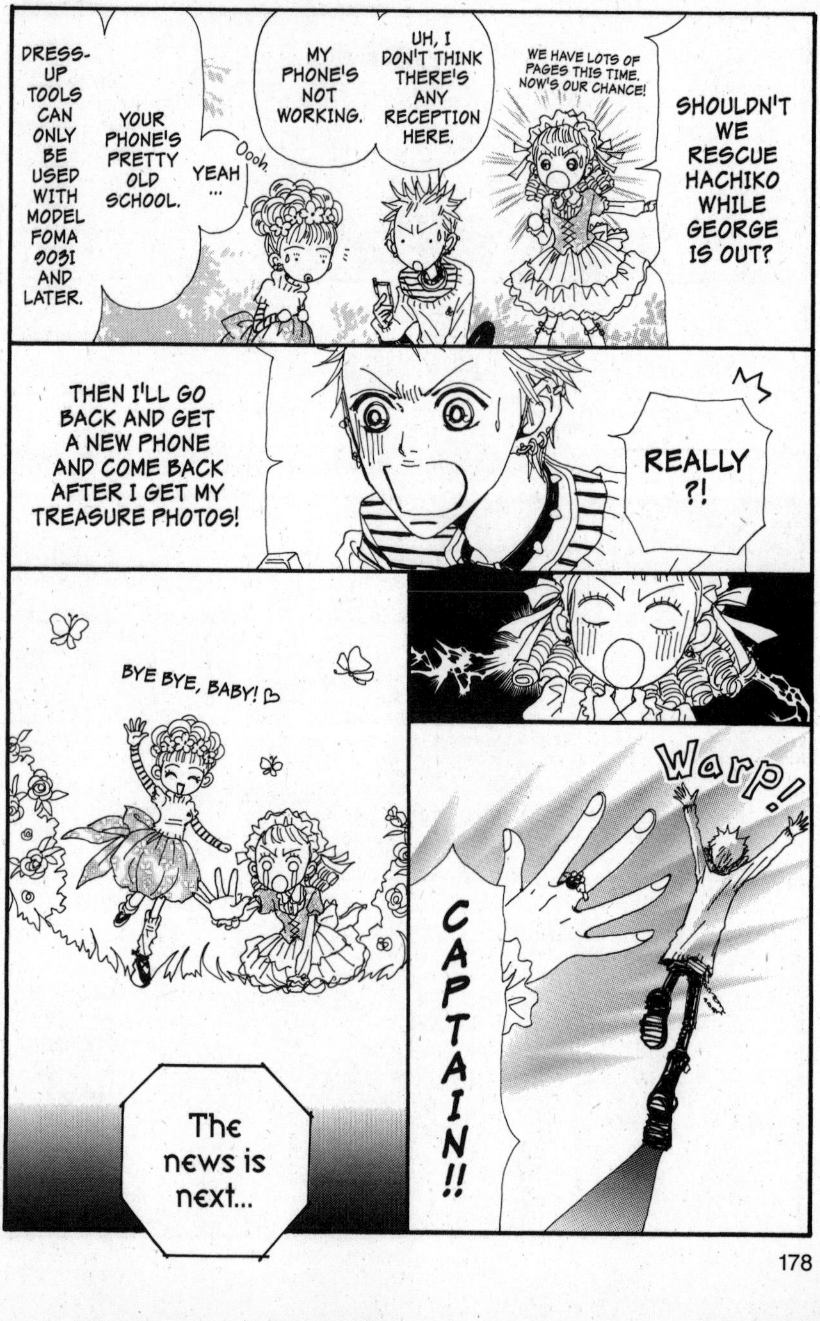
SHOULDN'T WE RESCUE HACHIKO WHILE GEORGE IS OUT?
WE HAVE LOTS OF PAGES THIS TIME. NOW'S OUR CHANCE!
UH, I DON'T THINK THERE'S ANY RECEPTION HERE.
MY PHONE'S NOT WORKING.
Oooh.
YEAH ...
YOUR PHONE'S PRETTY OLD SCHOOL.
DRESS-UP TOOLS CAN ONLY BE USED WITH MODEL FOMA 903I AND LATER.
THEN I'LL GO BACK AND GET A NEW PHONE AND COME BACK AFTER I GET MY TREASURE PHOTOS!
REALLY ?!
Warp!
CAPTAIN!!
BYE BYE, BABY! ♡
The news is next...

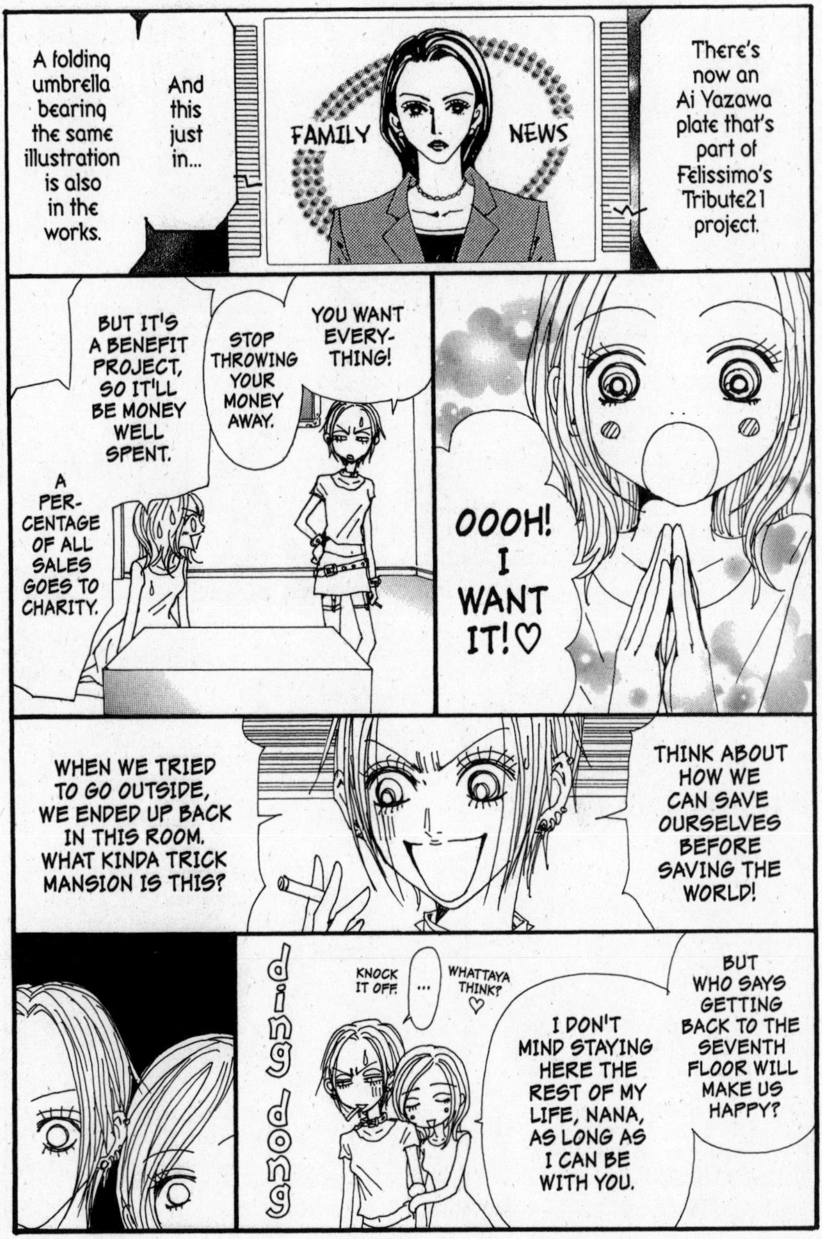
There's now an Ai Yazawa plate that's part of Felissimo's Tribute21 project.
FAMILY NEWS
And this just in...
A folding umbrella bearing the same illustration is also in the works.
OOOH! I WANT IT!♡
YOU WANT EVERY-THING!
STOP THROWING YOUR MONEY AWAY.
BUT IT'S A BENEFIT PROJECT, SO IT'LL BE MONEY WELL SPENT.
A PER-CENTAGE OF ALL SALES GOES TO CHARITY.
THINK ABOUT HOW WE CAN SAVE OURSELVES BEFORE SAVING THE WORLD!
WHEN WE TRIED TO GO OUTSIDE, WE ENDED UP BACK IN THIS ROOM. WHAT KINDA TRICK MANSION IS THIS?
BUT WHO SAYS GETTING BACK TO THE SEVENTH FLOOR WILL MAKE US HAPPY?
WHATTAYA THINK? ♡
...
KNOCK IT OFF.
I DON'T MIND STAYING HERE THE REST OF MY LIFE, NANA, AS LONG AS I CAN BE WITH YOU.
ding dong

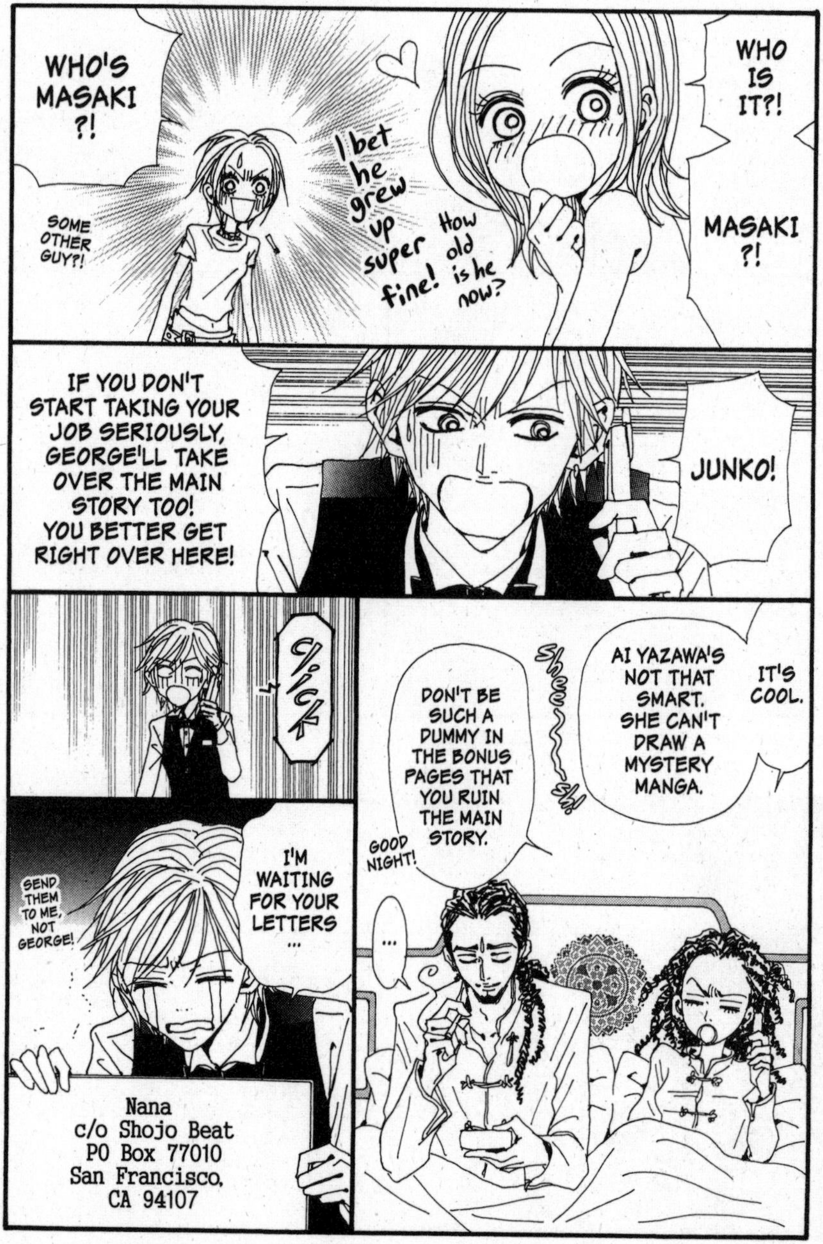
WHO IS IT?!
MASAKI?!
How old is he now?
I bet he grew up super fine!
WHO'S MASAKI?!
SOME OTHER GUY?!
JUNKO!
IF YOU DON'T START TAKING YOUR JOB SERIOUSLY, GEORGE'LL TAKE OVER THE MAIN STORY TOO! YOU BETTER GET RIGHT OVER HERE!
IT'S COOL.
AI YAZAWA'S NOT THAT SMART. SHE CAN'T DRAW A MYSTERY MANGA.
Sheesh
DON'T BE SUCH A DUMMY IN THE BONUS PAGES THAT YOU RUIN THE MAIN STORY.
GOOD NIGHT!
...
Click
I'M WAITING FOR YOUR LETTERS ...
SEND THEM TO ME, NOT GEORGE!
Nana
c/o Shojo Beat
PO Box 77010
San Francisco,
CA 94107

☆ DON'T FORGET SHOJI! LET'S HOPE THE BAR'LL BE OPEN IN VOLUME 22 TOO!

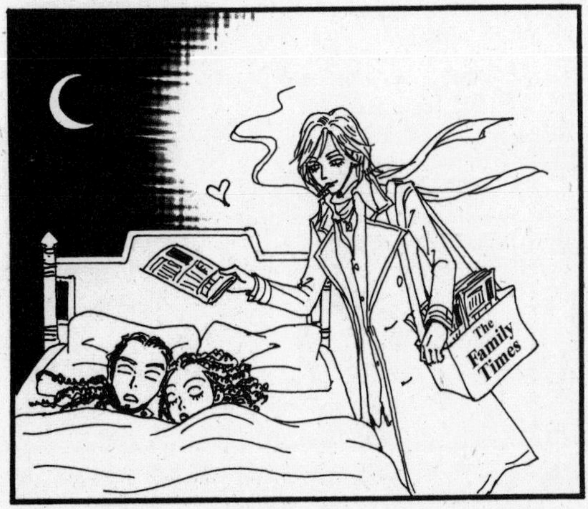
The Family Times

The Family Times

Mar. 13, 2009

NANA 21 & the May Issue of *Cookie* Joint Project!!

(Hits stands March 26, 2009)

Special Primography Present♡

To enter, you need coupons from both *NANA* 21 and the May issue of *Cookie*. For details, see the May issue♥... Now you gotta buy *Cookie*!

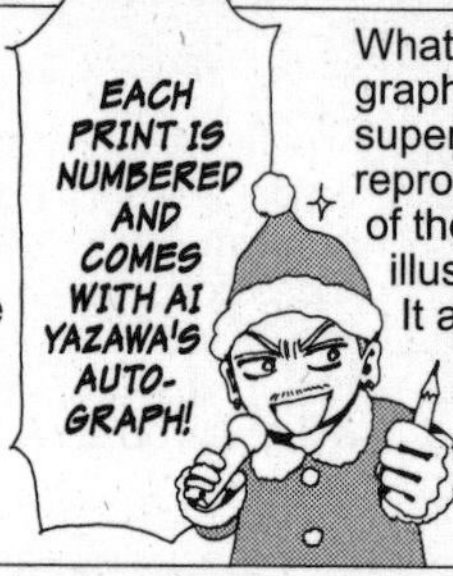
EACH PRINT IS NUMBERED AND COMES WITH AI YAZAWA'S AUTO-GRAPH!
Heh heh♥

What's primography? It's a super-fine reproduction of the original illustration. It almost looks like the original! And this time...

Ⓐ Nana + Hachi Ⓑ Nana + Ren Ⓒ Nana

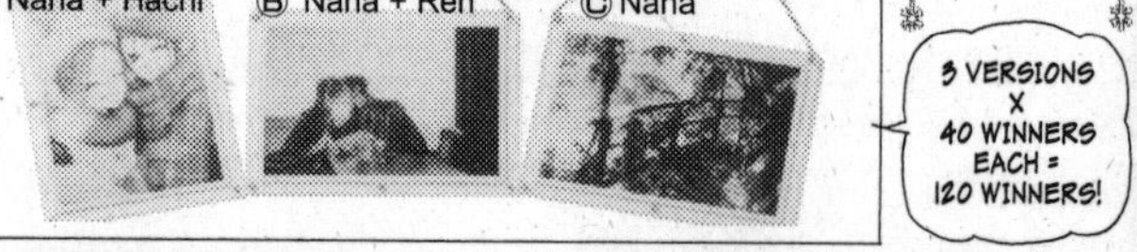
3 VERSIONS X 40 WINNERS EACH = 120 WINNERS!

Shueisha Shopping Plaza

mekke!

http://mekke.shueisha.co.jp

NANA stuff still on sale!

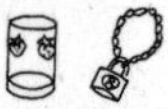

Official Website

NANA Online

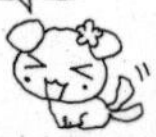
CHECK THIS SITE FOR ALL THE LATEST!

http://www.s-nana.com/

Ai Yazawa Designer Plate in Felissimo's "Tribute21" LOVE PLATES!!

Felissimo's "Tribute21" is a charity project to make the dreams of children all over the world come true. Now there's a plate featuring an Ai Yazawa illustration. The concept is "PandA (Philosophy & Action)," and the plate is really cute♡. Get several and use them every day! Yes, ma'am!

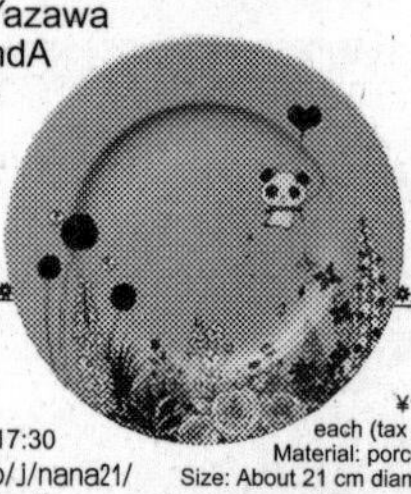

■ Contact:
Tel: 0120-055-820 or
Kobe 078-791-8635
■ Hours:
Weekdays (Mon-Fri) 9:30-17:30
http://www.felissimo.co.jp/j/nana21/

¥1500 each (tax incl.)
Material: porcelain
Size: About 21 cm diameter

"Have You Seen Me?"

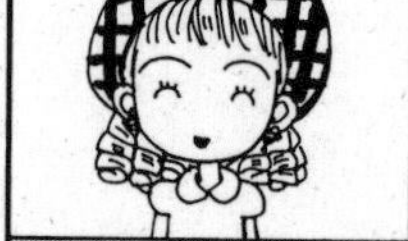

Misato Uehara (alias)

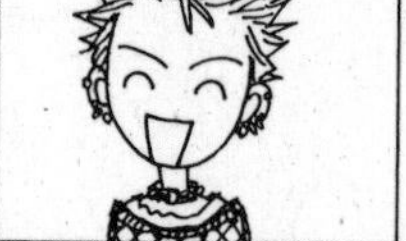

Nobuo Terashima

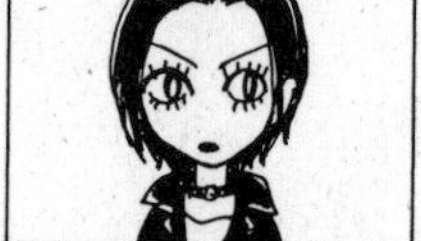

Nana Osaki

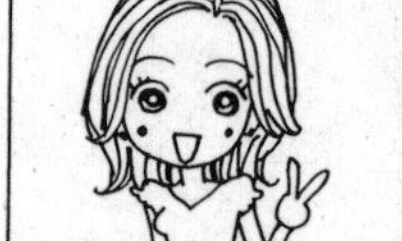

Nana Komatsu

The Family Times Mar. 13, 2009

Mobile *NANA* book

~ A Happy Collaboration between *NANA* and cell phones! ~

Mobile *NANA* started in March 2005. These extremely popular features have been squeezed into this book.♥

The cover features a new illustration by Ai Yazawa!
What—even Ginpei's weight?!
With the latest complete character profiles!
Includes lots of limited(?) edition standby displays!
Special Gallery
SHIN
Readers' choice: Great Scenes & Great Lines!
Popularity poll results!
How many questions can you answer?
Quiz *NANA* exam
The author answers the readers' questions!
"Ai Yazawa Answers, extended version"
NOBU

Both mobile *NANA* members and non-members can get this book! It also contains stickers of popular standby displays! Keep it on hand along with Fanbook 7.8!

★ Released to Critical Acclaim! ★

¥780 (tax incl.)

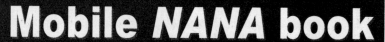

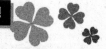

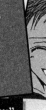

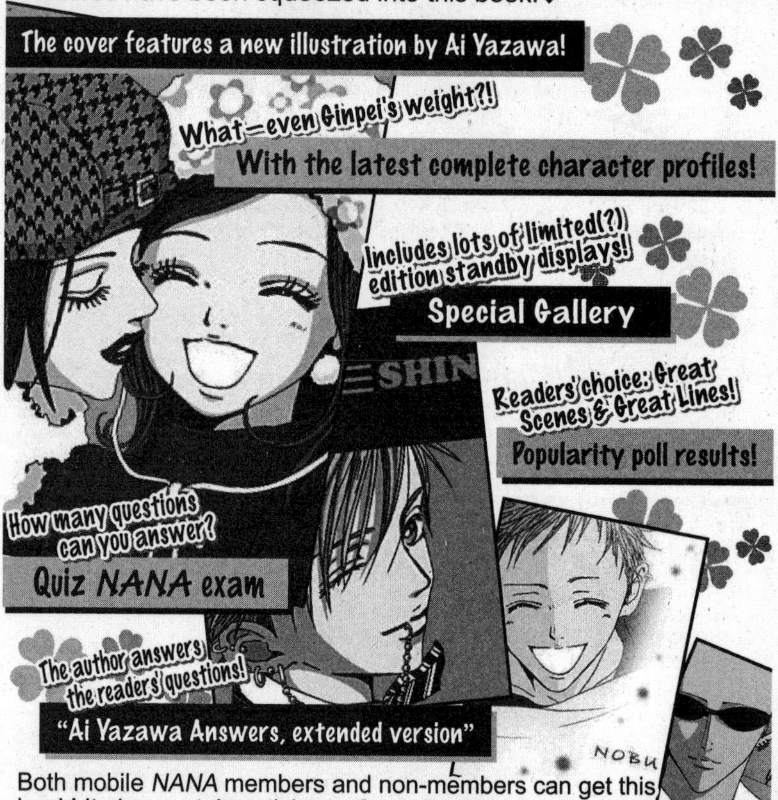

The Family Times Mar. 13, 2009

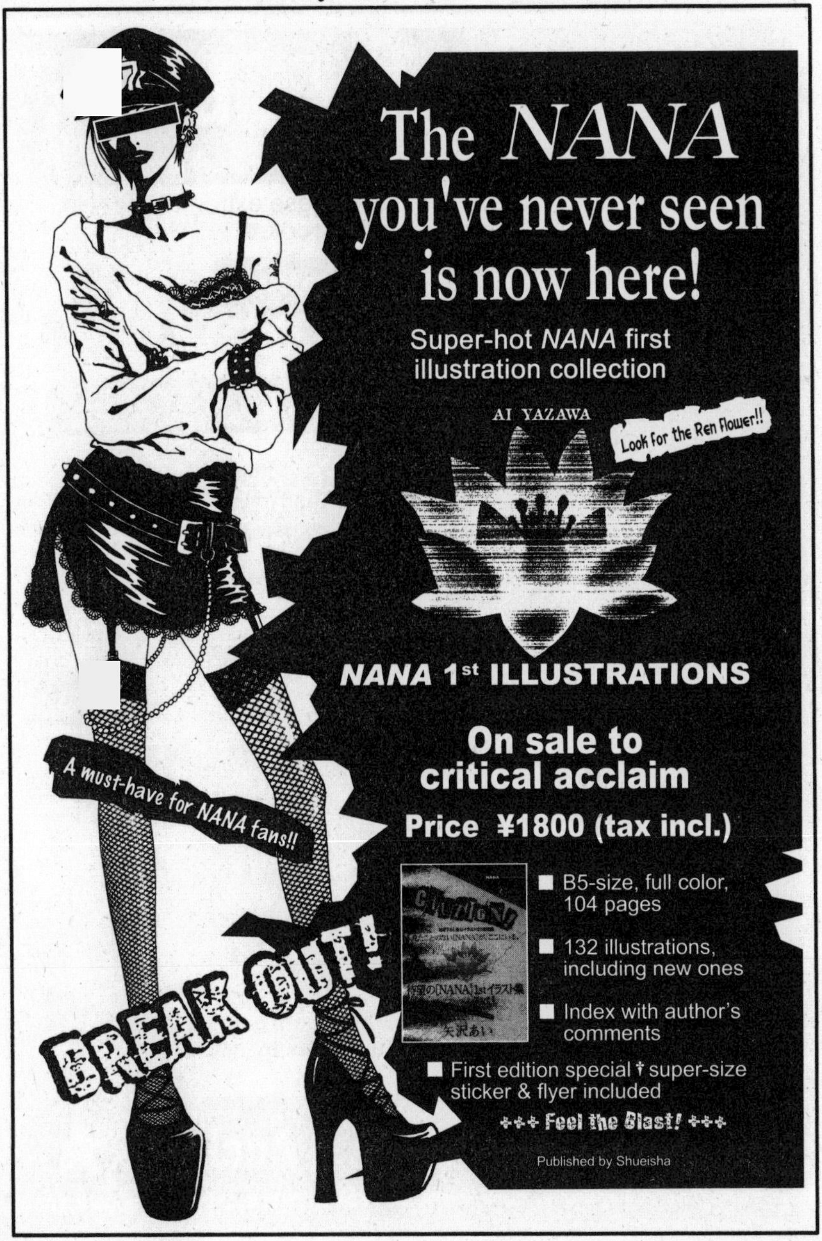
The NANA you've never seen is now here!
Super-hot NANA first illustration collection
AI YAZAWA
Look for the Ren Flower!!
NANA 1st ILLUSTRATIONS
On sale to critical acclaim
Price ¥1800 (tax incl.)
B5-size, full color, 104 pages
132 illustrations, including new ones
Index with author's comments
First edition special † super-size sticker & flyer included
+++ Feel the Blast! +++
Published by Shueisha
A must-have for NANA fans!!
BREAK OUT!

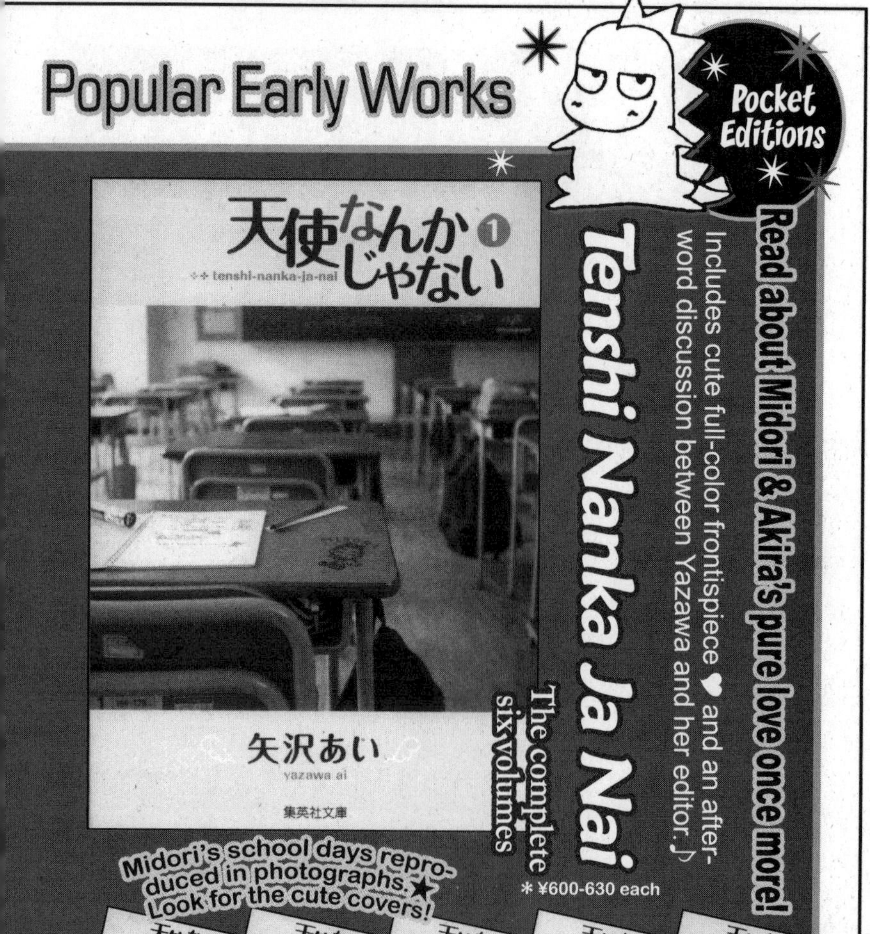
Popular Early Works
Pocket Editions
Read about Midori & Akira's pure love once more!
Tenshi Nanka Ja Nai
Includes cute full-color frontispiece ♥ and an after-word discussion between Yazawa and her editor.♪
The complete six volumes
* ¥600-630 each
天使なんかじゃない 1
tenshi-nanka-ja-nai
矢沢あい
yazawa ai
集英社文庫
Midori's school days reproduced in photographs.★ Look for the cute covers!

The Family Times Mar. 13, 2009

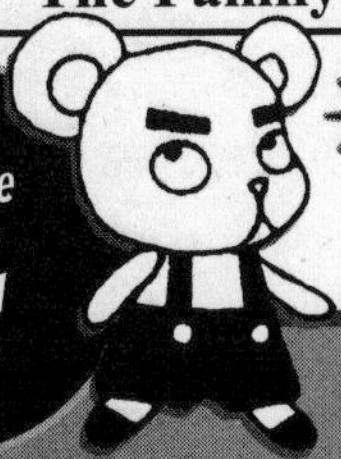

The Complete Edition Special Edition

Ai Yazawa's

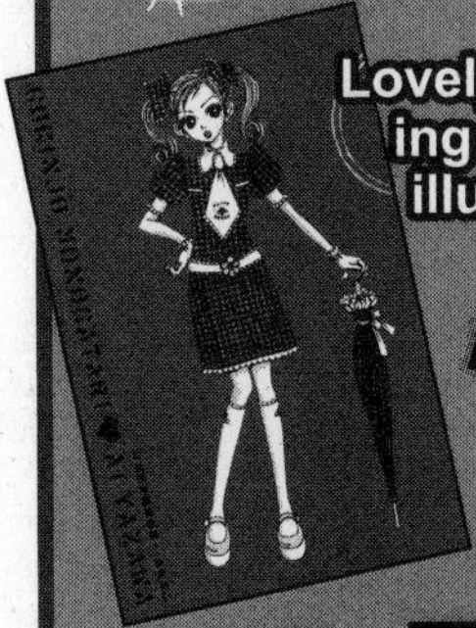

GOKINJO MONOGATARI ♥ AI YAZAWA

Lovely new binding & full-color illustrations★

Gokinjo Monogatari

The Complete Edition of four volumes

＊¥1260 each

A must-have for fans. Super-gorgeous, keep-forever version!

Kagen no Tsuki *Last Quarter*

Special Edition

Two volumes

＊¥1200 each

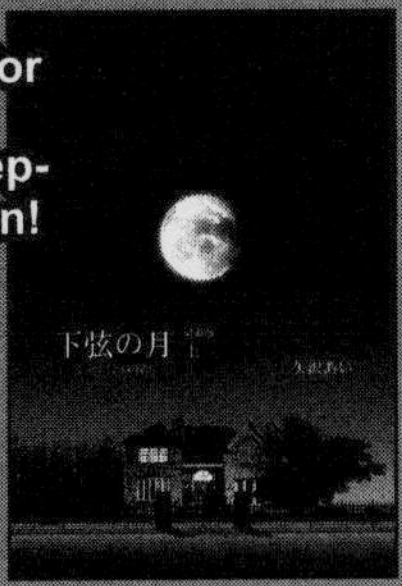

下弦の月

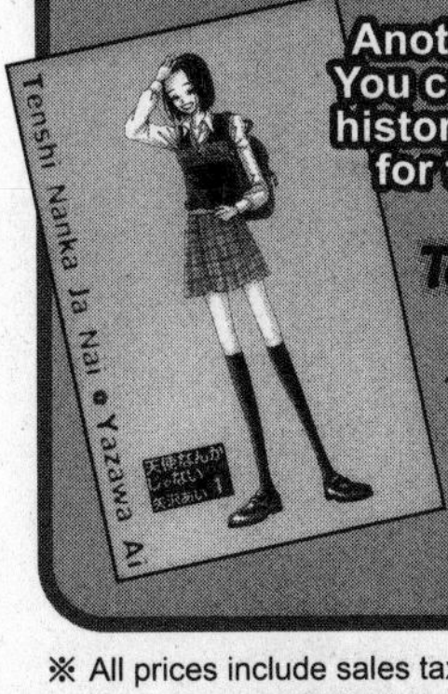

Tenshi Nanka Ja Nai ● Yazawa Ai

Another “Tennai!” You can read secret histories drawn just for this version!

Tenshi Nanka Ja Nai

The Complete Edition

Four volumes

＊¥1260 each

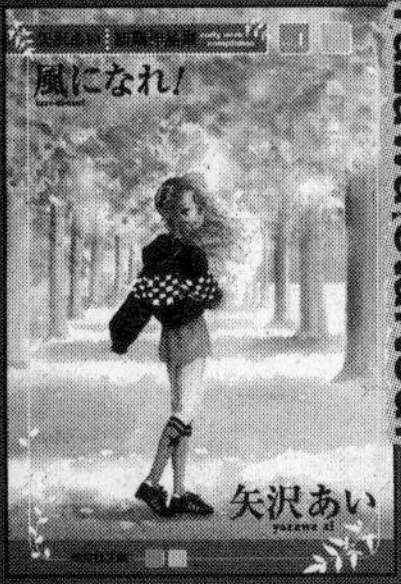

風になれ!
矢沢あい

This is where Ai Yazawa started!

Ai Yazawa's Early Works

vol.1 *Kaze ni Nare!*

vol.2 *Ballad Made Sobani Ite*

vol.3 *Usubeni no Arashi / Escape*

＊¥630 each

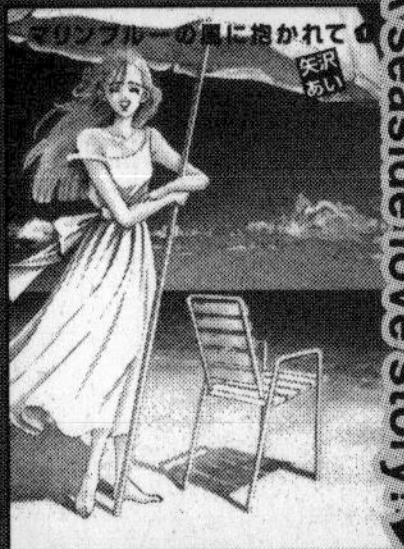

マリンブルーの風に抱かれて
矢沢あい

Makes your heart flutter! A seaside love story!♥

Marine Blue no Kaze ni Dakarete

The complete three volumes ＊¥590 each

※ All prices include sales tax.

☆ All products listed in this newspaper really exist. Please don't be afraid to buy them!

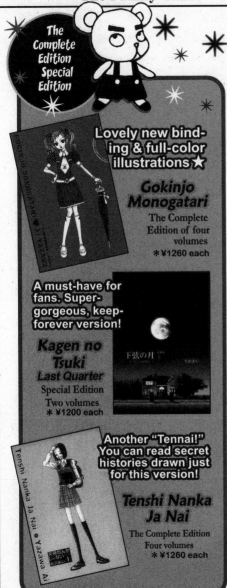

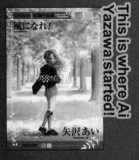

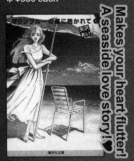

Hello, Yazawa here. With this volume, no matter what scene I was drawing, I was heartbroken. I had a hard time, and it took me longer than usual to draw. So it was such a relief when Satsuki appeared. Somehow the panel with Satsuki and Yasu together felt especially soothing. I never envied any of Yasu's girlfriends or Nana, whom Yasu protects, but I'm totally jealous of Satsuki, whom Yasu's taken under his wing since she was a baby.

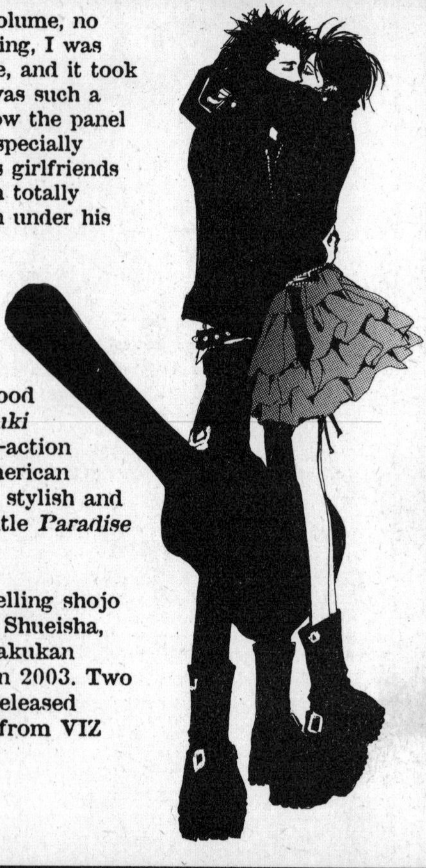

Ai Yazawa is the creator of many popular manga titles, including *Tenshi Nanka Janai* (I'm No Angel) and *Gokinjo Monogatari* (Neighborhood Story). Another series, *Kagen no Tsuki* (Last Quarter), was made into a live-action movie and released in late 2004. American readers were introduced to Yazawa's stylish and sexy storytelling in 2002 when her title *Paradise Kiss* was translated into English.

Nana has become the all-time best-selling shojo title from Japanese publishing giant Shueisha, and the series even garnered a Shogakukan Manga Award in the girls category in 2003. Two live-action *Nana* movies have been released in Japan and are available on DVD from VIZ Pictures in the U.S.

NANA
VOL. 21

Shojo Beat Edition

STORY AND ART BY AI YAZAWA

English Adaptation/Allison Wolfe
Translation/Tomo Kimura
Touch-up Art & Lettering/Sabrina Heep
Design/Julie Behn
Editor/Pancha Diaz

VP, Production/Alvin Lu
VP, Sales & Product Marketing/Gonzalo Ferreyra
VP, Creative/Linda Espinosa
Publisher/Hyoe Narita

Printed in the U.S.A.

Published by VIZ Media, LLC
P.O. Box 77010
San Francisco, CA 94107

10 9 8 7 6 5 4 3 2 1
First printing, July 2010

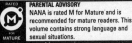

www.viz.com   www.shojobeat.com

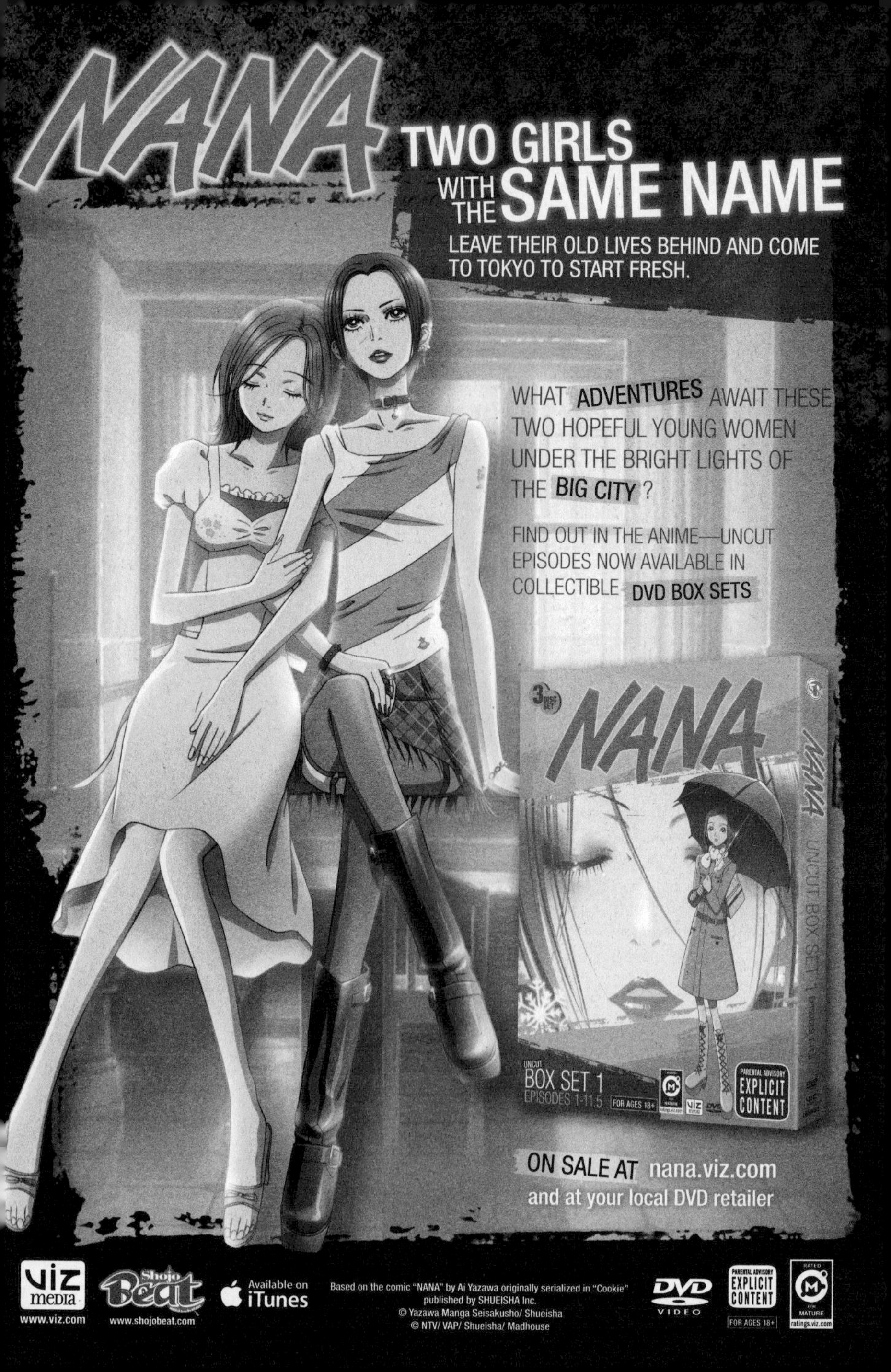
NANA
TWO GIRLS
WITH THE SAME NAME
LEAVE THEIR OLD LIVES BEHIND AND COME TO TOKYO TO START FRESH.
WHAT ADVENTURES AWAIT THESE TWO HOPEFUL YOUNG WOMEN UNDER THE BRIGHT LIGHTS OF THE BIG CITY?
FIND OUT IN THE ANIME—UNCUT EPISODES NOW AVAILABLE IN COLLECTIBLE DVD BOX SETS
3 DISC SET
NANA
NANA UNCUT BOX SET 1
UNCUT
BOX SET 1
EPISODES 1-11.5
FOR AGES 18+
PARENTAL ADVISORY EXPLICIT CONTENT
ON SALE AT nana.viz.com
and at your local DVD retailer
viz media
www.viz.com
Shojo Beat
www.shojobeat.com
Available on iTunes
Based on the comic "NANA" by Ai Yazawa originally serialized in "Cookie" published by SHUEISHA Inc.
© Yazawa Manga Seisakusho/ Shueisha
© NTV/ VAP/ Shueisha/ Madhouse
DVD VIDEO
PARENTAL ADVISORY EXPLICIT CONTENT
FOR AGES 18+
RATED M FOR MATURE
ratings.viz.com